HARMONY AND VOICE LEADING

SECOND EDITION

HARMONY
AND
VOICE
LEADING

SECOND EDITION

EDWARD ALDWELL
The Curtis Institute of Music
The Mannes College of Music

CARL SCHACHTER
Queens College of the City University of New York

HBJ

Harcourt Brace Jovanovich, Publishers
San Diego   New York   Chicago   Austin   Washington, D.C.
London   Sydney   Tokyo   Toronto

PREFACE

Although this Second Edition of *Harmony and Voice Leading* is one instead of two volumes, the book itself pursues the goals and retains the approach of the First Edition in dealing with tonal organization in the music of the eighteenth and nineteenth centuries. It offers a thorough and comprehensive course of study in harmony, and, at the same time, it emphasizes the linear aspects of music as much as the harmonic, with relationships of line to line and line to chord receiving as much attention as relationships among chords. Large-scale progressions —both harmonic and linear—are introduced at an early stage so that students can gain an understanding of the connection between detail and broad, inclusive plan in a musical composition. They learn that "harmony" is not merely the progression from one chord to the next and that "voice leading" is much more than the way two consecutive chords are connected.

This single-volume edition is not an abridgment. In order to conserve space and to facilitate reading, a number of musical citations have been reduced from full- to two-stave score, but the contents of the book have actually been expanded. The one-volume format will give teachers greater flexibility in pacing their classes and in making semester divisions suit their students' needs. Students will find it easier to review earlier material, and teachers will be able to introduce at least some concepts sooner than the book does (for example, some of the material on figuration in Units 20 and 21).

In preparing this new edition, we have reviewed the entire text to improve our manner of presentation, our examples from the literature, our use of terminology, and our exercises. We hope that these changes will make the book more effective for both teacher and student. Among the new features are the following:

A new section on setting melodies (Unit 7)

More hints for working out exercises (see especially the table on page 192)

Expanded treatment of harmony and rhythm (Units 7 and 9)

Simpler and clearer presentation of the resolution of VII^6 (Unit 7)

More comprehensive treatment of V as a key area (Unit 14, which now introduces applied dominants)

Step-by-step and more approachable explanation of suspensions and figured bass (Unit 21)

More help with diatonic modulation (Unit 26, particularly section 4, which introduces new material)

Expanded treatment of symmetrical divisions of octave (Unit 31), a topic that can form a bridge to the study of twentieth-century music (sections 14-18, especially section 17)

More consistent and more clearly explained terminology and use of symbols throughout the book

The book is suitable either for a self-contained course in harmony or for an integrated program combining harmony with other aspects of music. *Harmony and Voice Leading* touches on many of these aspects, including rhythm, melody, counterpoint, and form. It can function, therefore, as the basic text for an integrated program, and can serve as a convenient point of departure for systematic work in the other areas, with or without a supplementary text. Many theory programs are returning to the study of species counterpoint, usually at an early stage. This book would combine very well with work in species counterpoint; such a combination would provide an excellent basis for the understanding of tonal music. But counterpoint need not precede or accompany work in *Harmony and Voice Leading;* this is a completely self-contained and self-sufficient text.

In most theory programs, instruction in harmony or counterpoint usually follows a review of fundamentals: scales, key signatures, intervals, and so forth. This initial phase can pose difficult problems for instructors. Students vary widely—even wildly—in the quality of their previous training. And even those with a reasonably secure grasp of the fundamentals seldom understand the significance of the material they have learned by rote. The first three units of *Harmony and Voice Leading* attempt to deal with these problems. They offer both a review of the fundamental materials and a glimpse—a first glimpse for most students—of their significance for musical structure. Thus these opening units attempt to provide both a practical and a conceptual basis for the students' later work. For students deficient in their knowledge of fundamentals, we have provided a large number of written drills in the accompanying workbook as well as a smaller group in the text itself. Better prepared students will not need to devote much time to these drills, but they will profit from reading through the first three units and from classroom discussion of their contents.

If *Harmony and Voice Leading* is used for the harmony phase of a comprehensive theory program, four semesters will suffice to work through it; of course, other aspects of music would also be covered during that time. If the book is used for a self-contained harmony course, less time will be required— about three semesters depending on the number of class hours a week and the amount of time spent reviewing fundamentals. The remaining months could be devoted to an intensive study of form, to larger compositional projects, or to twentieth-century music. The text and the two workbooks contain far more exercise material than could be covered in any single course. Instructors can thus choose the number and type of exercises that best meet the needs of their particular class. The remaining exercises will provide valuable material for classroom demonstration, exams, and review.

The order in which important materials and procedures are presented differs from that found in any other text. After a discussion of chord vocabulary, chord construction, and voice leading (Units 4 and 5), the fundamental harmonic relationship between tonic and dominant is introduced, and the discussion then proceeds quickly to the most frequent linear expansions of tonic harmony. Confining students' work in these initial stages to a single harmonic relationship and to a number of closely related contrapuntal ones makes it much easier for them to *hear* what they are doing than if they are confronted immediately with seven root-position chords, each with a different sound and function. In subsequent units students learn new usages a few at a time, in a way that relates to and expands on the techniques they have already mastered. This order of presentation also makes it possible to show examples from the literature at a much earlier stage than in other approaches—and without including usages that students have not yet learned. Thus they develop their ability to hear in a logical and orderly fashion, and they can begin their analysis of music of the highest quality much sooner than in other approaches. The book's order of presentation also makes it possible to pursue a number of fundamental concepts, such as tonic-dominant relationship, voice exchange, and 5-6 technique, by starting with their simplest manifestations and gradually revealing more complex developments and ramifications. By relating new material to large inclusive ideas, rather than simply piling rule upon rule, we hope to help students to begin thinking about music in productive ways that will benefit their analysis, writing, and performing.

Although *Harmony and Voice Leading* probably covers more material than any comparable text, it does not require an inordinate amount of time to complete. Nonetheless, this book offers no shortcuts. There are no shortcuts in learning music theory—especially in the development of writing skills. If twentieth-century students wonder why they need to master such skills—why they need to take the time to learn a musical language spoken by composers of the past—they can be reminded that they are learning to form the musical equivalents of simple sentences and paragraphs. The purpose is not to learn to write "like" Mozart or Brahms, but to understand the language the great composers spoke with such matchless eloquence, the language that embodies some of the greatest achievements of the human spirit.

Late in the ninth decade of the twentieth century, no one can minimize the importance of a thorough study of twentieth-century music. But we believe that to combine in a single text an intensive study of tonal harmony with an introduction to twentieth-century techniques would fail to do justice to either subject. For one thing, some of the simplest and most fundamental principles of earlier music—the functioning and even identity of intervals, for example—become radically altered in twentieth-century usage, so that it is impossible to proceed directly from one kind of music to the other. And the twentieth century has seen the development of compositional styles that sometimes differ from one another so profoundly as to amount to different languages. To deal adequately with this disparate and often complex material requires a separate text.

Many readers will realize that this book reflects the theoretical and analytic approach of Heinrich Schenker, an approach many musicians recognize as embodying unique and profound insights into tonal music. *Harmony and Voice Leading* is not a text in Schenkerian analysis—no knowledge of it is presupposed for either instructor or student—but the book will lay a valuable foundation in Schenker's approach for students who wish to pursue it later.

In preparing this Second Edition, we profited from the advice of many colleagues, students, and friends; and we wish to thank all of them, including the large number we are not able to list here. We are very grateful to the following reviewers of the Second Edition: David A. Damschroder, University of Minnesota; Michael Eckert, University of Iowa; Donald Gibson, Baylor University; Patrick McCreless, University of Texas, Austin; Paul Wilson, University of Miami; and Eric Ziolek, University of Iowa. Robert Cuckson, David Gagné, Erez Rapoport, and Eric Wen offered much valuable criticism; Frank Samaratto greatly helped in correcting galleys; and Debbie Kessler prepared the index with meticulous care. We extend special thanks to David Stern who was particularly helpful in the revision of the text and preparation of the manuscript. The staff of Music-Book Associates provided the expert book composition.

We also wish to thank the staff of Harcourt Brace Jovanovich—especially Julia Berrisford, under whose expert guidance the Second Edition took shape, production editors Pat Zelinka and Jon Preimesberger, book designer Diane Pella, and production manager Lynne Bush.

We continue to benefit from the assistance we received from those who helped us with the First Edition, and we thank them once again. Two of them we must mention: David Loeb, who went through the entire book and offered many valuable suggestions, and Natalie Bowen, who took time from her busy schedule to edit this new version of a book whose shape and character owe so much to her.

Edward Aldwell
Carl Schachter

CONTENTS

PART

I

THE PRIMARY MATERIALS AND PROCEDURES

1

Key, Scales, and Modes

1-1   Mozart, Piano Sonata, K. 545, I

TONAL RELATIONSHIPS; MAJOR KEYS

1. Key. We'll begin by considering the opening of Mozart's familiar Sonata in C major, K. 545 (Example 1-1). The piece obviously contains many tones besides C. Why, then, do we call it a "Sonata in C major," or say that "it's written in the key of C"? Most people would answer that music is "in a key" when its tones relate to one central tone—the one that has the same name as the key—and when the functions of the other tones result from the ways in which they relate to the central one. According to this answer, the Mozart sonata is in C because C is the central tone; we hear the other tones as subordinate to C. (Why it's not simply in C but in C *major,* we'll discuss presently.)

This explanation of key is certainly correct as far as it goes, but it tells us little about the *kinds of relationships* that exist between the central tone and the others. (A definition of chess as "a game played on a board by two people, each with sixteen pieces" would be correct in the same way. But it wouldn't help anyone to learn to play chess.) Let's now look more closely at these relationships.

2. The tonic. We call the central tone of a key the *tonic.* In Example 1-2, which shows the most prominent tones of the Mozart, both hands begin on the tonic, C. The left hand stays around C for most of bars 1-4 and moves on to C as the lowest point in the downward motion F-E-D-C, bars 5-8. The right-hand part does not return to C after the opening bars, but its subsequent course points to C as its eventual goal. In bars 3 and 4, the melody moves from the high A down as far as E. The sixteenth-note scales that follow repeat, in varied form, the melodic line A-G-F-E but then carry it one step further, to D (bar 9). In listening to the melody, we are led to expect it to finish on C, to complete the circle by ending where it began. But it doesn't—not yet, at any rate. Instead the D is taken up again in bars 11 and 12; the first part of the piece closes without having arrived at its melodic goal.

1-2

And, in fact, C's function as a goal is not fulfilled until almost the end of the piece (Example 1-3). Generalizing from the Mozart, we can state that the tonic, the central tone of the key, forms the *point of departure* from which the other tones move and the *goal* to which they are directed. As in bars 1-12, the music does not always reach its goal at the moment we expect it to; by ending a part of the piece in a state of suspense, a composer can enhance the feeling of finality at the very end.

1-3   Mozart, Piano Sonata, K. 545, I

3. Scales. In Example 1-1, Mozart uses only some of the tones that the piano keyboard can produce. Almost all the sounds in these twelve bars result from playing the white keys; of the nearly 200 notes, the only exceptions are two C♯'s (bar 9) and one F♯ (bar 10). And if we were to look at other pieces in C major, we would find similar tonal materials. For the most part the pieces would contain the tones C, D, E, F, G, A, and B, and any other tones would play a subordinate role.

When all the tones that belong to a key occur in consecutive order, each one next to those closest to it in pitch, the result is a *scale* (Latin *scala,* steps, staircase, or ladder). In bars 5-8 of the Mozart, C major scales occur beginning on A, G, F, and E. The basic form of a scale, however, is the one that begins and ends on the tonic. A scale in this basic form can be thought of as a symbol of, or abstraction from, the natural flow of music—at least of music that is written "in a key." For such a scale begins on the tonic as its point of departure and concludes on the tonic as its goal (Example 1-4).

1-4   scale degrees in C*

The capped numbers above the notes in Example 1-4 indicate *scale degrees* (sometimes called *scale steps*) and will be used for this purpose throughout the book. In addition to numbers, the following traditional names are used so often for the scale degrees that you should memorize them:

$\hat{1}$	tonic
$\hat{2}$	supertonic
$\hat{3}$	mediant
$\hat{4}$	subdominant
$\hat{5}$	dominant
$\hat{6}$	submediant
$\hat{7}$	leading tone

4. The octave. The beginning and ending tones of Example 1-4 are both C, but they are not one and the same tone. The last tone sounds considerably "higher" in pitch than the first. Yet despite this marked difference in register, the sounds of the two C's are very similar; that's why we call them both by the same letter name. When two tones are separated by an *octave* (Latin *octava,* eighth) they are equivalents—that is, they are variants of the same sound. This phenomenon of *octave equivalence* is one of the most important aspects of pitch organization in music. In technical writing about music, it is frequently helpful to indicate the register in which a tone occurs. Example 1-5 shows how this can be done.

---

*Throughout the examples, the exercises, and the Workbook, capital letters are used for major keys and lower-case letters are used for minor keys. Thus, G and g indicate the keys of G major and G minor respectively.

1-5   registers

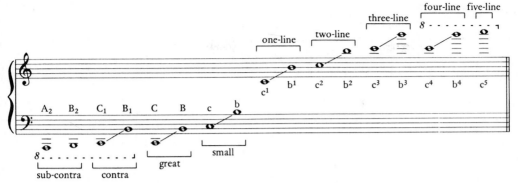

5. Major scales; whole steps and half steps. If we play a white-key scale from C to C on the piano, we can easily see that there is a black key between most of the adjacent white keys—between C and D, D and E, F and G, and so on. However no black key appears between E and F or between B and C. The distance between one tone of a scale and the next is usually called a *step*. The scale from C to C contains two kinds of steps: small ones between E and F and between B and C, larger ones between the other adjacent tones. The small ones occur where there is no intervening black key; the larger ones where there is a black key.

We call the smaller steps *half steps* (or *semitones*) and the larger ones *whole steps* (or *whole tones*). The half steps occur between $\hat{3}$ and $\hat{4}$ and between $\hat{7}$ and $\hat{8}$; all the others are whole steps:

1 w 2 w 3 h 4 w 5 w 6 w 7 h 8

A scale with half steps and whole steps arranged in the above order is called a *major scale*. Only the major scale has half steps between $\hat{3}$ and $\hat{4}$ and $\hat{7}$ and $\hat{8}$. Any piece whose tones form the same pattern of whole and half steps, starting with the tonic, is a piece in a major key.

The major scale is one kind of *diatonic scale*. All diatonic scales contain five whole steps and two half steps within the octave, but each of the different types of diatonic scale has the half steps in different places. From the time of the ancient Greeks through the nineteenth century, most Western art music was based on diatonic scales. Other kinds of scales are used in some Western folk music, music of non-Western cultures, and much twentieth-century music.

6. Intervals. Example 1-6a shows the tones that begin each of the first four bars of the Mozart sonata in both the left-hand and the right-hand parts. We call the relationship between two tones heard in a single context an *interval*. Intervals formed by simultaneously sounding tones are called *vertical* (because they are written one above the other). Intervals formed by tones that sound one after the other are called *horizontal* (Example 1-6b). The terms *harmonic* and *melodic* are sometimes used instead of vertical and horizontal.

1-6

(a) vertical intervals   **(b) horizontal intervals**

We can describe intervals by ordinal numbers arrived at by counting letter names up from the lower to the higher tone, or down from the higher to the lower. Thus C up to G is a *5th,* because it spans five letter names, C, D, E, F, and G. From B to C is a *2nd,* because it spans two letter names. From G to the next G above is an *octave* (not an "eighth," though it has the same meaning as "octave"). Finding the numerical size of an interval does not identify it completely. For example, B-C and C-D are both 2nds. Yet C-D (a whole step) is larger than B-C (a half step). Later on we will be specifying intervals more exactly; for now, it is enough to be able to determine the numerical size.

7. Chords; triads. Compare the first and last bars of the Mozart (Examples 1-1 and 1-3). Both bars contain the same three tones (with octave duplications); the tones are C, E, and G ($\hat{1}$, $\hat{3}$, and $\hat{5}$). These three tones are very closely associated, the basis of their association being membership in the same chord. A *chord* is a group of three or more tones that functions as a *simultaneity*—that is, the tones make sense played all at the same time. In essence a chord is a vertical unit; the simplest and most basic way to present it is as a *block chord,* with all the tones sounding at once (as in the last bar of the Mozart, second beat). But a composer can also present the tones one after the other, as Mozart does in bar 1. Because our ear and memory can group the tones into a unit, we still hear a chord. But not a block chord; it is a *broken chord* or *arpeggio.*

The chord C-E-G contains three tones; the upper two form the intervals of a *5th* and a *3rd* from C, the lowest. A three-tone chord formed in this way is a *triad.* The triad is the basic chord in Western music from the fifteenth through the nineteenth centuries. All other chords are derived from it. In every key the triad $\hat{1}$-$\hat{3}$-$\hat{5}$ has the tonic as its lowest tone. Since the lowest tone, called the *root,* functions as the basis of the chord, we call this triad the *tonic triad* or *tonic chord.*

8. Active tones; stable tones. Among the many mysterious powers of music is its ability to suggest *motion.* In listening to a piece of music, we do not hear a succession of static tones; rather, we hear tonal motions, one tone moving to another. In part this impression comes from rhythm, for musical rhythm has close relationships to some of the physical activities—walking, for instance—that form our primary experience of motion. But the impression of motion also arises from tonal organization. We have already seen that $\hat{1}$, the tonic, functions as the goal to which the other tones are directed. (And musical motion is essentially *directed* motion, motion to a goal.) We might say that all the other scale degrees, in different ways, are *active* in the direction of $\hat{1}$, that they tend to move to this stable, central tone. However $\hat{3}$ and $\hat{5}$ can also function as stable tones, though they are less stable than $\hat{1}$. They can serve as goals to which other, still more active tones can move because they are members of the tonic triad and thus closely associated with $\hat{1}$. Motion to $\hat{3}$ or $\hat{5}$ will not have the same finality as motion to $\hat{1}$.

Many melodies begin on $\hat{3}$ or $\hat{5}$ rather than on $\hat{1}$. If these melodies are harmonized, the tonic will almost always appear in the lowest part. Thus the music will still move from a tonic at the beginning to a tonic as final goal even if $\hat{1}$ does not serve as the initial *melodic* tone.

9. Passing tones; neighboring tones. Example 1-7 contains a diagram of the C major scale. The stable tones, $\hat{1}$, $\hat{3}$, $\hat{5}$, and $\hat{8}$, are shown as whole notes; the more active tones are written with black noteheads.

1-7

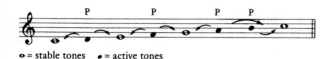

○ = stable tones   ● = active tones

As the diagram indicates, the active tones lead from one stable tone to another: up from $\hat{1}$ to $\hat{3}$, $\hat{3}$ to $\hat{5}$, and $\hat{5}$ to $\hat{8}$; down in the reverse order. A tone that forms a stepwise connection between two stable tones is called a *passing tone* (abbreviation, P); the term clearly conveys the transitional character of these tones. We can readily hear this transitional character if we play the scale in the right hand while holding the tonic triad in the left. Note that a single passing tone connects $\hat{1}$ with $\hat{3}$ and $\hat{3}$ with $\hat{5}$ but that two passing tones are needed to connect $\hat{5}$ with $\hat{8}$.

Motion along the scale—that is, motion with passing tones—is by no means the only type of melodic progression, though it is the basic type. Example 1-8 shows another important possibility. Here the active tones decorate a single stable tone rather than move from one to another. A tone that moves by step away from and back to a stable tone is called a *neighboring tone,* or simply *neighbor* (N). Sometimes it is helpful to specify the direction of a neighboring tone by referring to it as an upper or a lower neighbor (UN or LN).

1-8

To begin to see how passing and neighboring tones work in a musical composition, look at the two excerpts of Example 1-9. In the Brahms, the accompaniment sustains $\hat{1}$ and $\hat{3}$; with the melody's prominent $\hat{5}$ (opening upbeat and long notes in bars 1 and 2), a complete tonic chord seems to form the background of the whole line. Against this background, two segments of the descending E♭ scale create melodic motion: the first one leads from $\hat{8}$ down to $\hat{5}$ (bar 1) and the second from $\hat{5}$ to $\hat{1}$ (bars 1-2). In listening to the first segment, we experience no stability until the line comes to rest on $\hat{5}$; the transitional, "passing" character of $\hat{7}$ and $\hat{6}$ is very evident. In the second segment, $\hat{4}$ and $\hat{2}$ receive more rhythmic emphasis than $\hat{3}$ and $\hat{1}$, but the dissonances they form against the "background" tonic direct them strongly toward the more stable tones.

In the *Messiah* excerpt, the scalar motion leads from $\hat{1}$ up to $\hat{5}$, and it decorates the goal $\hat{5}$ with its upper neighbor, $\hat{6}$. This upward motion is balanced by a line that moves down, but only as far as $\hat{3}$, not $\hat{1}$. Note that bar 2 contains the motion $\hat{5}$-$\hat{4}$-$\hat{3}$ on two different levels. The main note of the first beat, G, moves on to F and E on beats 2 and 3, but a smaller version of the same line fills out beat 1. In music, as in language, we perceive connections between elements that are not right next to one another. We hear $\hat{5}$ in the Handel moving to the $\hat{4}$ of beat 2 despite the two notes in between, just as we connect the subject and verb of a sentence even if they are separated by many words.

1-9

(a) Brahms, Intermezzo, Op. 117/I

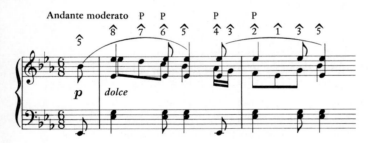

(b) Handel, Pastoral Symphony   (from *Messiah*)

10. Half steps as melodic intensifiers. When an active tone, P or N, lies a half step from the stable tone to which it is attracted, its motion to the goal tone has a particularly intense character. The closeness in pitch between the two tones draws the active tone into the gravitational field, as it were, of the stable one and enhances the attractional power of the latter. In major, therefore, $\hat{4}$ tends to move more readily to $\hat{3}$ than to $\hat{5}$, the other possible goal tone. And $\hat{7}$ is very strongly attracted to $\hat{8}$; in fact the term *leading tone* refers to the active way in which $\hat{7}$ "leads into" $\hat{8}$. The half steps are very well situated in major; the instability of $\hat{7}$ and $\hat{4}$ helps to strengthen $\hat{1}$ and $\hat{3}$ and leads to a clear definition of the key. Play the right-hand part of Example 1-1, extending the duration of B (bar 2) and F (bar 4). Notice how urgently the ear demands a continuation to C and E.

11. Incomplete neighbors; double neighbors. Sometimes a neighboring tone will connect with only one statement of the stable tone rather than two; it will move either to the stable tone or from it, but not both. In the melodic fragment shown in Example 1-10, the stable tones are A, C#, and E ($\hat{1}$-$\hat{3}$-$\hat{5}$ of A major). The G#, D, B, and F# are active tones that precede or follow (but not both) one of the main tones. We use the term *incomplete neighbor* (IN) to denote neighboring tones connected with one rather than two main tones.

1-10 **Mozart, Piano Concerto, K. 488, I**

Also derived from the neighbor is a four-note group consisting of a stable tone, both the upper and the lower neighbor (in either order) and a return to the stable tone. Two neighbors occurring together are called a *double neighbor* (DN), as in Example 1-11.

1-11 **Haydn, Symphony No. 98, II**

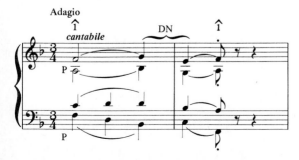

12. Transposition; key signatures. In bar 42 of the Mozart movement with which we began this unit, the opening idea returns; the technical name for such a return in a sonata movement is *recapitulation.* Usually a recapitulation is in the same key as the beginning of the movement, but most exceptionally, Mozart does not begin his recapitulation in C. Instead of C, F functions as the central tone; the music has moved to F major. Example 1-12 quotes the opening few bars of this F major recapitulation; observe that every time a B occurs, it is modified by a flat. A moment's reflection (and, perhaps, a glance at the keyboard) will show why the B♭ is needed. Without it, there would be a whole step between $\hat{3}$ and $\hat{4}$; the music would no longer be in F major.

1-12   Mozart, Piano Sonata, K. 545, I

Putting a piece (or section) of music into another key is called *transposing* it. If we transpose a piece from C to any other major key, we have to use flats or sharps to preserve the half steps between $\hat{3}$ and $\hat{4}$ and $\hat{7}$ and $\hat{8}$. These sharps or flats are gathered together into a *key signature* that occurs at the beginning of each line of music. Sometimes a change of key within a piece is accompanied by a new key signature, but very often, as in the Mozart, the necessary flats, sharps, naturals, and so on, occur in the body of the music as *accidentals,* like the flats before the B's in Example 1-12.

Example 1-13 shows the signatures of the fifteen major keys. Note that the keys with sharps move *up* in 5ths; the tonic of each new key lies a 5th above the preceding tonic. And that the keys with flats do just the opposite—they move *down* in 5ths.

1-13   major key signatures

(a)

(b)

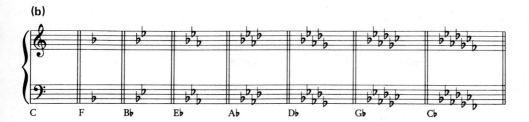

C   F   B♭   E♭   A♭   D♭   G♭   C♭

If you have not already done so, memorize these key signatures *immediately*. Not doing so will cause you unnecessary difficulties in studying music theory. And, by the way, memorizing them means being able to recall them *instantly and automatically*.

13. Chromaticism; chromatic half steps. In the recapitulation of the Mozart, the use of an accidental—B♭—results from a change of key to F major. However accidentals do not always signal a change of key; most often, in fact, they do not do so. Very often they occur when a composer wishes to emphasize a scale degree by means of the melodically intense half-step progression. In Example 1-1, the F♯ in bar 10 (left hand, last tone) intensifies the G that follows. Example 1-14 shows the specific function of this F♯ by leaving out some of the less important tones and simplifying the use of registers. It reveals that the F♯ leads from the F♮ of bars 9 and 10 to the G of bar 11; it functions, therefore, as a kind of passing tone.

1-14

P

The use of tones that normally do not belong to a key is called *chromaticism;* Mozart's F♯, therefore, is a *chromatic passing tone.* Chromatic elements embellish a basically diatonic substructure; the term *chromatic* (Greek *chroma,* color) clearly conveys the decorative character of these tones. As Example 1-14 indicates, the use of chromatic tones creates the possibility for a new kind of half step, the *chromatic half step.* The half step F♮-F♯ involves two tones with the same letter name, whereas the *diatonic half step* (for example, B-C) involves two tones with adjacent letter names. Chromatic passing tones divide a whole step into a chromatic half step plus a diatonic one (F♮-F♯-G). The chromatic half step normally comes first; the chromatic passing tone uses the same letter name as the preceding diatonic tone. Thus a chromatic passing tone from A down to G would be A♭; the melodic progression, therefore, would be A♮-A♭-G. Chromaticism sometimes involves the use of double sharps and double flats. A chromatic passing tone between F♯ and G♯, for example, would be F✗; one between B♭ and A♭ would be B♭♭.

Not every chromatic tone produces a chromatic half step. The C♯'s in bar 9 of Example 1-1 do not. They intensify the motion to D through the half-step progression, but they lie a whole step above the preceding tone, B.

MINOR KEYS; MODES; TONALITY

14. Minor keys. Example 1-15 is the beginning of a variation movement by Handel. The key signature contains two flats, but this composition is clearly not in B♭ major. The lowest part begins and ends on G; the highest begins on D and ends on G; the opening chord contains the tones G, B♭, and D. All of this points to G as the tonic and to G-B♭-D as the tonic triad. And, in fact, the piece is in the key of G, but G *minor*, not G major.

1-15 **Handel, Passacaglia**   (from *Harpsichord Suite No. 7*)

Why this piece is in minor becomes very clear if we compare its tonic triad with the tonic triad of G major (Example 1-16).

$\hat{1}$ and $\hat{5}$ are the same in both chords; only $\hat{3}$ varies. The B♭ is closer to G than is the B♮; the 3rd G-B♭, therefore, is smaller than the 3rd G-B♮. *Minor* and *major* simply mean smaller and larger. A minor key is a key containing a small or minor 3rd between $\hat{1}$ and $\hat{3}$; a major key is a key containing a large or major 3rd between $\hat{1}$ and $\hat{3}$. There are other significant differences between major and minor, but the contrast in sound between the two kinds of 3rds marks the fundamental distinction between them.

1-16

15. **The natural form of minor.** Example 1-17a shows the beginning of a later variation from the Handel Passacaglia. The right-hand part contains descending scales that follow the key signature exactly; no chromatic alterations occur. Example 1-17b is a diagram of the scale Handel uses, showing its stable and active tones as well as the location of its two half steps. The scale in this diagram is the *natural* (or *pure*) *minor scale*.

1-17

(a) Handel, Passacaglia

(b) natural minor scale

The contrast with major is striking. The minor 3rd between $\hat{1}$ and $\hat{3}$ lends its characteristic color to the scale. The half steps between $\hat{2}$ and $\hat{3}$ and $\hat{5}$ and $\hat{6}$ create an intensity in the motions from $\hat{2}$ to $\hat{3}$ and from $\hat{6}$ to $\hat{5}$ quite different from the corresponding progressions in major. Finally—and very significantly—the whole step between $\hat{7}$ and $\hat{8}$ fails to lead into the tonic with the same conviction as in major. For this reason, the term leading tone is not used to indicate the seventh degree of the minor scale in its natural form. We use the term *subtonic* instead.

When the minor scale descends (as in Example 1-17a), the lack of a leading tone does not present a problem, for $\hat{7}$ leads away from $\hat{8}$ rather than toward it. But when the scale ascends, the whole step between subtonic and tonic can constitute a real defect because $\hat{8}$ does not sound like a goal; its power to act as the central tone of the key is impaired. For this reason, $\hat{7}$ in minor must be raised to create the necessary half step whenever it moves to $\hat{8}$ as goal, or whenever the composer wishes to suggest such a motion, even if it is not immediately fulfilled. That is why Handel uses F♯ instead of F♮ in bars 3 and 4 of Example 1-15.

16. The harmonic form of minor. Raising the seventh degree but leaving the others unaltered produces the scale shown in Example 1-18. This scale is called the *harmonic minor,* for many important chord progressions use the tones it contains. However one characteristic of this scale makes it unsuitable for normal melodic progression. The interval between $\hat{6}$ and $\hat{7}$ is larger than a whole step; it is equivalent, in fact, to a step and a half. This larger interval creates a gap in the continuity of the scale that can be destructive of melodic flow. As Example 1-18 shows, the harmonic minor has three half steps: between $\hat{2}$ and $\hat{3}$, $\hat{5}$ and $\hat{6}$, and $\hat{7}$ and $\hat{8}$. In the keys of G♯ minor, D♯ minor, and A♯ minor, raising $\hat{7}$ will necessitate the use of a double sharp; in A♯ minor, for example, the leading tone is G𝄪.

1-18 harmonic minor scale

17. The melodic form of minor. If we raise $\hat{6}$ as well as $\hat{7}$, we gain a leading tone, but without creating an awkwardly large interval between $\hat{6}$ and $\hat{7}$. In a melodic line in minor, therefore, if $\hat{6}$ comes before the leading tone (raised $\hat{7}$), it too will be raised. Note, for example, the E♮ in bar 4 of Example 1-15, used instead of the E♭ called for by the key signature.

   The minor scale that raises $\hat{6}$ and $\hat{7}$ ascending is called the *melodic minor scale* (Example 1-19a). Example 1-19b, still from the Handel Passacaglia, illustrates its use in a composition. Note that it contains two half steps, between $\hat{2}$ and $\hat{3}$ and $\hat{7}$ and $\hat{8}$.

1-19 (a) melodic minor scale

(b) Handel, Passacaglia

Since $\hat{6}$ and $\hat{7}$ are raised in order to lead convincingly to $\hat{8}$, the raised forms of these degrees will normally occur only when the scale goes up. The descending form of the melodic minor, therefore, reverts to the natural form, with the accidentals for $\hat{6}$ and $\hat{7}$ canceled.

18. The three forms of minor. Beginning students sometimes have the misconception that the three forms of minor constitute three independent and unrelated scales. Actually, the harmonic and melodic forms are variants of the natural minor scale. The fact that the key signature *always* corresponds to the natural minor indicates that this is the basic form of the scale.

Most compositions in minor will contain elements of all three forms of the scale. Some successions of chords will come from the natural form (Example 1-15, bars 1 and 2); others from the harmonic (Example 1-15, bars 3 and 4). Melodic lines that ascend $\hat{6}$-$\hat{7}$-$\hat{8}$ tend to use the ascending melodic scale; descending lines tend to use the descending melodic (or natural) form (Examples 1-17 and 1-19).

19. Key signatures in minor. Like C major, A minor has neither sharps nor flats. As we move up in 5ths from A, we must add one sharp each time to the key signature to preserve the correct pattern of whole steps and half steps. As we move down in 5ths, we add flats. Example 1-20 shows the signatures for the fifteen minor keys, which you should memorize.

1-20 minor key signatures

(a)

a   e   b   f♯   c♯   g♯   d♯   a♯

(b)

a   d   g   c   f   b♭   e♭   a♭

20. Relative major and minor. The terms *relative major* and *relative minor* are often used to denote a major key with the same signature as a given minor one, and vice versa. Thus, C major would be the relative major of A minor, and D minor would be the relative minor of F major. These terms sometimes confuse students, who might think that F major and D minor, for instance, are the same key. Nothing could be more misleading; F major and D minor have different tonics; therefore they are different keys.

Knowing the relative major can help you learn the minor key signatures. Remember that the tonic of the minor key is $\hat{6}$ in the relative major. For example, the tonic of G♯ minor is $\hat{6}$ in B major; the key signature of G♯ minor, therefore, contains five sharps.

21. Parallel major and minor; mixture. Major and minor keys with different signatures but with the same tone as tonic are called *parallel*. G minor would be the parallel minor of G major. Actually, parallel major and minor keys are much more closely related than are relative majors and minors. In G minor as in G major, tonal activity is directed to the same goal, to G. In many compositions, elements from major and minor occur in very close proximity; in such cases we speak of a *mixture* of major and minor. Using raised $\hat{6}$ and $\hat{7}$ in minor constitutes one kind of mixture, for these tones are the same as the corresponding ones in the parallel major.

22. Modes; the diatonic order. Writers on music often refer to major and minor as *modes.* If we build scales starting on each of the white keys of the piano as a tonic, and using only white keys for the other tones, the result will be seven scales, each with a different pattern of five whole steps and two half steps within its octave. We will have created seven different tonal systems, for in each of these scales, the different arrangement of whole and half steps creates a different tonal structure.

The seven "white-key" scales constitute segments of the *diatonic order,* the pattern of whole and half steps that has given rise to most of the tonal systems of Western music. Like major and minor, these segments are known as *modes.* The seven patterns are shown in Example 1-21, together with their traditional names. Some of these modes had great importance in music before the eighteenth century, but some did not. The Locrian mode was scarcely more than a theoretical possibility, and the Lydian, at least in polyphonic music, made such regular use of B♭ as to be indistinguishable from Ionian (or major). Much great music was composed in the Dorian, Phrygian, and Mixolydian systems, and to understand early music, you must certainly investigate the way the modes were used. General information appears in any standard history of music and in some counterpoint texts. However, the study of early music is still a fairly new discipline, and we are far from having a complete understanding of specific techniques of tonal organization in early music.

1-21 seven diatonic modes

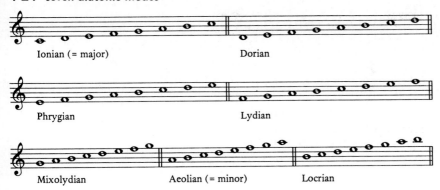

Ionian (= major)   Dorian

Phrygian   Lydian

Mixolydian   Aeolian (= minor)   Locrian

In the music we are dealing with in this book—the music from the Baroque through the Romantic periods—there are only two modes of any importance: major and minor. In this music, elements from some of the other modes—especially Phrygian—will sometimes appear. But they do so, for the most part, in a larger context of major or minor.

23. Tonality. Many musicians and writers use the term *tonal* to describe any piece or type of music organized around a central tone. And the principle of organization would be called *tonality*. Under these broad definitions of tonal and tonality, many—indeed, most—kinds of music would be tonal: music in major and minor keys, modal music, much non-Western music, and a good deal of twentieth-century music. The presence of a tonal center is an important common feature of these different kinds of music. But the ways in which the other tones function with respect to the central tone may vary considerably. Since the music we will deal with in this book is based, for the most part, on major and minor, the term *major-minor tonality* is the most accurate, though it is fairly unwieldy. So we will sometimes use the words "tonal" and "tonality" in a narrower sense as an abbreviated form of major-minor tonality.

24. The contrast between major and minor. Many people feel that music in a major key is "happy" and that music in minor is "sad." Sophisticated musicians often question this association, believing that it is a purely arbitrary one based on nothing except, perhaps, habit. And of course it is true that the emotional character of a piece depends on many factors in combination. Light and even comical pieces—some of Mendelssohn's scherzos, for instance—are in minor. And some very solemn pieces are in major, for example the "Dead March" in Handel's *Saul*. But it is a mistake to ignore the likelihood that choice of mode is one of the factors that determine the character of a piece. And sometimes it may be the most important factor.

For one thing the association of mode and emotion is a very old one; it goes back at least 400 years. Writing in 1558, Gioseffo Zarlino, the greatest theorist of the late Renaissance, remarks that melodies (and modes) featuring a major 3rd above the central tone sound cheerful and that those with a minor 3rd sound sad.* Any cultural tradition that has persisted for so long takes on a certain importance even if it is based on nothing more than custom. That the great composers of the eighteenth and nineteenth centuries believed in this association is evident to anyone who studies their songs and other music they composed to texts. And (as you will see in Unit 2) there is a strong possibility that the emotional connotations of major and minor may reflect more than habit or conditioning—that they may arise out of qualities inherent in tonal relationships.

EXERCISES

1. Be able to write from memory and to recite fluently the fifteen major key signatures in the order shown in Example 1-13.
2. Be able to write from memory and to recite fluently the fifteen major key signatures in the following order: C, C♯, D♭, D, E♭, E, F, F♯, G♭, G, A♭, A, B♭, B, C♭.
3. Be able to write from memory and to recite fluently the fifteen minor key signatures in the order shown in Example 1-20.
4. Be able to write from memory and to recite fluently the fifteen minor key signatures in the following order: c, c♯, d, d♯, e♭, e, f, f♯, g, g♯, a♭, a, a♯, b♭, b.
5. Recite as quickly as possible the names of the major keys indicated by the key signatures in each numbered row (horizontal and vertical) in the diagram on page 21. Do not *write* the answers.
6. Using the same diagram, recite as quickly as possible the names of the minor keys indicated by the key signatures in each row. Do not write the answers.
7. Using the order of major keys in Exercise 2, name the relative minor of each of these keys.
8. Using the order of minor keys in Exercise 4, name the relative major of each of these keys.
9. Using the order of major keys in Exercise 2, name the key signature of the parallel minor of each of these keys. Which keys lack a parallel minor? Why?
10. Explain: key, tonic, scale, octave equivalence, diatonic, interval, horizontal interval, vertical interval, chord, triad, passing tone, neighboring tone, transposition, chromatic half step, diatonic half step, relative major, parallel minor, Phrygian mode.

*Gioseffo Zarlino, *The Art of Counterpoint,* translated by Guy A. Marco and Claude V. Palisca (New Haven, Conn.: Yale University Press, 1968), pp. 21-23.

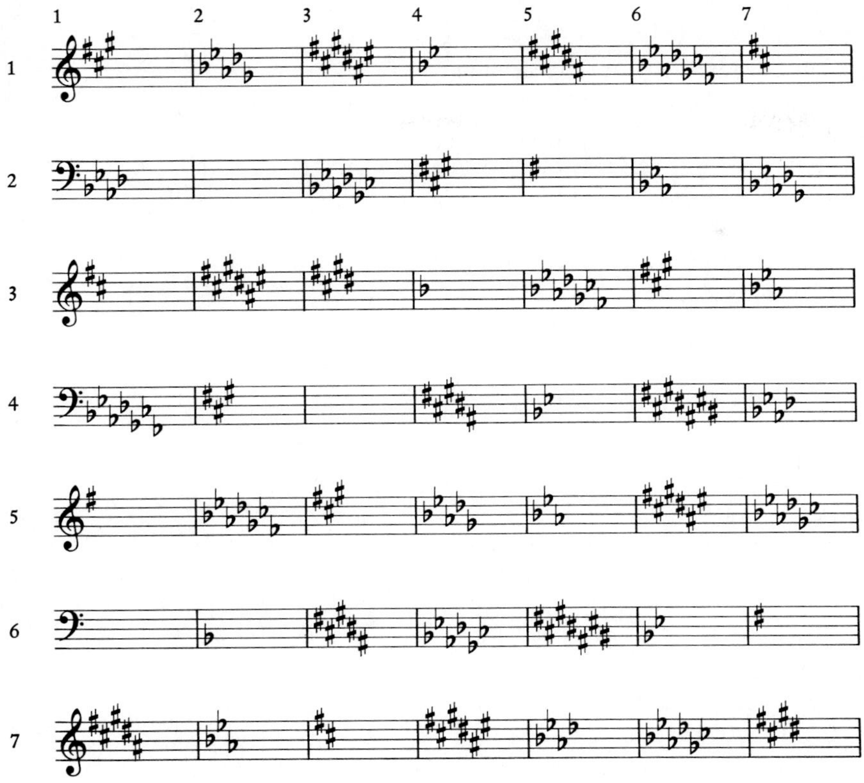

2

Intervals

2-1

(a)

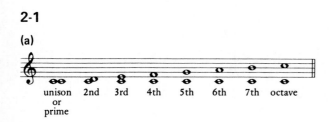

unison   2nd   3rd   4th   5th   6th   7th   octave
or
prime

(b) Verdi, Recordare   (from the *Requiem,* Dies Irae)

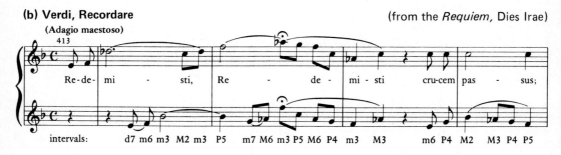

Re-de- mi - sti,   Re - de - mi - sti   cru-cem pas - sus;

intervals: d7 m6 m3 M2 m3 P5   m7 M6 m3 P5 M6 P4 m3   M3   m6 P4 M2   M3 P4 P5

translation: You have redeemed [me] through your suffering on the cross.

RECOGNIZING AND CONSTRUCTING INTERVALS

1. Numerical size; quality. As you'll remember from Unit 1 (section 6), the *numerical size* of an interval depends on the number of letter names the two tones span (Example 2-1a). But numerical size alone is not enough for the complete identification of an interval. For example, the intervals from C down to G♯, G♮, and G♭ are all 4ths, for they all have the same letter names. Yet the three intervals are different in size and *very* different in sound or *quality.* The complete identification of an interval, therefore, depends on both its numerical size and its quality.

22

Example 2-1b shows the intervals between two melodic lines labeled both by size and by quality. Intervals come in five qualities:

major (M)
minor (m)
perfect (P)
augmented (A)
diminished (d)

(Occasionally one encounters *doubly* augmented or *doubly* diminished intervals.)

For purposes of classification, intervals may be divided into two groups:

Group 1: unisons, 4ths, 5ths, and octaves
Group 2: 2nds, 3rds, 6ths, and 7ths

The intervals belonging to the first group are basically *perfect;* they are never major or minor. The intervals belonging to the second group are basically *major* or *minor;* they are never perfect. Thus musicians never speak of a "major 5th" or a "perfect 6th." Intervals belonging to both groups are sometimes *augmented* or *diminished.*

Group 1. If the upper tone of the interval belongs to the major scale of the lower tone, the interval is *perfect.* If the interval is a chromatic half step larger than perfect, it is *augmented;* if it is a chromatic half step smaller than perfect, it is *diminished* (Example 2-2).

2-2

Group 2. If the upper tone belongs to the major scale of the lower tone, the interval is *major.* If the interval is a chromatic half step larger than major, it is *augmented.* If it is a chromatic half step smaller than major, it is *minor.* And if it is a chromatic half step smaller than minor, it is *diminished* (Example 2-3).

2-3

Identifying and building intervals is easy if the lower tone normally begins a major scale and if the interval is built up from the lower tone. It is slightly more difficult if the lower tone is the tonic of an improbable major scale or if the interval must be built down from the upper tone. The two problems on page 24 show the way to proceed.

PROBLEM 1: IDENTIFY THE FOLLOWING INTERVAL.

Since few of us are familiar with the exotic key of B♯ major, we'll disregard the sharp for a moment. From B♮ to A is a minor 7th. (B to A♯ would be a major 7th, for A♯ belongs to the B major scale. B-A♮ is a chromatic half step smaller than major; therefore it is minor.) If B-A is a minor 7th, then B♯-A must be a *diminished* 7th, for raising the lower tone makes the interval a chromatic half step smaller than minor.

PROBLEM 2: WRITE AN AUGMENTED 6TH BELOW D.

To solve this problem we must first find the letter name of the lower tone. In this case, it is F, since F-D forms a 6th. From F♮ to D would be a major 6th, for D fits into the F major scale. An augmented 6th is a chromatic half step larger. Since we cannot change the given tone, D, we can enlarge the interval only by lowering the F. The correct answer, therefore, is F♭.

2. Compound intervals. *Compound intervals* are those larger than an octave. Owing to the principle of octave equivalence (see Unit 1, section 4), compound intervals are functionally the same as the corresponding simple ones. As Example 2-4 demonstrates, a *12th* is simply an expanded 5th, a *15th* an expanded octave, and so forth. And such intervals are almost always called 5ths and octaves rather than 12ths and 15ths. The only compound intervals whose names we need for our present purposes are the *9th* and the *10th*.

2-4   compound intervals

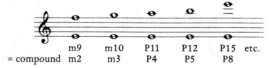

3. Interval inversion. We invert an interval of an octave or less by bringing the lower tone up an octave or the upper tone down an octave while leaving the other tone in place (Example 2-5); with compound intervals one of the tones would have to be displaced by two or more octaves. The numerical size of an interval plus that of its inversion adds up to 9. Thus the inversion of a unison is an octave (1 plus 8 equals 9), the inversion of a 3rd is a 6th (3 plus 6 equals 9), and so on.

2-5

The inversion of a perfect interval is also perfect. Inversion changes the other qualities to their opposites:

major	becomes	minor
minor	becomes	major
augmented	becomes	diminished
diminished	becomes	augmented

Because interval inversion results from the octave displacement of one of the interval's tones, an interval and its inversion form a related pair; this relationship is another consequence of octave equivalence.

THE OVERTONE SERIES

4. Composite sounds and overtones. Most musical tones are *composite sounds.* Their pitch results from the frequency with which the sounding body vibrates. (The sounding body may be a string, as on a violin; or an air column, as inside an oboe; and so forth.) As it vibrates, the sounding body divides itself into segments that vibrate independently. The vibration of the segments produces *overtones.* Normally we are not conscious of these overtones for they and the *fundamental tone* (the pitch we hear) blend into a single sound. But if you have a good musical ear you can easily train yourself to hear overtones, especially when the fundamental tone is in a low register. Overtones help to determine the *timbre* (or tone color) of the various instruments; they make possible the playing of harmonics on string instruments and the technique of overblowing on wind instruments.

The *intensity* (loudness) of the different overtones will vary depending on the instrument and on how it is played, but almost all musical sounds of any pitch contain the same group of overtones; we call this group the *overtone series.* Example 2-6 shows the series from Great C through the 16th tone (or *partial*). The series continues infinitely, the intervals between successive partials becoming smaller and smaller. But the higher partials are so weak as to lose any musical significance. Note that the partials are numbered from the fundamental, which is the first partial. All the other partials, or overtones, are literally "over" the fundamental.

2-6   the overtone series

5. The overtone series and the tonal system. It is clear from Example 2-6 that the overtone series contains elements that coincide with some of the most important materials of the tonal system. Between the fundamental and its upper partials we find:

> the perfect octave (partials 2, 4, 8, and 16)
> the perfect 5th (partials 3, 6, and 12)
> the major 3rd (partials 5 and 10)
> the major triad (partials 1-6)

However, the tonal system does not make use of all the sounds that occur in the overtone series. The partials shown by black noteheads in Example 2-6 (7, 11, 13, and 14) do not form part of major or minor scales, and their notation in the example is only an approximation of their true pitch. Furthermore, some of the important elements of tonal music—the minor triad, for example—do not relate directly to the overtone series.

The significance of the overtone series for the theory of tonal music is a matter of controversy. In the past, many theorists went to absurd extremes in their attempt to use the series as a "scientific" basis for music, contorting it in various ways to extract a minor triad from it and making it the basis for arbitrary "rules" of composition—rules that no great composer has ever followed. And even where the series and the tonal system correspond very closely—as with the major triad—there is no proof that the acoustical relationship causes the musical one.

Nowadays most musicians would maintain that the foundations for music theory should lie in the works of great composers, not in the laboratories of acousticians. But the following characteristics can be observed in the works of the great composers of tonal music:

1. The major triad functions as the most stable chord. From the Renaissance on, composers showed a marked preference for the major triad as final chord even in modes containing the minor 3rd. This tendency was strongest in the earlier stages of triadic music, but it never died out altogether.
2. In major-minor tonality, the major mode is normally the positive, happy, bright one, and the minor is the negative, sad, dark one. This again points to the greater stability of the major triad.
3. Two tones a 5th apart are in a particularly close relation.
4. The most stable intervals are the octave, 5th, and 3rd (the major 3rd more so than the minor).
5. A triad is generated from its root, or lowest tone, much as overtones are generated from the fundamental.

All these characteristics are at least compatible with the view that some of the most important features of tonality give expression to relationships that are inherent in a single musical tone. As noted before, it is impossible to demonstrate a causal connection between the overtone series and these aspects of tonal music. But if it is a coincidence, it is a most remarkable one.

CONSONANCE AND DISSONANCE

6. Stable and unstable intervals. Some intervals produce the impression of stability; others, the effect of activity or tension. We call the stable intervals *consonances* or *consonant intervals;* the unstable ones are *dissonant.* The consonant intervals are:

> the perfect unison
> the perfect octave
> the perfect 5th
> the perfect 4th (sometimes)
> major and minor 3rds
> major and minor 6ths

The dissonant intervals are:

> all 2nds
> all 7ths
> all augmented and diminished intervals
> the perfect 4th (sometimes)

For the moment, in discussing consonance and dissonance, we will concentrate on vertical intervals, those whose tones sound simultaneously. Melodic intervals can also be characterized as consonant or dissonant, as we will discuss in later units.

7. The consonant intervals. In major-minor tonality, the consonant intervals are the unison and octave, plus all the intervals that make up major and minor triads. The most stable triadic intervals are those that lie between the lowest tone (root) of a triad and one of the upper tones; these are the perfect 5th, the major 3rd, and the minor 3rd. The remaining consonances—the major 6th, the minor 6th, and the perfect 4th—result from the inversion of the more stable ones. Example 2-7 illustrates the consonant intervals in an order that proceeds from the more to the less stable.

2-7   consonant intervals

P1	P8	P5	M3	m3	M6	m6	P4
							(sometimes)

The unison and octave are the most stable of all the consonances; in the unison the two tones agree completely and in the octave they differ only in register. The lack of tension in these intervals is reflected in the tendency of composers to end pieces on unisons or octaves.

Next comes the perfect 5th. In music based on the triad, the 5th is uniquely important, for its upper tone defines the lower one as the root of a chord. Thus if we hear the bare 5th F-C, we understand F as the root, for F-C occurs in no triads except F major and F minor, in both of which F is the root. And since our feeling for key rests in part on the stability of the tones of the tonic triad, the 5th between $\hat{1}$ and $\hat{5}$ plays a most significant role in defining the key.

Composers have tended to treat the major triad as more stable than the minor. The major 3rd, therefore, which characterizes the major triad, is a more stable interval than the minor 3rd, which characterizes the minor triad. Both 3rds are more active intervals than the 5th.

Still more active are the major and minor 6ths, inversions of the 3rds. Differences in stability between the two kinds of 6th are not particularly significant. Their fluid character is reflected in the fact that they are not used to end pieces except for special and unusual effects.

The perfect 4th—the only interval that is sometimes consonant and sometimes dissonant—is in a category of its own and will be discussed in section 11.

8. Perfect and imperfect consonances. We call unisons, octaves, and 5ths *perfect consonances;* we call major and minor 3rds and 6ths *imperfect consonances.* In two-part textures (music containing two melodic lines), composers prefer the more stable perfect consonances for important *points of articulation*—beginnings and endings of phrases, sections, or pieces. Because of their less stable, more fluid character, the imperfect consonances normally predominate in places where the music moves from one point of articulation to another. In textures of more than two parts, imperfect consonances tend to occur between the highest and the lowest parts (the most prominent lines), except at points of articulation.

9. The dissonant intervals. Unlike the consonances, all of which form part of major or minor triads and therefore function as chordal elements, dissonant intervals between two parts arise out of melodic activity in one or both of the parts. In Unit 1, section 9, we saw that *passing tones* move by step from one stable tone to another and that *neighboring tones* arise from the stepwise decoration of a single tone. In Example 2-8, the passing and neighboring tones in one part create dissonant intervals between the two parts.

2-8

All the dissonant intervals in Example 2-8 arise out of stepwise motion. This is a fundamental characteristic of dissonance treatment in tonal music. Approaching and leaving the dissonance by step ensures a close connection between it and the surrounding consonances. The stepwise connection channels the tension and energy of the dissonant intervals so that dissonance becomes a powerful force for musical direction. On the other hand, isolated dissonances—those without a close connection to consonances—run the risk of creating tensions that serve no musical purpose because they lead to no goals.

10. Dissonance and activity. In Unit 1, we saw that $\hat{2}$, $\hat{4}$, $\hat{6}$, and $\hat{7}$ function as active tones tending to move to $\hat{1}$, $\hat{3}$, and $\hat{5}$. The division of scale degrees into stable and active tones relates directly to the phenomenon of consonance and dissonance, for the active tones are those that form dissonances with one or more tones of the tonic chord, whereas $\hat{1}$, $\hat{3}$, and $\hat{5}$ (the tonic chord) are all consonant with each other. The simplest and most basic use of consonance and dissonance, therefore, would be $\hat{1}$, $\hat{3}$, and $\hat{5}$ as consonances and the other scale degrees as dissonances against the other part or parts (Example 2-9).

2-9

$\hat{4}$, $\hat{2}$, and $\hat{7}$ form dissonances

For composers to restrict themselves to the simplest possibilities, however, would be far too limiting. A most important compositional resource, therefore, is stabilizing the normally active tones by giving them the support of consonant intervals; at the same time, normally stable tones may become unstable by appearing as dissonances (Example 2-10). Note that $\hat{4}$, $\hat{2}$, and $\hat{7}$, the active tones stabilized by consonant support, do not altogether lose their active character, as we can ascertain by playing the example and stopping on one of those tones. The music does not sound at rest until it arrives at the final $\hat{1}$.

2-10

active $\hat{4}$, $\hat{2}$, and $\hat{7}$ given consonant support

11. The perfect 4th. In the early stages of medieval polyphony, the perfect consonances formed the basis for music composition. Not only unisons, octaves, and 5ths, but perfect 4ths as well, functioned as stable intervals.

Over the course of several centuries, composers experimented with the possibilities made available through the use of 3rds and 6ths; the most important of these possibilities were the complete triads, major and minor, that became the basis for later music. Using complete triads effected a fundamental change in musical structure; one consequence of this change threatened the consonant status of the 4th. Once the 3rd became a pervasive element in musical texture, many situations arose in which the 4th sounded less like an inversion of the 5th— and thus a more or less stable interval—than like an active interval gravitating to the 3rd. In such situations, the 4th takes on the character of a dissonance (Example 2-11).

2-11 dissonant 4ths

However if the 4th occurs in close proximity to the 5th of which it is an inversion, it sounds perfectly stable and consonant; it has no tendency to move to a 3rd. The same is true in situations where the 4th appears in the course of an arpeggiated triad. Example 2-12 illustrates the 4th as a stable, consonant interval.

2-12 consonant 4ths

Unlike any other interval, therefore, the 4th is sometimes consonant, sometimes dissonant. It is consonant whenever the context shows it to function as an inverted 5th; otherwise it is dissonant. In simple textures, the 4th is mostly dissonant when it occurs in a two-part setting or between the lowest part and one of the upper ones in a setting of more than two parts.

INTERVALS IN A KEY

12. Intervals between scale degrees. Using the tones that belong to the major or the natural minor scales, we can produce the following intervals: perfect unisons and octaves, perfect and diminished 5ths, perfect and augmented 4ths, major and minor 3rds and 6ths, and major and minor 2nds and 7ths. No other intervals can be generated from these tones. Example 2-13a lists the intervals that contain $\hat{3}$ in G major, and 2-13b lists those that contain $\hat{6}$ in the same key. The two groups of intervals are almost the same, but not quite: $\hat{3}$ forms a minor 2nd and major 7th, whereas $\hat{6}$ does not. The fact is that every scale degree generates a unique collection of intervals; thus each tone of the diatonic scale has its own distinctive character.

2-13

(a)

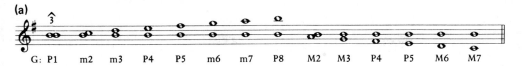

| G: | P1 | m2 | m3 | P4 | P5 | m6 | m7 | P8 | M2 | M3 | P4 | P5 | M6 | M7 |

(b)

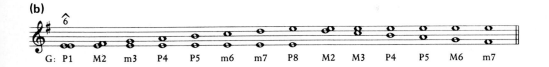

| G: | P1 | M2 | m3 | P4 | P5 | m6 | m7 | P8 | M2 | M3 | P4 | P5 | M6 | m7 |

13. The diminished 5th and augmented 4th in major. Among the intervals found in major and in natural minor are six perfect 5ths and six perfect 4ths (inversions of the 5ths). But there is only one diminished 5th and only one augmented 4th. In major, the diminished 5th occurs between $\hat{7}$ and $\hat{4}$; the augmented 4th, between $\hat{4}$ and $\hat{7}$. In Unit 1, we saw that $\hat{4}$ and $\hat{7}$ gravitate to the stable tones $\hat{3}$ and $\hat{1}$ owing to the particularly intense character of the half-step relationship. When $\hat{4}$ and $\hat{7}$ occur at the same time, their melodic tendencies remain; in fact, they are considerably enhanced by the tension of the dissonant interval they form. The motion of a dissonant interval to the consonance that acts as its goal is called a *resolution*. The diminished 5th resolves by moving in to a 3rd; the augmented 4th resolves by moving out to a 6th (Example 2-14).

2-14

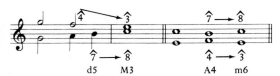

The resolution of the diminished 5th and augmented 4th to $\hat{1}$ and $\hat{3}$ creates a strong drive toward the tonic triad and helps to orient the listener as to the position of the tonic; for this reason we call it a *key-defining progression*. The key-defining function of these intervals is connected with the fact that any particular diminished 5th or augmented 4th occurs in only one major key. Thus, the minor 2nd E-F occurs in two major keys: C and F; the major 3rd C-E occurs in three: C, F, and G. But the diminished 5th B-F (and the augmented 4th F-B), unlike any other interval, occurs in one major key alone—the key of C.

Traditionally, the augmented 4th is called the *tritone*, which means three whole steps, thus: F-G, G-A, and A-B. (Strictly speaking, the diminished 5th is not a tritone, for it contains not three whole steps but a diatonic half step, two whole steps, and another diatonic half step: B-C, C-D, D-E, and E-F. However, for convenience, the term tritone is often used to mean the diminished 5th as well as the augmented 4th.)

14. The diminished 5th and augmented 4th in minor. In the natural minor, the diminished 5th lies between $\hat{2}$ and $\hat{6}$, the augmented 4th between $\hat{6}$ and $\hat{2}$. They resolve to $\hat{3}$ and $\hat{5}$, expressed as a 3rd (resolution of diminished 5th) or as a 6th (resolution of augmented 4th). Although $\hat{3}$ and $\hat{5}$ are members of the tonic triad, these resolutions do not define the key nearly as successfully as do the corresponding resolutions to $\hat{1}$ and $\hat{3}$ in major. When $\hat{3}$ and $\hat{5}$ are heard without $\hat{1}$, $\hat{3}$ tends to be heard as the root of a triad. Thus the progression shown in Example 2-15 suggests E♭ as tonic rather than C. It is partly because of this implication that the minor mode tends to gravitate to its mediant degree (or relative major).

2-15

does *not* define c

Raising $\hat{7}$ in the harmonic and melodic minor creates an "artificial" tritone between $\hat{4}$ and $\hat{7}$ that resolves to $\hat{1}$ and $\hat{3}$ as in major. The use of this tritone (or diminished 5th) lends to minor the clear definition of the key that occurs naturally in major (Example 2-16).

2-16

defines c

The raised $\hat{6}$ of the ascending melodic minor scale creates another tritone, in this case with $\hat{3}$. This tritone occurs much less often than the other two and has no significant influence on key definition.

15. The diminished 7th and augmented 2nd. The interval between raised $\hat{7}$ and natural $\hat{6}$ in the harmonic minor is a diminished 7th; inverted, it becomes an augmented 2nd. Like all diminished and augmented intervals, these are dissonant. As Example 2-17 indicates, they resolve to $\hat{1}$ and $\hat{5}$. The diminished 7th is the more useful of the two intervals, for it resolves to a 5th. The interval of the 4th, to which the augmented 2nd resolves, is itself often dissonant. Therefore the augmented 2nd cannot occur very freely; as a rule, it is used in those situations where the 4th to which it resolves is consonant.

2-17

This pair of dissonant intervals has a very strong key-defining power. The resolution to $\hat{1}$ and $\hat{5}$ unmistakably points out the location of the tonic. Furthermore, among the intervals in major and minor scales, the diminished 7th and augmented 2nd appear *only* between raised $\hat{7}$ and natural $\hat{6}$. Thus the diminished 7th C♯-B♭, for example, immediately points to D as tonic, for no other tonic can generate this particular interval. Because of its powers of key definition, the diminished 7th often appears in major as a consequence of mixture (see Unit 1, section 21). We can bring the diminished 7th C♯-B♭ into the key of D major by introducing B♭, $\hat{6}$ of the parallel minor (Example 2-17c).

16. The remaining intervals. We have already mentioned most of the intervals that are significant in the study of music theory. Of those not yet mentioned, one pair, the augmented 5th and diminished 4th, occurs in the inflected forms of minor; these intervals arise from the combination of $\hat{3}$ and raised $\hat{7}$ (Example 2-18).

2-18

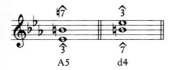

Another pair, the diminished 3rd and augmented 6th, is the product of chromaticism. These intervals normally come about as a consequence of raising $\hat{4}$ in minor; the intervals between raised $\hat{4}$ and natural $\hat{6}$ are the diminished 3rd and augmented 6th. As Example 2-19 indicates, raised $\hat{4}$ functions as a lower neighbor to $\hat{5}$ or as a chromatic passing tone leading from $\hat{4}$ to $\hat{5}$.

2-19

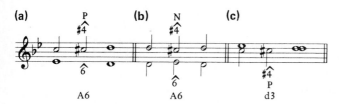

Chromaticism sometimes produces other intervals, but they are of less significance. The diminished octave and augmented 3rd of Example 2-20 are formed by melodic ornamentation in one of the parts; the intervals are mere by-products of this ornamentation.

2-20

17. Enharmonically equivalent intervals. On the piano, we depress the same key to produce C♯ and D♭, A♯ and B♭♭, and so on. In order to facilitate playing in all keys and to make possible an extensive use of chromaticism, keyboard instruments are tuned to the *equally tempered scale,* a scale that divides the octave into twelve equal semitones. Tempered tuning eliminates the minute differences in pitch between, say, G♯ and A♭ or B♯ and C♮. Two tones with different names but the same pitch (or, in nontempered tuning, almost the same pitch) are called *enharmonic equivalents.* The use of enharmonically equivalent tones makes it possible to construct two intervals of different size and quality, but whose tones have the same pitch in tempered tuning. Example 2-21a shows some of these enharmonically equivalent intervals. In isolation, an interval is indistinguishable from its enharmonic equivalent. In context, however, the two can sound very different indeed (2-21b).

2-21

(a) enharmonic equivalents

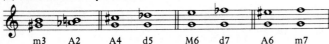

m3   A2   A4   d5   M6   d7   A6   m7

(b)

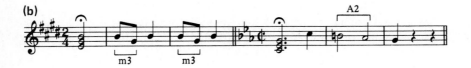

EXERCISES

1. Construct the following intervals above D: m2, M3, A4, d5, m6, M7, P8, m10, A2, P5. Do the same thing above F♯ and E♭.
2. Construct the following intervals below G: P4, A6, d7, A3, M2, m7, M6, m9, M10, m3. Do the same thing below C♯ and A♭.

3. Name the following intervals:

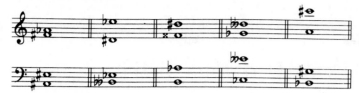

4. Name the inversions of the intervals in Exercise 3.
5. Name the major keys in which the following intervals would occur:

6. Name the minor keys in which the following intervals would occur:

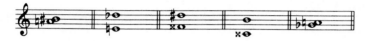

7. The overtone series. Memorize the series starting on Great C at least as far as the 8th partial and preferably through the 16th. Then, write the series on other tones, as below. Proceed either by interval above the fundamental (P8, P5, P8, M3, P5, m7, and so on) or by melodic interval from one partial to the next (P8, P5, P4, M3, m3, m3, and so on). The method not initially chosen can be used to check your results.
   a. Write the series up through the 16th partial, starting on Contra G♭.
   b. Write the series of which g^1 is the 10th partial.
   c. Write the series of which a♭^{2} is the 12th partial.
   d. Write the series of which c♯^{2} is the 5th partial.
8. Explain: numerical size, interval quality, compound interval, interval inversion, partial, imperfect consonance, resolution, key-defining progression, tritone, enharmonically equivalent intervals.

3

Rhythm and Meter

3-1 **Mozart, Piano Concerto, K. 467, II**

RHYTHMIC ORGANIZATION

1. The beat. Music moves in time; musical rhythm organizes the flow of time. This organization involves many factors, the most important being duration, accent, and grouping. The basic unit of duration is the pulse or *beat*. A beat is a span of time that recurs regularly; a succession of beats divides the flow of time into equal segments.*

We are aware of the beat even if it is not always expressed in the music. Thus, in the Mozart piano concerto passage of Example 3-1, the quarter note

---

*Actually, the segments are approximately, rather than strictly, equal, for in performance, slight deviations from exact measurement are the rule rather than the exception. And the word "beat" is often used to denote the point in time where the span begins, rather than the span itself.

takes the beat. But the music does not move only—or even mainly—in quarter notes. Beats combine into half notes; they divide into eighths, triplets, and sixteenths; and additional time values are produced by dots, double dots, and ties. In the Mozart, we relate these other values to the quarter note as basic unit, so the beat persists as a background against which we hear the varied rhythms of the piece.

The simplest way both to divide and to combine beats is by twos (Example 3-2). Thus a quarter note divides into two eighths, an eighth into two sixteenths, a sixteenth into two thirty-seconds, and so on. Similarly, two quarters combine into a half note and two half notes into a whole note. The division and combination of rests follow exactly the same principle.

3-2

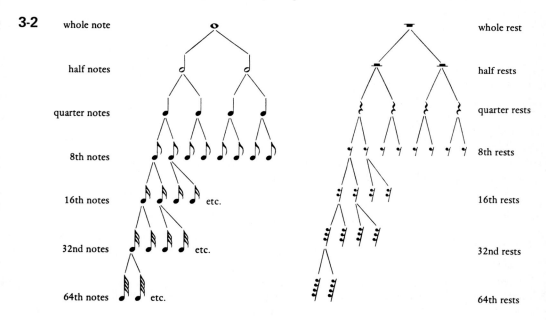

The use of dots permits more complex divisions and combinations (Example 3-3). A dot following a note or rest adds half its value to it; a second or third dot adds on half the value of the preceding dot.

3-3

A division of the beat into three (*triplets*) is indicated by the numeral *3* above or below the notes. Other divisions can also be indicated through the use of the appropriate numerals. Example 3-4 shows some possibilities.

3-4

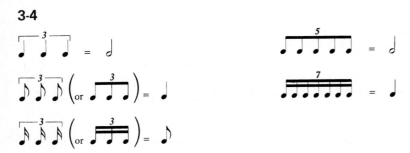

Using *ties* makes it possible to combine notes across a bar line and to create durations that cannot be achieved through note values or dots (Example 3-5). Sometimes two tied notes will replace a single dotted note to make for easier reading or a clearer expression of the rhythmic structure.

3-5

(a)   (b)

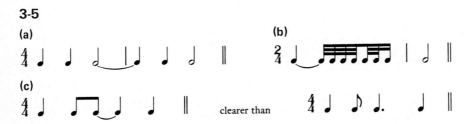

(c)

2. **Tempo.** The musical term for the pace of a composition is *tempo* (Italian, time). In music whose rhythms are based on beats, the impression of a quick, moderate, or slow tempo comes from the pace of the beats, not from the speed of the quickest notes. A slow tempo such as an Adagio or Largo may contain passages in, say, 64th notes that move very quickly indeed. Yet we do not hear a change to a quicker tempo; as long as the beats move slowly, the tempo remains slow. The pace of the beats relates to tonal movement, to the frequency with which chords change, or to the rate of motion of the main tones of the melody.

The fact that music moves at different tempos relates to an important aspect of our notational system: note values indicate relative rather than absolute durations. A quarter note that occupies a beat in a Largo lasts much longer than a quarter note that gets the beat in a Presto. But no matter what the tempo, a quarter note equals two eighths or four sixteenths.

3. **Accent.** *Accent* means emphasis. A note that receives more emphasis than the ones surrounding it is heard as accented. Accents often arise in performance when a note is stressed by being played more loudly than those around it or when the performer emphasizes the beginning (attack) of the note. Other kinds of accents are, so to speak, built into the composition itself. In general, long notes attract accents, for their long duration creates an emphasis. Unusually high

or low notes come across more strongly than those in a normal register. Dissonant or chromatic elements, because of the tensions they create, tend to sound accented compared to consonant or diatonic elements.

4. Meter and metrical accent. A repetitive pattern that combines accented and unaccented beats is called *meter.* Usually we speak of *strong beats* and *weak beats* to distinguish beats with and without accents. If the first of every two beats is strong, the meter is *duple;* if the first of every three is strong, the meter is *triple. Quadruple meter* (derived from duple) has a primary emphasis on the first beat and a weaker emphasis on the third beat of four. In normal musical notation, the bar line appears just before the strong beat; the accent that falls on the first beat of the bar is called the *metrical accent.*

Meters containing five or seven beats are frequent in twentieth-century music and occur occasionally in earlier music. Often these meters result from the combination of duple and triple meter. Changing meters (such as $\frac{2}{8}$, $\frac{3}{8}$, $\frac{3}{16}$, $\frac{5}{8}$, $\frac{4}{8}$, and so on) also occur in a good deal of twentieth-century music—much less often in music of the nineteenth century.

The inner organization of a divided beat mirrors in miniature the metrical organization of a measure. The beginning of a beat is stronger than the subdivisions that follow it. Within a divided quarter note, for example, the accent will fall on the first of two eighths, the first of three triplet eighths, or the first of four sixteenths. If the tempo is slow, the third of four sixteenths may get a subsidiary accent, just like the third beat in a bar of quadruple meter.

5. Time signatures. Composers indicate meter by means of *time signatures* placed at the beginning of a piece after the key signature and at any subsequent point where the meter changes. The time signature contains two numbers, one above the other. The lower number normally indicates the note value of the beat; the upper one indicates the number of beats per measure. Most often the quarter note gets the beat. Therefore duple, triple, and quadruple meter usually have the time signatures $\frac{2}{4}$, $\frac{3}{4}$, and $\frac{4}{4}$ (or its equivalent, **C**). However, composers can suggest the character and, sometimes, the tempo of a piece by using another note value, usually a half note or an eighth, for the beat. Time signatures like $\frac{2}{2}$ (**¢**), $\frac{2}{8}$, $\frac{3}{2}$, $\frac{3}{8}$, $\frac{4}{2}$, and $\frac{4}{8}$ occur frequently.

Some meters contain accentual patterning on more than one level. This is especially true of the so-called *compound meters,* those with beats grouped in multiples of three ($\frac{6}{8}$, $\frac{9}{8}$, $\frac{12}{8}$, $\frac{6}{4}$, and so on). In a bar of $\frac{6}{8}$ time, for instance, the first eighth note of each three receives an accent; the strong eighth notes, therefore, are the first and fourth. At the same time, a larger pattern of half bars is superimposed on this one; of the two dotted quarters in the bar, the first is the stronger. If the tempo is slow, we hear six beats in the bar arranged in two groups of three beats each; the beginning of the first group is stronger than the beginning of the second. If the tempo is quick, however, the $\frac{6}{8}$ has only two real beats; it sounds exactly like $\frac{2}{4}$ with triplet subdivisions.

6. Rhythmic accent versus metrical accent. Very often a composer underscores the metrical accent by making it coincide with some other kind of emphasis. In

Example 3-1, long notes appear at the beginnings of bars 1, 2, 4, and 5. At these points, the rhythmic accents caused by longer note values coincide with the metrically strong beats. In general, the simplest and most natural kinds of rhythm are those whose emphases fit into the metrical pattern.

Sometimes, however, a rhythmic emphasis contradicts the meter. The presence of a rhythmic accent at a metrically weak place is called *syncopation*. Syncopations arise in various ways; for our purposes the most important are those caused by a note that begins on a weak beat (or part of the beat) and is held through the next strong beat (or part). Since the beginning of a note is heard as stronger than its continuation, a note held from a weak through a strong beat conflicts—sometimes very strongly—with the meter. In Example 3-6 the syncopated notes are those tied over from the third to the first beat; the conflict between rhythmic emphasis and meter is evident.

3-6   Beethoven, Cello Sonata, Op. 69, II

Rhythmic emphases that contradict the meter sometimes set up such a consistent pattern of their own that we hear a temporary change of meter. A passage from Brahms's violin concerto sounds as if it is in $\frac{5}{4}$ time, though the composer continues to notate the section in the basic $\frac{3}{4}$ meter of the movement (Example 3-7).

3-7   Brahms, Violin Concerto, Op. 77, I

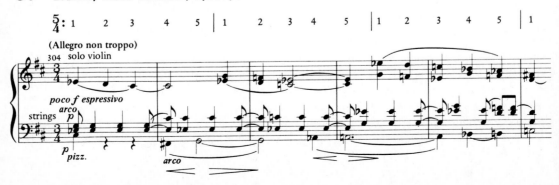

In triple and compound meters, shifted accents sometimes transform two groups of three beats into three groups of two beats. Such is the case in bars 8 and 9 of the Mozart sonata quoted in Example 3-8; the two bars of $\frac{3}{4}$ sound like a larger bar of $\frac{3}{2}$. The technical name for this rhythmic device is *hemiola*.

3-8   Mozart, Piano Sonata, K. 283, I

7. Rhythmic groups. Musical tones coalesce into small figures or *rhythmic groups;* such groups form an important element in the design of a composition. Sometimes, as in the opening melody of our Mozart C major sonata, rhythmic groups begin on a strong part of the measure (Example 3-9a). Often, however, they begin on an unaccented beat, as in the opening of another Mozart sonata (3-9b). Longer rhythmic groups are frequent, sometimes extending for more than a bar (Example 3-10). And one rhythmic group can merge into another; this happens when the last note of one also functions as the first note of the next. Such groups are said to *overlap* (Example 3-11).

3-9

(a) Mozart, K. 545, I

(b) Mozart, K. 283, I

3-10   Mozart, K. 545, II

3-11   Mendelssohn, Song Without Words, Op. 85/4

8. Measure groups and phrases. The principle of meter—regular and periodic groupings of weak and strong beats—often extends to groups of measures. Thus in a group of four measures, the first and third will normally be heard as strong compared to the second and fourth. The two excerpts shown in Example 3-9 can serve as illustrations. The normal organization of measure groups is duple; as in Examples 3-9 and 3-10, strong and weak measures alternate. However, grouping in threes is also possible (Example 3-12).

3-12   Beethoven, Bagatelle, Op. 126/6

Very often the end of a group of measures coincides with a goal of tonal motion. In such cases the group is tonal as well as rhythmic, and we call it a *phrase*. In Example 3-13, the arrival at the tonic in the eighth bar signals the end of the phrase.

3-13   Beethoven, Piano Sonata, Op. 14/1, II

Phrases of eight bars, as in Example 3-13, are very common; so are four-bar phrases. But other groupings often occur, including asymmetrical ones of five or seven bars (Example 3-14).

3-14   Schubert, Impromptu, Op. 90/1

RHYTHM AND DISSONANCE TREATMENT

9. Dissonance, duration, and accent. The effective functioning of a dissonant element depends on its relation to the consonances surrounding it. We have already seen that dissonances normally arise out of stepwise motion; this rule governs the melodic aspect of dissonance treatment. There is a rhythmic aspect as well: dissonances tend to occur in notes of relatively brief duration and (with one important exception) in metrically unaccented places. This rhythmic aspect of dissonance treatment is of particular importance in the polyphonic music of the Renaissance, a period when composers subjected dissonance to stringent controls.

In and after the Baroque period, from about 1600 on, composers became more willing to extend the duration and highlight the prominence of dissonances. Nevertheless, brief duration and placement on unaccented beats remained the norm. Thus passing and neighboring tones—the types of dissonance we have already encountered—will normally appear on weak beats or weak parts of divided beats. When they appear in a strong metric position we call them *accented* passing or neighboring tones. Accented incomplete neighbors are feequently called *appoggiaturas.* Example 3-15 illustrates.

3-15

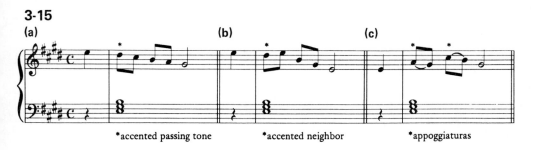

*accented passing tone   *accented neighbor   *appoggiaturas

10. Suspensions. One important type of dissonance, however, almost always appears in metrically accented positions; we call it the *suspension.* Suspensions originated as a consequence of syncopation. Tones in one part are shifted out of their normal rhythmic position with their beginning displaced from the strong beat to the following weak one; consequently they extend through the next strong beat. Example 3-16 shows how this process introduces dissonances (7ths) into a passage that consists, basically, of 6ths.

3-16

Suspensions also result from lengthening a tone so that it usurps part of the duration of the following tone (Example 3-17a). Or the suspended tone can be struck again rather than held over (3-17b). And in a texture of more than two parts, a suspension can delay the appearance of one of the tones belonging to a chord (Example 3-18).

3-17

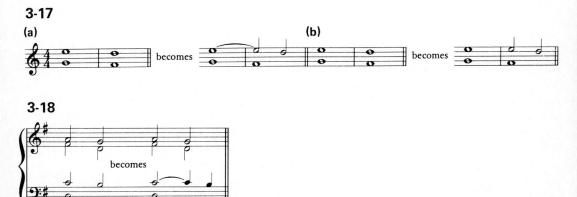

3-18

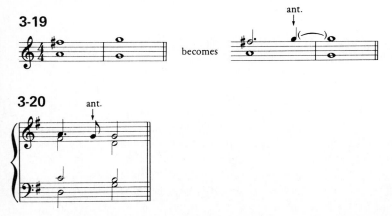

11. Anticipations. Syncopation can also give rise to unaccented dissonances. If a tone is shifted out of its normal rhythmic position by beginning *before* the strong beat, a dissonance can arise. We call such a tone an *anticipation* (Example 3-19). Anticipations are not always held over into the consonance that follows; often, the main tone is restruck. In textures of three and more parts, a chordal tone—most often in the highest part—can be anticipated. Example 3-20 shows both possibilities.

3-19

3-20

EXERCISES

1. Add bar lines to the following examples. None of the three begins with a complete measure; the final measure, also, may be incomplete.

(a)

(b)

(c)

2. Add rests to the following examples where indicated by x's. Some of the x's may indicate more than one rest. The final bar must be complete.

(a)

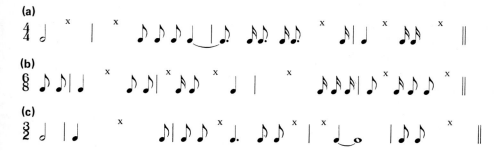

(b)

(c)

3. The following examples are melodic fragments from the literature. Supply time signatures and bar lines, bearing in mind that neither the opening nor the final measures are necessarily complete. Finally, supply a tempo you consider appropriate.

(a) Beethoven

(b) Haydn

(c) Mozart

(d) Mendelssohn (Excerpt begins on downbeat.)

4. Explain: beat, tempo, accent, meter, syncopation, hemiola, rhythmic group, phrase, appoggiatura, suspension, anticipation.

4

Triads and
Seventh Chords

4-1   Clementi, Piano Sonatina, Op. 36/2, I

(a)

(b) reduction

TRIADS

1. The triad as basic chord. Example 4-1 shows a phrase from a sonatina by Clementi. Under the music is a *reduction* (simplification) of its contents, with the left-hand part written in block chords and only the most essential tones of the melody shown. The purpose of this reduction is to help us concentrate on the chords that occur in this phrase. As Example 4-2 shows, the chords are of three types, which are determined by the intervals between the lowest tone and the upper ones. Omitting octaves (which merely duplicate one of the other tones) we find the following intervals:

1. 5th and 3rd
2. 6th and 3rd
3. 6th and 4th

The arabic numerals written under the chords refer to these intervals.

4-2

Only the first of these types is a triad as defined in Unit 1: a three-tone chord consisting of a 5th and 3rd above the lowest tone. But the other two types are derived from triads. In this unit we will discuss how the triad—the basic chord of tonal music—generates other consonant and dissonant chords.

2. Triad qualities. As we know, triads consist of two intervals—a *5th* and a *3rd*—above the lowest tone (the *root*). Since there are different kinds—or qualities—of 5ths and 3rds, there are different qualities of triads. Example 4-3 shows the four types of triads, which are followed by a summary of their qualities.

4-3   triad types

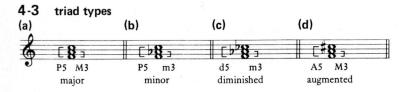

	TRIADS	
triad quality	*5th quality*	*3rd quality*
major	perfect	major
minor	perfect	minor
diminished	diminished	minor
augmented	augmented	major

Of the four qualities, the major and minor are by far the most important; because they contain only consonant intervals (perfect 5ths, major and minor 3rds), they are consonant chords. Diminished and augmented triads are dissonant because each contains a dissonant interval—a diminished or augmented 5th. Of the two dissonant triads only the diminished has any importance for the beginning stages of music theory.

3. The use of roman numerals. The chordal vocabulary of tonal music has as its basis a group of seven triads, each constructed on a different degree of the diatonic scale. Example 4-4 shows this group of triads in the key of C major. Note that the group contains three major triads, three minor triads, and one diminished triad.

4-4 triads in major

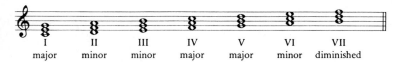

I	II	III	IV	V	VI	VII
major	minor	minor	major	major	minor	diminished

As we saw in Unit 2, section 5, the major triad is the most stable of all chords. If music were merely a succession of stable, well-balanced chords, it might well contain nothing but major triads. But such a procedure would contradict the unity and continuity that form an essential aspect of musical composition. In D major, for example, if the chords on F♯ and B were expressed as major triads, they would contain the tones A♯ and D♯, tones that do not belong to the D major scale and that would conflict with the D♮ and A♮ of the tonic triad. In order to avoid such contradictions, the basic chordal vocabulary of tonal music confines itself to diatonic elements—those belonging to the scale.

The roman numerals under the chords in Example 4-4 designate the scale degrees on which the triads are built. These scale degrees are the roots or fundamental tones of the triads. (Remember that the roman numerals refer to scale degrees only as the roots of chords, not as elements in a melodic line; for the latter purpose we use the capped arabic numerals.)

Here are the seven major-scale triads grouped in terms of qualities:

major triads	I, IV, and V
minor triads	II, III, and VI
diminished triad	VII

4. Triads in natural minor. Example 4-5 shows the triads on the degrees of the C minor scale. Note that each triad's quality differs from that of the corresponding triad in major.

4-5   triads in natural minor

I	II	III	IV	V	VI	VII
minor	diminished	major	minor	minor	major	major

Here are the minor-scale triads grouped in terms of qualities:

minor triads	I, IV, and V
major triads	III, VI, and VII
diminished triad	II

Note that I, IV, and V are major triads in the major mode and minor triads in the minor mode. The characteristic color of each mode comes not only from the quality of the tonic triad—though that is the most important factor—but also from the fact that IV and V, the other major triads in the major mode, are minor triads in the minor mode.

5. Triads in the inflected forms of minor. The lack of a leading tone in the natural minor makes it necessary to raise $\hat{7}$ whenever a motion to $\hat{1}$ is expected; the raising of $\hat{7}$ frequently necessitates raising $\hat{6}$ to avoid the awkward melodic interval of an augmented 2nd (see Unit 1, sections 15-17). When $\hat{7}$ and $\hat{6}$ occur as members of chords, raising them changes the quality of the chords. Example 4-6 shows the three chords containing $\hat{7}$ in its raised form. The qualities of these chords are:

III	augmented
V	major
VII	diminished

4-6   triads with raised $\hat{7}$

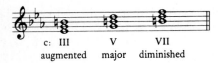

c: III	V	VII
augmented	major	diminished

Note that V and VII become just the same as in the parallel major key, reinforcing the idea that the inflected forms of minor result from mixture with major. As an augmented triad, III is more visible in harmony books than audible in real music. The basic form of III as it occurs in composition—a major rather than an augmented triad—is the one derived from the natural form of minor. On the other hand, V and VII occur frequently in both forms; in fact they occur more frequently with raised than with natural $\hat{7}$.

Example 4-7 illustrates what happens to II, IV, and VI when $\hat{6}$ is raised. The chords become:

II   minor
IV   major
VI   diminished

4-7   triads with raised $\hat{6}$

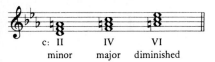

c: II   IV   VI
minor   major   diminished

II, IV, and VI with raised $\hat{6}$ occasionally make a fleeting appearance in musical compositions. But the characteristic form of these chords is the one with natural $\hat{6}$. The following summary shows the qualities of triads in minor and indicates the typical usage of each.

TRIADS IN MINOR		
	in natural minor	*other quality*
I	minor	none
II	diminished	minor (with raised $\hat{6}$)—infrequent
III	major	augmented (with raised $\hat{7}$)—infrequent
IV	minor	major (with raised $\hat{6}$)—infrequent
V	minor	major (with raised $\hat{7}$)—very frequent
VI	major	diminished (with raised $\hat{6}$)—infrequent
VII	major	diminished (with raised $\hat{7}$)—very frequent

The problematic character of minor compared with major is reflected in the presence of these alternative forms of triads—especially of V and VII. Only as we begin to work with these chords will we be able to learn how to use the two forms of V and VII. But the basic principle is simple: a motion to $\hat{1}$, or the expectation of such a motion, requires the raising of $\hat{7}$ and the accompanying change in the quality of V and VII.

6. Triads in inversion. The normal position of the triad, with the root as the lowest tone, is called the *root position*. Like intervals, however, triads can be *inverted*. A triad is in inversion when a tone other than the root is the lowest. If the 3rd of the triad is the lowest tone, the triad is in *first inversion;* if the 5th is the lowest tone, the triad is in *second inversion*. Whether a triad is in root position or one of the inversions depends solely on which tone is the lowest; the upper tones can be in any position (Example 4-8).

4-8   **triad inversions**

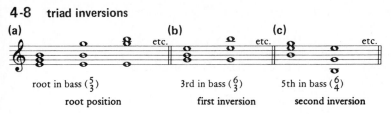

(a)	(b)	(c)
root in bass ($\frac{5}{3}$)	3rd in bass ($\frac{6}{3}$)	5th in bass ($\frac{6}{4}$)
root position	first inversion	second inversion

Just as the 3rd G-B and its inversion, the 6th B-G, form a pair of related intervals, so do the triad G-B-D and its inversions, B-D-G and D-G-B, form a group of related chords. And just as a 3rd and a 6th, though related, are not completely equivalent (the 6th is less stable), so, too, a root-position triad and its inversions are by no means completely equivalent. Learning to distinguish their various functions will form a significant part of later units.

7. $\frac{5}{3}$, $\frac{6}{3}$, and $\frac{6}{4}$ chords; figured bass. We know that the intervals between the lowest and the upper tones of a root-position triad are a 5th and 3rd. As Example 4-8 shows, the intervals between lowest and upper tones in a first-inversion triad are a 6th and a 3rd; in a second-inversion triad, they are a 6th and a 4th. Musicians frequently use the term *five-three chord* (written $\frac{5}{3}$) when referring to a triad in root position. The terms *six-three chord* ($\frac{6}{3}$) and *six-four chord* ($\frac{6}{4}$) denote triads in first and second inversion.

This terminology comes from the old practice of *figured bass,* sometimes called *thorough bass.* During the Baroque period, composers did not normally write out the accompaniments to solos and ensemble music, but indicated them instead in a kind of musical shorthand. The accompanist (usually a keyboard player) would play from a part containing the bass line of the composition; the bass line was supplemented by numbers (or figures, hence figured bass). The numbers denote intervals above the bass, and indicate the chords the accompanist must play. Thus the sign $\frac{6}{4}$ indicates that the bass tone and a 6th and 4th above it are to be played at the same time. The resulting chord would be a $\frac{6}{4}$ chord. Often the figures are abbreviated. Triads in root position occur so frequently that the symbol $\frac{5}{3}$ is usually omitted; the omission also reflects the fact that a bass tone, heard alone, tends to sound like a root. If the lowest tone of a chord is not figured, therefore, the chord is a $\frac{5}{3}$. Also the symbol $\frac{6}{3}$ is frequently shortened to 6. Sometimes other symbols—sharps or flats, for example—modify the figures.

By means of the figured bass the composer indicated the essentials of the accompaniment, but in the execution (or "realization"), many of the details were left to the accompanist, who would sometimes contribute extensive improvised elaborations. People trained to play from a figured bass, therefore, received an excellent preparation for improvisation and for composition. And long after composers stopped including figured-bass accompaniments (or *continuo* parts) in their compositions, they used the figured bass in their preliminary sketches. Indeed, realizing figured basses both on paper and at the keyboard is an incomparably useful and convenient way to master the basic materials and procedures of tonal music.

Example 4-9 shows the basic figured-bass symbols for $\frac{5}{3}$, $\frac{6}{3}$, and $\frac{6}{4}$ chords. During the time that figured bass was an essential part of musical performance, a variety of symbols were used at different times and places or by different composers.* The procedures we follow in this book are fairly standard:

1. Key signatures apply to figures as well as to notes.
2. Modifications of key signatures (accidentals) are indicated by the appropriate sign (♭, ♮, ♯, ♭♭, and so on) next to the figure.
3. An accidental standing alone (not next to a figure) always affects the third above the bass.
4. Sometimes the raising of a tone is indicated by a slash through the figure (δ) or a little vertical line (4, 2, or 5) rather than by a ♯ or ♮.
5. Figures do not specify the arrangement of the upper voices. Thus a ⁶₄ chord can be played with either the 6th or the 4th on top; the choice is the accompanist's.

4-9   figured-bass symbols

(a)

(b)

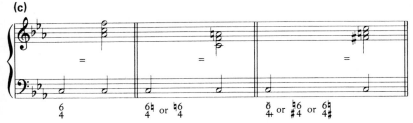

(c)

8. **⁶₃ and ⁶₄ chords as products of melodic motion.** It is convenient to think of ⁶₃ and ⁶₄ chords as inversions of root-position triads. This is certainly the case in Example 4-10a where a ⁶₃ chord comes about through inverting the chord on

*For an exhaustive account of figured-bass practice see one of the standard works dealing specifically with figured bass. An excellent source is F. T. Arnold, *The Art of Accompaniment from a Thorough-Bass* (Oxford: Oxford University Press, 1931), reprinted in two volumes (New York: Dover, 1965).

the downbeat. Quite often, however, the context in which these chords occur makes another explanation far more musically convincing, as a look at 4-10b will show. The piece is in D major, and D is the first bass tone we hear. Since this tone happens to be the tonic, it would make little sense to understand the opening chord as an inversion of a B minor triad. Instead, one hears the B of the melody as a tone that ornaments and delays A, the 5th of the tonic triad. In this situation, therefore, the $\frac{6}{3}$ chord D-F♯-B results from melodic activity in one of the parts rather than from chord inversion.

4-10

(a) Beethoven, Piano Sonata, Op. 110, I

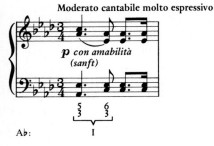

(b) Schubert, Piano Sonata, D. 664, II

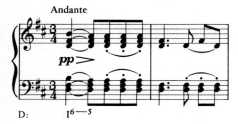

What the Schubert excerpt indicates is that $\frac{6}{3}$ chords—and the same is true of $\frac{6}{4}$'s—can derive from $\frac{5}{3}$'s through melodic motion above a stationary bass as well as through inversion. Example 4-11 shows these two contrasting possibilities. It also shows how such melodic motions are indicated in figured bass: by figures placed next to each other horizontally above a stationary bass tone. Such figures (5-6, 6-5, $\frac{5\text{-}6\text{-}5}{3\text{-}4\text{-}3}$) are normally executed by keeping the melodic motions in the same voice or pair of voices.

4-11

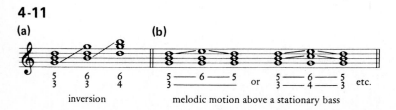

9. Harmonic analysis. Roman numerals and figured-bass symbols show very different things. Roman numerals indicate the *roots* of chords and the scale degrees on which they fall. Figured-bass symbols are calculated from the *bass tones,* not the roots, so that we do not need to think of the chord roots in order to realize a figured bass. But it is possible to combine elements from both approaches; the roots can be indicated by means of roman numerals, and the inversions, if any, by figured-bass symbols. Thus, E-G-C in C major would be I⁶—I because the root is C and 6 because the chord is in $\frac{6}{3}$ position. Example 4-12 consists of a short chord progression in C major; underneath the progression is a *harmonic analysis* that combines roman numerals and figured-bass symbols.

4-12

This kind of harmonic analysis is the usual one, and it is useful up to a point. However, such an analysis has serious limitations, one of which we can already perceive. Placing a roman numeral under each chord implies that all the $\frac{6}{3}$ and $\frac{6}{4}$ chords are the products of inversion. But we have already seen that some of these chords arise from melodic motion over a stationary bass. In such cases—and they are very frequent—a harmonic analysis like the one shown in Example 4-12 can be misleading, for it ignores the origin, behavior, and function of some of the chords. Thus, although roman numerals constitute an important tool at every stage of harmony study, the further you advance, the less you will need to label every chord.

Theorists follow two different approaches in naming the tones of inverted chords; Example 4-13 illustrates these approaches. In discussing a $\frac{6}{3}$ chord, for instance, some refer to the tones as "3rd, 5th, and root," just as if the chord were in root position (4-13a). Others, following a figured-bass approach, name the tones from the bass and call them "bass, 3rd, and 6th" (4-13b). In general, we follow the second approach. Our reason is the fact—already familiar—that F is the "root" of A-C-F only when that chord is the product of inversion, not when it comes from melodic activity. When the chord clearly functions as an inversion, however, it is sometimes necessary to refer to its "root" or "5th." One can always avoid confusion by specifying "3rd above the bass" or "5th of the root position," and so on.

4-13

(a)   **(b)**

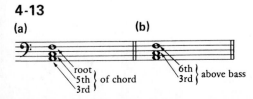

10. An easy way to remember triads. In music theory, it is vital to be able to recognize and construct triads instantly and to relate them to major and minor keys. In this connection it helps to remember that only seven combinations of letter names form the intervals of a 5th and a 3rd; only these seven groups, therefore, form triads. They are:

C-E-G   D-F-A   E-G-B   F-A-C   G-B-D   A-C-E   B-D-F

Thus the first sonority shown in Example 4-14 is not a triadic chord, for it cannot be reduced to one of the seven groups. The second one is, however; it can be reduced to B-D♯-F♯ or, without the sharps, to B-D-F.

4-14

SEVENTH CHORDS

11. The melodic origin of seventh chords. All the consonant chords of tonal music are triads in root position or inversion (though not all triads are consonant—some $^6_4$ chords and all diminished and augmented ones are not). Most of the dissonant chords used in tonal music belong to the category of *seventh chords*. The name reflects the fact that all these chords contain the interval of a 7th above the root.

Example 4-15 shows how seventh chords originated. In 4-15a, the 7th is formed by a passing tone that leads down from an octave to the 3rd of the following chord. The figured-bass sign 8-7 symbolizes this motion from the octave through the passing 7th to the following consonance. Around the beginning of the Baroque period, composers began to intensify the effect of the dissonance by omitting the octave and allowing the 7th to occupy the full duration of the chord, a process called *contraction* or *elision*. That the dissonant 7th still represents a passing tone is indicated by the basic rule governing the use of seventh chords: the dissonance moves down by step to resolve (4-15b), just as it would if it were a normal passing tone.

4-15

(a)   **(b)**

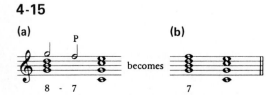

Every seventh chord consists of a triad plus the interval of a 7th. The triad —especially if it is a major or minor one—is the stable part of the chord. The 7th is the active, unstable, dissonant element that must resolve by stepwise descent.

12. Qualities of seventh chords. The quality of a seventh chord depends on the qualities of the triad and 7th it comprises. And since all seventh chords are unstable and all follow the same basic rule of resolution (the 7th moves down by step), the quality of a seventh chord has less influence on its function than is the case with triads. Example 4-16 lists the most important types of seventh chords; using the names by which they are usually called. The term *dominant seventh* reflects the fact that this chord appears on the 5th degree (dominant) of the major and inflected minor scales; it is the most important of all the seventh chords. A summary of seventh-chord qualities follows the example.

4-16   seventh-chord types

| major | minor | dominant
or
major-minor | diminished | half-
diminished | augmented | minor-major |

SEVENTH CHORDS

important qualities	*triad quality*	*7th quality*
major	major	major
minor	minor	minor
dominant or major-minor*	major	minor
diminished	diminished	diminished
half-diminished	diminished	minor

less important qualities		
augmented	augmented	major
minor-major†	minor	major

*called "major-minor" when it occurs on scale degrees other than $\hat{5}$

†hardly ever a real seventh chord; why not? (see Example 4-16)

13. Seventh chords on scale degrees. Seventh chords, like triads, appear on all degrees of the major and minor scales. Like triads, they are identified by roman numerals (showing roots), but with an arabic 7 added. Thus a seventh chord built on the subdominant would be called IV^7. Example 4-17 shows the seventh chords on the degrees of the E major and C♯ minor scales. The alternative forms of minor make possible a bewildering array of qualities; we have indicated only the most important possibilities.

4-17

(a) seventh-chord qualities in major

E: I⁷   II⁷   III⁷   IV⁷   V⁷   VI⁷   VII⁷
   major   minor   minor   major   dominant   minor   half-
                                                                                diminished

(b) seventh-chord qualities in minor

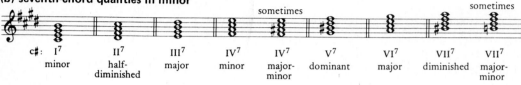

c♯: I⁷   II⁷   III⁷   IV⁷   IV⁷   V⁷   VI⁷   VII⁷   VII⁷
    minor   half-   major   minor   major-   dominant   major   diminished   major-
               diminished   minor   minor

14. Inversions of seventh chords. Since seventh chords contain four tones—root, 3rd, 5th, and 7th—they occur in three inversions as well as in root position (Example 4-18). In the first inversion, the 3rd appears as the lowest tone; in the second inversion, the 5th is the lowest tone; in the third inversion, the 7th is lowest.

4-18   seventh-chord inversions

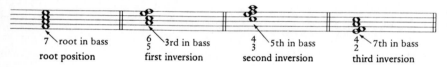

7 ╲root in bass   6 ╲3rd in bass   4 ╲5th in bass   4 ╲7th in bass
   root position   5 first inversion   3 second inversion 2 third inversion

15. Figured-bass symbols for seventh chords. The complete figures for a seventh chord and its inversions are $\frac{7}{5}_3$, $\frac{6}{5}_3$, $\frac{6}{4}_3$, and $\frac{6}{4}_2$. Usually these figures are abbreviated to 7 (sometimes $\frac{7}{5}$ or $\frac{7}{3}$), $\frac{6}{5}$, $\frac{4}{3}$, and $\frac{4}{2}$ (or 2). It is easiest to memorize the figures as "seven, six-five, four-three, two," but $\frac{4}{2}$ is used more frequently than 2 to indicate the third inversion. Sometimes the figure appears in complete rather than abbreviated form—for example, if one of the numbers is modified by a sharp or flat.

Just as with triads, one can indicate the roots of seventh chords by using roman numerals and the root position or inversion by figured-bass symbols. Example 4-19 illustrates.

4-19

A: I   V⁴₃   I⁶   V⁶₅   V⁴₂ - III⁷   I⁶   IV   V⁷   VI⁷   V⁶₅   I

16. Remembering the seventh chords. Again, as with the triads, only seven combinations of letter names form seventh chords. They are:

C-E-G-B   D-F-A-C   E-G-B-D   F-A-C-E   G-B-D-F   A-C-E-G   B-D-F-A

Note that the first three letters of each group correspond to the seven triads.

TEXTURE AND STRUCTURE

17. Note-against-note and figurated textures. Music in a simple chordal style usually proceeds in a *note-against-note* texture; all the voices or parts maintain the same rhythm. In the simplest form of this style, only tones that are chord members will appear. Example 4-20 illustrates such a texture. Real music, however, seldom maintains this kind of simplicity for long. More often, the texture will be enlivened by *figuration,* quicker notes in one or more of the parts. These quicker notes sometimes arpeggiate the chord that is sounding at the time; that is, they leap from one chord tone to another. At other times, the play of figuration introduces tones that do not form part of the chord against which they sound. The most important of these figuration tones are the passing tone, neighboring tone (complete and incomplete), suspension, anticipation, and appoggiatura, which were discussed in Units 1 and 3 and which will frequently appear in the examples of later units. The progression shown in Example 4-21 is the same as the one in 4-20, but the texture is figurated.

4-20   **note-against-note texture**

4-21   **figurated texture**

18. The progression of chords. The material in this unit will enable you to recognize and label all the chords that appear frequently in tonal music, except those modified by chromatic alteration. The ability to identify and construct chords is an important and necessary step toward the goal of musical understanding; but by itself it does not guarantee such understanding. Far more important is learning—with both ear and mind—how these chords function, how they relate to each other, how they interact to create musical motion. The principles that regulate the progression of chords form a large part of the subject matter of this book, and they do not lend themselves to quick summary. However, two of these principles—*harmony* and *voice leading*—are sufficiently general and broad in their application to be mentioned appropriately at this point.

By harmony we mean that aspect of music concerned with relationships among chords. By voice leading we mean that aspect of music concerned with the simultaneous motion of two or more parts. The unit of harmony is the chord; the unit of voice leading is the melodic line. However, the simultaneous motion of several lines necessarily creates chords. And it is hard to conceive a progression of chords without the explicit or implicit presence of melodic lines. In practice, therefore, the two principles interact with and influence each other.

19. Harmony; the 5th relationship; tonic and dominant. In tonal music, harmonic progression is organized by the *5th relationship*. We have already mentioned the close affinity that exists between two tones pitched a perfect 5th apart. The 5th is the first "new" tone in the overtone series; in triadic music the 5th is uniquely able to define the root or fundamental tone of a triad. The 5th forms the basis of organization not only of elements within a single chord but of movement from one chord to another. That the interval of the 5th dominates harmonic progression is reflected in the use of the term *dominant* to denote the scale degree a 5th above the tonic and the chords built on that degree. Since relationships in tonal music are organized around the tonic, the basic harmonic relationship is that between tonic and dominant—between the chord built on the central tone and the one built on its upper 5th.

This relationship controls not only many immediate successions from one chord to the next, but large-scale connections as well. In the Mozart C major sonata (Example 1-1), for instance, the opening theme moves from the tonic to the dominant of bars 11 and 12; the tonic begins the motion and the dominant is its goal. The large-scale progression from I to V forms the framework within which the numerous details are organized. And at the end of the piece (Example 1-3), V—this time as a seventh chord (V^7)—precedes the final tonic of bar 71. Beginning in Unit 6, you will have many opportunities to observe the overriding importance of the 5th relationship and, in particular, of the connection between tonic and dominant harmonies.

20. Voice leading. Many chord progressions of tonal music arise out of voice leading or counterpoint—that is, the chords result from the simultaneous motion of several melodic lines. This principle of organization is older than harmony; composers became aware of the possibility of relating chords to each other after centuries of contrapuntal music in which the chords arose as by-products of the voice leading. Just as the basis of harmonic progression is motion by 5th, so the basis of melodic progression is motion by step. In successions of chords controlled by voice leading (*contrapuntal progressions*), stepwise motion predominates.

You will begin to understand the manifold elaborations of harmony and voice leading and the countless ways in which they join forces to create musical textures when you study the basic techniques of four-part writing in Unit 5.

EXERCISES

1. On E build major, minor, augmented, and diminished triads in root position. Do the same on B♭, G♯, and A♭.

2. Major key and roman numeral given. Write root-position triads as indicated.

B:	II	F♯:	VII
G:	VI	E♭:	III
A♭:	IV		

3. Minor key given. Write root-position triads as indicated, using natural form.

f:	III	d♯:	VI
c♯:	IV	e♭:	VII

4. On E build major, minor, augmented, and diminished $\frac{6}{3}$ chords.

5. On B♭ build major, minor, augmented, and diminished $\frac{6}{4}$ chords.

6. On G♯ build all four qualities of $\frac{6}{3}$ chords.

   On A♭ build all four qualities of $\frac{6}{4}$ chords.

7. Major key and roman numeral given. Write triads as indicated.

E:	IV^6	G:	III$^6_4$
B♭:	II^6	C♯:	I$^6_4$
F:	VII^6	A♭:	VI$^5_3$
B:	V^6	D:	IV$^6_4$
G♭:	III^6	A:	II$^6_4$

8. Minor key given. Write triads as indicated, using natural form.

c:	VII$^6_4$	e♭:	VI^6
f♯:	V$^6_4$	a:	IV$^5_3$
c♯:	III^6	e:	II$^6_4$
g:	I^6	b♭:	VII$^5_3$
d:	VI$^6_4$	f:	V^6

9. On F♯ build all qualities of root-position seventh chords. Label each chord, using the following symbols:

major	M	diminished	o
minor	m	half-diminished	∅
dominant	X	augmented	A
minor-major	m/M		

10. Do the same on A♭.

11. Major key and roman numeral given. Write root-position seventh chords as indicated, labeling each chord with the symbols given in Exercise 9.

$$E\flat: IV^7 \qquad C: V^7$$
$$A: VI^7 \qquad F\sharp: VII^7$$
$$B: II^7 \qquad A\flat: III^7$$
$$F: IV^7 \qquad C\sharp: V^7$$
$$E: VI^7 \qquad D: I^7$$

12. Minor key given. Write root-position seventh chords as indicated, using harmonic form.

$$g: VII^7 \qquad g\sharp: V^7$$
$$a: VII^7 \qquad b\flat: V^7$$
$$b\flat: VII^7 \qquad b: V^7$$

13. Major key and roman numeral given. Write inverted seventh chords as indicated and label the quality of each.

$$A: II^6_5 \qquad B: VII^4_3$$
$$D\flat: VI^4_2 \qquad E\flat: V^7$$
$$F: IV^6_5 \qquad G: III^4_3$$
$$A\flat: II^4_2 \qquad B\flat: I^7$$
$$C: VII^6_5$$

14. Minor key given. Write inverted seventh chords as indicated, using natural form.

$$d: VI^4_3 \qquad e: IV^4_2$$
$$f\sharp: III^7 \qquad g\sharp: II^6_5$$
$$b\flat: I^4_3 \qquad c: VII^4_2$$
$$c\sharp: VI^7 \qquad d\sharp: IV^6_5$$

15. Minor key given. Write inverted seventh chords as indicated, using harmonic form.

$$f: V^6_5 \qquad g: V^4_3$$
$$a: V^4_2 \qquad b: V^7$$
$$c: VII^7 \qquad d: VII^6_5$$
$$e\flat: VII^4_3 \qquad f\sharp: VII^4_2$$

16. Explain: root position, triad in inversion, figured bass, $^6_3$ (or $^6_4$), chord by melodic motion, note-against-note texture, figured texture, 5th relationship.

5

Procedures of Four-Part Writing

5-1   Bach, Chorale 293, phrase 1

CHORD CONSTRUCTION

1. Four-part vocal texture. To study harmony and voice leading is to study how chords and lines interact—chord with chord, line with line, and line with chord. For you to concentrate on these essentials, particularly in written exercises, the simplest rhythm and texture is the most desirable. In this respect four-part vocal writing—the traditional medium for harmony exercises—has many advantages. By its very nature, vocal music is simpler than instrumental: many complexities of rhythm, extremes of range, and changes in register that are easy on an instrument are difficult or even impossible for voice. At the same time, a setting in four parts, using the natural combination of high and low men's voices plus high and low women's or children's voices, provides a texture in which complete chords occur easily. Indeed, since the sixteenth century the four-part texture has come to represent the norm, especially in vocal music.

   Four-part vocal writing is an ideal medium for the study of harmony not only because of its simplicity, but also because of its applicability to music of greater complexity. Much instrumental music—though often more elaborate on the surface—is based on a framework of four voices. Example 5-1, a phrase from J. S. Bach's Chorale 293, illustrates certain principles of chord construction. Bach's 371 chorales are universally acknowledged to be among the masterpieces of four-part choral writing. Although they are in many ways complicated little pieces, their complexities are not those of rhythm, texture, and register, all of which remain relatively simple. For this reason the chorales have served as models for generations of music students, from Bach's day to yours.

As with nearly all the 371 chorales, Example 5-1 is set for four voices:

soprano—women's or children's high voices
alto—women's or children's low voices
tenor—men's high voices
bass—men's low voices

When notated on two staves, as in the example, the two upper voices (soprano and alto) are written on the treble staff and the two lower ones (tenor and bass) on the bass staff.* The stems of the soprano and tenor voices always point up; those of the alto and bass always point down. The soprano and bass are referred to as *outer voices;* the alto and tenor, *inner voices.*

2. Vocal range. In simple four-part vocal writing, each voice is set in a range that it can sing without strain. The usual ranges are shown by the whole notes of Example 5-2; the smaller noteheads represent allowable extensions. The greater part of each line will normally lie within the middle of the range rather than at the extremes.

5-2   vocal ranges

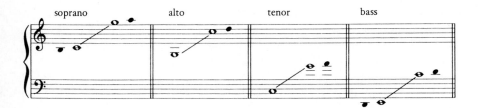

3. Doubling. In Example 5-1, all but one of the chords—the V^7 just before the fermata—are triads. Since a triad consists of only three tones, one of its tones must appear twice—that is, it must be doubled. Example 5-3 indicates the doublings that occur in the first phrase of Chorale 293. Note that doublings can occur at the unison as well as at the octave or multiple octave.

---

*Bach himself notated his chorales in an open score for four staves, using soprano, alto, tenor, and bass clefs. If you are familiar with these clefs, you will find it valuable to write some of your exercises in open score.

5-3   Bach, Chorale 293

brackets indicate doubled tones

"Rules" for doubling are formulated on the basis of an ideal vertical sonority. In practice, however, doublings are very much influenced by the way the voices move. Therefore, most of the rules of doubling can be applied flexibly; violations, however, should always occur for a reason, not arbitrarily. One rule must be regarded as virtually absolute: the leading tone, because of its active tendency toward $\hat{1}$, should never be doubled when it is part of V or VII or their inversions. Thus, to construct the third chord of Chorale 293 in the way shown in Example 5-4 would be wrong.

5-4

wrong (doubled
leading tone)

With root-position chords the tendency is to double the more stable parts of the triad; thus with major and minor triads, the root is most often doubled, as in the excerpt from Chorale 293. The root of a final tonic chord is virtually always doubled. Seventh chords, since they already contain four tones, contain no doublings if they are complete chords (Example 5-3, V^7 just before fermata). Sometimes the root is doubled and the 5th omitted. Since the chord 7th always forms a dissonance, it must never be doubled.

4. Complete and incomplete chords. The best vertical sonority is achieved when, as in our opening example, all the tones of a triad are present in the chord. The 5th of a major or minor root-position triad, however, may be omitted without confusing the identity of the chord. Owing to the strength of the second overtone, the ear assumes a 5th above the bass unless there is some other interval present that contradicts the 5th. Most often when the 5th is omitted the root is tripled and the chord 3rd not doubled. Example 5-5 illustrates. Because of the empty sound and the lack of major or minor quality, the 3rd of the triad is never omitted except for special effects. Triads in inversion are usually complete.

Root-position seventh chords frequently omit the chord 5th and double the root. Inversions of seventh chords are usually complete, exceptions occurring even less often than with inversions of triads.

5-5   Bach, Chorale 250

*incomplete chords

5. Spacing. Except for special effects, the voices of a multivoiced texture should blend. Too great a distance between the soprano and alto or the alto and tenor, especially if continued beyond one or two chords, may create an impression of thinness. Normally, adjacent upper voices should not be more than an octave apart, as in both the Bach excerpts (Examples 5-1 and 5-5). However, it is perfectly acceptable for the tenor to be separated from the bass by as much as two octaves. The resulting high tenor register gives a particularly intense choral sound. On the other hand, to have the alto and tenor in a low register and separated from the soprano often produces muddiness. Play the three "rewritten" versions of Chorale 293 (Example 5-6) and compare their effect with each other and with the original.

5-6

soprano and alto too far apart; alto out of range   inner voices too far apart

possible in keyboard style (why not for voices?)

6. Open position and close position. Strict observance of the rule of spacing still leaves room for considerable variety in the construction of a chord. Of the many "correct" possibilities, two general types are commonly distinguished: *open position* and *close position* (Example 5-7). Close position occurs when the three upper voices are as close together as possible—no additional chord tone can be inserted between adjacent voices. In open position, the upper voices are separated so that a chord tone could be inserted between either alto and soprano, or tenor and alto, or both pairs of voices, as in Example 5-7b. Open position tends to give a full but clear and well-balanced sound. Both open and close position can be used within a single phrase, as in Example 5-1, where the first two chords are in close position and the rest are in open position. Changing from close to open position, or the reverse, is often necessary for good voice leading; the change can also give a welcome variety of sound.

5-7

(a) close position   **(b) open position**

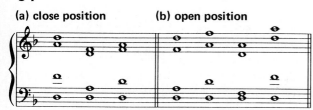

7. Position of the soprano. Although not as crucial as the bass tone, which determines whether a chord is in root position or inversion (Unit 4, section 6), the soprano tone also exerts a strong influence on the sound of a chord. The reason is that the soprano is usually the most prominent of the four voices. The effect that the soprano tone creates depends on several factors in combination: the interval from the bass, the stability or activity of the scale degree, the context in which it appears. For instance, $\hat{1}$ over tonic harmony tends to give a stable—indeed, sometimes a static—impression; it forms an octave with the bass and is the least active degree of the scale. Thus, this position of the soprano will be most useful at points of articulation. A particularly beautiful sonority often results from placing the 3rd of a triad (especially a major triad) in the soprano. This disposition mirrors the overtone series, in which the 3rd (5th partial) appears above the octave (2nd and 4th partials) and the 5th (3rd partial). In a tradition that dates back to the sixteenth century (Zarlino cites it), composers have tended to favor this position of the soprano.

8. Keyboard style. As far back as the late seventeenth century, a figured bass was normally realized at the keyboard with the right hand playing the three upper parts and the left hand playing the bass only. This would mean that the distance between soprano and tenor could not exceed an octave, a comfortable stretch for most hands. Except for its notation, then, keyboard style is similar to close position. In this instrumental style, the limitations of vocal range need not be followed strictly. The tenor, in particular, tends to move higher than would be practical for voices.

Example 5-8 illustrates two conventional notations for keyboard style. In both notations the bass is alone on the lower staff with the stems pointing up or down depending on whether the note is above or below the third line. In 5-8a, the three right-hand parts are stemmed together. The direction of the stems is determined by whether the majority of tones are above or below the third line. In 5-8b, all the soprano tones are stemmed up, while a stem pointing down connects the inner voices.

5-8   keyboard style

(a)   **(b)**

9. Unusual spacing. Like the rules for doubling, the rule of spacing refers to a norm and is therefore not absolutely binding. Even in chorale style, Bach's settings clearly show that melodic considerations and motivic development may make a departure from the rule logical or even necessary. In a chorale, exceptional spacing is of brief duration, most often just a chord or two, as in the second phrase of Chorale 293 (Example 5-9) where the stepwise descent in the alto causes a gap between it and the soprano. In the even simpler texture of written exercises, such spacings are best avoided.

5-9   Bach, Chorale 293, phrase 2

At the same time it is important to realize that, particularly in solo instrumental compositions, extremes of spacing and register can be a most important expressive factor. In the beginning of the Arietta from Beethoven's Piano Sonata, Op. 111 (Example 5-10), the left hand is written an octave below its normal register so that the inner parts are separated by as much as two octaves. The great distance between the upper and the lower parts suggests an immensity of space that could not be achieved otherwise. And the extreme register of the lower parts gives by contrast an ethereal quality to the upper parts, which are written in a normal register.

5-10   **Beethoven, Piano Sonata, Op. 111, II**

Adagio molto semplice e cantabile

VOICE LEADING

Voice leading, unlike chord construction, involves motion—the motion of each of the four voices considered individually and the sense of progression created by their combination. First, we will discuss the melodic motion of the single voice and then proceed to the consideration of several voices moving simultaneously.

10. Melodic motion. In addition to sustaining or repeating a tone, a line may move by step (*conjunct* motion) or by skip or leap (*disjunct* motion). The proportion of conjunct to disjunct motion varies according to the function of the line. In a simple four-part setting, such as the first two phrases of Chorale 293 (Examples 5-1 and 5-9), we can distinguish three types of function: that of the top voice (soprano), of the bass voice, and of the inner voices.

As the highest, and therefore most exposed, voice, the soprano carries the main melodic line. Most good soprano lines contain a preponderance of conjunct motion, but the inclusion of one or two leaps will help greatly in adding interest and variety to the line. On the other hand, too much disjunct motion may keep the line from holding together and may make it difficult to sing. The first two phrases of Chorale 293 illustrate a good balance of conjunct and disjunct motion within a simple vocal melody. Note that this soprano line has no repeated tones. In general, excessive repetition of a single tone can result in a static melodic line, but an occasional repetition can create a good effect, especially if the other voices move.

Because the lowest tone is the crucial member of the chord, the bass voice has the special function of regulating the succession of chords. Bass and soprano lines are interdependent. The bass must make explicit the harmonic meaning of the soprano. For example, in the opening phrase of Chorale 293 (Example 5-1), the soprano D could stand for the root of V, the 3rd of III, or the 5th of I. The bass G shows that the soprano D means the 5th of I. For its part, the top voice must move in such a way as to allow logical harmonic direction in the bass. Bass lines are often quite disjunct, particularly at the ends of phrases, as Example 5-1 illustrates, but stepwise motion, such as at the beginning of the second phrase of the same chorale, can give a welcome melodic quality to the line.

Inner voices sometimes have a melodic interest of their own, particularly in places where the soprano does not move very much. Their main function, however, is to complete the tones of the chord framed by the bass and soprano. The position of the outer voices may limit the melodic possibilities of the inner voices, so that extensive repetition of one or two tones may be unavoidable. Such repetition is not injurious to the total effect if the bass and soprano are good. In general, the inner voices will have a less distinct profile than the soprano and bass. Smooth voice-leading connections make likely a preponderance of conjunct motion, as in the tenor voice of Chorale 293, but the alto voice of the same two phrases shows that skips are also a possibility, if they occur for a valid reason.

11. Treatment of leaps. Disjunct motion gives variety and tension to a melodic line, but can be disruptive if used carelessly. The effect a leap produces depends largely on its size and on whether it is consonant or dissonant. (In context, other factors may be of importance, for instance whether or not there is a chord change.)

Consonant leaps—upward or downward—occur fairly frequently even in the simplest vocal textures (Example 5-11). The smaller the leap, the less it tends to disrupt the continuity of the line. Thus a leap of a major or minor 3rd interferes least with melodic continuity, especially where it is preceded or followed by stepwise motion (5-11a). A leap of a 6th or octave, on the other hand, generates considerable tension, and should usually be followed by a change of direction, preferably by step (5-11b). Leaps larger than an octave are not permitted. Large leaps must be used sparingly in a short harmony exercise; although their occasional use creates interest and variety, too many will create a disconnected, meaningless line. The melodic perfect 5th and perfect 4th (as a melodic interval the perfect 4th is always consonant) are more moderate in their effect than the octave or 6th but far more noticeable than the leap of a 3rd. It is best often to change direction after such a leap, but stepwise motion in the same direction, as in the opening of Chorale 293 (Example 5-1, soprano), is a good possibility (5-11c).

5-11

(a)

all good

(b)

good   good   poor   poor   good   poor   forbidden

(c)

good   good   usually good   usually good

Two or more leaps in a row and in the same direction are usually avoided except when a 3rd combines with another 3rd or with a 4th to arpeggiate a chord (Example 5-12). The sparing use of arpeggiation, within a limited range, is a good source of variety in vocal music, but excessive use will destroy the vocal character.

5-12

poor   good   good   good

Dissonant leaps represent a more advanced stage of complexity than consonant ones; consequently they are excluded entirely from the simplest vocal styles. In a four-voice chordal setting, certain types of chords—particularly the dominant seventh—and certain harmonic progressions make dissonant leaps logical and attractive, and we will discuss their use in a later unit. The augmented 2nd, an interval traditionally excluded from four-part chorale settings and figured-bass realizations, should not be used.

12. Simultaneous motion. The motion of one voice relates to the motion of another in one of the four following ways:

Parallel motion: Both voices move in the same direction and maintain the same numerical interval (Example 5-13).

Similar motion: Both voices move in the same direction but the interval between them changes (Example 5-14).

Oblique motion: One voice remains stationary while the other moves (Example 5-15).

Contrary motion: Both voices move in opposite directions (Example 5-16).

5-13   parallel motion

3   3   3   3   6   6   6   5   5   5

5-14   similar motion

5-15   oblique motion

5-16   contrary motion

Contrary motion creates the greatest contrast between the two voices and helps to give each an individual contour. Each voice is independent of the other in a way that adds to the listener's interest. Of the remaining types, oblique motion is the next most independent, similar motion less so, and parallel motion least of all. Since there are only two directions, up and down, all four voices cannot be going in contrary motion to each other; thus the other types of motion are not only permissible but necessary and desirable. In particular, parallel motion in 3rds, 6ths, and 10ths can be among the most useful types of voice leading.

13. Forbidden parallel motion. In any multivoiced setting, the voices must join forces to create an overall sense of movement and direction. Within this unified web of sound, however, each voice must maintain its own individuality as much as possible. Certain types of parallel motion interfere either with the individuality of parts or with the forward momentum of the voice leading. Consequently, the following types of parallel motion are forbidden:

Parallel unisons: Here individuality does not exist, since the one part merely duplicates the pitch, register, and motion of the other (Example 5-17).

Parallel octaves: Here one part duplicates the pitch and motion of the other in a different register; this provides some contrast but not enough to give the feeling of two individual voices (Example 5-18).

Parallel perfect 5ths: The perfect 5th is unique in that it is the only interval that can define a triadic root (see Unit 2, section 7). This quality gives the interval a very strong stability and resistance to forward momentum. Composers from the fifteenth through the nineteenth centuries have excluded parallel 5ths from their writings, as well as unisons and octaves (Example 5-19).

5-17

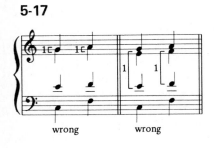

5-18

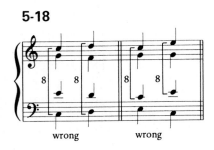

5-19

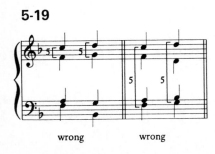

Motion from a perfect 5th to a diminished 5th is acceptable. Motion from a diminished 5th to a perfect 5th does not constitute parallel 5ths but is normally avoided since the dissonant interval does not resolve (Example 5-20).

The prohibition of parallel unisons, 5ths, and octaves refers only to motion within the *same* pair of voices. Example 5-21 shows two chords, one with an octave between bass and alto, the other with an octave between bass and soprano. Progressions like this do *not* contain parallel octaves.

The exact repetition of a unison, octave, or perfect 5th does not create motion and is therefore not a case of forbidden parallels (Example 5-22).

5-20

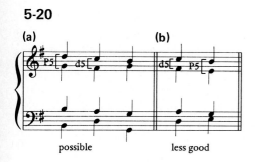

5-21   **5-22**

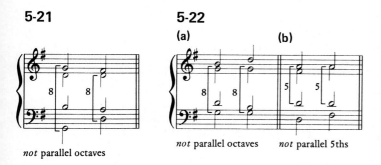

14. Doubling in free textures. In instrumental pieces, in which the number of parts will change from time to time, doublings at the octave may occur, usually in order to obtain variety of sound or for emphasis. Such doublings are *not* parallel octaves. Example 5-23, an excerpt from a piano piece of Brahms, illustrates octave doubling. The reduction shows that the piece begins with three real parts; at the repetition of the theme, the texture changes to four parts and contrasts with the first statement by the absence of doublings, the change of register, and the different harmonization.

5-23   Brahms, Intermezzo, Op. 76/7

(a)

(b) reduction

Doublings at the unison occur frequently in chamber and orchestral music. This is shown in the Schumann passage in Example 5-24. Where the number of voices must remain the same, as in a chorale or harmony exercise, such doublings should be strictly avoided.

5-24   Schumann, Trio, Op. 63, I

15. 5ths and octaves by contrary motion. Consecutive 5ths and octaves by contrary motion (Example 5-25) are not, strictly speaking, illegal, although they are best avoided in most cases, since the succession of two perfect intervals in the same pair of voices tends to cause unwanted accents. (The same applies to motion between a unison and an octave.) In compositions—usually those with a free texture—octaves in the outer voices may occur at the end of a phrase for purposes of emphasis (5-25a). 5ths in the outer voices are less frequent (5-25b), but sometimes occur between an outer and an inner voice, as in 5-25c.

5-25

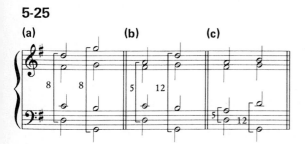

16. Hidden 5ths and octaves. 5ths or octaves approached by similar motion are called *hidden* (or *direct*) 5ths or octaves. The term "hidden" reflects the old theoretical idea that hidden 5ths or octaves conceal actual parallels that would occur if the intervals were filled in (Example 5-26).

5-26

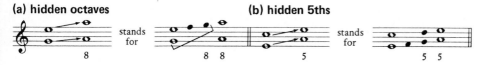

Hidden 5ths and octaves are far less drastic in their effect than parallels, and theorists disagree about their effect in four-part writing. In this respect, keep the following in mind:

1. The fewer the voices, the stronger and more problematic the effect. (Thus hidden 5ths and octaves are forbidden entirely in two-part writing.)
2. The more complex the texture, the milder, and therefore less problematic, the effect.
3. The greater the concentration of dissonance, the weaker the effect.
4. Hidden octaves tend to be more obtrusive than hidden 5ths.
5. Hidden octaves and 5ths are most noticeable in outer voices, least so in inner voices.
6. They are most noticeable where there is no common tone between the two chords, least so where they occur within a single chord.
7. Skips in both voices emphasize hidden 5ths and octaves; stepwise motion in the upper voice minimizes their effect.
8. And most important: Bach, in his chorales, avoids hidden octaves in the outer voices except where the soprano moves by step (Example 5-27a). Follow this practice, use your ear in doubtful cases, and otherwise don't worry.

5-27

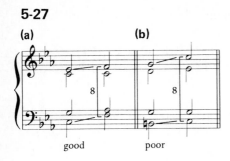

17. **Voice crossing.** If two voices exchange position—if the alto moves below the tenor, for instance—the voices are said to cross (Example 5-28). Voice crossing occurs for a variety of reasons; it is least problematic when it involves only inner voices, and it is best when of very brief duration. A soprano or bass line may become obscured if crossed by an inner voice; you should therefore avoid such crossings.

5-28   voice crossing

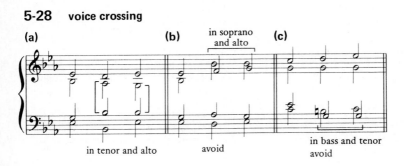

18. **Overlapping.** Example 5-29 illustrates overlapping. Here the two voices do not cross, but the lower voice moves above the former position of the upper voice or vice versa. Such voice leadings may be confusing, particularly if a melodic stepwise connection can be made between the two voices. In the interest of clarity, overlaps, while not strictly forbidden, should be avoided wherever possible in four-part vocal style. They occur more appropriately in keyboard style; indeed, they are unavoidable if the soprano leaps any great distance.

5-29   voice overlapping

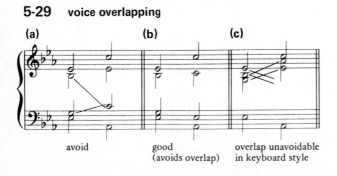

POINTS FOR REVIEW

1. The ranges of the four vocal parts are: soprano—c^1 to g^2; alto—g to c^2; tenor—c to g^1; bass—E to c^1. (See Example 5-2 for possible extensions.)

2. The soprano and alto are notated on the upper staff with treble clef; the tenor and bass are notated on the lower staff with bass clef. The soprano and tenor stems always point up; the alto and bass stems always point down.

3. It is usually best to double the most stable tone(s) of a chord. Therefore, the leading tone in V or VII and the 7th of seventh chords should not be doubled.

4. Complete chords create the best sonority. The 5th of major or minor root-position triads may be omitted, but *not* the 3rd. If the 5th is omitted, the root is often tripled. Similarly, the 5th may be omitted from root-position seventh chords and the root doubled.

5. Except for bass and tenor, the distance between adjacent voices should not exceed an octave. In close position, the upper three voices are as close together as possible. In open position, the upper voices are separated so that a chord tone could be inserted between alto and soprano or alto and tenor. In keyboard style, the distance between soprano and tenor is an octave or less and vocal ranges—particularly in the tenor—need not be strictly observed. (See Example 5-8 for notation.)

6. There are two types of melodic motion: conjunct and disjunct. In disjunct motion the augmented 2nd is forbidden, as is a leap larger than an octave. After any large leap, it is best to change direction.

7. There are four types of simultaneous motion: parallel, similar, oblique, and contrary.

8. Parallel unisons, parallel octaves, and parallel perfect 5ths are forbidden.

9. Hidden 5ths or octaves occur where the 5th or octave is approached by similar motion. Hidden octaves in the outer voices should be avoided unless the soprano moves by step.

10. Voice crossing (Example 5-28) is best avoided where it involves an outer voice. Overlap (Example 5-29) is also best avoided except in keyboard style.

EXERCISES

1. Explain: conjunct and disjunct motion; parallel, similar, oblique, and contrary motion; 5ths and octaves by contrary motion; hidden 5ths and octaves; voice crossing; overlapping.

2. Define, and know the rules for: vocal range; complete and incomplete chords; spacing; open position, close position; keyboard style.

3. Write at least five different versions of each of the following chords. Vary the spacing, the doubling, and the position of the soprano. Name the major key to which (e), (f), and (g) belong; name the minor key to which (h) belongs.

   a. F major $\frac{5}{3}$
   b. C# minor $\frac{5}{3}$
   c. F# diminished $\frac{6}{3}$
   d. A♭ major $\frac{6}{4}$
   e. D dominant 7th

   f. E dominant $\frac{6}{5}$
   g. B♭ dominant $\frac{4}{2}$
   h. A# diminished 7th
   i. D# half-diminished $\frac{6}{5}$
   j. D♭ major 7th

4. There are many mistakes of voice leading and chord construction in the following example. Indicate each one you can find.

I-V-I AND ITS ELABORATIONS

6
I, V, and V⁷

6-1   Kuhnau, Biblical Sonata No. 5

Gideon incoraggia i suoi soldati

TONIC AND DOMINANT

1. I-V-I. Example 6-1 is a rather special piece. It is from the fifth of a set of six Biblical Sonatas for keyboard composed by Bach's predecessor in Leipzig, Johann Kuhnau (1660-1722). This sonata is entitled "The Savior of Israel: Gideon," and the Italian subtitle at the beginning of the movement means "Gideon encourages his soldiers." Kuhnau may have wanted to indicate that Gideon was a man of few words, for in all its 33 measures the piece uses only two chords, a curious and unusual procedure. The two chords are I and V, and the choice is not an accident; it would be scarcely possible to compose a coherent piece of tonal music with any other combination of two chords. Only the V chord can contrast with the tonic and, at the same time, lead to and affirm it so convincingly.

V leads to I by both *harmonic* and *contrapuntal* motion. The harmonic motion is that of the descending 5th (or its inversion, the ascending 4th), discussed in Unit 4. At the same time the 5th and 3rd of V, $\hat{2}$ and $\hat{7}$, stand in a stepwise *contrapuntal* relation to $\hat{1}$. The progression V-I, therefore, combines the strongest possible harmonic motion (in the bass) with the strongest possible melodic motion (Example 6-2). The progression from an opening tonic through a dominant to a closing tonic constitutes the harmonic nucleus of many phrases, sections, and, as with the Kuhnau, complete pieces. It is *the* basic progression of Western music.

6-2

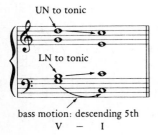

bass motion: descending 5th
      V — I

2. Expanding I and V. Obviously, if I-V-I is to become the basis for an entire piece, the progression must somehow be expanded. The basic way to accomplish this expansion is by using the harmonies as the source for more or less extended melodic lines. Look at the first 14 bars of the Kuhnau. Three bars of block chords suggest a kind of call-to-attention, with changes of tones within the chord creating a bit of melodic interest. With the upbeat to bar 4, a more distinct melody begins in the left hand. Despite the low register, the tones of this melody do not actually function as the bass of this chord, which is simply the low C, sustained by implication from the opening bars. Kuhnau probably wanted to depict Gideon's exhortation to his troops in a booming baritone, hence the register. The melody itself is nothing more than a simple arpeggiation of the tonic chord, its resemblance to a bugle call giving it a distinctly martial character. With the upbeat to bar 8, the soldiers begin to respond with the same tune, but in a much higher register (perhaps their voices hadn't yet changed). According to the Bible, there are three hundred of them, so the response supports the melodic line with additional tones, all of them belonging to the I chord. Starting with the last eighth note in bar 11, passing tones in the upper voices fill in the 3rds between chord tones. After the double bar, the dominant is expanded in an almost identical way, but with the opening melody inverted. The tonic returns in bar 28 and continues to the end except for the V of bar 31, which we shall discuss in the next section. The Kuhnau piece demonstrates the simplest way to expand a chord: *arpeggiating above a sustained bass.* This technique forms the basis for many of the more advanced procedures we shall explore in later units.

3. Cadences. Music has its punctuations and groupings, roughly comparable to the sentences and paragraphs of language. In bar 15 of the Kuhnau, the impact of the change of harmony, the slower rhythm, and the stepwise descent of the melodic line from G to D make us hear the arrival of V as a goal and mark the end of an important group. But there is still more to follow: we have reached the end of a sentence, so to speak, not a paragraph. Having reached V and $\hat{2}$, we feel the need to continue to I and $\hat{1}$. This doesn't happen right away. After the double bar, dominant harmony continues, and the rhythmic activity increases again. The tonic returns in bar 28, but without a feeling of repose: the melody is on $\hat{3}$, and the rhythm becomes more active, as it did in bars 12-13. V and $\hat{2}$ are once more reached in bar 31, beat 2, but this time the motion continues to the final goal: tonic chord and $\hat{1}$.

We call a succession of chords that marks the end of a musical phrase or section, as in bars 14-15 and 31-32 of the Kuhnau, a *cadence* (Latin *cadere*, to fall). Because it creates a halt in the musical motion, a cadence is a rhythmic as well as a tonal event. Many cadences, as in the Kuhnau, show a broadening of time values; in most the final chord falls on a strong beat. The Kuhnau piece illustrates the two most important types of cadence: the *authentic cadence* (V-I) in bars 31-32, and the *semicadence*, or *half cadence* (ends on V), in bars 14-15. Example 6-3 illustrates typical cadential patterns in four voices.

6-3   cadential patterns

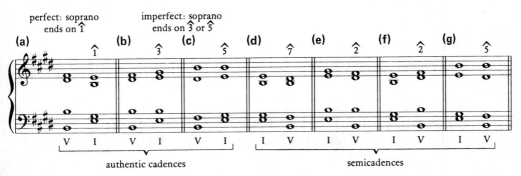

perfect: soprano ends on $\hat{1}$ imperfect: soprano ends on $\hat{3}$ or $\hat{5}$

authentic cadences   semicadences

Authentic cadences (6-3 a-c): 6-3a is the most final sounding and is often called a *perfect* authentic cadence. This cadence is used mostly at the end of a piece, but it is possible earlier. 6-3b and c are *imperfect* authentic cadences; that is, they are less final sounding than 6-3a. Of the two, 6-3b occurs much more frequently than 6-3c.

Semicadences (6-3 d-g): 6-3g occurs somewhat less frequently than 6-3d, e, and f because of lack of melodic activity in the soprano.

4. Different functions of I and V. Chords derive their meaning—as opposed to their label—from the way they function. In the Kuhnau, the tonic functions first as an *opening tonic,* establishing the tonality and serving as a point of departure. At the end it is a goal of motion, thus a *closing tonic.* The V has three different functions in this piece. In bars 15-16, V is the goal chord of the cadential progression I-V (semicadence) and articulates the close of the first section. In bars 17-27, V is expanded so that it becomes a significant portion of the piece; V thus helps to shape the form. And in bar 31, V functions as part of an authentic cadence leading to the final tonic and thus identifying it as goal. Finally, the Kuhnau illustrates an important fact about harmonic progression—namely, that it operates over both large and small spans. As Example 6-4 illustrates, the expanded I and V chords create a large-scale harmonic progression, whereas the quicker successions of chords at the cadences mark important points of arrival.

6-4

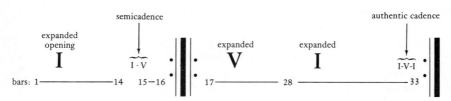

5. Doublings. (For doublings of I and V, review Unit 5, section 3.) Most often the root is doubled both in I and in V, but the 5th and 3rd of I and the 5th of V are also possibilities. *Never* double the leading tone (3rd of V)!

6. I-V-I in four parts. (Review Unit 1, sections 9-10.) The progression I-V-I makes possible many important melodic and voice-leading techniques. In Unit 1 you learned that $\hat{2}$ and $\hat{7}$ can function as neighbors to $\hat{3}$ or $\hat{1}$ and that $\hat{2}$ can function as a passing tone between $\hat{1}$ and $\hat{3}$. All these melodic figures frequently occur harmonized by I-V-I. Writing the progression with these different possibilities in the soprano voice can provide valuable practice. Don't feel obliged to memorize every detail of voice leading shown in the following examples, but do refer to them from time to time, especially when working out the exercises. What you *must* remember is that I supports $\hat{1}$, $\hat{3}$, and $\hat{5}$; V supports $\hat{5}$, $\hat{7}$, and $\hat{2}$.

Lower-neighbor figures (Example 6-5): These figures occur frequently and present no voice-leading problems. The common tone $\hat{5}$ is kept in the same voice; other voices move to the nearest position.

6-5   lower-neighbor figures

(a) $\hat{1}$ in soprano

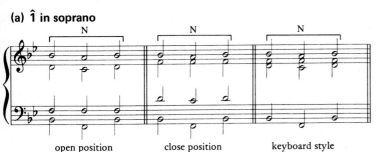

open position   close position   keyboard style

(b) $\hat{3}$ in soprano

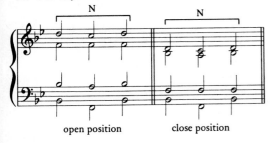

open position   close position

(c) $\hat{5}$ in soprano

open position   close position

Descending passing motion (Example 6-6): The very important melodic progression $\hat{3}$-$\hat{2}$-$\hat{1}$ often supports the cadential progression I-V-I, as at the end of Example 6-1. $\hat{3}$ and $\hat{1}$ are stable tones belonging to the tonic triad; $\hat{2}$ is a passing tone, dissonant against the tonic triad. The V provides consonant support for this passing tone. With this soprano line the common tone does not always remain in the same voice. In 6-6a the 5th of the final tonic chord is omitted in order to allow the leading tone (in the tenor) to move to the tonic. In 6-6b the leading tone descends to the 5th of I in order to make possible a complete chord. In 6-6c the common tone $\hat{5}$ is kept in the alto throughout. The tenor leaps from the leading tone to the 3rd of the tonic chord.

6-6   descending passing tones

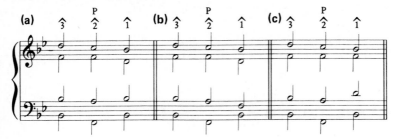

Upper-neighbor figures (Example 6-7): Compare the voice leading here with that of Example 6-5.

6-7   upper-neighbor figures

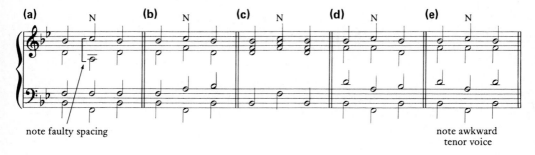

note faulty spacing

note awkward tenor voice

Other figures (Example 6-8).

6-8   other figures

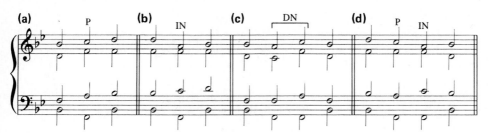

7. I-V-I in minor. (Review Unit 4, section 5.) In any progression where V goes to I, or creates the expectation of such a motion, $\hat{7}$ must be raised to form a leading tone, so that V becomes a major triad as in Examples 6-9b and c; the progression shown in 6-9a is *wrong*. It will be good practice for you to rewrite Examples 6-5 through 6-8 in various minor keys. Only one detail of voice leading requires comment: the progression shown in Example 6-9c will contain a diminished 4th in the tenor voice. Although melodic dissonances are generally to be avoided in the inner voices, this progression, which occurs frequently in the Bach chorales, is permissible.

6-9

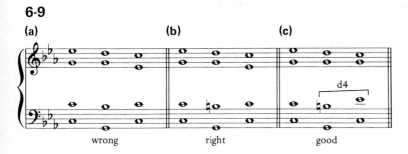

8. Expanding I and V in four parts. In the Kuhnau we saw how I and V were expanded by changing the position of all the upper voices, so that when the soprano moved, the alto and tenor followed in parallel or similar motion. The inner voices need not always follow the soprano, however; sometimes considerations of vocal range make it better for one or both of them not to. In moving from one chord position to another it is not necessary to keep the chord complete: the 5th may be omitted, but take care not to omit the 3rd (Example 6-10).

6-10

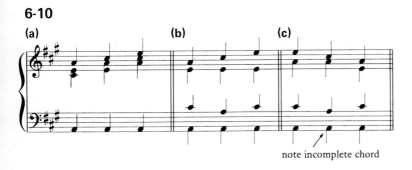

THE DOMINANT SEVENTH

9. V^7 as dissonant chord. Example 6-11, the beginning of the trio from a minuet by Haydn, provides an excellent introduction to the use of V^7. In bars 3-5, and in bar 7, $\hat{5}$ is in the bass, but the chord contains a 7th above the bass as well as a 3rd and a 5th. Because of the 7th, V^7, unlike V$^5_3$, is a *dissonant* chord; the 7th, which represents a descending passing tone, must therefore resolve (review Unit 4, section 11). Thus, in the Haydn, the $\hat{4}$ (7th of V^7) of bars 3-5 resolves to $\hat{3}$ in bar 6; likewise the inner-voice $\hat{4}$ of bar 7 moves to $\hat{3}$ in bar 8. V^7 has the same harmonic meaning as V, but the dissonance (a contrapuntal factor) intensifies its drive to the tonic. V^7 is therefore often part of an authentic cadence, as in bars 7-8 of the Haydn.

6-11   Haydn, Symphony No. 97, III (simplified)

10. V⁷ and the soprano voice. (Review Unit 1, sections 9-11, especially in reference to use of $\hat{4}$.) One very important function of V⁷ is to support $\hat{4}$ in the soprano. In bars 3-5 of the Haydn, $\hat{4}$ is part of a somewhat elaborated stepwise descending line—in other words $\hat{4}$ functions as a passing tone; Example 6-12a shows this in reduced form. $\hat{4}$ supported by V⁷ can also appear as a neighbor to $\hat{3}$, either complete (6-12b) or incomplete (6-12c).

6-12

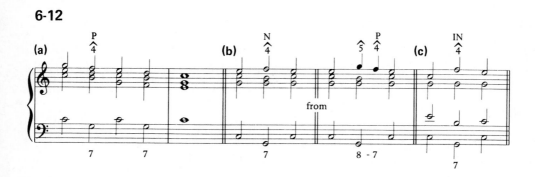

V⁷, like V⅗, can also support $\hat{7}$, $\hat{2}$, and $\hat{5}$ in the soprano. If $\hat{5}$ is in the soprano, the V⁷ will be incomplete, as in Example 6-13c. Sometimes, however, V⅗ is a better choice for supporting these tones. If the melodic line comes to rest on $\hat{7}$, $\hat{2}$, or $\hat{5}$, V will generally produce a better effect than V⁷, which conveys an inappropriate feeling of activity. *For this reason, V⁷ is rarely used in a semicadence.*

11. V⁷ in four voices: doubling. In four parts, V⁷ may appear as a complete chord ($\frac{7}{5}$), in which case there is no doubling, or as an incomplete chord with root doubled and fifth omitted ($\frac{8}{7}$). Example 6-14 illustrates. In this example the figures represent *all* the intervals above the bass. In actual figured basses of the Baroque period incomplete chords are not necessarily indicated by special symbols.

6-13

6-14

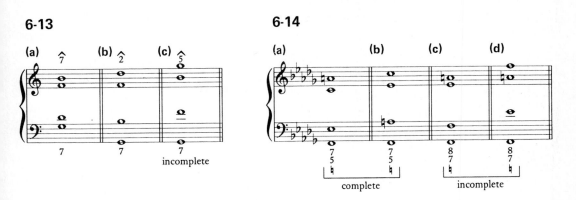

12. V⁷-I: voice-leading techniques. V⁷ contains two "tendency" tones: $\hat{4}$ and $\hat{7}$, the scale degrees that form a tritone in major and in the inflected forms of minor. (Like V$\frac{5}{3}$, V⁷ in minor *must always contain a leading tone.*) As we have seen, $\hat{4}$, which forms a dissonance with the bass, *must* move down by step to $\hat{3}$. $\hat{7}$ tends strongly to move to $\hat{8}$, and if it appears in the soprano voice (an exposed position), it must do so. Where both these tendency tones resolve, one of the chords in the progression V⁷-I will be incomplete. In Example 6-15a, for instance, where the V⁷ is complete, the I will be incomplete; in 6-15b, where the V⁷ is incomplete, the I will be complete. However, since $\hat{7}$ is consonant with the bass, it may move to $\hat{5}$ if it is an inner voice; this procedure makes it possible for both V⁷ and I to be complete chords (6-15c). The last is the voice leading preferred by Bach in his chorale settings, especially at cadences, but all three possibilities are good.

6-15

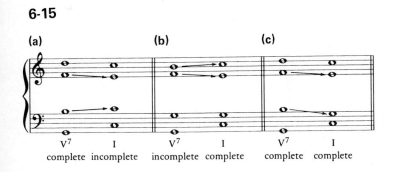

Normal resolution of the 7th combined with the melodic motion $\hat{2}$-$\hat{3}$ will result in a tonic with a *doubled 3rd*, as shown in Example 6-16a. Despite the irregular doubling, the contrary motion into the doubled 3rd has a good effect, and the motion up to $\hat{3}$ often helps to produce a beautiful soprano line. This doubled 3rd, therefore, is far preferable to the one in Example 6-16b, where the similar motion into the octave on $\hat{3}$ creates an unpleasant effect, at least in the simple and transparent textures of beginning harmony exercises.

Sometimes a melodic interpolation decorates the resolution; this occurs most frequently in the soprano voice (Example 6-17).

6-16   **6-17**

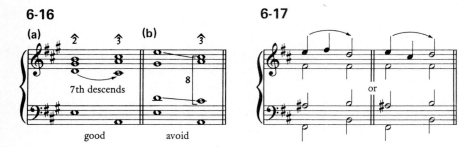

13. V⁸⁻⁷. Dominant harmony is often extended and intensified by moving from $\frac{5}{3}$ to 7, as shown in Example 6-18. This happens frequently in an authentic cadence, where the introduction of the 7th can be emphasized by a *downward* leap of an octave in the bass. Note that the 7th sometimes comes from $\hat{5}$ rather than $\hat{8}$.

6-18

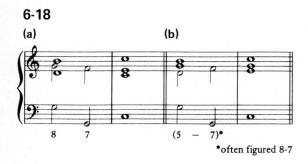

14. Expanding V⁷. Like I and V⁵₃, V⁷ may be expanded by changing the positions of the upper voices. This may result in a *transfer* of the dissonant 7th from one voice to another; the 7th will resolve in the last voice in which it occurs, as in Example 6-19.

6-19

Extending V^7 creates the possibility of dissonant melodic leaps of the 7th, diminished 5th, and augmented 4th, which we will discuss in Unit 8.

15. Harmony and rhythm. (Review Unit 3, sections 6-7.) Patterns of chord change create groupings and accents, and consequently exert a strong influence on our impression of rhythm. Especially in simple styles with more or less uniform note values and few changes in texture, the succession of chords can be the most important factor in defining the rhythm. In general, repeating a chord attracts very little accent. Because there is minimal contrast, the ear tends to hear the repeated chord as an extension of the preceding one. Changing a chord, on the other hand, tends to attract an accent; a "new" chord, therefore, tends to sound rhythmically stronger than a repeated one.

Although conflict between rhythm and meter is a very important compositional resource, it is one that demands a good deal of skill and experience—and usually a more complex texture than occurs in harmony exercises. For the time being, therefore, organize your written work so that the changes of chord support the meter. Avoid repeating a chord from a weak to a strong beat, for this contradicts the meter (Example 6-20). Repeating a chord from a strong beat to a weak beat is permissible, and repetition from a strong beat, through a weak beat, to the next strong beat is also possible. Weak-strong repetition of an *initial* tonic emphasizes the tonality and is therefore justifiable.

6-20

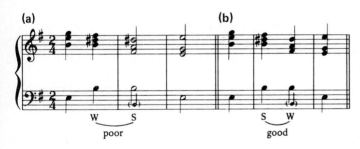

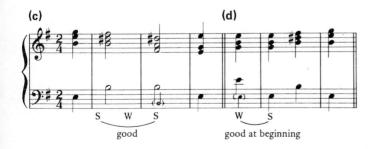

Sometimes the segmentation of a musical idea into rhythmic or melodic groups creates patterns that also justify weak-strong repetition; in such cases we hear the weak beat as the end of one pattern rather than as an upbeat to the next (Example 6-21).

6-21

good   etc.

POINTS FOR REVIEW

1. I-V-I is the basic harmonic progression. V leads to I by harmonic motion in the bass and by contrapuntal motion in the upper voices.

2. I and V (and every other major or minor root-position triad) can be expanded by changing the position of the upper voices over a sustained bass.

3. I supports $\hat{1}$, $\hat{3}$, and $\hat{5}$. V supports $\hat{5}$, $\hat{7}$, and $\hat{2}$.

4. V-I at the end of a phrase is an authentic cadence; if the soprano leads to $\hat{1}$, the result is a *perfect* authentic cadence. I-V is a semicadence.

5. In doubling I or V, the root is best; next best is the 5th; the 3rd of I is possible. The leading tone (the 3rd of V) must not be doubled.

6. In minor, the 3rd of V must be raised to form a leading tone.

7. V⁷ is V$\frac{5}{3}$ plus a 7th above the bass. This 7th is dissonant and must resolve *downward by step* ($\hat{4}$-$\hat{3}$). When moving from V⁷ to I, avoid similar motion into doubled $\hat{3}$.

8. V⁷, which supports $\hat{4}$, $\hat{5}$, $\hat{7}$, and $\hat{2}$, intensifies motion to I. V⁷-I is therefore good at an authentic cadence, but V⁷ is not normally the goal of a semicadence.

9. V⁷ may be complete, with no tone doubled, or the 5th may be omitted and the root doubled.

10. V⁸⁻⁷ is a common way of expanding V at authentic cadences. If the 7th of V⁷ is transferred from one upper voice to another, it must resolve in the last voice.

11. When repeating a chord, strong-weak repetition is good; weak-strong repetition is poor; strong-(weak)-strong repetition is good.

EXERCISES

NOTE. Beginning in this unit, avoid chords and techniques in your written work that have not yet been explained in the text.

Learn to *hear* what you write. Sing the given melody or bass so that you know what it sounds like; sing the individual lines of your harmonizations, and play your completed exercises at the piano. When you check for errors in voice leading, be sure to test all six combinations of voices: bass-tenor, bass-alto, bass-soprano, tenor-alto, tenor-soprano, and alto-soprano.

REALIZING FIGURED BASSES. First make sure you know what chords are demanded by the figures. Next give your attention to the soprano; try to invent a top voice that is interesting and, if possible, beautiful—one with a good balance between stepwise motion and leaps.

HARMONIZING MELODIES. Remember that $\hat{5}$ belongs both to I and $V^{(7)}$. In deciding which to use, remember to avoid weak-strong repetitions of the same chord.

We do not recommend the addition of passing tones, neighboring tones, suspensions, and the like for the exercises in this unit.

1. Preliminaries. Complete the following melodic fragments and set for four voices in note-against-note texture, so that each melody tone gets a chord.

2. Figured bass with some melody tones. Complete the soprano and add inner voices.

3. Melody. Set for four voices; harmonize each tone of the melody.

transferred 7th

4. Melody.

7
I^6, V^6, and VII^6

7-1

(a) Chorale melody, Das neugeborne Kindelein

(b) Bach, Chorale 178

I^6 AND V^6

1. New possibilities for the bass line. Example 7-1 shows two settings of the first phrase of a chorale melody. The first setting, done by us for purposes of illustration, uses only I, V, and V^7, the chords discussed in Unit 6. The second, a harmonization by Bach, adds three important $^6_3$ chords: I^6, V^6, and VII^6. There is a considerable difference, to put it mildly, in the effect of the two bass lines. The first is rather primitive. Confined to two tones, it can provide only the minimal harmonies implied by the melody. On the other hand, Bach's bass with its three new scale degrees ($\hat{3}$, $\hat{7}$, and $\hat{2}$) is far more sophisticated. Here the listener can sense a distinction between goals of motion and intermediate steps. In addition, the bass has a partly melodic or contrapuntal character arising out of the stepwise line (review Unit 4, section 20). Both these characteristics relate directly to the use of $\frac{6}{3}$ chords.

2. I⁶ and V⁶ expanding I and V. In Example 6-1 we saw how chords can be extended by changing tones in the soprano line. However useful that possibility is, musical composition would not have evolved very far if composers had not learned to extend a chord by changing its bass tone. Perhaps the most frequent and important way of expanding *any* major or minor triad is by moving the bass between the root and 3rd of the chord (Example 7-2). This, of course, changes the position of the chord from $\frac{5}{3}$ to $\frac{6}{3}$ (or the reverse). In this context $\frac{6}{3}$ functions as an inversion of $\frac{5}{3}$. Such a procedure creates a melodic activity in the bass that makes it possible to continue the same harmony without monotony. Thus in bar 1 of the Bach excerpt the initial tonic is expanded by a motion in the bass from $\hat{1}$ to $\hat{3}$ and back, producing the succession $\frac{5}{3}$-$\frac{6}{3}$-$\frac{5}{3}$. The second eighth note of each pair in the bass is a passing tone. These tones do not affect the harmony. (Note the imitation in the alto of the bass figure G-A-B♭, which causes the two upper parts to cross.) At the beginning of a Handel variation (Example 7-3a), both I and V are expanded. Here the $\frac{6}{3}$ chords come first, producing a pattern of descending 3rds (7-3b and c).

7-2 $\frac{6}{3}$ **expands** $\frac{5}{3}$

7-3

(a) Handel, Double IV
   (from *Harpsichord Suite No. 5*)

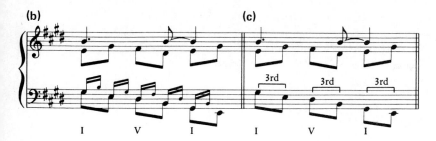

I   V   I   I   V   I

3. $\frac{6}{3}$ **expanding** $\frac{5}{3}$. Example 7-4 shows the most important possibilities for the soprano over the bass progression I-I⁶ (which could also be V-V⁶, and so on). Particularly important, because of their far-reaching compositional applications, are parallel 10ths between the outer voices (7-4a) and voice exchange (interchanging two tones between two voices, as in 7-4c). Example 7-5 shows characteristic voice leadings in four parts.

7-4   I-I⁶ and soprano

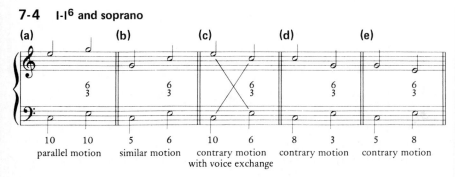

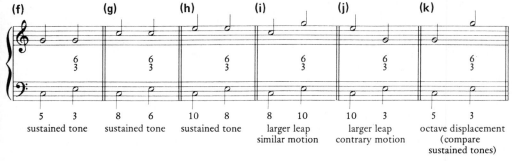

7-5   in four voices

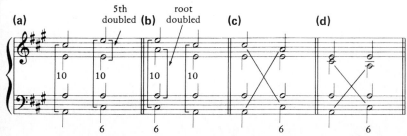

4. $\frac{6}{3}$ substituting for $\frac{5}{3}$. I⁶ and V⁶ can support the same melody tones as I and V; they imply the same harmonic function, though less strongly. They can, therefore, substitute for $\frac{5}{3}$ in some circumstances. For example, I⁶ may replace I where the greater stability of the root position chord is not needed, as in Example 7-6, a fragment from Schumann's *Papillons.*

7-6   Schumann, Papillons, Op. 2, Finale

However, the two positions are by no means completely interchangeable. $\frac{6}{3}$ chords attract less accent than their root-position equivalents and give a more flowing effect; their use imparts a melodic character to the bass line. This is largely because the 6th, the most characteristic interval of the $\frac{6}{3}$ chord, is a much less stable consonance than the 5th, which occurs in root position. Therefore, where stability is needed, as in most beginnings and virtually all endings, $\frac{6}{3}$ is *not* a satisfactory substitute for $\frac{5}{3}$.

A further limitation on the use of I⁶: avoid the progression V⁷-I⁶ where the soprano moves $\hat{4}$-$\hat{3}$, since the similar motion of the outer voices into $\hat{3}$ will cause a bad set of hidden octaves, particularly if I⁶ is in a rhythmically strong position (Example 7-7). Compare Example 6-16b, page 90.

7-7

5. I-I⁶-V; arpeggiation in the bass. A bass motion from I to V can alight on $\hat{3}$ along the way. If tonic harmony is sustained above the $\hat{3}$, a I⁶ chord will result, as in Example 7-8a. Although the harmony changes from I to V, the bass line *arpeggiates* the tonic triad, a feature that helps the listener relate the whole progression to the governing tonic. The easiest way to accomplish this arpeggiation is simply to move up from $\hat{1}$ to $\hat{3}$ and from $\hat{3}$ to $\hat{5}$, but a motion down a 6th from I to I⁶ is also possible (7-8b). Continuing on to I (7-8c) produces a larger arpeggiation, and one that sounds more self-contained, ending as it does on the tonic note. Bass arpeggiations like these are an important way of expanding the initial tonic harmony of the basic I-V-I progression.

7-8

(a) Bach, Little Prelude, BWV 924

(b) Brahms, Symphony No. 3, Op. 90, III

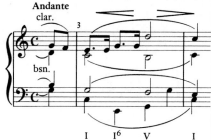

(c) Telemann, Die durstige Natur

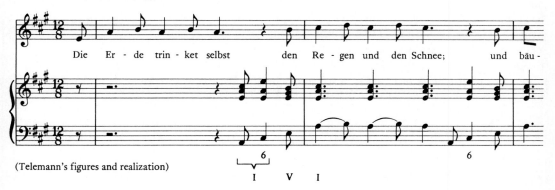

(Telemann's figures and realization)

translation: The earth itself drinks rain and snow.

6. Passing tones. A bass line leading from I to I^6 or from I^6 to V will often contain passing tones that fill in the 3rds between chord tones. Example 7-9 illustrates. Although the exercises in this book don't yet require you to use passing tones in your written work—in later units we'll study figuration in detail—you might want to add one occasionally to create a more flowing bass line between $\hat{1}$ and $\hat{3}$ or $\hat{3}$ and $\hat{5}$. (Soprano passing tones between the same scale degrees are also possible.) *Warning:* Parallel 5ths lurk in the progression from I^6 to V with a bass passing tone unless I^6 occurs with bass tone doubled, as in Example 7-9.

For the time being, use only unaccented passing tones—that is, those that fall on weaker beats or parts of the beat than the chordal tones they connect. Make sure that any passing tones you use sound appropriate. In an exercise that contains only half notes and quarters, for example, a passing tone that divides a beat into two eighth notes may sound out of place; if the exercise contains eighth-note motion in other places, however, the passing tone has a better chance of success.

7-9   bass passing tones

Bach, Chorale 166

7. **V⁶ within expanded tonic.** Using V⁶ between two root-position tonics produces the stepwise bass line $\hat{8}$-$\hat{7}$-$\hat{8}$ and makes possible a contrapuntal expansion of tonic harmony. Here the specific function of V⁶ is that of a neighboring chord. Where a clear expression of the harmonic 5th relationship is needed (as in most cadences), root-position V should appear; but in other situations, especially near the beginning or the middle of phrases, V⁶ often functions more effectively. Compare bars 1-2 of the two chorale settings shown in Example 7-1.

Example 7-10 shows three characteristic uses of V⁶ within an expanded tonic. In 7-10a, V⁶ supports $\hat{2}$ in a rising soprano line, the kind that frequently occurs at the beginning of a phrase. In 7-10b, V⁶ forms an effective support for $\hat{5}$; the stepwise bass balances the disjunct soprano. The same is true of 7-10c where the melodic progression would be virtually impossible with root-position I-V-I, because of the consecutive octaves.

7-10   V⁶ within an expanded tonic

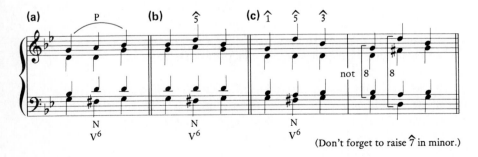

(Don't forget to raise $\hat{7}$ in minor.)

I⁶ can replace the initial tonic in the progression I-V⁶-I (Example 7-11). Here the bass of V⁶ functions as an incomplete neighbor to I. In minor, the progression produces a perfectly allowable diminished 4th in the bass line (compare Example 6-9c, tenor). Because $\hat{7}$ is active in the direction of $\hat{8}$, V⁶ normally continues on to I$\frac{5}{3}$, not I⁶.

7-11   I⁶ replacing I⁵₃

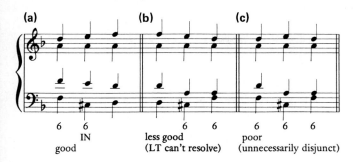

8. **⁵₃ expanding ⁶₃.** In most cases where the ⁶₃ and ⁵₃ positions of a chord appear together or in close conjunction, ⁵₃ is the principal chord, owing to the stability of its perfect 5th. However rhythmic and melodic factors may cause the reverse to be true. In an excerpt from Handel's G minor Oboe Concerto (Example 7-12), both the strong rhythmic position of the first F♯ and its stepwise connection to the tonic, G, make the V⁵₃ chord subordinate to its first inversion. (Note that the incomplete chords in this example would be filled in by the continuo player.)

7-12   Handel, G Minor Oboe Concerto, IV

Brief expansions of ⁶₃ chords occur fairly often; however, for large-scale expansions where the chord becomes the basis of an entire section (like the V in Example 6-1, bars 17-27), the stable sonority of the root position is necessary.

9. **Doubling I⁶ and V⁶.** Any tone of I⁶ may be doubled; doubling the soprano often gives a good sonority. In V⁶ the leading tone must *never* be doubled. Both the remaining tones of V⁶ (2̂ and 5̂) are possible choices.

VII⁶ (LEADING-TONE TRIAD)

10. **2̂ in the bass line.** As we saw in section 6, a bass line that expands tonic harmony by moving from 1̂ to 3̂ (or from 3̂ to 1̂) can take on a more melodic character by passing through 2̂. The passing 2̂ can become more prominent if it forms

part of a chord; in this case we speak of a *passing chord*. A particularly useful passing chord built on $\hat{2}$ is VII⁶; go back to Example 7-1 and notice how convincingly the VII⁶ of bar 3 leads from I⁶ to I. The two stepwise motions to $\hat{1}$—from the adjacent pitches $\hat{2}$ and $\hat{7}$—combine with the descent of $\hat{4}$ to $\hat{3}$ and produce a strong sense of directed motion. VII⁶ contains the three upper tones of V⁷ and, like it, can support $\hat{7}$, $\hat{2}$, and $\hat{4}$ in the soprano. Because of the stepwise bass, however, it functions more typically as a melodic, contrapuntal chord than a cadential, harmonic one. Example 7-13 shows some typical outer-voice possibilities for a VII⁶ that passes from I to I⁶. Very often, as with I-I⁶ or I⁶-I, the soprano will form parallel 10ths and a voice exchange with the bass (7-13a and b). Because the soprano moves by step between two tones of the I chord, it participates in expressing the expanded tonic harmony. Thus, both outer voices join forces to create a counterpoint that animates an extended or *prolonged* tonic. Because it produces stepwise motion in the bass and permits it to occur in the soprano as well, VII⁶ effects a contrapuntal expansion of the disjunct, arpeggiated progressions shown in Example 7-4a and c. Other possibilities for the soprano are shown in 7-13c, d, and e; they are by no means the only ones. In addition to its basic function of passing between I and I⁶, VII⁶ has another important function: it can form a neighboring chord to I or I⁶ (Example 7-14).

7-13   passing VII⁶ and soprano

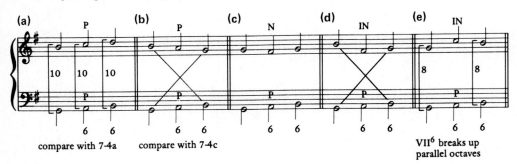

compare with 7-4a   compare with 7-4c

VII⁶ breaks up
parallel octaves

7-14   neighboring VII⁶ and soprano

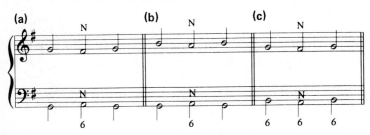

11. Doubling VII⁶. It is usually best to double the bass tone, $\hat{2}$, since this is not part of the tritone; however, voice-leading considerations may make doubling $\hat{4}$ preferable. The leading tone must never be doubled.

12. Resolution of tritone. VII⁶ contains an augmented 4th or diminished 5th in the upper voices. Because the bass of VII⁶ is consonant with both the other tones, the effect of the dissonance is considerably softened. Very frequently the tendency of the tritone to resolve regularly ($\hat{7}$ to $\hat{8}$ and $\hat{4}$ to $\hat{3}$) is offset by other considerations such as achieving a complete tonic chord or stepwise voice leading. Examples 7-15 to 7-18, taken from Bach chorales, illustrate some typical voice leadings, and you will find it useful to consult them when doing your written work.

The dissonance will often resolve normally, as in Example 7-15. However, if the dissonance is an augmented 4th, it can move to a perfect 4th, $\hat{4}$ moving up to $\hat{5}$ (Example 7-16).

7-15   **VII⁶: normal resolution of dissonance**

Bach Chorales

(a) No. 80   **(b) No. 51**

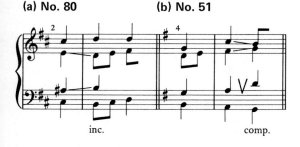

7-16   **VII⁶: A4-P4**

Bach Chorales

(a) No. 72   **(b) No. 40**

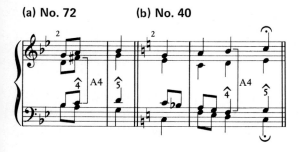

If the dissonance is a diminished 5th, Bach tends to resolve it normally (Example 7-15), for the progression diminished 5th-perfect 5th creates hidden 5ths. As part of the diminished 5th, $\hat{4}$ will normally move up to $\hat{5}$ *only* if the bass moves up to $\hat{3}$ in parallel 10ths, thereby bringing in the tone of resolution in another voice but very prominently (Example 7-17). This voice leading occurs frequently.

7-17   VII⁶: d5-P5

Bach, Chorale 47

Quite often Bach doubles $\hat{4}$, a strategy that permits resolution of one of the tritones, stepwise voice leading, and a complete chord (Example 7-18a and b). If doubling $\hat{4}$ results in both a diminished 5th and an augmented 4th, as in 7-18b, resolve the diminished 5th.

7-18   VII⁶: $\hat{4}$ doubled

Bach Chorales

(a) No. 69   **(b) No. 281, simplified**

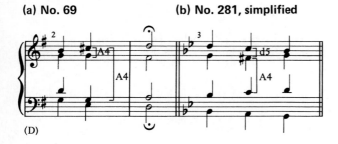

SUMMARY

If the dissonance is a diminished 5th, it must resolve unless VII⁶ moves to I⁶; if it is an augmented 4th, $\hat{4}$ may move either to $\hat{5}$ or to $\hat{3}$.

VII$^5_3$ occurs much less frequently than VII^6 owing to the dissonance (diminished 5th) involving the bass. Its use will be explained in Unit 15; until then avoid it.

13. Avoiding unwanted cadential effect. In a chorale, the unvarying rhythmic pulse (and to some extent the shortness and irregularity of the phrase lengths) often makes the progression V$^{(7)}$-I undesirable except at cadential points, especially if the soprano moves to $\hat{1}$. For the moment, most of your exercises will be chorale-like in rhythm and texture, so you should generally seek alternative progressions except where a cadence is needed. Using VII^6 or V^6 instead of root-position V, or using I^6 instead of I$^5_3$, will also help you become more familiar with these new chords.

14. Harmony and rhythm. In Unit 6, section 15, we saw that repeating a chord from a weak to a strong beat tends to neutralize the metrical accent. Moving between two positions (for example, $^5_3$ and $^6_3$) of the same chord from a weak to a strong beat can also cause contradiction of the meter (V, V^7, and VII^6 count as the same chord). Thus, in Example 7-19a, maintaining the same chord across the bar line creates an unintended syncopation; the weak beat (new chord) actually sounds stronger than the following strong beat (same chord).

Example 7-19b shows how this problem can be avoided. Note that in setting $\hat{5}$ as a melody tone, the choice between I$^{(6)}$ or V$^{(6)}$ is often decided by the rhythmic position of $\hat{5}$ and the melody tone that follows. Example 7-19c, on the other hand, demonstrates a situation where a weak-strong motion within the same harmony is possible. Here the repeated motive in the soprano creates enough emphasis on the downbeat to offset the lack of contrast between V^6 and VII^6. Compare Example 6-21.

Awareness of these rhythmic implications of chord progression is of great importance for harmonizing melodies, setting unfigured basses, and writing phrases. This is especially true in simple textures where there are no quickly moving passing or neighboring tones to enliven the rhythm and to produce a contrast in sonority lacking in the progression of chordal tones.

7-19   chord progression and rhythm

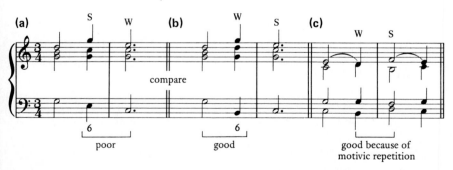

POINTS FOR REVIEW

1. I^6 and V^6 expand root-position I and V. Important voice leadings in the progression I-I^6 or V-V^6 are parallel 10ths or voice exchange in the outer voices. I-I^6-V, possibly continuing to another I, produces an arpeggiation of tonic harmony in the bass. Bass passing tones often connect the chordal tones.

2. I^6 and V^6 may substitute for I and V where the stability of the root-position chord is not needed. V^6 functions as a neighboring chord (N) within an expanded tonic (bass: $\hat{8}$-$\hat{7}$-$\hat{8}$) or as an incomplete neighbor (IN) in the progression I^6-V^6-I.

3. Any tone of I^6 and V^6 may be doubled *except* the leading tone of V^6.

4. VII^6 functions as a passing chord between I and I^6 or as a neighboring chord to I or I^6.

5. In VII^6, either $\hat{2}$ or $\hat{4}$ may be doubled, but never $\hat{7}$ (the leading tone).

6. The tritone in VII^6 often resolves normally ($\hat{7}$-$\hat{8}$ and $\hat{4}$-$\hat{3}$), with all voices tending to move by step. $\hat{7}$ virtually *always* moves to $\hat{8}$, but $\hat{4}$ may sometimes move to $\hat{5}$ if the dissonance is an augmented 4th; if it is a diminished 5th, $\hat{4}$ may move to $\hat{5}$ *only* if the bass moves to I^6 ($\hat{3}$). See Examples 7-15 through 7-18.

7. Avoid VII^5_3 for the time being.

8. To avoid an unwanted cadential effect, don't use $V^{(7)}$-I^5_3 in the middle of a phrase if the soprano goes to $\hat{1}$. Use VII^6 or V^6 instead of root-position $V^{(7)}$, or use I^6 instead of I.

9. Avoid contradicting the meter: don't move between two positions of the same chord from a weak to a strong beat.

EXERCISES

NOTE. Beginning in this unit, the soprano and bass lines in the exercises frequently include idiomatic figures associated with chord progressions discussed in the unit. You will find it helpful, therefore, to review the musical examples in the text before and while you work on the exercises.

With the new chords in this unit, you can now make a distinction between cadential and noncadential functions. Therefore, in harmonizing a bass—figured or unfigured—look for indications of cadences and direct the soprano line to points of repose at these cadences. To prevent the bass from creating an unwanted cadential effect, lead the soprano to a $\hat{3}$ or $\hat{5}$ in preference to $\hat{1}$. In harmonizing a given soprano, also look for melodic halts that might indicate a cadential progression.

The somewhat larger vocabulary of chords that you now have permits more attractive melody harmonizations than were possible with the exercises in Unit 6, but the greater number of choices open to you imposes certain difficulties. The least productive way to respond to these difficulties is by proceeding one or two chords at a time. Try instead to think in larger units, so that you learn to "speak" in musical sentences rather than in single words or syllables. To do this, first scan the entire melody and determine where phrases begin and end;

melodic halts that suggest cadences are your surest guide to phrasing. The sample melody below, for instance, divides into two four-bar units, ending with a half cadence and an authentic cadence, respectively. Sketching in the bass notes of the cadence will prove helpful even though you may wish to modify your original plan as you continue working.

Sample Melody

The next step is to become aware of groups of melody notes that combine to express an underlying harmony. Writing the scale degrees above the melody will help you perceive these groups. In our example, the $\hat{3}$-$\hat{7}$-$\hat{1}$ of bar 1 suggests a tonic chord as basic harmony for the entire bar; the skip from $\hat{2}$ to $\hat{5}$ in bar 2 suggests an expanded V. Bars 3 and 4 arpeggiate a tonic chord, but expanding only one harmony will prevent your writing a cadence, so changing to V for bar 4 is your only sensible option. In Sample Solution 1, we have sketched in the main chords.

Sample Solution 1

After determining the large harmonic structure, fill in the bass line and the subordinate chords that help to expand the basic underlying harmonies; add figured-bass symbols to specify these chords. In Sample Solution 2, we have sketched in a possible harmonization. Note that the soprano above the prolonged tonics in bars 1, 3, and 6 moves between $\hat{3}$ and $\hat{1}$ or $\hat{1}$ and $\hat{3}$. These melodic patterns suggest the possibility of voice exchanges, with I⁶ helping to extend tonic harmony. In bars 1 and 6, an active tone—$\hat{7}$ or $\hat{2}$—occupies the second beat; the $\hat{7}$ of bar 1 is an incomplete neighbor, and the $\hat{2}$ of bar 6 is a passing tone. To harmonize these tones, we would use VII⁶, functioning as a passing chord between I and I⁶.

The voice exchange in bar 3, on the other hand, results from a simple arpeggiation, and the voice exchange would lead to a motion I⁶-I without an intervening chord. The I⁶, by the way, is a particularly good choice for the first beat of bar 3. Since the melody note is $\hat{1}$, a root-position tonic might produce an inappropriate cadential effect, and it might also lead to consecutive octaves from the V of the preceding bar. In bar 7, the downward octave leap in the bass and the $\hat{8}$-$\hat{7}$ passing motion in an inner voice help to intensify the harmonic resolution into the final tonic through rhythmic activity. Note how the use of register—in particular the contrast between the $\hat{5}$ above and the $\hat{5}$ below the tonic—helps to give shape and direction to the bass line.

Sample Solution 2

Check your work at the keyboard, but only after you have written at least a few bars. *Before writing the alto and tenor,* play the outer voices to make sure that these two crucial lines create a good counterpoint, with mainly imperfect consonances except at points of articulation (see Unit 2, section 8). When you add the inner voices, be sure that you check carefully for possible errors. This final stage can sometimes present problems that call for flexibility and resourcefulness. The very beginning of this sample exercise is a case in point. The soprano's downward leap against the rising bass carries with it the threat of parallel octaves, a doubled leading tone, or awkward leaps if the root of I is doubled. The best, though not the only, way to avoid these dangers is to double the 3rd of the opening tonic, as shown in Sample Solution 3b.

Sample Solution 3 (bar 1)

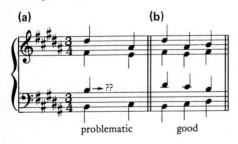

1. Preliminaries. Using a different major or minor key for each, write short progressions (no more than six chords) that end with an authentic cadence and show the following chord combinations:

   a. tonic expanded by $\frac{6}{3}$; outer voices in parallel 10ths
   b. tonic expanded by $\frac{6}{3}$; outer voices exchange
   c. V expanded by $\frac{6}{3}$; outer voices in parallel 10ths
   d. V⁶ as neighbor to I
   e. V⁶ as incomplete neighbor to I
   f. VII⁶ passing between I and I⁶ with voice exchange

g. VII^6 passing between I and I^6 with parallel 10ths
h. VII^6 passing between I and I^6 with soprano $\hat{7}$ as IN
i. VII^6 passing between I^6 and I with soprano $\hat{4}$ as IN

2. Figured bass. Add three upper voices. (This exercise does not use VII^6.)

3. Melody. Use I, V, V^7, I^6, V^6. No VII^6!

4. Outer voices given. Provide figures for the bass and add alto and tenor. Be able
   to describe the function of each chord.

5. Figured bass given. Add three upper voices.

6. Melody given. Add three lower voices.

8

Inversions of V⁷

8-1 Schubert, Impromptu, D. 935

8-1 Schubert, Impromptu, D. 935

V⁶₅, V⁴₃, AND V⁴₂

1. New ways to expand I. It is hard to imagine a better introductory illustration of the inversions of V⁷ than the opening eight bars of Schubert's Impromptu in A♭, D. 935 (Example 8-1). This eight-bar phrase contains only tonic chords (in ⁵₃ and ⁶₃ position) and dominant chords in inversion; all the dominant chords are inversions of V⁷. The phrase unmistakably expands an underlying tonic; the important stable tones of the melody and bass, for example, are A♭ and C, both elements of the tonic triad. A sense of movement is contributed by the active outer-voice tones G, B♭, and D♭. In the bass, B♭ (bar 2) is a passing tone between A♭ and C; G (bar 3) forms an incomplete neighbor to the following A♭, and D♭ (bar 6) is an incomplete neighbor leading to C. These three active tones support

110

the three inversions of V^7 in the order in which they appear in the Schubert —$^4_3$, $^6_5$, and $^4_2$. Like V^6 and VII^6, the inversions of V^7 serve to prolong an underlying tonic through melodic-contrapuntal activity. Their bass tones function as neighbors (complete or incomplete) to the bass tones of I or I^6 or as passing tones leading from one to the other. Compared to V^6 and VII^6, the inversions of V^7 have an even stronger urgency to move to the tonic. This is because of the dissonances—2nd or 7th (as well as tritone)—that they contain. Starting with the late Baroque period these are among the most frequently used of all chords. They fulfill several important compositional functions. In this unit we will concentrate on the most characteristic of these: to create movement within an extended tonic harmony, often (as in the Schubert example) the opening tonic of a large-scale harmonic progression.

2. Descending resolution of $\hat{4}$. In the inversions of V^7, as in the root position, the contrapuntal function of the chord 7th ($\hat{4}$) imposes a descending stepwise resolution to $\hat{3}$. As in the root position, the 7th can appear as a descending passing tone, an upper neighbor, or an upper incomplete neighbor entering by leap Example 8-2). The one frequent exception to the normal descending resolution of the 7th will be discussed below.

8-2   function of $\hat{4}$

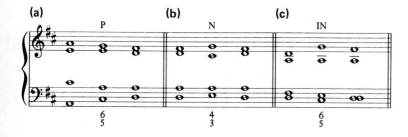

3. V$^6_5$. V$^6_5$, like V^6, has the leading tone as its bass and functions similarly as a neighboring chord to I (Example 8-3a). Any of the remaining chordal tones can appear in the soprano; perhaps the most characteristic soprano progression is $\hat{4}$-$\hat{3}$, as in the Beethoven excerpt (8-3b). Bar 3 of the Schubert Impromptu shows another characteristic function: there the bass of V$^6_5$ forms an incomplete neighbor leading from I^6 to I. The bass of V$^6_5$ is involved in a dissonant relationship (diminished 5th) with $\hat{4}$ in one of the upper parts. Because the diminished 5th involves the bass it must resolve according to rule. Consequently the bass of V$^6_5$ always ascends to $\hat{1}$ except in those cases where it forms part of an expansion of V^7.

8-3

(a) V$\frac{6}{5}$ as N to I

(b) Beethoven, Piano Sonata, Op. 2/1, I

4. V$\frac{4}{3}$. Like VII⁶, V$\frac{4}{3}$ has $\hat{2}$ as its bass. V$\frac{4}{3}$, in fact, resembles VII⁶ so closely that they are almost interchangeable chords. The bass of V$\frac{4}{3}$ is a more neutral tone than that of V$\frac{6}{5}$ (or, as you will see, V$\frac{4}{2}$) and can move convincingly either to $\hat{1}$ or to $\hat{3}$. Consequently V$\frac{4}{3}$, like VII⁶, forms a natural connection between I and I⁶ and appears very frequently as a passing chord within an extended tonic, as in bars 1-3 of the Schubert example—bars that illustrate a most important detail of voice leading: the D♭ of bar 2 (right-hand part) moves up to E♭ in bar 3 rather than down to C. In other words, $\hat{4}$—the 7th of the root position—moves up to $\hat{5}$ rather than down to $\hat{3}$. This is by no means an unusual case. Very frequently when V$\frac{4}{3}$ leads from I up to I⁶ with parallel 10ths (less often 3rds) above the bass, $\hat{4}$ ascends in order to complete this motion. In the Schubert, the 10ths above the bass lie in an inner part. More often, as in Example 8-4, they occur in the soprano. This usage of V_3^4 corresponds to the usage of VII^6 shown in Example 7-13a. Note that other uses of V_3^4 require the normal descending resolution—for example, its function as a neighbor of I, or (very frequent) as a passing chord leading down from I^6 to I (Example 8-5).

8-4   Mozart, Non ti fidar   (from *Don Giovanni*, K. 527)

translation: O miserable one, don't trust that villainous heart.

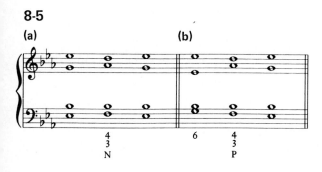

8-5

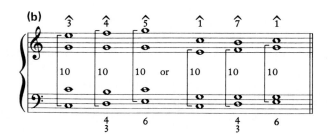

Like VII^6, V_3^4 most often occurs in a stepwise bass line. It can, however, form part of a double-neighbor figure, together with V^6 or V_5^6, as in Example 8-6.

8-6

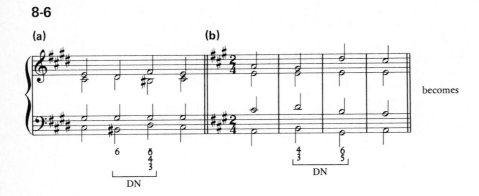

(c) Beethoven, String Quartet, Op. 131, IV

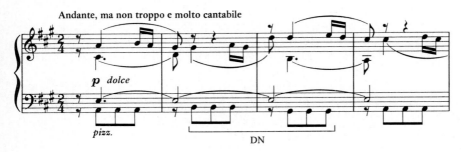

5. **V⁴₂.** V⁶₅ and V⁴₃ resemble chords we already know: V⁶ and VII⁶. V⁴₂, however, functions differently from any chord we have previously encountered. Since $\hat{4}$ is its bass tone, V⁴₂ must move to a chord whose bass tone is $\hat{3}$ in order to resolve the dissonance by stepwise descent. For the present the only possibility is a progression to I⁶. But even later when other chords become available the progression V⁴₂-I⁶ will remain by far the most frequent one. The bass of V⁴₂ has two characteristic functions: descending passing motion from V to I⁶ and upper neighbor—complete or incomplete—to I⁶. These are shown in the chord progressions and the Bach chorale excerpt of Example 8-7. Very characteristic: the soprano leaps up a 4th from $\hat{5}$ to $\hat{8}$ or—more frequently—from $\hat{2}$ to $\hat{5}$.

8-7   functions of V⁴₂

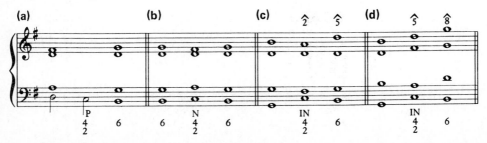

(e) Bach, Chorale 67

note stepwise bass

V$^4_2$ occasionally passes from V^7 (rather than V$^5_3$) to I^6. The 7th of V^7 transfers from one of the upper voices to the bass of V$^4_2$ and, of course, resolves in the bass. This provides a convenient way of moving from V^7 to I^6 (which cannot be done directly—compare Unit 7, section 4). Example 8-8 (including the excerpt from a Mozart quartet) illustrates this possibility.

8-8

(a)   **(b) Mozart, String Quartet, K. 428, IV**

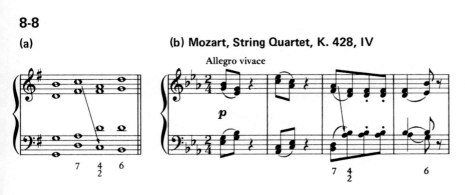

6. Double-neighbor and passing figures. As we saw in Examples 8-6 and 8-8, double-neighbor and passing figures in the bass create opportunities for moving from V^7 to an inversion or from one inversion to another. Such progressions occur frequently. The chordal 7th ($\hat{4}$) will resolve in the last voice in which it appears (see Example 6-19).

7. Incomplete chords. In Example 8-1, bar 6 contains an incomplete V$^4_2$. The special texture that Schubert creates here—in particular the E♭ sustained in both hands and in the octave doubling of the soprano line—makes it impossible to introduce the missing G gracefully. In general, however, inversions of V^7 almost always appear as complete chords unless there are fewer than four parts; incomplete chords are seldom necessary or desirable.

8. Common tones. In the inversion of V^7, $\hat{5}$ appears in one of the upper parts and is available as a common tone (with I). Repeating this common tone in the same voice produces a smooth connection with I and helps to reduce voice-leading

hazards (review Examples 8-1 through 8-7). (If the soprano line demands the skip
$\hat{5}$-$\hat{8}$, as in 8-7e, repeating the common tone becomes impossible unless the inversion of V⁷ is incomplete.) One caution: do not proceed in similar motion to $\hat{3}$
doubled at the octave or unison; the interval successions 2-1 and 9-8 usually
produce awkward voice leading in moving from an inversion of V⁷ to I (Example 8-9). Review Examples 6-16b and 7-7.

8-9

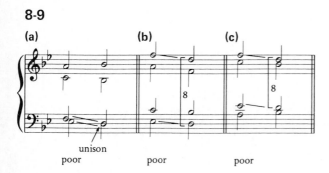

poor   poor   poor

CONTRAPUNTAL EXPANSIONS OF TONIC AND DOMINANT

9. Typical figures for bass and soprano. Examples 8-10 through 8-13 illustrate
some of the most important possibilities for expanding tonic harmony through
the use of V⁶, V⁷ and its inversions, and VII⁶. In a sense these examples summarize the contents of this unit and the preceding one. They are grouped according
to typical bass-line figures. The possibilities shown for the soprano are by no
means the only ones, but they are among the most important; notice the great
number of different soprano figures possible over the same bass. The more familiar you are with these progressions, the easier it will be for you to harmonize
melodies, realize basses, and write phrases. Work with them, try to understand
the principles they exemplify, and refer to them when you do your written work.
Playing them at the keyboard (and supplying the inner voices) is also of great
value, but trying to memorize them is not necessary.

Passing chords: VII⁶ and V$^4_3$ are often used as passing chords between I
and I⁶ (Example 8-10).

8-10

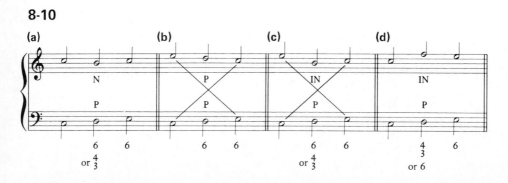

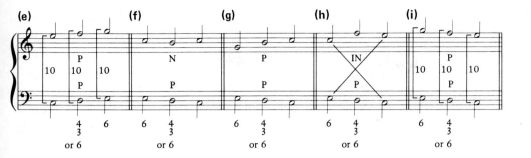

Neighbor chords: V^6 or V^6_5 can be used as LN to I^5_3; V^4_3 and VII^6 as UN to I^5_3 as well as LN to I^6; V^4_2 as UN to I^6 (Example 8-11).

8-11

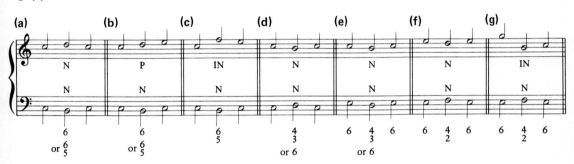

Incomplete-neighbor chords: V^6_5 and V^4_2 can be approached by leap as long as they resolve correctly. This produces the incomplete-neighbor figure in the bass (Example 8-12).

8-12

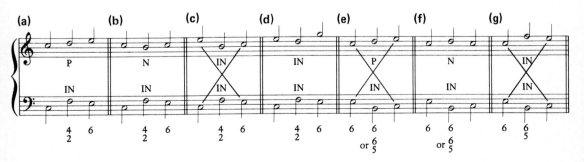

More elaborate figures: These involve leaps from one inversion of V^7 to another (Example 8-13).

8-13

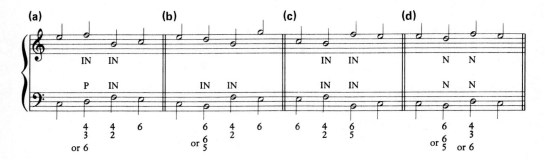

10. Contrapuntal cadences. A root-position V or V^7 normally precedes the I at an authentic cadence, the leap of a 5th or 4th in the bass strongly articulating the phrase ending. A stepwise bass motion to I—from VII^6, V^6, V^6_5, or V^4_3—produces a much weaker articulation. Very occasionally, as in bars 7-8 of Example 8-1, a contrapuntal cadence of this sort (contrapuntal because it is based on a stepwise progression) will end a phrase or a group of measures within a larger phrase. Such cadences are virtually never used at the end of a piece (or exercise).

11. "I" as a neighboring or passing chord. We have seen that $\hat{1}$, $\hat{3}$, and $\hat{5}$—normally the stable degrees of the scale—can become active tones if the context makes them dissonant (review Unit 2, section 10). In a similar fashion, the triad formed by these three tones—normally the most stable of all triads—can function as a passing or neighboring chord subordinate to another chord. Example 8-14 shows the end of the opening theme from the first movement of Mozart's "Jupiter" Symphony. It closes with a half cadence and reaches the goal, V, in bar 19. Since the dominant is clearly the goal, the "I" chords that appear in bars 19-21 do not demonstrate the typical tonic function of beginning or ending harmonic progressions; rather they serve to extend and intensify dominant harmony. Since they support a neighboring tone in the soprano, their specific meaning is that of neighboring chords.

8-14 Mozart, "Jupiter" Symphony, K. 551, I

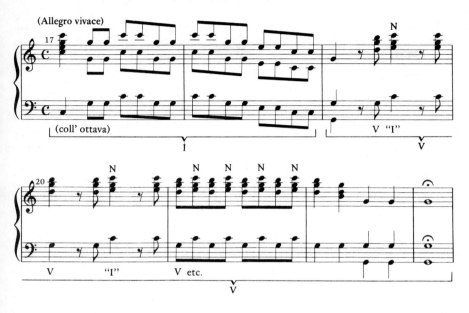

Example 8-15 shows "I" as a passing chord between V_3^4 and V^6. Compare the effect of the F minor chord in bar 3 with the one in bar 4. Melodic and rhythmic factors make it impossible to hear the first one as a goal; the same factors make it impossible to hear the second as anything else.

8-15 Beethoven, Piano Sonata, Op. 2/1, III

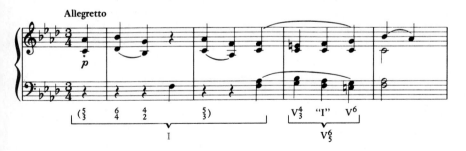

12. Melodic dissonance. The use of V^7 and its inversions presents a number of possibilities for the effective use of melodic dissonance (Example 8-16). In using such dissonances remember that changing direction after a leap—especially one that creates tension—helps to produce a satisfactory melodic line (see Unit 5, section 11).

8-16   melodic dissonance

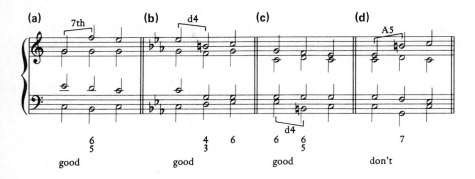

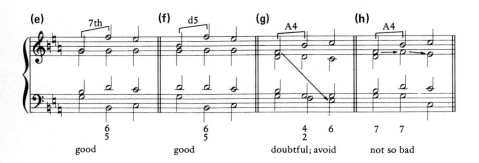

Leaps from I to V⁷: 8-16a shows the leap of an ascending 7th in the soprano. Note that resolving the 7th of V⁷ produces a desirable change of direction after the leap. 8-16b and c show the diminished 4th that occurs in minor with a downward leap from $\hat{3}$ to raised $\hat{7}$. The inversion of the diminished 4th—the augmented 5th—creates an unbalanced effect (8-16d); the tone following the leap does not change direction.

Leaps within V⁷: 8-16e shows a leap from the root of V⁷ to its 7th. Best in the soprano voice, but possible in the bass. As in 8-16f, the leap of a diminished 5th will work well in bass or soprano as long as the 7th resolves. The augmented 4th (8-16g and h) is unsatisfactory because the tone following the leap does not change direction. Of the two progressions 8-16h is better because the soprano F is taken over *in the same register* by the alto and resolves as expected.

Leaps in inner voices: At present they should be avoided, with the exception of diminished 4ths between I and V in minor (Example 6-9c).

POINTS FOR REVIEW

1. In moving from an inversion of V^7 to I (or I^6), $\hat{4}$ descends to $\hat{3}$; in inversions, the 7th resolves in the same way it does in root position. In moving to I, $\hat{5}$ should be kept as a common tone wherever possible. Avoid similar motion to $\hat{3}$ doubled at the octave or unison.

2. The three inversions of V^7 function as follows:

   V^6_5. Resolves to I; its bass functions as a neighbor to $\hat{1}$, either complete (I-V^6_5-I) or incomplete (at present I^6-V^6_5-I; other possibilities in later units).

   V^4_3. Functions as a passing chord between I and I^6, or I^6 and I. A less frequent function is as a neighboring chord to I or I^6.

   In the progression I-V^4_3-I^6 with parallel 10ths (3rds) above the bass, $\hat{4}$ may ascend to $\hat{5}$; otherwise the normal descending resolution occurs.

   V^4_2. Moves to I^6 to resolve $\hat{4}$. Functions as a passing chord between V and I^6 and as an upper neighbor to I^6.

3. Inversions of V^7 are almost always complete chords.

4. "I" can function as a passing or neighboring chord subordinate to V, V^7, or their inversions.

5. In moving from I to V^7 or within V^7 the following dissonant leaps in the bass or soprano are allowable: ascending minor 7th, diminished 4th, and diminished 5th.

EXERCISES

NOTE. With the chords available at present, you will sometimes find it impossible to avoid the frequent repetition of $\hat{5}$ in one of the inner voices. Don't worry about this; to try to achieve active inner voices often creates unnecessary problems in voice leading and may make it impossible to get a good soprano or bass line.

1. Preliminaries. Write short progressions (three or four chords each) showing characteristic uses of VII^6, V^6, V^6_5, V^4_3, and V^4_2. Each progression should begin and end with some form of the tonic and should be written in a different major key and in its parallel minor.

2. Write two 4-measure phrases, one in major, the other in minor. In both, expand an initial tonic contrapuntally by V^6, VII^6, and/or the inversions of V^7, omitting root position V, or V^7. End each phrase with an authentic cadence.

3. Melody.

4. Unfigured bass.

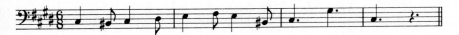

5. Melody.

6. Un igured bass.

9

Leading to V: IV, II, and II⁶

9-1 Schubert, Impromptu, D. 899

INTERMEDIATE HARMONIES

1. Moving to the dominant. Compare the opening phrase of Schubert's Impromptu in E♭ (Example 9-1) with the Schubert excerpt that begins Unit 8. Although they could hardly differ more in texture and in the way the piano is used, the two phrases are partly very similar in tonal design. Both begin with contrapuntal motion through an expanded tonic harmony; the first five bass tones are identical (compare bars 1-4 of Example 8-1 with bars 1-5 of Example 9-1). In one important respect, however, our present example differs from any of the previous ones. The harmony that fills bar 6 is a II in $\frac{6}{3}$ position; its function is to lead from the extended tonic of bars 1-5 to the cadential dominant of bar 7 and to intensify the latter chord. Because it connects the initial I and the V of the basic I-V-I progression, we call such a chord an *intermediate harmony*. Intermediate harmonies occur very frequently and can assume great significance in the structure of tonal music.

Although a number of different chords can function as intermediate harmonies, IV, II, and their derivatives form the most important possibilities. They are particularly well suited to lead into and intensify dominant harmony. Their roots lie between $\hat{1}$ and $\hat{5}$; both are active scalar elements, unlike $\hat{3}$, which has the stability of a tone belonging to tonic harmony. I-IV-V and I-II-V, therefore, are more intense progressions than I-I⁶-V, whose bass arpeggiates the stable tones $\hat{1}$, $\hat{3}$, and $\hat{5}$. Furthermore, the three chords of these new progressions contain all the notes of the scale. This helps to express the key, as does the inevitable juxtaposition of $\hat{4}$ (in II or IV) and $\hat{7}$ (in V), which, between them, produce the key-defining interval of the diminished 5th (Unit 2, section 13).

In moving from IV or II to V we can easily use a descending soprano line, so often appropriate at cadences. IV stands on the scale step just below V and leads into it by stepwise bass motion. II is the upper 5th of V and moves to it through the fundamental harmonic progression of the falling 5th (or rising 4th). Remember that the function of these intermediate harmonies is to lead *toward* V, not away from it. Thus: I-IV-V-I or I-II-V-I but *not* I-V-IV-I or I-V-II-I.

2. Cadential uses. IV and II can move either to a cadential V or to a noncadential V. In the former case they typically appear shortly before (often, as with the II⁶ in the Schubert Impromptu, *immediately* before) the cadential V, so that they form part of the cadence. Using them makes available to us the expanded cadences of Example 9-2.

9-2   cadences with IV, II, and II⁶

3. Subdominant harmony (IV). IV lies a 4th above or a 5th below the tonic; the progression I-IV is analogous to V-I (falling 5th), the I moving easily and naturally to IV. IV lies a step below V; there is a strong *melodic* connection between the two chord roots. Two triads with roots a 2nd apart share no common tones; in moving from IV to V, therefore, all four voices must proceed to a new tone. If you're not careful, you will soon find that the absence of common tones makes it dangerously easy to produce parallel 5ths and octaves; to avoid them, lead the upper voices in contrary motion to the bass, as in Example 9-3a. As with most $\frac{5}{3}$ chords, the root is usually the best tone to double.

9-3   using IV

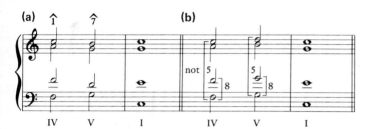

Any of the three tones that belong to IV ($\hat{4}$, $\hat{6}$, and $\hat{1}$) can appear in the soprano. At cadences $\hat{4}$ (moving to $\hat{2}$ over dominant harmony) and $\hat{1}$ (moving to $\hat{7}$) are the most usable. The same melodic tones can occur when IV moves to a noncadential V. In addition—and very characteristically—IV supports $\hat{6}$ as upper neighbor to $\hat{5}$ in the progression I-IV-V. Example 9-4, from Brahms's Third Symphony, shows this very frequent and important usage. The repetition (I-IV-I-IV) emphasizes the neighboring figure.

9-4   Brahms, Symphony No. 3, Op. 90, II

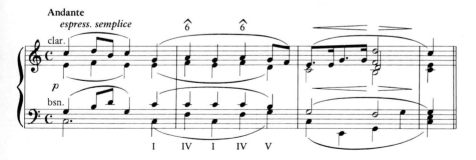

4. Supertonic harmony (II). II lies a 5th above V and a step above I. Thus its connection with V is a harmonic one (similar to V-I); its relation to I is melodic (similar to IV-V). I and II, like IV and V, have no tones in common. To avoid parallels, lead the upper voices in contrary motion to the bass—just as with IV-V.

II and V share $\hat{2}$ as a common tone. We can repeat the common tone in the same voice; the remaining two voices will normally move up by step (Example 9-5a). Very frequently, however, the upper voices will all descend (much as with IV-V). This allows $\hat{1}$ to be preceded by both its adjacent tones, $\hat{2}$ and $\hat{7}$.

9-5   using II

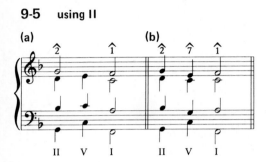

II tends to support $\hat{2}$ or $\hat{4}$ in the soprano more often than $\hat{6}$. Thus IV will harmonize $\hat{6}$ more frequently than II. At cadences the typical possibilities are $\hat{2}$-$\hat{7}$, $\hat{2}$-$\hat{2}$, and $\hat{4}$-$\hat{2}$, all over II-V. Unlike I-IV-V, I-II-V cannot harmonize the neighboring motion $\hat{5}$-$\hat{6}$-$\hat{5}$ because of the 5ths that would occur between I and II.

In minor, II is a diminished triad. Because of its unsatisfactory quality—at once harsh and thin—II$^5_3$ in minor is usually avoided and the $^6_3$ position used instead. However, circumstances sometimes justify the use of II$^5_3$ in minor, as we will see in section 12 of this unit (see also Example 16-9).

In major, II presents no problems of doubling. In minor, doubling the 3rd of II$^5_3$ improves its sonority, as the 3rd is the only tone that does not form a dissonance with one of the other chord members. However, if the soprano contains $\hat{2}$ the doubled root is obviously the only possibility.

5. II⁶. II⁶ leads very convincingly to V, occurring particularly often at cadences. As a cadential chord it is especially characteristic of the music of Mozart, Haydn, and Beethoven. Besides its obvious relation to II, II⁶ is also closely related to IV. The progression II⁶-V combines features of II-V and IV-V. It embodies the root progressions by falling 5th of II-V, though expressed less strongly, the root of II not being in the bass. And it has the stepwise bass line of IV-V.

In minor, II⁶ can occur freely; as with VII in major the diminished triad sounds much less harsh in $^6_3$ position.

In II⁶-V, the upper voices usually descend, $\hat{2}$ moving to $\hat{7}$. Very often the progression $\hat{2}$-$\hat{7}$ occurs in the soprano, as in Example 9-6a and c. The descending upper voices are almost mandatory in minor because of the augmented 2nd between $\hat{6}$ and raised $\hat{7}$ that would otherwise occur. In moving from II⁶ (or II) to V in minor, the diminished 5th or augmented 4th between $\hat{2}$ and $\hat{6}$ *cannot* resolve normally. $\hat{6}$ can (and usually should) descend to $\hat{5}$, but $\hat{2}$ cannot ascend to $\hat{3}$, for the V chord does not contain that tone. However the harmonic force of the progression is sufficiently strong to offset the melodic irregularity.

9-6   using II⁶

(c) Haydn, Piano Sonata, Hob. XVI/35, I

The bass of II⁶ is very frequently doubled, both in major and—especially—in minor. In major, the doubling of $\hat{2}$ is also quite frequent. The doubling of $\hat{6}$ is less frequent—particularly in minor where it will probably produce a melodic augmented 2nd. Example 9-7 illustrates.

9-7   doubling II⁶

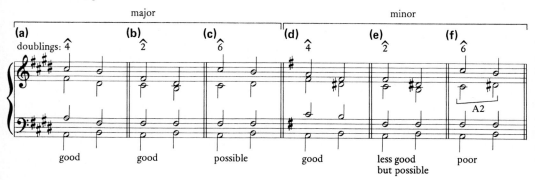

6. **Moving to V⁷.** IV, II, and II⁶ all lead very easily into V⁷. All contain $\hat{4}$; at the change of harmony, this tone becomes the 7th of V⁷. If we keep $\hat{4}$ in the same voice, first as a consonance, then as the dissonant 7th of V⁷, the dissonance is said to be *prepared*. Preparing the dissonance allows it to enter in a smooth and unobtrusive manner; if the prepared 7th is metrically strong, it functions as a

suspension. The good effect of preparing the 7th justifies irregular doubling, especially where the soprano moves away from $\hat{4}$ and cannot keep it as a common tone (Example 9-8d and e).

9-8   approaching V^7

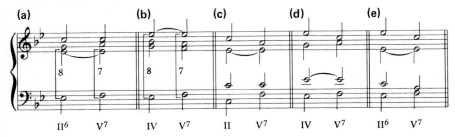

Especially in free, instrumental textures, but often in four-part vocal style as well, the 7th of V^7 can enter by leap, the preparation occurring in another voice (Example 9-9).

9-9   Beethoven, Bagatelle, Op. 33/2

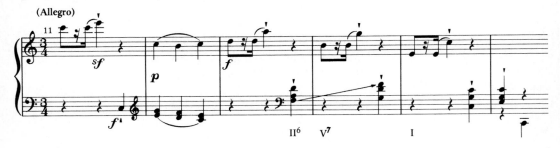

Note in 9-8a how V^7 eliminates the octaves that could occur with II⁶-V. In 9-8b the incomplete V^7 is the best way to avoid parallel 5ths between bass and alto.

The melodic leap of a diminished 5th from $\hat{4}$ down to $\hat{7}$ (normally moving on to $\hat{1}$) can create a beautiful soprano for the progression from IV or II$^{(6)}$ to V^7 (Example 9-10).

9-10   Schumann, Fantasy, Op. 17, III

7. Connecting I and V by stepwise bass. A bass rising by step from I to V is a natural and beautiful way to connect the initial tonic of a phrase with the cadential dominant. Using II^6 and IV (both with $\hat{4}$ in the bass) makes it possible to do this. In Example 9-11, notice the accelerating rate of chord change, which intensifies the drive toward the dominant.

9-11   Beethoven, Piano Sonata, Op. 2/1, I

stepwise bass connects I and V

In general II^6 lends itself to this progression more readily than IV; there are more good possibilities for the soprano and fewer voice-leading difficulties. But IV is also usable as is shown by Example 9-12b (and Example 10-1). Be careful about parallel octaves when moving from I^6 to IV!

9-12   II and IV in stepwise bass

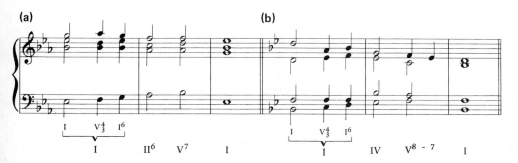

IV AND II IN CONTRAPUNTAL PROGRESSIONS

8. Moving to VII⁶, V⁶, and to inversions of V⁷. We have learned that VII⁶, V⁶, and the inversions of V⁷ can function as melodic, contrapuntal equivalents to root-position V and that these inverted chords are particularly useful in avoiding an unwanted cadential effect. IV, II, and II⁶ can move to any of these chords. One of the most useful possibilities is IV or II⁶ moving over a stationary bass to V$^4_2$, as in Example 9-13.

9-13   Mozart, Piano Sonata, K. 310, I

Moving from II to V$^6_5$ produces a particularly smooth bass line (Example 9-14a). Compare it to the much sharper effect of leading IV or II⁶ to V⁶ or V$^6_5$ (9-14b). These latter progressions necessarily result in a dissonant leap. Of the two possibilities (augmented 4th or diminished 5th) the diminished 5th is almost always better because the subsequent motion to $\hat{1}$ changes direction and produces a more flowing bass line.

9-14
(a) Chopin, Nocturne, Op. 62/2

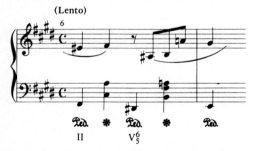

(b) Haydn, String Quartet, Op. 76/3, III

9. The melodic progression $\hat{5}$-$\hat{6}$-$\hat{7}$-$\hat{8}$. At the beginning or in the middle of a phrase (less often at the end) we might encounter a melodic progression ascending by step from $\hat{5}$ to $\hat{8}$. What might seem the most likely harmonization—I-IV-V-I—is difficult to achieve without parallels (Example 9-15a). One way of averting them is to use descending leaps in both the inner voices (9-15b), a solution that produces correct voice leading but not a very flowing effect unless there is a passing tone (9-15c).

9-15

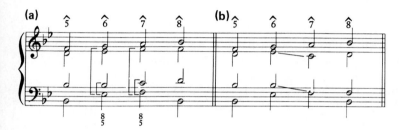

(c) Bach, Chorale 26

However, if we replace V by VII[6] (or its equivalent, V$^4_3$) all difficulties of voice leading disappear. And since the line $\hat{5}$-$\hat{6}$-$\hat{7}$-$\hat{8}$ usually occurs in places where a strong cadence is not needed (or might even be inappropriate) the absence of a root-position V is frequently an advantage (Example 9-16). I[6] can replace I$^5_3$ at the beginning or end of this progression.

9-16

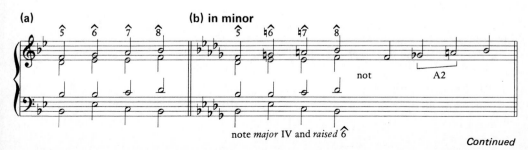

note *major* IV and *raised* $\hat{6}$

Continued

(c) Bach, Chorale 212

As we mentioned in section 4 of this unit, II tends to support $\hat{2}$ or $\hat{4}$ in the soprano more than $\hat{6}$. II or II⁶ will seldom support $\hat{6}$ in a melodic progression rising from $\hat{5}$ to $\hat{8}$; it is difficult (sometimes impossible) to avoid 5ths in moving from I. However, the succession I-IV-II$^{(6)}$-V$^{(7)}$-I works well if the rhythm of the melodic line allows it—that is, if $\hat{6}$ lasts long enough to serve as the top-voice tone of both IV and II (Example 9-17; also Example 16-7).

9-17

EXPANSIONS OF II AND IV

10. Expanding supertonic harmony. Supertonic harmony is often expanded by moving from II to II⁶, or the reverse, in a manner exactly analogous to the expansions of I and V by I⁶ and V⁶ discussed in Unit 7. A passing "I⁶" often appears between II and II⁶ as in the Mozart excerpt of Example 9-18a. Such a chord is a "tonic" in appearance only—not in function. It is neither the beginning nor the goal of a harmonic motion, but rather a detail within the unfolding of the II chord: Example 9-18b and c, shows two possible applications to four-part writing. Note that such "I⁶" chords are usually in a relatively weak rhythmic position.

9-18

(a) Mozart, Piano Concerto, K. 271, II

(b)   **(c)**

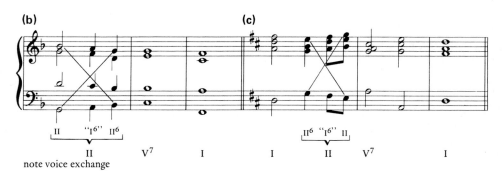

note voice exchange

Passing from II to II⁶ gives us another possibility for a rising stepwise bass from I to V (Example 9-19).

9-19

11. IV-II⁶: the 5-6 technique. IV and II share two common tones and are thus closely associated. The basis of this association is contrapuntal: a melodic motion above a sustained bass as discussed in Unit 4, section 8. If we start with a IV chord and move its 5th up to a 6th (thus: F-A-C to F-A-D), we produce a II chord in $\frac{6}{3}$ position, a procedure called the *5-6 technique;* this process occurs very often in composition and can fulfill a variety of functions (for example, breaking up parallel 5ths). In Example 9-20, a 5-6 progression transforms the IV into a II⁶; the II⁶ is then expanded by its own root position before moving on to V. It is not immediately apparent, but there would be 5ths between the two lowest parts in the progression from IV to V were it not for the change to II⁶.*

9-20   Mozart, String Quartet, K. 387, III

(a)

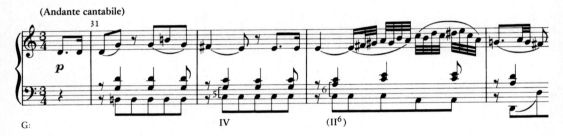

(b) reduction

Sometimes the bass will leap down a 3rd at the same time that the 5th of IV moves up to a 6th; this produces the succession IV-II. In Example 9-21 the basic progression is IV-V; the II results from a 5-6 motion together with a leap in the bass to the root of II.

---

*The parentheses in Example 9-20 indicate that this II⁶ chord is an offshoot of the IV. In general, we use such parentheses to show that the enclosed chords are incidental to a governing harmony or harmonic progression.

9-21   Beethoven, Piano Concerto, Op. 58, III

(a)

(b) reduction

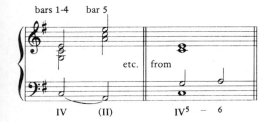

12. II$_3^5$ in minor. We mentioned in section 4 of this unit that II$_3^5$ seldom occurs in minor because of the harsh quality of the diminished triad in root position. If it follows II^6 or IV and occurs without rhythmic stress, the chord loses much of its unpleasant quality, as in Example 9-22.

9-22   Schubert, Piano Sonata, D. 279, Menuetto

RHYTHMIC IMPLICATIONS

13. More about chord progression and rhythm. We have already seen that repeating a chord from a weak to a strong beat can neutralize the metric accent (Unit 6, section 15) and that changing the bass tone of an extended chord can have a similar effect (Unit 7, section 14). Another procedure that can contradict the meter is repeating a *bass tone* from a weak to a strong beat, while changing the chord it supports—for example, IV-II⁶. You must therefore avoid progressions like the one in Example 9-23a. In 9-23b, on the other hand, the weak-strong repetition of the bass tone $\hat{4}$ is good; the $\frac{4}{2}$ chord arises from a dissonant suspension (9th against the alto) in the bass. Suspensions, by definition, are held over or repeated from a weak to a strong beat; the dissonance produces enough contrast to give an accented quality to the downbeat despite the static bass.

9-23   chord progression and rhythm

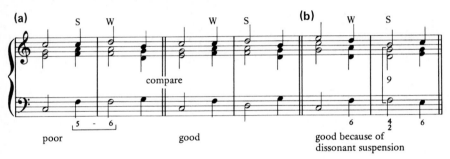

14. Subordinate and incomplete progressions. The chords in this unit will enable you to write more varied and interesting musical phrases, and will enhance your understanding of the techniques found in the works of great composers. One new possibility is to extend the initial tonic of a phrase through IV, II, or II⁶ moving to a noncadential V⁽⁷⁾. In Example 9-24 the first four chords constitute a harmonic progression clearly subordinate to the larger I-II⁶-V⁷-I (note how $\hat{3}$ in the soprano at the beginning of measure 2 prevents too strong a cadential effect); we therefore refer to the first succession of chords as a *subordinate harmonic progression* (Example 9-24; compare Example 9-4).

9-24

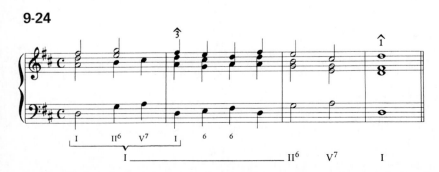

If the subordinate progression threatens to produce an inappropriate cadential effect, I^6 can be used in place of the final I, or an inversion of V$^{(7)}$ or VII^6 in place of the V, or both (see again Example 9-13).

Sometimes IV, II, or II^6 will begin a phrase—or even, as in Example 9-25, a piece. Here the opening progression is II^6-V^7-I. Because it lacks an initial tonic we call such a chord succession an *incomplete harmonic progression*. (Compare with Example 9-21, which also contains an incomplete progression.) Regardless of the actual metrics, phrases like that of Example 9-25 often produce the effect of beginning with an upbeat; the lack of a tonic can weaken the rhythmic stress of the first downbeat. Omitting an initial tonic is a device especially characteristic of Chopin, Schumann, Brahms, and other composers of the nineteenth century.

9-25   Schumann, Davidsbündlertänze, Op. 6/5

15. **Harmony and phrase rhythm.** Countless phrases of tonal music—especially those that begin pieces—open with an expansion of I that leads to an authentic or half cadence with IV, II, or II^6 before its dominant. Although this pattern would seem to impose a certain uniformity on the shape of the phrases that follow it, the interaction among harmony, melody, counterpoint, and meter (and other compositional elements as well) can lead to an almost limitless variety in emphasis and pacing. In Example 9-11, for example, the stepwise bass drives up to V. The cadential II^6 gets no special emphasis, for it falls on a weak beat between the melodic climax on c^3 (bar 7) and the goal dominant. In Example 9-1, on the other hand, the skip to the bass note of II^6 and the right hand's melodic high point combine to accentuate the II^6 even though it occupies the normally weak second bar of its four-bar group.

POINTS FOR REVIEW

1. The intermediate harmonies IV, II, and II^6 lead from I to V—*not* from V to I. They can appear immediately before a cadential dominant, forming part of the cadence.

2. In IV-V or I-II, lead the upper voices in contrary motion to the bass to avoid parallel 5ths and octaves.

3. In general, IV is better than II or II^6 as support for $\hat{6}$.

4. Avoid II$^5_3$ in minor except on a weak beat following II^6 or IV.

5. The best doubling of IV and of II (in major) is the root; of II in minor (if used), the 3rd; of II^6, the bass or root. *Warning:* Be careful of parallel octaves in II^6-V if the bass of II^6 is doubled.

6. IV, II, and II^6 allow the 7th of V^7 to be prepared as a common tone; they also make possible a stepwise bass ascent from I to V.

7. The following expanded usages can precede V; II-II^6 or II^6-II, possibly connected by a passing "I^6"; IV-II^6, or IV-II (from 5-6 technique).

8. As alternatives to root-position V or V^7, the following are possible: VII^6 or V$^4_3$, especially with melodic line $\hat{5}$-$\hat{6}$-$\hat{7}$-$\hat{8}$; V$^4_2$; V^6 or V$^6_5$.

9. Avoid the following types of progression, which can cause a contradiction of the meter: a weak-strong progression within the same chord, such as II-II^6; a weak-strong bass repetition, such as IV-II^6 (exception: IV or II^6 to V$^4_2$ is good).

EXERCISES

NOTE. In Units 6 through 8, we have been studying tonic chords and those chords that resolve directly into tonic harmony, whether in harmonic progressions based on the fifth relationship (V and V^7) or contrapuntal progressions based on stepwise motion (V^6, VII^6, and the inversions of V^7). All of these nontonic chords share as a common element the leading tone with its powerful drive to $\hat{1}$; in addition, many of them contain the key-defining interval of the tritone. With this unit we arrive at a wholly new type of chord: intermediate harmonies whose function is to lead into and intensify dominant and contrapuntal leading-tone chords.

This expanded vocabulary increases the number of choices you will have to make in writing your exercises, for a given scale degree might belong to two chords of radically different function. For example, $\hat{1}$ in the soprano could indicate I or IV; $\hat{2}$ in the bass could indicate II or VII^6. When working out the exercises, use the procedures explained at the end of Unit 7, but integrate these new chords into your work. In your preliminary sketches, incorporate cadential IV, II, and II^6 chords. When setting melodies, look for idiomatic patterns that suggest progressions including these chords. $\hat{5}$-$\hat{6}$-$\hat{7}$-$\hat{8}$, for example, usually implies I-IV-VII^6-I or a variant thereof (perhaps using I^6 or V$^4_3$); in general, $\hat{6}$ tends to evoke subdominant harmony. $\hat{4}$-$\hat{2}$, $\hat{2}$-$\hat{4}$, $\hat{4}$-$\hat{3}$-$\hat{2}$, and $\hat{2}$-$\hat{3}$-$\hat{4}$ might well call for an expansion of supertonic harmony, perhaps with a voice exchange.

Rhythmic considerations will often determine whether one possibility is better or less good than another. Think of a soprano line $\hat{3}$-$\hat{2}$-$\hat{7}$-$\hat{1}$. You might harmonize it with I-V-V-I or with I-II$^{(6)}$-V-I. If the $\hat{2}$-$\hat{7}$ is in a weak-strong relation, however, only the second possibility is good: repeating dominant harmony will contradict the meter. (Of course even if the $\hat{2}$-$\hat{7}$ is in a strong-weak relation, the II might well be preferred simply because it defines the key more strongly.)

1. Preliminaries.

   a. Write a phrase that begins with a contrapuntal expansion of I (omitting root-position V); lead it to a cadence that includes IV, II, or II^6.
   b. Write a phrase that begins with a subordinate harmonic progression ending on I^6; lead it to a cadence that includes IV, II, or II^6.

2. Figured bass.

3. Melody.

bass: whole note

4. Figured bass.

5. Unfigured bass.

*Begin the soprano a compound 5th above the bass.

6. Melody.

(I^6)

10

The Cadential $\frac{6}{4}$

10-1   Beethoven, String Quartet, Op. 18/3, I

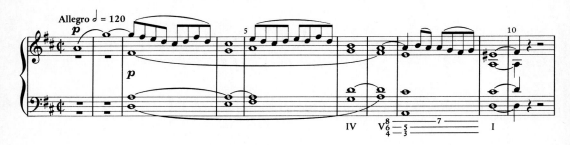

AN INTENSIFICATION OF V

1. Nontonic function. Example 10-1 begins with a bass that rises by step from I to V in a manner familiar to us from the preceding unit. When the bass arrives at the goal tone, A, in bar 7, however, the upper parts do not play a dominant chord. Instead they sound the tones D, F♯, and A, thus producing a $\frac{6}{4}$ chord above the bass. In the next bar the bass leaps down an octave, and the upper voices move to a cadential dominant. The $\frac{6}{4}$ chord of bar 7 contains the same tones as the tonic triad; for this reason most harmony books label such chords "I$\frac{6}{4}$." This label may be helpful for purposes of identification but it contradicts the meaning and function of a $\frac{6}{4}$ chord used in this way. The chord does not act as an inversion of I$\frac{5}{3}$; it serves neither to extend it nor to substitute for it (play the Beethoven with a D in the bass in bar 7 and hear how different the chord sounds). The purpose of this $\frac{6}{4}$ is to embellish and intensify the dominant; therefore we shall use the notation V$^{6\text{-}5}_{4\text{-}3}$ or, when appropriate, a variant of it—in the

Beethoven, $V_{6\text{-}5\text{-}}^{8-7}$ $_{4\text{-}3\text{-}}$. This type of $\frac{6}{4}$ is very frequently and very appropriately termed *cadential* $\frac{6}{4}$ for it most characteristically decorates the V chord at an authentic or half cadence. Although the cadential use is the most typical, a $\frac{6}{4}$ on the dominant is not restricted to cadences.

2. Origin of the cadential $\frac{6}{4}$. It is easiest to understand the cadential $\frac{6}{4}$ if you realize that it developed out of a very old voice-leading technique: delaying the leading tone at a cadence by means of a suspension. This suspension frequently decorates a cadential V, as in Example 10-2a; the suspension and its resolution form a 4th and a 3rd, and the intervallic progression is called a "4-3" suspension. If we delay the 5th of the V chord by first using a sixth, we obtain the complete $\frac{6}{4}$ chord moving to V in $\frac{5}{3}$ position (10-2b). (In working out the exercises, you might occasionally wish to introduce a simple 4-3 suspension over V and to compare its effect with that of the cadential $\frac{6}{4}$. The suspension is particularly useful in cadences where V supports $\hat{2}$ in the soprano.)

10-2

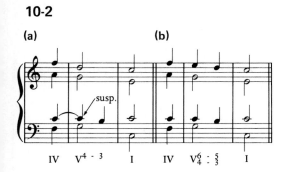

3. Voice leading. The stepwise descending resolution of a 4th to a 3rd forms the basis for the correct treatment of the cadential $\frac{6}{4}$. Stepwise descent is the normal way to resolve suspensions and other accented dissonances, and the 4th is dissonant when it sounds between the bass and one of the upper parts. Because it contains the 4th in this position, the $\frac{6}{4}$ functions as a dissonant chord; thus its resolution requires as much care as that of V^7.

As we noted, the 4th will most often enter as a suspension—held over or repeated from the preceding chord. When this is not possible (for example, coming from II or II⁶) the 4th can enter by stepwise descent as an accented passing tone (APT). In either case, it will resolve by step to the 3rd of dominant harmony (Example 10-3). In simple textures, the 4th will not usually enter by leap. And even in more complex instrumental styles, the 4th normally enters as a common tone or by stepwise motion. Sometimes the stepwise introduction of the 4th is masked by figuration, as in Example 10-3c.

10-3   voice leading and the cadential $\frac{6}{4}$

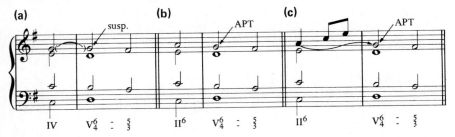

4. Doubling. The bass is the best tone to double, for it is the root of the prevailing harmony—V—to which the $\frac{6}{4}$ resolves. If this doubling is impracticable—as is the case in Example 10-4b, where moving from II⁶ in open position threatens parallel fifths—the 6th should be doubled. The 4th is not doubled except in very free or complex textures. The cadential $\frac{6}{4}$ moves easily to V⁷. Usually all the upper voices descend by step, thus: $\begin{smallmatrix}8\text{-}7\\6\text{-}5\\4\text{-}3\end{smallmatrix}$ (Example 10-4d). Less frequently the 6th above the bass (especially when in an inner voice) can move up to the 7th (10-4e). With the less usual doubled 6th, still another possibility arises: $\begin{smallmatrix}6\text{-}7\\6\text{-}5\\4\text{-}3\end{smallmatrix}$ (10-4f).

10-4 $\frac{6}{4}$ doublings

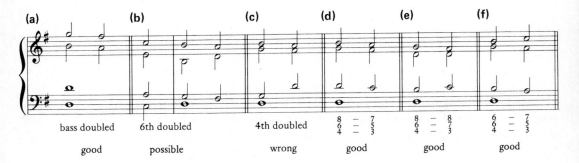

5. Rhythm. Because it grows out of a suspension (which, by definition, is metrically accented) and because it resolves over a stationary bass, the cadential $\frac{6}{4}$ *must* appear in a metrically strong position; no weak-to-strong bass repetitions are permitted. If the chords change every beat or so, the $\frac{6}{4}$ will appear on a strong beat and will resolve on the following weak beat (duple meter) or on one of the two following weak ones (triple meter). In triple time the second beat is sometimes stronger than the third; therefore a resolution from second to third beat can be a possibility. If the $\frac{6}{4}$ resolves within a divided beat, the $\frac{6}{4}$ will appear on the strong part of the beat and its resolution on a weaker part. Sometimes chord changes occur more slowly than one per beat. In such cases the $\frac{6}{4}$ will appear on a strong beat and its resolution either on a weak or another strong one (for example, from the first to the third quarter of $\frac{4}{4}$ time). Example 10-5 illustrates the metrical relation between the cadential $\frac{6}{4}$ and its resolution. Note that the strong-to-weak rhythm can be underscored by the leap of a *descending* octave in the bass.

10-5   rhythmic position of cadential $\frac{6}{4}$

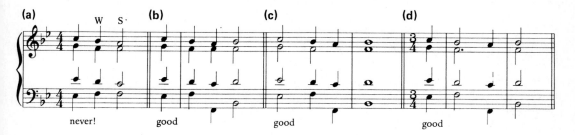

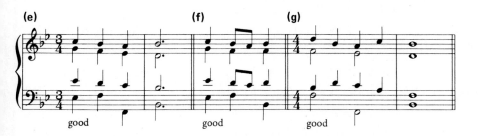

In many musical phrases (for example, the Beethoven excerpt that begins this unit), strong and weak *measures* alternate, creating a metrical pattern similar to strong and weak beats within the measure. In the Beethoven observe that the $\frac{6}{4}$ falls on a strong measure and its resolution on a weak one; also note how the descending bass octave emphasizes the rhythm. Cadential $\frac{6}{4}$ chords that last a whole bar fall, in principle, on a strong or accented bar.

On occasion, cadential $\frac{6}{4}$ chords will last a very long time. Long duration does not alter the meaning or function of the chord; it is still dependent on the dominant to which it resolves. Extending the $\frac{6}{4}$ can generate a great deal of tension, as in Example 10-6, where the musical tension relates directly to Shakespeare's text.

6. Stepwise melodic lines. An important use of the cadential $\frac{6}{4}$ is the stepwise melodic line it permits when IV or II moves to V with $\hat{4}$-$\hat{2}$ or $\hat{2}$-$\hat{7}$ in the soprano. The two excerpts of Example 10-7—one of them from the same Haydn song as our last example—illustrate this. The one necessary condition is that $\hat{3}$ and $\hat{1}$ —the passing tones belonging to the $\frac{6}{4}$—must fall on an accented beat or part of the beat.

10-6   Haydn, She Never Told Her Love

10-7

(a) (Haydn)

(b) Bach, Well-Tempered Clavier II, Fugue 9

Using the cadential $^6_4$ effects a significant (though temporary) reversal in the melodic functions of $\hat{1}$ and $\hat{7}$. $\hat{1}$ is, of course, the most stable melodic tone and normally serves as a goal of motion; $\hat{7}$ is an unstable tone with a marked tendency to move to $\hat{1}$. In the cadential $^6_4$, however, $\hat{1}$ functions as a dissonance (4th). It cannot serve as a goal of motion; instead, it must resolve to $\hat{7}$ by stepwise descent. In this situation, therefore, $\hat{7}$ becomes a temporary goal; $\hat{1}$ loses its stability and becomes an active tone dependent on $\hat{7}$. To the perceptive listener, $\hat{1}$ in a cadential $^6_4$ and $\hat{1}$ in a tonic $^5_3$ chord have such contrasting functions that their identical pitch becomes of secondary importance (much as the words "son" and "sun" mean very different things heard in context, though they sound the same). In the cadential $^6_4$, $\hat{3}$ (6th above the bass) also becomes more unstable than $\hat{2}$ (5th of V) to which it normally descends; the relationship between these tones resembles that between $\hat{1}$ and $\hat{7}$. After the resolution of the cadential $^6_4$ to V, $\hat{7}$ and $\hat{2}$ retain their tendency to move on to $\hat{1}$; they function as temporary, not final, goals.

7. Noncadential uses. In Example 10-8, $^6_4$ chords embellish noncadential dominants (bars 95 and 97). With regard to rhythm and voice leading these chords function in the same way as cadential $^6_4$'s.

10-8 **Mozart, Piano Sonata, K. 332, I**

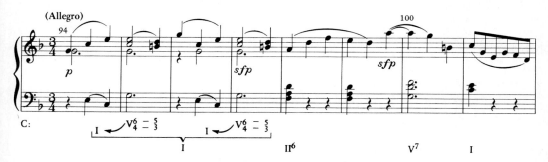

If a cadential effect is not wanted, the $^6_4$ can move to a $^4_2$ (Example 10-9). A $^6_4$ moving to a $^4_2$ occurs in the last movement of Mozart's String Quartet, K. 499 (Example 10-10). Here Mozart avoids a formal cadence at the end of the phrase and continues the motion into the next group of measures.

10-9

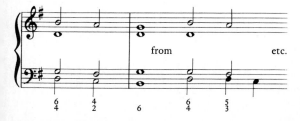

10-10   Mozart, String Quartet, K. 499, IV

Example 10-10 illustrates the technique of forming a larger unit from two phrases by suppressing the first cadence. You can use a similar procedure to extend the duration of a single phrase, as in Example 10-11.

10-11

(a) 4 bars

(b) 7 bars

(phrase extended)

8. Back-relating dominants. Cadential $\frac{6}{4}$'s frequently embellish *back-relating dominants*, that is, V chords that function as offshoots of a preceding tonic but that do not resolve into a goal tonic. Turn back to Example 10-8. Because of the rhythmic and melodic groupings, we do not hear the V chords of bars 95 and 97 as moving forward; they close off a musical idea without leading it to a definitive conclusion. We learned in Unit 9 that IV and II lead to V rather than coming from it. The Mozart excerpt would seem to contradict this principle, but the contradiction is apparent rather than real, for there is no *progression* of a V to a II. The V grows out of an expanded tonic that in turn forms part of the harmonic framework I (bars 94 and 96)-II^6 (bars 98-99)-V^7 (bar 100)-I (bar 101).

9. Antecedent-consequent construction. Two interdependent phrases that form a larger unit or *period* are in *antecedent-consequent* relation; the first phrase is called the antecedent, and the second is called the consequent. In Example 10-12, two factors working together create the impression of a unified period rather than of two separate phrases. These factors are repetition and the delayed resolution of tonal tension. The second phrase repeats (in slightly varied form) much of the material of the first; the repetition helps to connect the two phrases. An equally important, though less obvious, source of unity is the relationship between the two contrasting cadences. The first phrase closes on V; the tension produced by this semicadence is not dissipated by the tonic of bar 5, which is a new beginning, not a goal. Not until the arrival of I and $\hat{1}$ in bar 8 is tonal equilibrium restored. Cadential $^6_4$'s often occur prominently in antecedent-consequent groups; by intensifying the dominant chords, they give emphasis to the cadences.

10-12   Mozart, The Magic Flute, Act I   ART

POINTS FOR REVIEW

1. The cadential $\frac{6}{4}$ is *not* an inversion of I; it is an embellishment and intensification of V.
2. The 4th of the cadential $\frac{6}{4}$ is dissonant and must resolve downward by step. The 6th usually descends by step as well, thus: $\begin{smallmatrix}6\text{-}5\\4\text{-}3\end{smallmatrix}$. The 4th normally enters as a common tone (suspension) or by stepwise descent from $\hat{2}$ (accented passing tone).
3. The cadential $\frac{6}{4}$ occurs on a strong beat relative to the chord of resolution.
4. The bass is the most frequently doubled tone; *never* double the 4th.
5. The normal resolution to V^7 is $\begin{smallmatrix}8\text{-}7\\6\text{-}5\\4\text{-}3\end{smallmatrix}$. Also possible but less frequent is $\begin{smallmatrix}6\text{-}7\\6\text{-}5\\4\text{-}3\end{smallmatrix}$.

6. Melodically, the cadential $\frac{6}{4}$ permits a stepwise descending soprano—$\hat{4}$-$\hat{3}$-$\hat{2}$-$\hat{1}$ or $\hat{2}$-$\hat{1}$-$\hat{7}$-$\hat{1}$—in progressions from $II^{(6)}$ or IV to V.
7. A $\frac{6}{4}$ on the dominant is not restricted to cadences; the alternative resolution $\begin{smallmatrix}6\text{-}4\\4\text{-}2\end{smallmatrix}$ avoids a cadential effect.
8. Cadential $\frac{6}{4}$'s often occur in antecedent-consequent construction, in which two interdependent phrases form a larger group or period. The antecedent ends with a semicadence, the consequent with an authentic cadence.

EXERCISES

NOTE. With the melodic figures $\hat{3}$-$\hat{2}$, $\hat{3}$-$\hat{2}$-$\hat{1}$, $\hat{1}$-$\hat{7}$, and $\hat{1}$-$\hat{7}$-$\hat{1}$, remember that the first melodic tone may require the cadential $\frac{6}{4}$—*not* tonic harmony, particularly at cadential points. And don't forget that the cadential $\frac{6}{4}$ must be metrically strong relative to its resolution.

1. Preliminaries.

   a. Write three cadential $\frac{6}{4}$ progressions, each in a different key, containing:
      1. II
      2. IV $\Big\}$ $V^{\begin{smallmatrix}6\text{-}5\\4\text{-}3\end{smallmatrix}}$ or $\begin{smallmatrix}8\text{-}7\\6\text{-}5\\4\text{-}3\end{smallmatrix}$-I
      3. II^6

      Be sure the $\frac{6}{4}$ falls on a strong beat!
   b. Write two phrases of at least four measures in length—one in major, one in minor, one in $\frac{2}{4}$, one in $\frac{3}{4}$—each using II, IV, or II^6 moving to a cadential $\frac{6}{4}$.

2. Figured bass.

3. Melody.

*don't harmonize passing tones

4. Melody.

bass: ♩·

11

VI and IV⁶

11-1   Schubert, Impromptu, D. 899

USES OF VI

1. VI-IV or VI-II⁶ (bass arpeggio). To study harmony and voice leading is to study the expansion of simple patterns into more complex and differentiated ones, creating the possibility for new kinds of tonal motion and new tonal goals. For example, IV and II⁶—chords whose primary purpose is to move on to V—can themselves function as temporary goals of motion. At the beginning of Example 11-1, a bass motion in 3rds—a kind of broken chord or arpeggio—leads down from the tonic to the bass of II^6 in bar 3: G♭-E♭-C♭. The chord on E♭ is VI, a particularly versatile triad with many possible functions. The function illustrated in the Schubert is one of the most important and characteristic: to connect I with IV or II^6 by means of an arpeggiated descending motion in 3rds. Usually IV or II^6 will move on to V (as in the Schubert);* sometimes, however, they lead to an inversion of V$^{(7)}$ or to VII^6 for a more contrapuntal bass line. Example 11-2 shows some of the most typical possibilities.

11-2   VI leading to IV or II^6

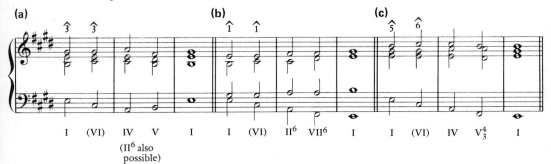

A particularly beautiful feature in the Schubert is the way VI makes it possible to retain the melody tone $\hat{3}$ for six beats without monotony. Since VI and I have both $\hat{1}$ and $\hat{3}$ as common tones, it frequently is the case that the bass arpeggio using VI will begin with the repetition of one of these tones in the soprano, as in Examples 11-2a and b. Another useful possibility for the soprano is shown in Example 11-2c.

2. VI-II (descending-5th progression). Another very important function of VI is exemplified in the opening idea of Beethoven's "Spring" Sonata for piano and violin (Example 11-3). Two statements of VI occur in this ten-bar phrase (bars 3 and 8); both move to II, the first in root position and the second in $^6_3$ position. The close connection that one feels here between VI and II—especially in bars 3-4—is largely due to the strong harmonic relationship between these chords. VI is built on the scale degree a 5th above II and thus gravitates to it, as II does to V and V to I. This harmonic connection is most strongly evident when both chords are in root position; the "harmonic" motion of a 5th (or its inversion, a 4th) will then occur in the crucial bass part. But a weaker harmonic connection can also be implied when II is in first inversion, as in bar 9 of the Beethoven.

*In the Schubert, the ultimate destination of the II^6 is the V of bar 4, the chords in between forming a kind of subordinate progression. The C♮ on the second beat of bar 4 functions as a leading tone to V.

11-3   Beethoven, Violin Sonata, Op. 24 ("Spring"), I

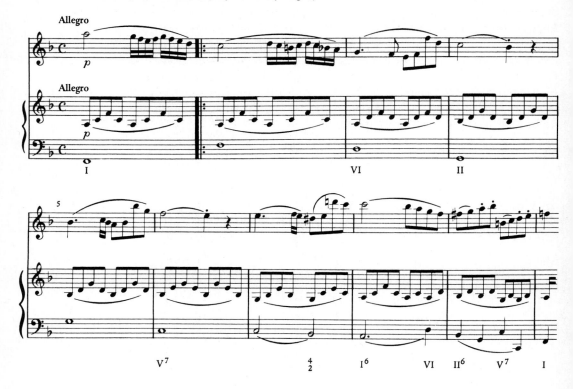

As you add to your vocabulary of chords you will see that progression by falling 5th constitutes a norm—indeed *the* norm of harmonic motion. Thus using VI is the most natural way to lead to II.

Because II^5_3 in minor is a problematic diminished triad, and because the roots of VI and II in minor form a diminished, rather than a perfect, 5th, the progression VI-II^5_3 does not have the significance in minor that it does in major. However VI-II^6—where the vertical diminished 5th is softened and the horizontal one eliminated—can and does occur as freely as in major.

In addition to its harmonic role, as discussed above, VI can also fulfill a voice-leading function. It often breaks up the parallel 5ths or octaves that would otherwise occur between I and II, a possibility we will explore closely in Unit 16.

3. VI approaching V from above. I can move to V with either a rising or a falling bass. Both possibilities are good, and both occur frequently, but the rising bass is the more "natural"—that is, it relates more directly to fundamental properties of the tonal system. $\hat{5}$ lies above $\hat{1}$ in the tonic triad and in the overtone series; the normal position of $\hat{5}$, therefore, is *above* $\hat{1}$, and the bass line of a I-V progression will most naturally ascend. The most frequently used intermediate harmonies— II, IV, and II^6—have bass tones that lie between $\hat{1}$ and the $\hat{5}$ above it; these harmonies help to fill in, and thus make partially stepwise, the ascending 5th from $\hat{1}$ to $\hat{5}$.

However, music would not have reached a very high level of development
if composers had confined themselves to the simplest and most basic possibilities.
Thus, as we know, we can invert the rising 5th and produce a descending 4th.
And we will now investigate the possibility of using an intermediate harmony
within this descending 4th, thus approaching V from above. The most important
of these chords are VI and IV^6.

VI does not lead directly to V as often as it does to II, IV, or II^6 but the
progression VI-V is nonetheless an extremely useful one. It is particularly well
suited to a rising top voice, such as the $\hat{1}$-$\hat{2}$-$\hat{3}$ in Example 11-4. Note that in
minor, the 3rd of VI must be doubled to avoid a melodic augmented 2nd (Ex-
ample 11-5).

11-4   Chopin, Scherzo, Op. 39

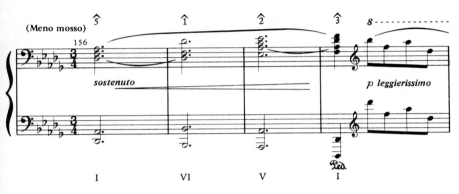

11-5

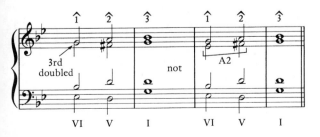

A less frequent possibility for the top voice is $\hat{5}$-$\hat{6}$-$\hat{7}$-$\hat{8}$ in major, which produces an unusually large number of perfect consonances. Don't use this combination in minor: if VI from natural minor is used, a melodic augmented 2nd is the result, whereas #VI (from melodic minor) forms a very ugly diminished $\frac{5}{3}$ chord (Example 11-6b and c). (If you want to set $\hat{5}$-$\hat{6}$-$\hat{7}$-$\hat{8}$ in minor, use the progression you learned in Unit 9, section 9.)

11-6

(a) Chopin, Impromptu, Op. 36

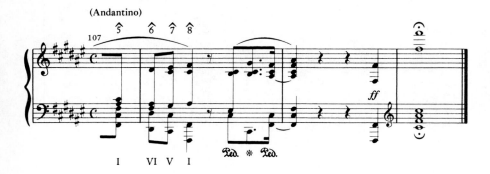

(b)   (c)

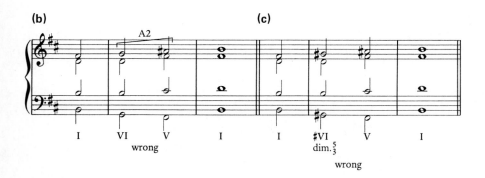

In a progression from VI to V, the top voice can move in parallel 10ths with the bass. This voice leading can be beautiful and is especially suitable for cadential points where a descending soprano is often desirable. It carries with it, however, the threat of parallel 5ths and octaves. To prevent these, *double the 3rd of VI* and move *both* inner voices up, as in Example 11-7.

If VI moves to the cadential $\frac{6}{4}$, doubling the 6th of the cadential $\frac{6}{4}$ will help avoid parallel octaves (Example 11-7b).

11-7

(a) parallel 10ths   **(b)**

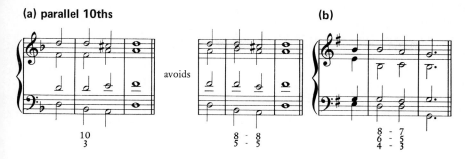

USES OF IV⁶

4. IV⁶-V. The second important chord whose bass descends by step to V is IV⁶. VI and IV⁶ often appear in similar situations; they relate to each other exactly as do IV and II⁶, sharing two common tones (one of them the bass). To change VI to IV⁶ we use the 5-6 technique, moving the 5th of VI up one step, exactly like changing IV to II⁶.

The two excerpts shown in Example 11-8 demonstrate a most important function of IV⁶: preceding V in a semicadence in minor. This makes a stronger effect than in major because of the bass motion by half step, which intensifies V. The term *Phrygian cadence* is often applied to the semicadence IV⁶-V in minor, not because the piece in question is even partly in the Phrygian mode, but merely because a similar chord progression often appears at cadences in genuine Phrygian compositions (Example 11-9).

11-8

(a) Bach, Chorale 281

(b) Handel, Adagio   (from *Harpsichord Suite No. 2*)

11-9   Bartolomeo Tromboncino (fl. 1500), Non val aqua

Phrygian
cadence

When used as a semicadence in minor, the Phrygian cadence occurs most typically in compositions from the Baroque period. Like any semicadence it will most naturally appear within a piece (as in the Bach chorale excerpt of Example 11-8). Quite frequently, however, composers of the Baroque era ended slow movements with such a cadence (thus ending on V rather than I), if the slow movement was not an independent composition but part of a larger work. This is the case in the Handel excerpt of Example 11-8, which ends with a Phrygian cadence on an A major chord. It is followed in the suite by an Allegro in F major, a connection by descending major 3rd that was quite frequent during this period.

When IV^6 is used in a Phrygian cadence, the usual tone to double is the 3rd above the bass, as in 11-8b and 11-9; this permits a completely stepwise progression into V and reduces the danger both of parallel octaves and of a melodic augmented 2nd (Example 11-10).

11-10   Phrygian cadence; doubling

(a)   (b)   (c)   (d)   (e)

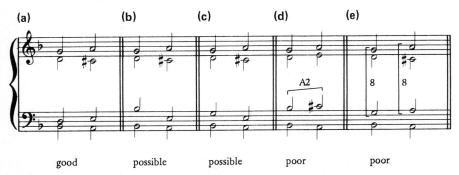

good   possible   possible   poor   poor

Perhaps you have noticed that all our examples of IV^6-V include the top-voice progression $\hat{4}$-$\hat{5}$. This is not invariable, but it is typical both for Phrygian cadences and for many other situations where IV^6 moves to V. IV$^5_3$ could never move to V under a soprano line $\hat{4}$-$\hat{5}$ because of the inevitable parallel octaves. The two excerpts of Example 11-11 illustrate this most useful feature of IV^6; neither, of course, is a Phrygian cadence.

11-11

(a) Bach, Chorale 256

(b) Brahms, German folksong

translation: The moon rises stealthily, little blue, blue flower!

Leading to V with the top-voice progression $\hat{4}$-$\hat{5}$ is a specialized function of IV⁶, one that it fulfills more readily than any other chord. In addition to this special function, IV⁶ can serve to *expand* IV (just as I⁶, II⁶, and V⁶ can expand I, II, and V); see the Mozart excerpt in Example 11-12a. IV⁶ can also *substitute* for IV where a lighter sonority, a descending bass, or both are desired (as in the Handel excerpt of 11-12b). In addition, IV⁶ can appear instead of VI in a bass arpeggio leading to IV (11-12a) or II⁶ (11-12c, from the same Handel Air).

11-12

(a) Mozart, Overture to Così fan tutte, K. 588

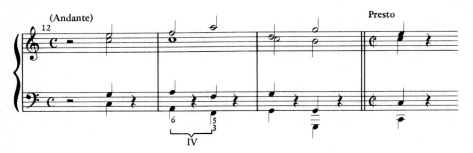

(b) Handel, Air   (from *Leçon No. 1*)

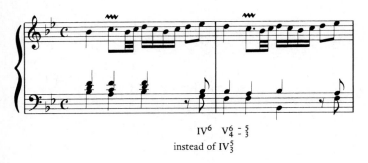

IV⁶   V⁶₄ - ⁵₃
instead of IV⁵₃

(c) (Handel)

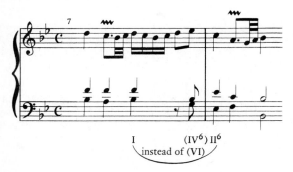

I   (IV⁶) II⁶
instead of (VI)

5. VI and IV⁶ ascending to V⁶ ($^6_5$). VI and IV⁶ normally move to root-position V, but their use is by no means restricted to such a progression. In major, if a melodic, noncadential bass is appropriate, both chords can move to V⁶ ($^6_5$) and then on to I (Example 11-13). Be careful, though, when you move from IV⁶ to

V_5^6. It's easy to get parallel 5ths (11-13d). In Example 11-13e, note the beautiful counterpoint between the descending arpeggio of the top voice and the ascending stepwise bass line.

11-13   bass line $\hat{6}$-$\hat{7}$-$\hat{8}$ in major

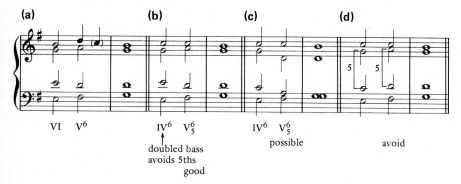

(e) Mozart, String Quartet, K. 458, III

In minor, IV⁶ (from *melodic* minor) may go to V⁶ ($_5^6$), but VI cannot. Example 11-14 illustrates.

11-14   bass line $\hat{6}$-$\hat{7}$-$\hat{8}$ in minor

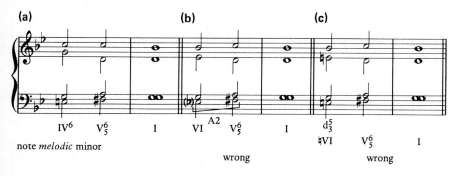

POINTS FOR REVIEW

1. VI makes possible the bass-arpeggio progression I-VI-IV or I-VI-II⁶.
2. I-VI often supports repeated $\hat{1}$ or $\hat{3}$ in the soprano. Another possibility is $\hat{5}$-$\hat{6}$.
3. VI leads to II in a descending-5th progression.
4. VI approaches V from above. In this progression, the top voice can ascend (in contrary motion to the bass to avoid parallels) or it can form parallel 10ths with the bass

(with the 3rd of VI doubled to avoid parallel 5ths).
5. IV⁶-V in minor forms a Phrygian cadence; a frequent soprano line (cadential or noncadential) is $\hat{4}$-$\hat{5}$.
6. The most frequent doubling of IV⁶ is the 3rd above the bass.
7. IV⁶ can extend or substitute for IV.
8. VI or IV⁶ makes possible the rising-bass progression VI or IV⁶-V⁶ ($^6_5$)-I.

EXERCISES

NOTE. In setting melodies, keep in mind that a repeated or sustained $\hat{1}$ or $\hat{3}$ may indicate the beginning of a bass arpeggio, that the melodic progression $\hat{4}$-$\hat{5}$ often suggests IV⁶-V, and that the progression $\hat{1}$-$\hat{2}$-$\hat{3}$ can be set VI-V-I.

1. Preliminaries. Melodic fragments.

*approach V from above

2. Melody.

bass:

$I^6 \longrightarrow IV$

3. Figured bass.

soprano: $\hat{5}$ $\hat{6}$ $\hat{7}$ $\hat{8}$

6 6   6   6   6   4 6 6   8   7
             or 4   2   6   5
                3   4   3

4. Melody.

5. Figured bass.

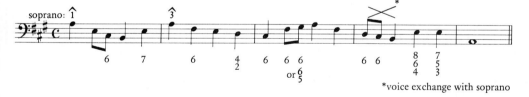

soprano: $\hat{1}$ $\hat{3}$ *

6   7   6   4   6 6 6   6 6   8   7
                     2   6   5
                  or 6   4   3
                     5

*voice exchange with soprano

12

Supertonic and Subdominant Seventh Chords

12-1　**Bach, Chorale 99**

1. II⁷ and IV⁷. If we add a 7th to II or IV, we produce II^7 or IV^7; these are among the most frequently used of all nondominant seventh chords. By far the most important positions are II^7, II^6_5, and IV^7. II^6_5, in particular, is an indispensable chord. It occurs in music of many styles and especially often in the works of Bach (Example 12-1). Adding a 7th to II and IV does not change their tendency to move to dominant harmony; on the contrary, the dissonance activates these chords and intensifies their motion toward V. Dissonance treatment greatly resembles that of V^7. As Example 12-1 shows, the process of resolution is exactly the same—*downward and by step*. The way the dissonance is introduced also resembles V^7 but tends to be stricter. Most frequently the 7th enters as a common tone held over or repeated from the preceding chord; it is usually accented and functions as a suspension. Where it is not prepared as a common tone, the 7th generally functions as a passing tone (8-7) within an extended II or IV. Except in rather free or complex textures the 7th will not enter by leap, as sometimes happens in V^7 when the 7th enters unprepared as an incomplete neighbor.

In four-part writing II^6_5, the other inversions of II^7, and the various positions of IV^7 are virtually always complete chords. However, root-position II^7, especially in major, will sometimes appear with 5th omitted and with doubled root or 3rd.

SUPERTONIC SEVENTH CHORDS

2. II^6_5. Example 12-1 shows II^6_5 in its most characteristic use: as an intermediate harmony connecting I with a cadential V. As the example indicates, the dissonant tone is the 5th above the bass, here the A of the alto. In any position of II^7, the dissonant tone is $\hat{1}$; as a dissonance, $\hat{1}$ cannot serve as goal of motion, but is dependent on $\hat{7}$, to which it resolves by stepwise descent. (We encountered the same reversal in the melodic functions of $\hat{1}$ and $\hat{7}$ with the cadential $^6_4$; see Unit 10, section 6.) Like the cadential $^6_4$, II^6_5 grows out of the suspension of $\hat{1}$ into a cadential leading tone; with II^6_5, however, two harmonies—II and V—accompany the suspension and its resolution. In keeping with its origin as a suspension, II^6_5 is normally accented relative to the V to which it moves, though exceptions to this norm are much more frequent with II^6_5 than with the cadential $^6_4$. The preparation of the dissonance as a common tone is another inheritance from the ancestral suspension. In the Bach, note how the alto leaps to A on the second beat. The sole purpose of leaping at this point is to prepare the suspension; keeping the E through the second beat would have produced an irregular leap into the dissonance.

II^6_5 can support $\hat{1}$, $\hat{2}$, or $\hat{6}$ in the soprano; $\hat{4}$ is possible in four parts only if II^6_5 is incomplete—a most unusual procedure. At strong cadences, II^6_5, like II^6, tends to support $\hat{2}$ in the soprano (as in the Bach chorale). In general II^6_5 resembles II^6, of course, but the two chords are not completely interchangeable. II^6_5 derives a much richer sonority from the added dissonant tone; its progression to V highlights the leading tone by resolving into it from a dissonance. These features often make it preferable to II^6. On the other hand, II^6 is often to be preferred if a light texture is appropriate. Sometimes the progression of the soprano will determine which of the two chords is better. If the soprano repeats or holds $\hat{2}$ (as in Example 12-1), II^6_5 frequently gives a better sonority and (in minor) prevents an augmented 2nd. If the soprano descends from $\hat{2}$ to $\hat{7}$, however (as in Example 12-2a), II^6_5 will not readily work—the resolution of the dissonance will be transferred into the wrong voice. For the present, therefore, II^6 remains the only possibility.

Another difference between II^6_5 and II^6 is that II^6_5 supports $\hat{6}$ in the soprano much more easily; the repetition of $\hat{1}$ (coming from a tonic) removes the danger of parallel 5ths (Example 12-2b).

12-2   II$^6_5$ **and soprano**

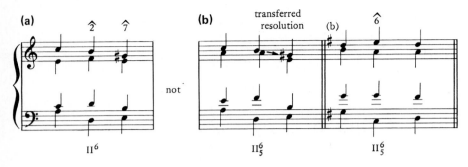

3. II^7. II^7 (the root position) occurs fairly frequently in composition (Example 12-3), but much less often than II$^6_5$ (just as II is less common than II^6, at least as a cadential chord). In the Mozart, the melody in the second half of bar 3 is an embellished G; the top voice of II^7, therefore, is $\hat{4}$. II^7, like II, very frequently supports $\hat{4}$ in the soprano; the 10th between the outer voices makes for a fluent contrapuntal setting. In the Schumann, the vocal part has the dissonant $\hat{1}$ as top-voice tone for II^7; this is another very frequent possibility and one where the prominence of the dissonance adds to the intensity of the chord. In the Schumann, notice how the addition of the 7th improves the sound of root-position II in minor.

12-3

(a) Mozart, Piano Sonata, K. 311, I

(b) Schumann, Ich will meine Seele tauchen (from *Dichterliebe,* Op. 48)

translation: I will dip my soul in the lily's cup.

II⁷ is easily approached by I⁶; in this progression a complete chord is possible in both major and minor (Example 12-4a and b). When approached by I⁵₃, however, II⁷ presents greater problems in voice leading than II⁶₅. In moving from I to II⁷ in major, the necessity of preparing the 7th and the danger of parallel 5ths make it almost obligatory to omit the *5th* of II⁷ and to double the *root* or *3rd* (Example 12-4c and d). In minor, the diminished 5th of II⁷ eliminates the danger of parallels and, at the same time, lends a characteristic sonority to the chord (12-4e). For these reasons the complete chord occurs more frequently in minor than in major. Nevertheless, securing a smooth introduction for the 7th of V⁷ often makes it advisable to use the incomplete chord in minor as well (12-4f).

12-4   II⁷: voice leading and doubling

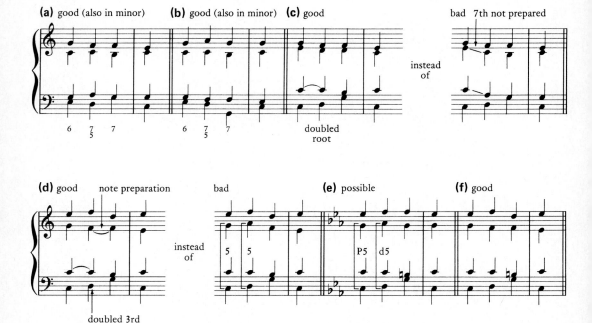

4. Moving to V⁷. In Examples 12-3 and 12-4, II⁷ moves to V⁷ rather than V⁵₃. If we move from II⁷ to V⁷ we interlock two dissonant chords; the immediate succession of two dissonant chords is perfectly correct as long as the dissonant *tones* resolve correctly. Especially when $\hat{4}$ is the soprano tone of II⁷, moving to V⁷ makes for logical and connected voice leading; $\hat{4}$ holds over to become the 7th of V⁷ and then resolves to $\hat{3}$, usually over I (Example 12-5a). And, in fact, if $\hat{4}$ in the soprano is not held as a common tone (if, for instance, it leaps down to $\hat{2}$), then it is usually best to double $\hat{4}$ (3rd of II⁷) in an inner voice in order to secure a good preparation for the 7th of V⁷ (12-4d and the piano accompaniment to 12-3b).

II⁶₅ can also move to V⁷, but it does so less readily than II⁷. In four-part texture, II⁶₅ does not contain $\hat{4}$ in any of the upper voices ($\hat{4}$, of course, is in the bass). This means that the 7th of V⁷ must enter through the leap of a 3rd (12-5b and c). Although not incorrect, these voice leadings are less smooth than the completely stepwise progression of II⁶₅ to V (as in Example 12-1), a voice leading that provides a particularly good accompaniment to the resolution of the suspension. Of the last two possibilities shown in Example 12-5, c is the more natural, in that the tendencies of the active notes are fulfilled. Leaping away from $\hat{6}$ (as in 12-5b), instead of leading it to $\hat{5}$, its normal goal, can sound forced in simple textures like those of four-part vocal music, but this device does sometimes occur, especially in instrumental style.

12-5   moving to V⁷

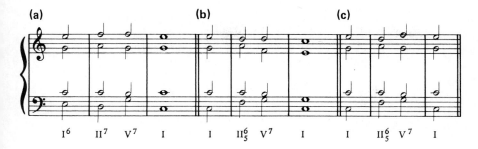

5. Metric position. In all the examples from the literature that we have presented so far, II$^6_5$ and II⁷ have appeared on strong beats, the dissonant tone functioning as a suspension. And the dominant chord that follows has been metrically weaker than the II⁷. This is the usual situation, but by no means an invariable one. Sometimes II⁷ ($^6_5$) appears on a weak beat and leads to an accented dominant. Such is the case in Example 12-6, an excerpt from a Schubert Impromptu. In this instance and in similar ones, although the dissonance is repeated as a common tone it is not really a suspension, for it is metrically weak. As the explanatory sketches indicate, the dissonance is derived from a passing tone within II⁶; the passing motion is contracted from three tones to two, through the omission of the first tone.

12-6   Schubert, Impromptu, D. 935

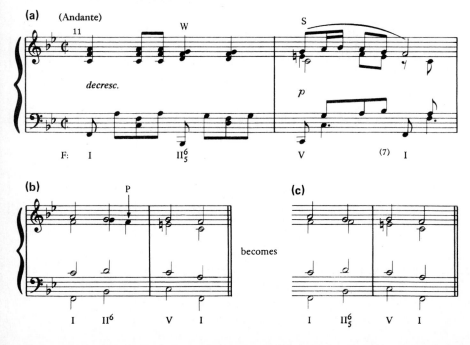

6. Moving to a cadential $^6_4$. II^7 or II^6_5 can move to a dominant embellished by a cadential $^6_4$ (Example 12-7). The 7th of II^7 ($^6_5$) is repeated *in the same voice* to become the 4th of the $^6_4$ chord before resolving down to the 3rd of V; thus the $^6_4$ effects a delay in the resolution of the dissonance. Both II^7 and the cadential $^6_4$ normally appear on a strong beat. The metric position of the $^6_4$, however, is less variable than that of the II^7, and we sometimes find II^7 on a weaker beat than the $^6_4$ that follows it.

12-7   Schubert, String Quartet, D. 804, III

(a)

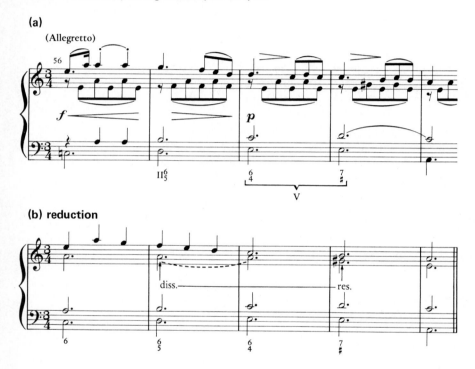

(b) reduction

some possibilities in 4 voices

7. VI-II$_5^6$. Any chord that can lead logically to II can also lead to II^7 or its inversions as long as it allows the dissonance to enter correctly. A particularly frequent and idiomatic progression is I-VI-II$_5^6$ with a bass descending in 3rds. We see an example of this progression in the closing cadence from Bach's Chorale 69 (Example 12-8); note that the bass of II$_5^6$ skips down to the root before moving on to V.

12-8   Bach, Chorale 69

$\qquad$ I $\quad$ (VI) $\qquad$ II$_5^6$ $\quad$ V $\quad$ I

8. II^7 expanding supertonic harmony. Composers often elaborate and extend supertonic harmony before moving on to V. In Example 12-9, also from a Bach chorale, II first appears in $_3^6$ position. On the second beat of the bar, the bass moves down to the root; at the same time, the soprano brings in the 7th as a passing tone.

12-9   Bach, Chorale 108

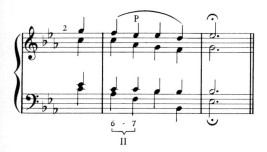

$\qquad$ 6 - 7

$\qquad$ II

$\qquad$A phrase from an etude of Mendelssohn (Example 12-10) shows II$_5^6$ moving to II^7 with voice exchange between the bass and melody (here the melody is in the middle, not at the top). Such motions between II$_5^6$ and II^7 (in either direction) occur frequently. In this excerpt the 4th of the cadential $_4^6$ moves up to the 5th of V; we will discuss such "irregular" resolutions of the $_4^6$ in Unit 19.

12-10   Mendelssohn, Etude, Op. 104/1

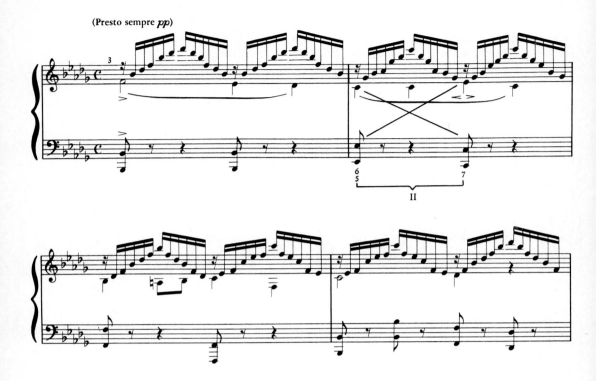

In general, dissonant chords have far fewer possibilities for extended duration than consonant ones. II⁷, however, is so strongly directed toward dominant harmony that it can be extended over fairly broad stretches of time without any loss to the music's coherence. In the latter part of Example 12-11, for example, the II_5^6 spans 2½ bars compared with just half a bar for the V_4^{6-7} to which it leads; also interesting is the voice exchange between the two lowest parts.

12-11   Mozart, String Quartet, K. 428, I

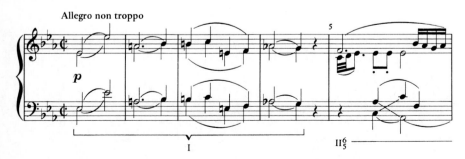

A passing "I⁶" can move between II⁷ and II⁶₅ or, as in Example 12-12, between II and II⁶₅; compare the very similar progression discussed in Unit 9, section 10. The reverse of this progression can also occur: from first inversion to root position (12-12c).

12-12   Chopin, Etude, Op. 10/II

(a) I⁶ connects II⁽⁷⁾ and II⁶₅

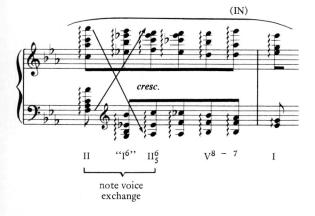

(b)   **(c)**

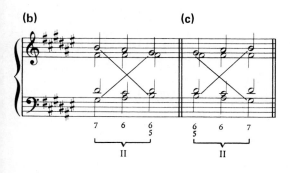

9. Noncadential uses of II^7 and II$_5^6$. II^7 and II$_5^6$ can lead to noncadential as well as cadential dominants. The noncadential ones need not be in root position. A particularly characteristic progression contains II$_5^6$ moving to V$_2^4$ over a common bass tone, as in Example 12-13. This progression is, in principle, the same as IV or II^6 moving to V$_2^4$; if the bass tone of the $_2^4$ receives an accent, it functions as a suspension.

12-13　Bach, Menuet　　　　　　　　　　　　　　　　　　　　(from *Partita No. 4*)

10. Other inversions of II^7. Of the two remaining inversions of II^7, $_2^4$ is the more important. It occurs very frequently in noncadential situations, especially at the beginning of a composition, where staying close to the tonic in the bass is often more appropriate than moving abruptly away from it. II$_2^4$ leads from I to V^6 or, more often, V$_5^6$. The opening of the first Prelude from *The Well-Tempered Clavier I* is a familiar example (Example 12-14).

12-14　Bach, Well-Tempered Clavier I, Prelude 1

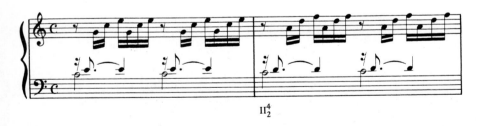

II$_3^4$, like VI or IV^6, can be used to lead to V$^{(7)}$ from above. In Example 12-15a, II$_3^4$ moves into a cadential $_4^6$; the eventual resolution of the $_4^6$ is not shown in the example.

12-15

(a) Mendelssohn, String Quartet, Op. 13, I

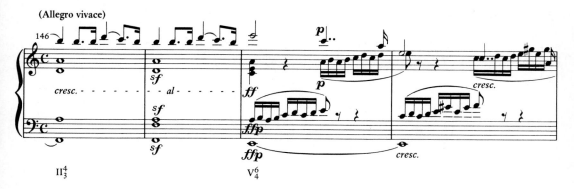

some possibilities in 4 voices

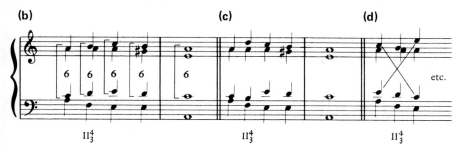

SUBDOMINANT SEVENTH CHORDS

11. IV^7. As we know, IV and II are closely associated; they share two common tones and a common goal—V. It follows as a logical consequence that the seventh chords based on these triads—II^7 and IV^7—will also have many features in common. The most important position of IV^7—the root position—differs by only a single tone from II$_5^6$ and moves to V in a very similar manner. Thus in Example 12-16, merely substituting an F♯ for the G in the IV^7 would transform it into a II$_5^6$. The harmonic direction of the phrase would remain much the same but the *sound* of the chord in question would change in a way easier to hear than to describe in words. And, in bars 2-3, Schumann's imitative counterpoint (the repetition of a melodic idea in different voices) would be impossible.

12-16   Schumann, Auf einer Burg, Op. 39

translation: The old knight has fallen asleep during his watch.

IV^7 shows less resemblance to II$^6_5$ when the 7th of the chord is in the so-prano, for this tone ($\hat{3}$) is the only member of the chord that does not also belong to II^7. As it happens, $\hat{3}$ occurs very frequently in the soprano, more frequently than any of the other tones. This disposition gives us an alternative to the caden-tial $^6_4$ when $\hat{3}$ moves to $\hat{2}$ at a cadence, as in Example 12-17. In this excerpt IV^7 comes from a IV^6 in the previous beat; the 7th functions as a passing tone with-in an expanded subdominant.

12-17   Bach, Chorale 117 (end)

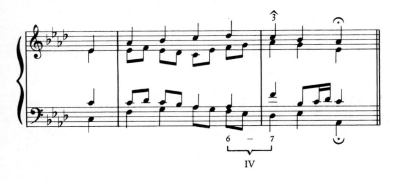

As Example 12-16 has shown, IV^7 can appear on a weaker beat than the V to which it moves; however it appears much more characteristically in strong metrical position, as in Example 12-17. The chord presents the problem of paral-lel 5ths in moving to V, especially when $\hat{3}$ occurs in the soprano. Example 12-18a and b show the most common way of avoiding 5ths. By the way, it is character-istic of IV^7 for its 5th to descend by step into the leading tone, thus moving to

V in parallel 3rds, 6ths, or 10ths with its 7th ($\hat{3}$). For this reason the voice leading of 12-18c, although not incorrect, is not often used. Examples 12-18d, e,
and f demonstrate some additional possibilities.

12-18   IV-V: $\hat{3}$ in the soprano

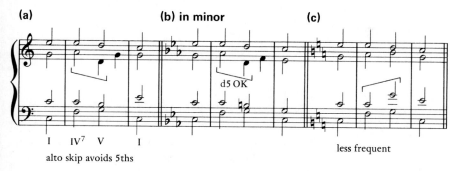

alto skip avoids 5ths

less frequent

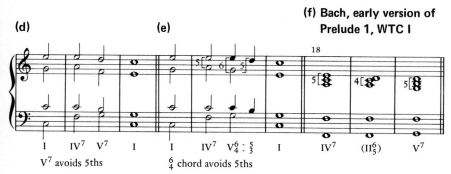

V^7 avoids 5ths

$^6_4$ chord avoids 5ths

The threat of parallel 5ths so often posed by IV^7 also looms when $\hat{3}$ occurs
as a soprano passing tone (8-7) over a progression from IV to V (Example 12-19).
This passing motion occurs very often in the approach to a cadence, especially if
$\hat{3}$ falls on a weak part of the measure or beat, thus excluding the cadential $^6_4$. The
strategies shown in Example 12-18 will save this situation as well; also compare
12-17, where an accented passing tone in the soprano produces the IV^7.

12-19 $IV^{8-7}V$

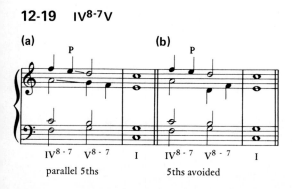

parallel 5ths

5ths avoided

12. Inversions of IV⁷. Of the three inversions, the $\frac{6}{5}$ is by far the most important. Its most useful function is to lead to V$\frac{6}{5}$ (less often V⁶) and I with a stepwise ascending bass—a beautiful alternative to IV-V-I where a strong harmonic cadence is not needed (Example 12-20). This use of IV$\frac{6}{5}$ is closely related to that of IV⁶ described in Unit 11, section 5.

12-20

(a) Bach, Chorale 117   (b) Bach, Chorale 100

IV$\frac{6}{5}$ V$\frac{6}{5}$ I   I⁶   V$\frac{6}{5}$ V⁶   I

POINTS FOR REVIEW

1. II⁷, IV⁷, and their inversions move to dominant harmony. All positions are usually complete except for root-position II⁷ in major. The most important position is II$\frac{6}{5}$; II⁷ and IV⁷ also occur frequently.

2. The motion to V is intensified by the dissonant 7th, which resolves downward by step. In four-part vocal writing, the 7th should be introduced either as a common tone (the most frequent possibility) or as a passing tone.

3. II$\frac{6}{5}$ is better than II⁶ if the soprano repeats $\hat{2}$; II⁶ is better if the soprano moves $\hat{2}$-$\hat{7}$. II$\frac{6}{5}$ provides better support for $\hat{6}$ than II⁶.

4. In minor, the 7th of II⁷ improves the root-position sonority of II.

5. Frequent progressions leading to a cadential dominant are I-VI-II$\frac{6}{5}$ (or II⁷) and I-VI-IV⁷. II$\frac{6}{5}$-V$\frac{4}{2}$ is an important noncadential progression.

6. A cadential $\frac{6}{4}$ frequently delays the resolution of II$\frac{6}{5}$(7) to V. The dissonant tone is held over in the same voice before resolving.

7. II$\frac{4}{2}$ (most often coming from root-position I) leads to V⁶ or V$\frac{6}{5}$. This progression is particularly frequent at the beginning of a piece. II$\frac{4}{2}$ can approach V from above.

8. IV⁷ is sometimes an alternative chord to II$\frac{6}{5}$ ($\hat{1}$ or $\hat{6}$ in soprano), but the most important use of IV⁷ is to support $\hat{3}$ in the soprano. *Warning:* Be careful of parallel 5ths in the progression IV⁷-V$\frac{5}{3}$ (see Example 12-18).

9. The most important inversion of IV⁷ is IV$\frac{6}{5}$ in the progression IV$\frac{6}{5}$-V$\frac{6}{5}$-I with ascending bass; compare IV⁶-V⁶($\frac{6}{5}$)-I.

EXERCISES

1. Preliminaries. Write the following progressions, each in a different major or minor key.

   a. I-II$^6_5$-V$^{6\text{-}5}_{4\text{-}3}$-I. II$^6_5$ should have $\hat{2}$ in the soprano.

   b. I-II$^6_5$-V$^{8\text{-}7}$-I. II$^6_5$ should have $\hat{6}$ in the soprano.

   c. I-VI-II$^6_5$-V-I. II$^6_5$ should have $\hat{1}$ in the soprano.

   d. II$^6_5$-noncadential V^7-resolution.

   e. I^6-II^7-V^7-I.

   f. I$^5_3$-II^7-V^7-I.

   g. I-II$^6_5$-II^7-V$^{6\text{-}5}_{4\text{-}3}$-I.

     voice
  exchange

   h. I-II$^4_2$-resolution-I.

   i. I-IV^7-V-I. IV^7 should have $\hat{3}$ in the soprano.

   j. I-IV$^6_5$-V$^6_5$-I.

2. Melody.

bass: arpeggio

II^6 or II$^6_5$?
*voice exchange, bass and soprano

3. Figured bass.

Marcia funebre

4. Melody.

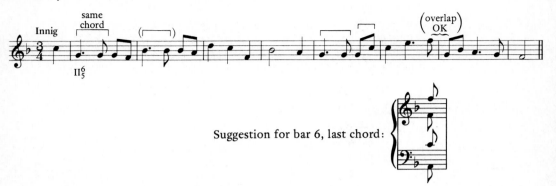

Suggestion for bar 6, last chord:

13

Other Uses of IV, IV⁶, and VI

13-1 Bach, Chorale 32

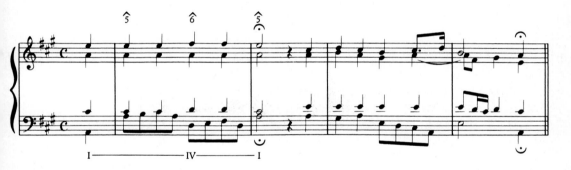

IV AND IV⁶

1. I-IV-I expanding tonic harmony. In the first two bars of Example 13-1, we encounter a new and characteristic function of IV. Instead of leading to V, this IV moves from tonic to tonic. Comparing the basses of I-IV-I and I-V-I (in A major, A-D-A and A-E-A), we discover that the latter unfolds the 5th of tonic harmony (A-E) whereas the former does not. For this reason, I-IV-I does not express the key nearly as strongly as I-V-I, and is thus a distinctly subordinate progression. I-IV-I generally occurs either before or after a progression in which the tonic is securely established by a strong dominant.

It would be quite possible to harmonize the tune in 13-1 with I-IV-V in the first two bars (Example 13-2). The effect, however, would differ greatly from that of Bach's setting; the temporary stop on V would introduce a much higher degree of tension. By extending tonic harmony without using V (or any chord containing the leading tone), I-IV-I constitutes an important source of variety; through contrast, it enhances the directional pull of dominant harmony once the latter arrives.

13-2

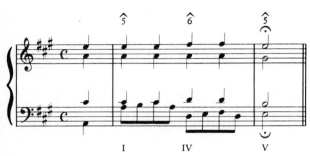

Our Bach chorale illustrates a most important aspect of I-IV-I: its frequent association with a neighboring progression in the melody, here the upper-neighbor figure $\hat{5}$-$\hat{6}$-$\hat{5}$. IV, which contains the upper neighbors to $\hat{3}$ and $\hat{5}$ plus $\hat{1}$ as a common tone, works particularly well as a neighboring chord to I. (II also contains $\hat{4}$ and $\hat{6}$ as upper neighbors to $\hat{3}$ and $\hat{5}$, but the absence of a common tone makes it almost impossible to secure good voice leading for the progression I-II-I.) Another important neighboring motion, $\hat{3}$-$\hat{4}$-$\hat{3}$, can also be supported by I-IV-I, as in the Schumann excerpt of Example 13-3.

13-3 **Schumann, Sheherazade**   (from *Album for the Young*, Op. 68)

Although I-IV-I most often supports a neighboring motion in the soprano, other possibilities exist. In bar 5 of Schubert's "Des Fischers Liebesglück" (Example 13-4), the neighbors are in the middle voices while the melody stays around $\hat{1}$. Here the effect is that of an incomplete progression IV-I rather than the usual I-IV-I. Although the preceding bar ends with I, the entrance of the singer, together with the fermata and rest, makes the IV sound like a new beginning. In bar 6, beat 2, the passing tone B transforms the IV into an apparent II⁶. This "II⁶" should be regarded as a contrapuntal derivative of IV (through the 5-6 technique) rather than representing supertonic harmony, for a root-position II would never occur in this context (review the relation of II⁶ to IV in Unit 9).

13-4   Schubert, Des Fischers Liebesglück

translation: Through the willows a glimmer winks and beckons.

In the progression I-IV-I, I⁶ can represent either or both of the tonic chords, frequently with 10ths between bass and soprano (Example 13-5).

13-5   Handel, Air   (from *Harpsichord Suite No. 5*)

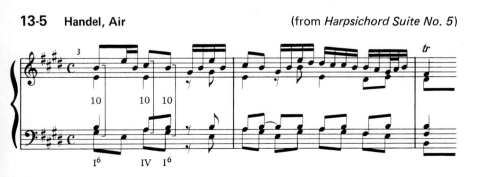

2. Plagal cadences. The progression IV-I, used as a cadential formula, is called a *plagal cadence*. Because motion between IV and I lacks the key-defining power of the V-I progression, plagal cadences have a much more limited function than authentic (V-I) cadences. They typically occur at the very end of a composition, as in the Amen at the close of a hymn. Emphasis on the subdominant can be very beautiful at the end of a piece, for this chord (a 5th below the tonic) often generates a feeling of repose (Example 13-6). In such cases the "finality" of the closing tonic has already been established by stronger tonal forces earlier in the piece.

13-6   Chopin, Nocturne, Op. 27/1

Often, as in Example 13-7, a plagal cadence follows immediately on an authentic one and gives added emphasis to the tonic.

13-7   Handel, And the Glory of the Lord   (from *Messiah*)

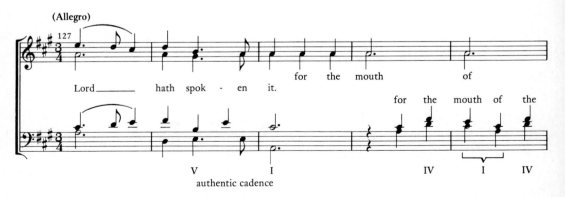

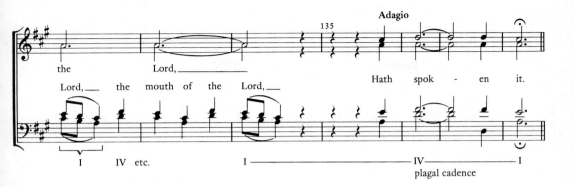

3. I-IV⁶-I⁶. IV⁶, like IV, can move within an expanded I, leading directly from one tonic to another. It does so in the context of a progression shown in Example 13-8, the beginning of the last movement of Haydn's "Clock" Symphony. In this very important progression, IV⁶ supports a passing tone ascending from $\hat{3}$ to $\hat{5}$; the bass moves from I to I⁶, not up a 3rd as is usual, but down a 6th.

13-8   Haydn, Symphony 101 ("Clock"), IV

This characteristic function of IV⁶ can be most valuable, especially if a leading-tone chord (VII⁶ or V⁴₃) is not wanted as the support for $\hat{4}$ (Example 13-9). Incidentally, IV⁵₃ does not work very well in this situation; the root-position chord following a large leap in the bass creates too heavy an effect for the passing function of the chord.

13-9

(a)

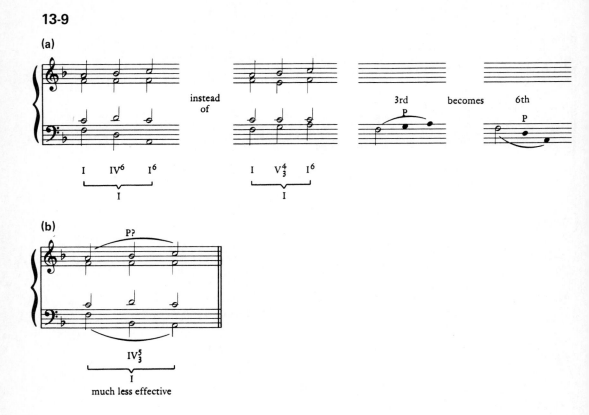

(b)

much less effective

Motion between I and I⁶ with a stepwise bass works well in both directions (I-VII⁶-I⁶ or I⁶-VII⁶-I). But the progression I-IV⁶-I⁶ is not reversible; I⁶-IV⁶-I does not occur. Nor will I-IV⁶-I⁶ appear with the bass rising a 5th from IV⁶ to I⁶. The reason is that $\hat{6}$ between two tonic chords is heard as upper neighbor to $\hat{5}$. Now if $\hat{6}$, as bass tone of IV⁶, leaps *down* to I⁶, we hear it resolving to an inner-voice $\hat{5}$, either actually present or implied. But if $\hat{6}$ leaps *up* (either to I or I⁶), it is left exposed and unresolved (Example 13-10). On the other hand, a leap of a 6th from IV⁶ down to I creates a needlessly discontinuous bass.

13-10   IV⁶ supports P within tonic harmony

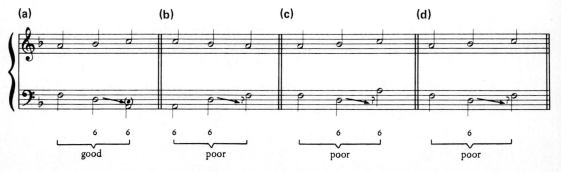

4. IV⁶ as a passing chord within V. Another contrapuntal function of IV⁶ is to move between the root position and the first inversion ($^6_3$ or, more frequently, $^6_5$) of dominant harmony. IV⁶ often introduces the 7th in an elaboration of V$^{8\text{-}7}$, as as in Example 13-11.

13-11   IV⁶ passing between V and V$^6_5$

(a)

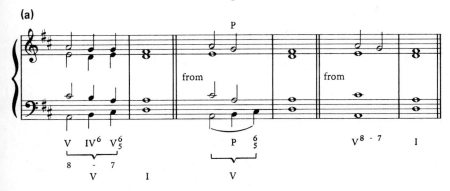

(b) Bach, Chorale 237

note melodic minor

VI

5. VI as substitute for I. VI and I share two common tones, $\hat{1}$ and $\hat{3}$. Therefore, VI can substitute for I where the latter might be expected—after V or V⁷. This substitution can forestall excessive repetitions of I, as in an excerpt from Beethoven's "Waldstein" Sonata (Example 13-12a), in which the soprano descends from $\hat{4}$ (over V⁷) to $\hat{3}$ (over VI), a frequent melodic pattern when VI substitutes for I. In addition, and most important, the VI of bar 15 carries the line *on* to the cadential II⁶ of the next bar—in contrast to the I at the end of bar 14, which creates less forward motion.

   Another quotation from the same sonata (13-12b) shows a different possibility for the top voice. Here the soprano for V⁷-VI is the same as for V⁷-I two bars later—both end on $\hat{1}$. The two contrasting haronizations of $\hat{1}$ create variety in a most beautiful way; in addition, using VI the first time prevents a cadential effect too early in the passage.

13-12

(a) Beethoven, "Waldstein" Sonata, Op. 53, II

(b) Beethoven, "Waldstein," I

In both Waldstein excerpts, the 3rd of VI is doubled. This is usual with $V^{(7)}$-VI because it allows $\hat{7}$ to move to $\hat{8}$ and prevents parallel 5ths or (in minor) an augmented 2nd (Example 13-13).

13-13

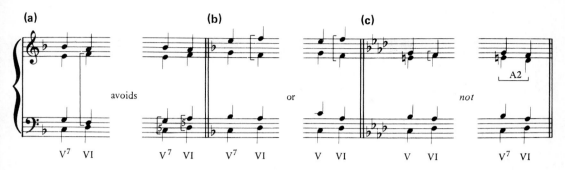

(a)   (b)   (c)

avoids   or   not

V⁷ VI   V⁷ VI   V⁷ VI   V VI   V VI   V⁷ VI

6. Deceptive cadences. If a substitution of VI for I occurs where a cadence is expected, we call the progression a *deceptive cadence* (V-VI or V⁷-VI). Deceptive cadences are inconclusive. They create no sense of repose; on the contrary, they produce a suspense that dissipates only when tonal stability is regained, usually through an authentic cadence. The deceptive effect is strongest if the soprano is the same as in a perfect authentic cadence—$\hat{2}$-$\hat{1}$ or $\hat{7}$-$\hat{8}$. In the music of the great composers, deceptive cadences fulfill a variety of functions. Examples 13-14 and 13-15 show two of the most important possibilities.

In Example 13-14, the deceptive cadence provides the impulse for a varied repetition of the whole four-bar phrase in a kind of antecedent-consequent grouping.

13-14   Mozart, Trio, K. 498, I

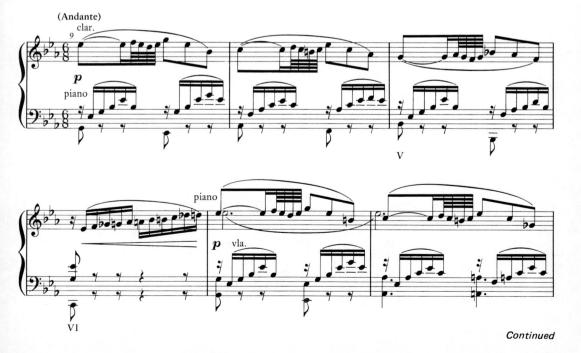

Continued

In Example 13-15, the VI of the deceptive cadence forms part of a rising-bass progression that leads chromatically from V to I. (The chords over D♮ and E♭ result from this chromatic progression; they will be discussed in later units.)

13-15   Handel, Courante   (from *Harpsichord Suite No. 8*)

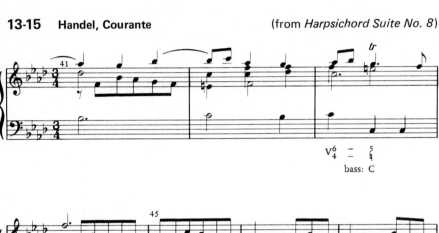

7. Relationship between IV⁶ and VI. As we noted in Unit 11, VI and IV⁶ are closely related chords that frequently appear in similar situations. Thus, IV⁶ will sometimes appear instead of VI at a deceptive cadence, where it has the effect of temporarily turning the 7th of V⁷ into a consonance, as in Example 13-16. Similarly, VI will sometimes replace IV⁶ in leading down a 6th from I to I⁶ (Example 13-17; compare 13-8).

13-16   Handel, Sonata No. 5 for Flute and Thoroughbass

13-17   Mozart, Piano Sonata, K. 545, II

As we saw in 13-15, VI, like IV⁶, can function as a passing chord between the root position and first inversion of V.

8. Harmonizing ascending scales. If you memorize the standard patterns for harmonizing scales shown in Examples 13-18 and 13-19—and, in particular, if you learn to play them in all keys—you will find it much easier to harmonize melodies, to realize figured and unfigured basses, and, eventually, to improvise at the keyboard. In these two examples, pay special attention to the treatment of $\hat{6}$ and $\hat{7}$ in minor.

13-18   harmonizing the ascending scale in the soprano

(a) major

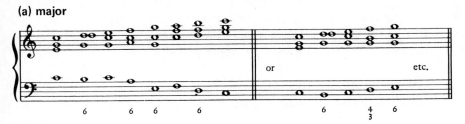

(b) minor

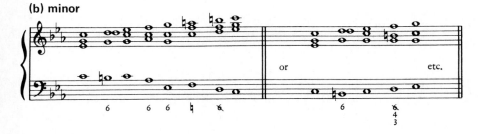

13-19   harmonizing the ascending scale in the bass

(a) major

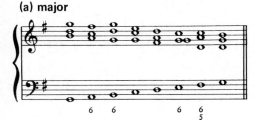

(b) minor

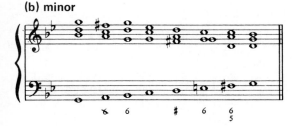

As is true with most formulas, the standard scale harmonizations offer only limited insight into the music of great composers. To be sure, the textbook patterns will sometimes appear in a composition. But the meaning—the inner groupings and the relation to larger context—will depend largely on the individual character of the passage. Thus in the last movement of Haydn's Symphony No. 98 (Example 13-20), we find a passage very similar to 13-18a except for the fact that I appears only in $\frac{6}{3}$ position. As it happens, this "exception" is one of the most significant aspects of the passage, which follows an extended V^7 with the 7th very prominent in the soprano (bars 64-71); the 7th then moves to the bass (bars 74-75), necessitating a resolution to I^6. That is why the scale in the soprano is harmonized in such a way that I^6 rather than I represents tonic harmony.

13-20 Haydn, Symphony No. 98, IV

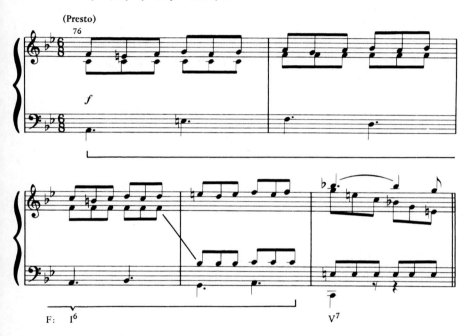

POINTS FOR REVIEW

1. I-IV-I expands tonic harmony, usually with a neighboring figure ($\hat{5}$-$\hat{6}$-$\hat{5}$ or $\hat{3}$-$\hat{4}$-$\hat{3}$) in the soprano. I^6 can replace either or both of the root-position tonic chords.

2. IV-I is the plagal (or Amen) cadence. It usually occurs at the end of a composition or section, often following an authentic cadence.

3. IV^6 leads from I *down* to I^6 with the melodic line $\hat{3}$-$\hat{4}$-$\hat{5}$. IV^6 also connects $V^{(7)}$ and V^6 ($\frac{6}{5}$).

4. VI substitutes for I following V or V^7, preventing excessive repetition of I. In the progression $V^{(7)}$-VI, the 3rd of VI should be doubled.

5. $V^{(7)}$-VI forms a deceptive cadence if it occurs where an authentic cadence is expected. This cadence is strongest with $\hat{2}$-$\hat{1}$ or $\hat{7}$-$\hat{8}$ in the soprano.

6. IV^6 and VI are sometimes interchangeable:

   a. IV^6 can replace VI in a deceptive cadence: $V^{(7)}$-IV^6.

   b. VI can replace IV^6 in moving down from I to I^6: I-VI-I^6.

   c. VI can replace IV^6 as a passing chord between $V^{(7)}$ and V^6 ($\frac{6}{5}$).

EXERCISES

NOTE. In setting both melodies and basses, keep in mind the relation between *characteristic soprano figures* and the chord progressions presented in this unit. You may find it helpful to refer to the following patterns while you do the exercises.

IDIOMATIC PATTERNS			
soprano	*progression*		
$\hat{3}$ $\hat{4}$ $\hat{3}$	I	IV	I
$\hat{5}$ $\hat{6}$ $\hat{5}$	I$^{(6)}$	IV	I$^{(6)}$
$\hat{1}$ $\hat{1}$ $\hat{1}$	I$^{(6)}$	IV	I$^{(6)}$
$\hat{7}$ $\hat{1}$	V$^{(7)}$	VI	(or IV^6)
$\hat{2}$ $\hat{1}$	V$^{(7)}$	VI	(or IV^6)
$\hat{4}$ $\hat{3}$	V^7	VI	
$\hat{3}$ $\hat{4}$ $\hat{5}$	I	IV^6	I^6
$\hat{5}$ $\hat{4}$ $\hat{4}$ $\hat{3}$	V	IV^6	V$^6(^6_5)$ I

1. Preliminaries.

   a. Write a phrase with a final tonic that is extended through a plagal cadence.
   b. Write a phrase with a deceptive cadence leading to an authentic cadence.

2. Unfigured bass.

soprano: $\hat{5}$

3. Melody. Set in keyboard style (overlaps OK).

4. Melody. Set in keyboard style. There should be one deceptive cadence.

5. Unfigured bass.

6. Melody.

14

V as a Key Area

14-1   **Schubert, Heidenröslein**

translation: A boy saw a wild rose, as fresh and lovely
as the morning. He ran to it quickly to gaze
on it closely with great joy. Little rose, little
red rose, little wild rose.

TONICIZATION AND MODULATION

1. Nontonic key areas. So far, all the chords we have studied result from harmonic progressions or voice-leading connections that are under the immediate control of the tonic triad. Most compositions, however, contain at least one passage that centers temporarily on a tone other than the tonic. In that new *key area* we hear another scale degree as $\hat{1}$ and another chord as the tonic triad. In Schubert's familiar song "Heidenröslein" (Example 14-1), the first phrase (bars 1-4) gravitates to the tonic G. The second phrase starts out as though it will simply repeat the first one. In its second bar, however (bar 6), a single change—C♯ instead of C♮—shifts the music temporarily into the orbit of D major. Until the end of the phrase, the progression of chords and the motion of the melodic line direct themselves to D. In making a chordal analysis of the phrase, we would count the D triad, not the G, as I; D has for the moment taken over the function of tonic. The Schubert song illustrates a new and most important way to emphasize nontonic chords: they can simulate the effect of a tonic and expand into temporary key areas; in the Schubert, the key area of the second phrase is the dominant.

2. Temporary tonics. We have two terms for the process of making scale degrees other than $\hat{1}$ sound temporarily like tonics: *tonicization* and *modulation*. The first implies a temporary "tonic" of brief duration; the second implies a longer-lasting and more significant change. The two terms overlap to a considerable extent; we cannot precisely determine where one stops and the other begins. From a broad perspective—one that takes in the composition as a whole—even the most firmly established key areas function as offshoots of the main key, if the composer has conceived the piece as a unified whole. In the Schubert song, which is only 16 bars long, it scarcely matters whether we think of the area in D as a large-scale tonicization of the dominant, or a brief modulation to it. This is often the case in very short pieces where there is hardly room for an extensive modulation.

3. Tonicizing (modulating to) V in major. Tonicizations and modulations can be organized around any scale degree and around any major or minor triad. Since V is the chord most closely related to I, pieces in major move to V as a key area more readily than to any other scale degree—one more instance of the controlling influence that the tonic-dominant relationship exerts on tonal structure. (Pieces in minor tend to move to III, as we shall see in the following unit.) In this unit we shall study only tonicizations of, and modulations to, V in major; however, most of the techniques that we shall discuss are easily applicable to other tonicizations and modulations.

4. Applied chords. The most frequent element of tonicization is the *applied dominant* or *leading-tone chord*—a chord that simulates the effect of a V or VII and "applies" it to a harmony other than the tonic. In Example 14-2, the C♯ in the bass of bar 3 functions like a leading tone to the D that follows. The motion from C♯ to D suggests the intense effect of $\hat{7}$-$\hat{1}$ in D major, and the chord containing the C♯ is equivalent to V$^6_5$ in D. The principle exemplified here is that any major or minor triad can be preceded by its own V or VII. In bars 3-4 of the Mendelssohn, we do not hear a real change of key—not even a temporary one; establishing a key requires time and musical content, not just one or two chords. What occurs here is the enrichment of the tonic key through the temporary intensification of a nontonic element. For a moment, this element (the V) acquires the color of a tonic chord without assuming its function.

14-2   Mendelssohn, Song without Words, Op. 62/1

$$V^6_5 \underline{\hspace{2cm}} 7 \qquad V$$

5. ♯4̂ as leading tone to V. All chords applied to V contain ♯4̂; this chromatic element is the tone that represents the dominant's leading tone. (The sharp before the 4̂—or any number indicating a scale degree—raises the pitch a chromatic half step: ♯4̂ in C = F♯; ♯4̂ in F = B♮.) Example 14-3 shows the applied chords to V that we can now use: V and its inversion V⁶, V⁷ and all of its inversions, and VII⁶. In speaking of these chords, we would refer to them as V⁴₂ of V, VII⁶ of V, and so forth; in the chordal analyses of this and subsequent units, a short curved arrow is used to replace the word "of." Raising 4̂ to ♯4̂ is what transforms the chords into applied V's or VII's; without this chromatic alteration, they would function as diatonic II's and IV's. *Note:* Since ♯4̂ functions (temporarily) as a leading tone, it must not be doubled.

14-3   chords applied to V

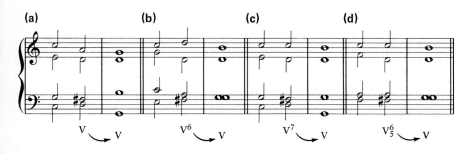

(a)   (b)   (c)   (d)

$$V \curvearrowright V \qquad V^6 \curvearrowright V \qquad V^7 \curvearrowright V \qquad V^6_5 \curvearrowright V$$

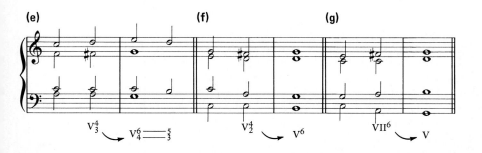

(e)   (f)   (g)

$$V^4_3 \curvearrowright V^6_4 {=} {}^5_3 \qquad V^4_2 \curvearrowright V^6 \qquad VII^6 \curvearrowright V$$

Among the most typical usages involving chords applied to V are those that emphasize dominant harmony (often at a cadence) by means of a rising chromatic progression, $\hat{4}$-#$\hat{4}$-$\hat{5}$, in the bass. Our Mendelssohn excerpt (Example 14-2) illustrates precisely this technique; note the beautiful effect of the chromatic line C-C#-D, embellished by the bass's skip down to A at the end of bar 3. In the Mendelssohn, II$^6_5$ is altered to become V$^6_5$ of V. As Example 14-3d shows, another point of departure for V$^6_5$ of V is IV (II^6); with both of them, as with II$^6_5$, $\hat{4}$ leads through #$\hat{4}$ to $\hat{5}$. Note that a cadential $^6_4$ can embellish the goal V.

Very frequently, chords applied to V harmonize #$\hat{4}$ in a top-voice line rising from $\hat{3}$ to $\hat{5}$; this device makes possible a particularly effective semicadence. Try playing Example 14-4 substituting IV^6 (the equivalent diatonic chord) for the applied VII (all you have to do is to play a B♭ instead of the B♮). The IV^6 moving to V sounds fine, but the V wants to continue moving; it doesn't sound nearly as much like a cadential goal as it does in the original excerpt.

14-4   Bach, Chorale 234

In Unit 25 we shall take up other usages of chords applied to V along with the remaining applied chords.

6. Larger tonicizations and modulations. If we are to transform V into a temporary tonic, we need more than a simple applied chord. Even a fleeting passage centered on a nontonic scale degree will require a progression of at least several chords, often culminating in a cadence. A long-lasting modulation will also frequently include a melodic line that gravitates to the new goal as if it were $\hat{1}$, a change in motivic design, and a punctuation in the music's flow that helps set off and emphasize the new tonic. The principle of the applied dominant, however, is still at work in even the most firmly established and abiding tonicization of V, for the tonic-dominant relationship is so fundamental to harmonic structure that no temporary tonic can long function as such without the participation of its own dominant. Often that dominant precedes the new tonic and helps to prepare it. At other times, the new tonic sets in without such preparation, and it is confirmed later by its dominant.

7. The pivot chord. Occasionally composers will introduce their new key area abruptly. More often, however, they will effect a smooth transition into the new key. An important way of achieving this transition is by using a *pivot chord,* a chord that occurs in both keys. Example 14-5 contains a particularly clear example of a pivot chord. We first hear the D minor chord of bar 3 as VI in F. But the continuation makes us reinterpret in retrospect the meaning of this chord: in relation to what follows it, the D chord functions as II in C, though in relation to what has preceded it, the chord is indeed VI in F. Because it effects the transition from one tonal area to the other, the D chord is the "pivotal" event of the modulation.

14-5   Freylinghausen, Figured-Bass Chorale, Morgenglanz der Ewigkeit

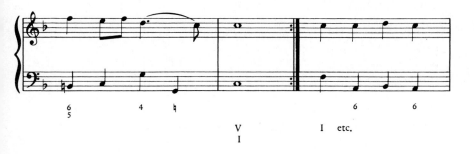

Among the most effective pivot chords are those that would normally lead into the V chord of the new key—II and IV, of course, being preeminent in this category. VI in the main key, becoming II in the key of the dominant (as in Example 14-5), makes a particularly smooth transition, but it is not the only possibility. In the Schubert song (Example 14-1), it is the main tonic triad itself that becomes the pivot (in bar 5), for subsequent events lead us to reinterpret it as IV in the dominant key.

8. Modulation through I$^{5\text{-}6}$. A technique with far-reaching consequences for modulation is illustrated in the two excerpts of Example 14-6, drawn from the first movement of a Mozart sonata. In the first four bars (14-6a), a harmonic framework I-II-V^7-I is expanded by a 5-6 motion over the opening tonic. Although one might think of the G minor chord thus produced as VI^6, the force of tonic harmony is so great that one tends instead to hear simply a sustained I modified by melodic motion, the 5-6 destabilizing the tonic and giving it a tendency to move forward. In addition, the common tone with II produces smoother voice leading and averts parallel 5ths. Example 14-6b, from slightly later on in the movement, begins similarly but uses a V^7 of F (the key of the dominant) instead of the II, thus initiating a tonicization of V. Here, the original tonic functions as the pivot chord since it receives so much more emphasis than the G minor $^6_3$. The lessening of stability caused by the 5-6 eases the process of modulation by impelling the original tonic onward to the dominant of F. The 5-6 technique is important for modulation precisely because it allows the tonic, itself normally a goal, to become an active element.

14-6　Mozart, Piano Sonata, K. 333, I

(a) beginning

(b) bars 10-14

In Example 14-7, from a Haydn quartet, we see a progression derived from the 5-6 technique. The C major and A minor chords of bar 2 (IV and II of G) constitute a 5-6 motion with a skip down to the root of the second chord (review Unit 9, section 11). Again the pivot chord is I of C becoming IV of G. Since the A minor chord, however, also belongs to both keys, one might read a group of two pivot chords rather than a single pivot.

14-7   Haydn, "Emperor" String Quartet, Op. 76/3, I

In Example 14-8, another excerpt from Haydn, the 5-6 motion is spread out over many measures, and the $\frac{6}{3}$ gets additional emphasis from the chromatic passing tone C#. For this reason, the D minor $\frac{6}{3}$ of bars 9-10 attracts much more attention than the corresponding chords in the two preceding examples. And the effect of destabilizing the tonic is much greater. Indeed the loss of tonic stability is so noticeable that we tend to hear a change of focus with the arrival on the D minor chord. This makes us feel it much more strongly as II^6 of C than as a chord belonging to F major. A pivot chord is more difficult to specify here than in the preceding examples, because the best candidate—the original F major tonic—does not connect immediately with the change of key (remember that the D minor chord already points to the coming C major). We might speak of a long-range, rather than a localized, pivot. This excerpt suggests a point of general validity: the boundaries between two key areas are not always sharply defined.

14-8   Haydn, String Quartet, Op. 77/2, Menuetto

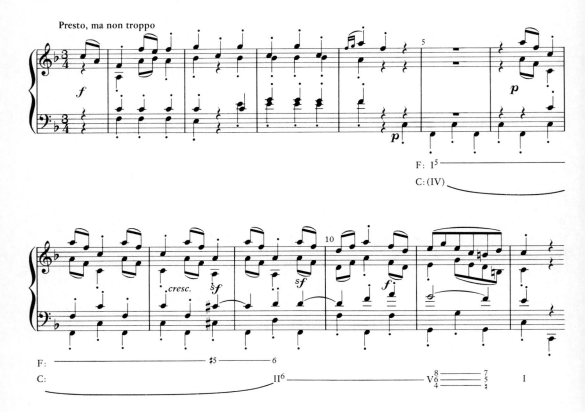

9. Cadencing in the new key. Most modulations and many of the more extensive tonicizations confirm the new tonic by means of an authentic cadence. In Example 14-7, the transitional chords—IV and II of G—lead directly to a V and form part of the cadence. Thus the pivot chord(s) can move immediately to the cadential dominant. At other times, however, the pivot chord will form part of a noncadential progression, and the cadence will occur later. In the Schubert song (Example 14-1), the pivot chord leads to V_2^4 and I^6 of the new key; the I^6 moves first to a deceptive, then to an authentic cadence. In the Freylinghausen (Example 14-5), the pivot chord leads to a noncadential V, with the cadential dominant coming later, in bar 4.

10. Returning to the tonic. After a brief sojourn in the area of the dominant, a return to the tonic requires no special preparation. If V has not been tonicized for long, the listener still feels the strong pull of the main tonic. The composer, therefore, can simply introduce the I chord in a place of some prominence and continue in the tonic. The last chord in the dominant area will have a double meaning: I of V and V of I. In Example 14-5 the tonic returns with the first chord of the new phrase that begins in bar 6.

If the dominant has been maintained as a key area for a longer time, it may be necessary to make it clear to the listener that the tonicized V is reverting to its permanent and basic function—that of dominant in the main key. This is best accomplished by turning the chord into a dominant seventh by adding a minor 7th ($\hat{4}$ in the main key). As a seventh chord, V no longer sounds like a tonic; besides, V^7 has so strong a drive toward I that the listener is prepared for the return of the tonic. And finally, $\hat{4}$ is the one scale degree in the tonic key that does not appear in the key of the dominant. Therefore the appearance of this tone helps to neutralize the temporary key at the same time as it prepares the return of the main one. In the Schubert song, the 7th appears as the bass of a V^4_2 chord (bar 11).

11. V as a key area and musical form. The *form* of a piece results from its articulation into parts of various dimensions—rhythmic groups, phrases, groups of phrases, sections—and from the relationship of part to part and of part to whole. A new key area makes for contrast with what has already happened; this contrast, in turn, can help to differentiate one section from another. Modulation, therefore, can be an important means of articulating the large divisions of form; tonicization can help to articulate some of the smaller segments. Because of the special importance of the tonic-dominant relationship, the use of V as a key area is of particular importance in creating musical form.

The form of Example 14-1, for example, grows out of its division into three phrases. The first of these moves within the tonic; the second tonicizes V and confirms it with a strong cadence; the third returns to the tonic and refers back to some of the opening material—note the resemblance between bars 11-12 and 3-4. The tiny *coda* or postlude rounds off the ending with a varied repetition of the final cadence. Without the contrast of the tonicized V, there would be no impression of departure and return; the form would lose much of its plasticity.

Tonicizations of V often occur within a group of two phrases in antecedent-consequent relation (see Unit 10, section 9). Sometimes, as in Example 14-9, the antecedent phrase closes with an authentic cadence in the dominant area, as an intensified replacement of the usual semicadence. (In the Chopin excerpt, a cadential $^6_4$ occurs on a weaker beat than the V^7 to which it moves; this rhythmic irregularity will be discussed in Unit 19, section 12.)

14-9 **Chopin, Prelude, Op. 28/13**

F#: I

C#: II   VI

V$^8_6{}_4$ —
                           —

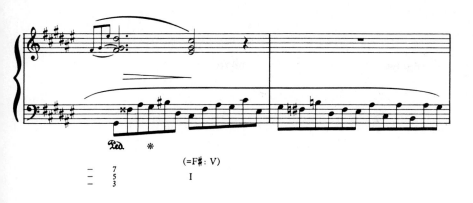

(=F♯: V)

I

(consequent phrase continues)

p *sempre legato*

etc.

F♯: I

Another possibility is for the *consequent* phrase to end with an authentic cadence in the dominant instead of the expected final tonic (Example 14-10). This procedure gives the consequent phrase a very different function from its usual one. It does not resolve the tension generated by the nontonic ending of the antecedent phrase; on the contrary, the level of tension is increased by the shift to a new key area. After such a modulating consequent phrase, the tonic may return immediately. But the dominant may also remain as a key area, or the ending of the consequent phrase may serve as a springboard for a modulation to yet another key area.

14-10   Mozart, In diesen heil'gen Hallen   (from *Die Zauberflöte,* K. 620)

translation: In these sacred halls revenge is unknown, and if a person
should be tempted, love will lead him to his duty.

A German dance by Mozart (Example 14-11) shows another important possibility: a tonicized V as the harmonic basis for the B section in an ABA or A :‖: BA :‖ form. In this piece, the middle (B) section starts off immediately in G, the dominant area (bar 9). This creates a more sharply sectionalized form than in the Schubert song, where the second phrase makes a gradual transition into the new key area. In analyzing a piece like the Mozart, the notion of a pivot chord is not very helpful. To be sure, the G chord of bar 9 might possibly be understood as a pivot, but the strong contrasts in rhythm and texture (and also the F♯ in the upbeat to bar 9) make it sound as though the section in G begins anew, without any transition from the preceding.

14-11   Mozart, German Dance, K. 509/6

Continued

Longer and more elaborate pieces than Examples 14-1 or 14-11 articulate their form by means of modulation to V. Among the most important are movements in sonata-allegro form in a major key. These usually modulate to the dominant in the bridge section that follows the first theme or thematic group. The latter part of the exposition remains in the dominant key; the return to the tonic is effected by the events of the development section.

APPLICATIONS TO WRITTEN WORK

12. Harmonizing modulating melodies; realizing modulating basses. Melodies sometimes signal a modulation with accidentals. In the Schubert song, for example, the C♯'s in the vocal line clearly indicate D as temporary tonic. Such melodies are not always easy to harmonize well, but at least recognizing that a modulation is taking place should not be a problem. Other melodies are less obliging. In the chorale of Example 14-5, for instance, the soprano line of bars 3-5 contains not a single accidental; the B♮ in the bass line is the only one. Harmonizing a melody of this kind can be difficult; you must use your ear and brain to recognize modulations where the melodic line does not hold up a sign, so to speak, to announce them. Always listen for the long-range goals of the line; in particular observe the cadential points. In the chorale melody, the motion from D to C (bars 4 and 5) implies $\hat{2}$-$\hat{1}$ in C rather than $\hat{6}$-$\hat{5}$ in F; strong cadences do not normally support the melodic progression $\hat{6}$-$\hat{5}$, but they *do* support $\hat{2}$-$\hat{1}$.

The realization of modulating figured and unfigured basses is usually easier than harmonizing melodies. The figured basses normally indicate all the necessary chromatic adjustments, and even in unfigured basses, modulations are easy to recognize because of the unmistakable V-I progressions, especially at cadences. But remember that a cadence is normally a melodic as well as a harmonic event, and try to shape your melody to support the cadence.

13. Writing phrase groups that tonicize V. Writing short phrase groups that begin on I, tonicize V, and return to and conclude on I can be one of the most valuable exercises for learning to hear and understand modulations. Example 14-12 includes two such groups that can serve as models. Both are eight bars long and have the following in common:

1. They establish the initial tonic (bars 1-2).
2. A pivot chord introduces the key change (bar 3).
3. An authentic cadence confirms the new key (bars 3-4).
4. The new "tonic" is transformed into a V (bar 5 in a; bar 6 in b).
5. The initial tonic returns and leads to a closing cadence.

14-12

Follow these procedures closely when you begin to write such phrase groups. You can vary the pacing of the tonal motions from one exercise to another, but you should achieve the cadence in the dominant key midway through the exercise. Strive for a clear texture in which the larger harmonic direction is not obscured by unnecessary complexities of voice leading or chord succession. You are writing exercises, not compositions, but they can sound very good if you direct your attention to the contour of the melodic line and to the balance among rhythmic groups.

POINTS FOR REVIEW

1. The terms *tonicization* and *modulation* refer to the process of making scale degrees other than $\hat{1}$ sound like temporary tonics. In major, V is the most frequently tonicized area.

2. The most frequent element of tonicization is the applied V or VII. At the present the following applied chords are available: V_3^5, 7, 6, $_5^6$, $_3^4$, $_2^4$ of V; VII^6 of V. All of these chords contain $\sharp\hat{4}$, the leading tone of $\hat{5}$. Don't double $\sharp\hat{4}$!

3. Characteristic bass line: $\hat{4}$-$\sharp\hat{4}$-$\hat{5}$, using V_5^6 (or sometimes V^6) of V.

4. Characteristic soprano line: $\hat{3}$-$\sharp\hat{4}$-$\hat{5}$, using VII^6, V_3^4, or V_2^4 of V.

5. A pivot chord belongs to both the original and new keys. Frequent pivot chords are II and IV in the new key (VI and I in the

old). Frequently a 5-6 progression over the main tonic leads to the dominant of the new key.

6. The new key area is often confirmed by an authentic cadence.

7. The return to the main tonic can be effected by adding a 7th to the tonicized V, so that it becomes V^7 of the main key.

8. There are several ways in which tonicizing V has an important influence on musical form. These include:

   a. using a tonicized V at the end of an antecedent or consequent phrase

   b. using a tonicized V for the middle section of ABA form

   c. modulating to V in the exposition of a sonata-allegro movement in major.

EXERCISES

1. Preliminaries. Using a different major key for each, write phrases that demonstrate

   a. the bass line $\hat{4}$-$\sharp\hat{4}$-$\hat{5}$

   b. the soprano line $\hat{3}$-$\sharp\hat{4}$-$\hat{5}$.

2. More preliminaries. Write short progressions in different major keys that begin on I and modulate to V. Show at least two different ways of using the following pivot chords.

main key		new key
a. I	=	IV
b. $VI^{(6)}$	=	$II^{(6)}$
c. V	=	I

3. Expand the progressions you wrote in Exercise 1 into phrase groups that incorporate the five features listed on page 209. See Example 14-12 for models.

4. Melody.

5. Figured bass.

6. Chorale melody.

7. Chorale melody.

8. Chorale melody.

15

III and VII

USES OF III

1. I-III-V in minor. Example 15-1 illustrates some of the most important characteristics of III and, in addition, shows a typical function of VII in minor. The section consists of two phrases in antecedent-consequent relation. In the first phrase the harmonic focal points are I (bars 1-2), III (bars 2-3), and V (bar 4). The second phrase retraces the same steps but adds a final tonic, thus answering the semicadence with an authentic one. Example 15-2 extracts the harmonic structure. Note that III forms a resting place almost midway between I and V (hence the term *mediant*).

212

15-2

As in the Schumann piece, III often forms an important part of a large-scale harmonic plan. Like II, IV, and sometimes VI, it leads from an opening tonic to a dominant. However, III differs from these other triads in important ways. The bass line of I-III-V arpeggiates the complete tonic triad, as can be seen very clearly in Example 15-2. In this way, III resembles I^6, which also produces an arpeggio between I and V. Although I and III have different roots, they share two common tones, and the root of III is one of the common tones. For this reason, a motion from I to III tends to sound less like a progression of two chords than like an expansion of I. This tendency characterizes any root progression by rising 3rd, even when chromatic inflection removes one of the common tones and adds more contrast, as in III-V in minor. Composers have treated these root progressions with care, almost as if they were repetitions of a single harmony. For the most part, they are avoided when moving from a weak to a strong beat. And when I-III-V is to form the harmonic framework of a section, intervening chords usually lead from I to III and from III to V. Unlike I-IV-V and I-II-V, therefore, I-III-V will seldom occur in direct succession.

Composers frequently move from I to III through VII. In the Schumann, the G triad has two meanings. On the one hand, it is an element of the A minor tonality (natural VII); on the other, it is the applied dominant of the C chord (V of III) and it makes III sound like a goal. In moving from III to V composers most often make use of a passing tone in the bass supporting IV or (as in the Schumann) II^6. The directional quality of the bass line and the elimination of $\hat{5}$ as a common tone intensify V and make the progression a very satisfactory one. As Example 15-3 shows, such a progression usually supports a top voice that descends by step. Other options exist, however. In the Schumann, for example, the leap of the diminished 5th in an otherwise conjunct melody enhances the poignant expression of the cadences.

15-3

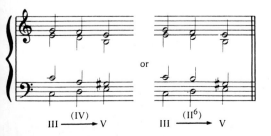

2. Modulation to III in minor. Because of the position of the diminished 5th in natural minor, the minor mode tends to gravitate to III. This tendency is reflected in the large structure of many pieces in minor: III is very frequently expanded into a key area. In addition, the major quality of III makes a welcome contrast to the minor tonic—a contrast beautifully evident in the Schumann excerpt of Example 15-1. Furthermore, the minor mode can tonicize III without any chromatic alteration; thus the chords in bar 2 of the Schumann suggest a cadential progression (VI-V-I) in C major without the use of any accidental signs.

Pieces in minor therefore tend to modulate to III more often than to V, but without any weakening of the tonic-dominant relationship, for the expanded III functions as a stopover on the way to V. In an excerpt from a figured-bass chorale of Bach (Example 15-4), III arrives in bar 3 and is confirmed by a strong cadence. Just as in the Schumann—only over a longer span—the III moves up by step to a strong V-I cadence.

15-4   Bach, Figured-Bass Chorale, No. 29

Because of the inherent tendency of minor to move to III, tonicizing it is much easier than tonicizing V in major. (Indeed, beginning students sometimes find it hard to prevent their exercises in minor from slipping into the relative major whether they want them to or not.) None of the applied chords that we are using require any accidental, for they all function as diatonic elements within the main key. As we have seen, V of III = VII; similarly, V^7 of III = VII^7, and VII^6 of III = II^6. Example 15-5 illustrates.

15-5   Applied chords to III

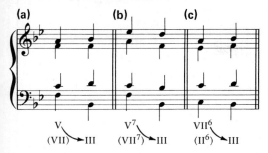

3. I-III-V in major. An excerpt from a Chopin etude (Example 15-6) shows III functioning as part of a broad harmonic progression in the major mode. This usage of III is much less common in major than in minor, especially in music before the nineteenth century. Unlike minor, the major mode contains no inherent tendency to gravitate to III; the tritone in major leads unequivocally to I. And III in major cannot be tonicized without the use of accidentals in the altered VII or V of III (note the F♯ in bar 7 of the Chopin; a complete chord would require a D♯ as well). A progression leading from III to V in major usually proceeds exactly as in minor—through a passing IV or II.

Sometimes, as in the Chopin, V in the progression III-V-I will appear in a weak metric position compared with III and I; this can occur both in major and in minor. The force of dominant harmony is so great that it does not always require special emphasis through duration or accent.

15-6   Chopin, Etude, Op. 10/7

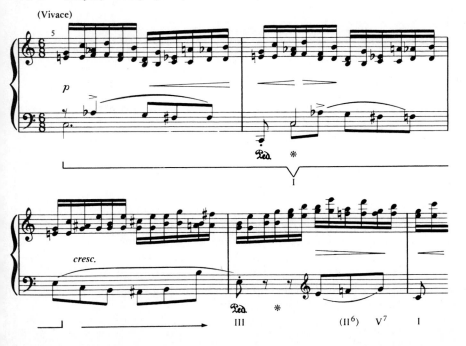

As we have seen, I-III-V does not typically occur in direct progression, especially in music written before the nineteenth century. During that century, composers increasingly began to exploit chord progression by ascending 3rds, sometimes moving directly from III to V without a passing IV or II^6. But they would seldom write the entire progression I-III-V without intervening chords. Brahms did, however, in his Intermezzo, Op. 119, No. 3 (Example 15-7), in a most unusual passage. With poetry and wit Brahms leads us from I to V^7 by almost imperceptible degrees, so that we are hardly aware that we have arrived at the dominant in the bass (beginning of bar 44) until the *sforzando* and the rush of quick notes bring the V^7 forcefully to our attention.

15-7   Brahms, Intermezzo, Op. 119/3

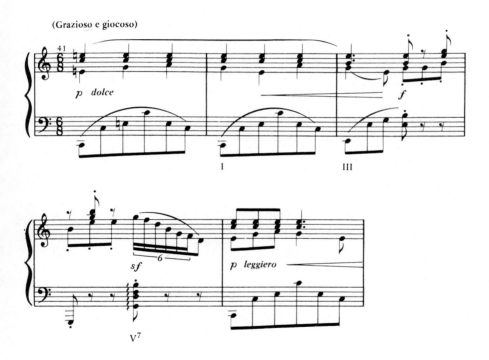

4. III moving to I through an inversion of V$^{(7)}$. The first main part of Mozart's Rondo in A minor, K. 511, divides into three subsections, the first and last in the tonic, the second in the mediant (C major) expanded into a key area. Example 15-8 shows the end of the C major section and the transition back to the tonic. Note that Mozart does not lead to I through a root-position V; the dominant chord is an inverted one, a $\frac{4}{3}$. As in the Mozart, III frequently moves to I through an inverted dominant (most often $\frac{4}{3}$, $\frac{6}{5}$, or $\frac{6}{3}$). The stepwise connection to I gives these progressions a decidedly melodic, contrapuntal character.

15-8   Mozart, Rondo in A Minor, K. 511

Inverted dominants do not normally constitute goals of motion and need not receive as much emphasis as those in root position, so intervening chords are not required here (Example 15-9). In major, there are two common tones between III and V; in minor, one common tone and one chromatic half step. The greater tonal contrast makes the progression stronger in minor than in major.

The use of V_3^6 or V_5^6 in minor creates a *cross-relation* between the bass and an upper part, that is, the chromatic succession takes place between *two* voices rather than in a single one. The cross-relation is unduly harsh if natural $\hat{7}$ occurs in the soprano voice (15-9c), but creates no problem if natural $\hat{7}$ is in one of the inner voices (15-9d).

15-9

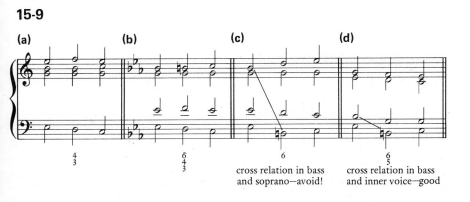

5. III as upper 5th of VI; III-VI-II-V-I. The addition of III to our vocabulary of chords allows us to add another link to the chain of progressions by descending 5th. III can move to VI in the same way that VI moves to II or II to V. As we know, VI does not usually function as a goal but instead moves on to some other chord—IV, perhaps, or II, or V. For this reason the descending 5th III-VI does not normally occur by itself but leads on through II to V and, often I. We can observe such a progression in Example 15-10. Note that II appears in $\frac{6}{3}$ position —partly, perhaps, to avoid a diminished $\frac{5}{3}$, but mainly to allow a large-scale stepwise bass line F-G-A (III-II⁶-V). In this excerpt the VI sounds subordinate to the other chords, which are emphasized by fuller texture and greater rhythmic activity. Incidentally, the root-position II (diminished $\frac{5}{3}$) and the dissonant bass progression VI-II (diminished 5th or augmented 4th) sound better in the middle of a progression (as in III-VI-II-V-I) than when the progression begins on VI. Handel avoids the root position here, but, as it happens, uses it in the next variation.

15-10   Handel, Air and Variations, Variation 3   (from *Suite No. 3*)

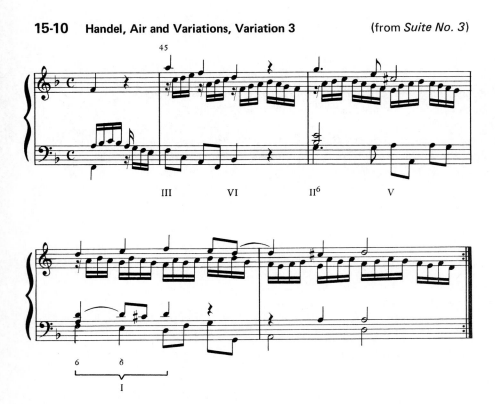

6. III in smaller contexts. Important though it is in large-scale progressions, III appears in smaller contexts much less frequently than II, IV, or VI. When it does so it usually follows I, and because of the common tones of the two chords, III sounds less like an independent chord than like an offshoot or extension of tonic harmony. As such, it has one highly important function: to support a passing $\hat{7}$ in a descending line, usually in the soprano. $\hat{7}$ lies a 5th above the bass of III, and the 5th, of course, is an exceptionally stable interval. This stability helps to diminish the intense upward drive of $\hat{7}$ in major and makes it more amenable to downward motion, as can be heard in Schubert's song "Im Frühling" (Example 15-11a). Schubert's succession of chords—I-(III)-IV—is the typical one; another important possibility is moving to II^6 with $\hat{8}$-$\hat{7}$-$\hat{6}$ in an inner voice (15-11b). Less frequently VI supports $\hat{6}$ (15-11c). III's effective support for $\hat{7}$ as a descending passing tone can be helpful in expanding a motion down from VI to IV, perhaps as part of a bass arpeggio (15-11d).

15-11   Schubert, Im Frühling

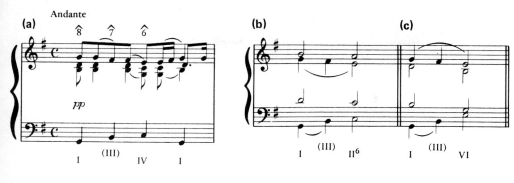

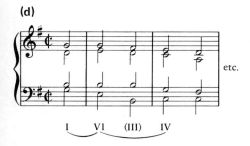

It is now possible for you to harmonize a descending scale in the soprano (Example 15-12). Note that in minor the natural form must be used.

15-12   harmonizing the descending scale in the soprano

(a) major

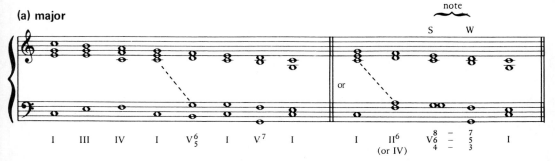

(b) minor

7. III as equivalent to I⁶. III is related to I⁶ through the contrapuntal motion 5-6 above a stationary bass (like IV and II⁶ or VI and IV⁶). Sometimes, therefore, III can occur in contexts where the bass would usually suggest I⁶. Such is the case in the opening of Bach's Chorale 365 (Example 15-13a) as well as in the other progressions of 15-13. In most situations where a choice between I⁶ and III exists, I⁶ is preferable; by unequivocally prolonging tonic harmony I⁶ can help to define the tonality. But III can be preferable when the stepwise descent 8̂-7̂-6̂ in the soprano or in an inner voice is wanted, or when excessive repetitions of 1̂ in any of the upper voices would otherwise result.

15-13

(a) Bach, Chorale 365

As a general rule, avoid moving from I to III in weak-to-strong rhythm. Because of the lack of tonal contrast, chord succession by ascending 3rd sounds almost like motion within the same chord; using it to move from a weak to a strong beat tends to contradict the meter.

8. III in minor as an augmented triad. III does not tend to move directly to I. In minor, therefore, there is usually no reason to raise 7̂ when it is part of III. This means that the augmented form of III—derived from the harmonic form of the minor scale—does not play an important role in pieces written in minor. Most of the apparent instances of III as an augmented triad are in $^6_3$ position and express dominant rather than mediant harmony (see Unit 18, section 8).

USES OF VII

9. Natural VII in minor. Example 15-1 shows root-position VII in minor (natural form) as V of III. This is an important usage. In first inversion, as in Example 15-14, the chord leads from I to III by stepwise ascent (passing function) and provides a new way to move from I up to V.

15-14

(a)

I   VII⁶   III   II⁶   V⁶₄ — ⁵♯   I

(b) Brahms, Intermezzo, Op. 76/7

Moderato semplice

mp   *p*

I   (VII⁶)   III   III

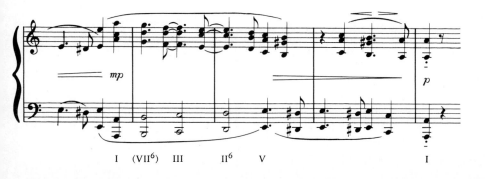

mp   *p*

I   (VII⁶)   III   II⁶   V   I

Sometimes—especially in Baroque music—natural VII appears as a chord leading to V^7. Because its two upper tones also belong to V^7 and because its lowest tone needs only a chromatic inflection to become the 3rd of V^7, natural VII becomes absorbed into the V^7 chord. Because of the contrast between natural $\hat{7}$ and raised $\hat{7}$, on the one hand, and the common tones, on the other, the progression natural VII-V^7 can sound both unexpected and, in retrospect, logical. And the chromatic inflection of $\hat{7}$ can produce a particularly expressive effect. Example 15-15 shows natural VII as part of a bass line descending from I to V^7; the 5th of natural VII ($\hat{4}$ in the soprano) forms a good preparation for the 7th of V^7.

15-15

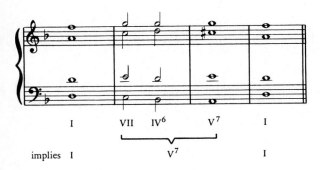

In Example 15-16, natural VII follows a tonicized III and functions, at first, as its dominant. Note the passing IV^6 to connect natural VII to V^7. This usage is very frequent; so is the use of parallel 10ths between the outer voices.

15-16   Handel, Concerto Grosso, Op. 3/1, II

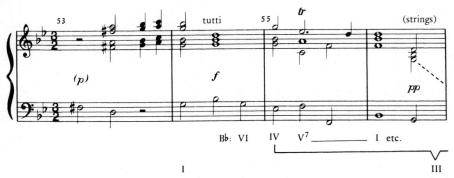

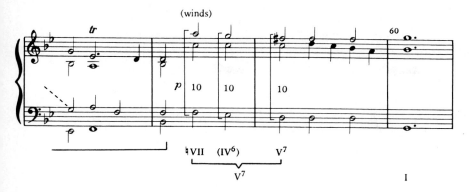

Natural VII often moves chromatically to I through V^6 or V^6_5, as in Example 15-17.

15-17

10. VII$^5_3$ in major; raised VII$^5_3$ in minor. Diminished triads on the leading tone are seldom satisfactory in $^5_3$ position. As we shall see in Unit 17, the diminished triad occurs freely in some sequential passages. In most other situations, V^6_5 (which contains all three tones of the diminished VII) creates a far more pleasing sonority and is to be preferred. In three-part writing, however, V^6_5 sometimes proves impracticable, and VII$^5_3$ forms the only possible alternative.

In the trio sonatas of the Baroque period, diminished VII chords sometimes appear in the three-part setting formed by the two melody instruments and the bass. This occurs in a passage from Corelli (Example 15-18) where VII clearly represents an incomplete V^6_5; the 6th above the bass tone must be sacrificed to allow the resolution of the dissonant 5th of the preceding IV$^6_5$ chord. A good continuo player, however, would supply the missing 6th in the accompaniment, knowing that composers of the period frequently wrote the figure 5♭ as an abbreviation for $^6_{5♭}$.*

*See C. P. E. Bach, *Essay on the True Art of Playing Keyboard Instruments,* translated and edited by William J. Mitchell (New York: W. W. Norton, 1949), pp. 222, 243-252.

15-18   Corelli, Sonata V, Op. 1, Allegro

In four-part writing IV_3^6 is generally best followed by V_5^6; occasionally VII_3^5 will occur for the sake of a smoother line in the inner voices. In Example 15-19 the vocal parts form a diminished $\frac{5}{3}$; Bach's figures expressly indicate that the missing 6th should be played in the continuo accompaniment. Note that Bach doubles the 3rd of the diminished chord; this is the preferred doubling, the 3rd being the one tone not involved in any dissonant relationship.

15-19   Bach, Chorale 83

(The figures are Bach's.)   note

In Example 15-20, also from a Bach chorale, the first bar consists of an extended dominant chord; the bass moves down a 6th from the root to the 3rd while the top voice ascends from $\hat{2}$ to $\hat{4}$. Normally the last beat of this bar would contain a $\frac{6}{3}$ chord. Here, however, Bach allows the tenor to accompany the bass at the upper 3rd, creating a "polarized" texture (SA up, TB down). This prevents the tenor from sounding the 6th, B♭, of the V_5^6 and produces a diminished $\frac{5}{3}$ as a substitute. Because it grows out of the strong V at the beginning of the bar, the diminished chord would be heard as representing a V_5^6 even if the continuo player failed to provide the missing 6th (the bass is unfigured).

15-20   Bach, Chorale 22

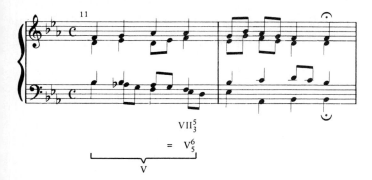

POINTS FOR REVIEW

1. In minor, III frequently leads from I to V in a large-scale harmonic progression. Typically introduced by natural VII, III is often expanded into a key area and generally moves to V through a passing IV or II^6 (descending stepwise soprano).

2. In major, a large-scale I-III-V is less common, as chromatic alteration is necessary to tonicize III. As in minor, III in major typically progresses to V through a passing IV or II^6.

3. III, in either a large- or small-scale progression, can move through an inverted V ($\frac{4}{3}$, $\frac{6}{3}$, or $\frac{6}{5}$) to I. In this progression, which is most frequent in minor, no intervening chord is necessary between III and V, and a cross-relation is acceptable if not between soprano and bass.

4. III functions most characteristically in large contexts. Its most important small-scale use is to support $\hat{7}$ in a descending soprano line while leading the bass from I (or VI) to IV. The progression III-VI-II-V-I is also possible.

5. In minor, natural VII often leads to III and functions as its dominant. In $\frac{6}{3}$ position, natural VII forms a logical passing chord between I and III; the bass line will often continue by step to V. Natural VII can also lead to V^7 through a descending bass (with passing IV^6) or up to I through a chromatically inflected bass supporting V^6 or V^6_5.

6. Because of their poor sonority, VII^5_3 in major and raised VII^5_3 in minor are to be avoided; a leading tone in the bass will generally support V^6_5. Sometimes, especially in three-part texture, VII^5_3 substitutes for V^6_5.

EXERCISES

1. Preliminaries. Write the following progressions:

   a. III moves to root-position V through a passing IV or II^6 (minor only—two versions)

   b. III moves contrapuntally through an inversion of V^7 to I (minor only—two versions)

c. $\hat{8}$-$\hat{7}$-$\hat{6}$
   I-(III)-IV (major and minor)
d. III-VI leading to a cadence (minor only)
e. I moves to III through a passing natural VII^6 (minor)
f. I moves to III through a natural VII$^5_3$ (minor)
g. natural VII moves to V^7 through a passing IV^6 (minor)

2. Melody.

3. Figured bass.

4. Melody.

5. Figured bass. Find a soprano line that will work for both bars 1-4 and 5-8.

PART

III

$\frac{5}{3}$, $\frac{6}{3}$, AND $\frac{6}{4}$ TECHNIQUES

16

$\frac{5}{3}$-Chord Techniques

Now that all seven diatonic triads have been introduced, we can begin to deal with some new procedures of harmony and voice leading and to broaden the application of those we have already discussed. For the moment we will discuss $\frac{5}{3}$ chords only; later units will show how the principles investigated here apply to work with other chords.

PROGRESSIONS BY 5THS AND 3RDS

1. The principle of descending 5ths. The basic harmonic progression is motion by 5th, and descending 5ths (V-I, II-V, VI-II, etc.) are strongly goal-oriented. Consequently, we can form a logical harmonic succession by arranging a group of triads in the order of descending 5ths. Sometimes, in fact, we encounter all seven triads so arranged: I-IV-VII-III-VI-II-V-I. When the complete progression occurs in a composition, some of the descending 5ths will appear in inversion as ascending 4ths in order to keep the bass in a reasonable register. We can see this quite clearly in Example 16-1. In the complete series of descending 5ths, one diminished 5th (or its inversion, the augmented 4th) must appear. In major it occurs between IV and VII; in minor, between VI and II. Without this diminished 5th, tones foreign to the key would appear, threatening the centrality of the tonic. Thus, in the Handel, substituting a perfect 5th for the diminished 5th would produce the bass line E♭-A♭-D♭-G♭ instead of E♭-A-D-G. In a chain of descending 5ths, some chords may be more significant than others. In the Handel the emphasized chords are I (beginning of motion, full voicing), III (low bass register, return to initial melody tone), and the cadential II-V-I (end of motion, bass register, increased rhythmic activity). The other chords do not function on an equal level of importance; IV and VII form a transition from I to III and VI leads from III to the final cadence.

16-1 **Handel, Passacaglia** (from *Harpsichord Suite No. 7*)

descending 5ths

The technique of descending 5ths is a most useful and important one. Variants of it can accommodate triads in $\frac{6}{3}$ position and seventh chords as well (in the Handel, II occurs as a seventh chord). It lends itself to contrapuntal elaboration of various kinds, ranging from suspensions to canonic imitation. And with chromatic alterations, the technique can produce applied dominants and can help to effect modulations. In later units we shall often use this technique.

2. The principle of ascending 5ths. Progressions of ascending 5ths occur much less frequently and play a much less important role in tonal composition. This is because they are not strongly goal-directed: in a motion from I to V, for example, the V is heard as an outgrowth of the I, and it tends to resolve back to I as its point of origin. The complete progression in rising 5ths—I-V-II-VI-III-VII-IV-I— is virtually useless, for the chords before the final I do not establish it as a goal. However, segments of the progression can lead convincingly to chords other than the tonic. The two main possibilities are I-V-II-VI-III in major (to be illustrated in Unit 17) and III-VII-IV-I-V in minor, as shown in Example 16-2. Both of these possibilities avoid the diminished triads VII in major and II in minor. In the less directional environment of these progressions, tritone dissonances are much more obtrusive than in the series of descending 5ths.

Example 16-2 shows the first two phrases of a Bach chorale. The ascending 5ths lead from III (tonicized in the first phrase) to the cadential V. The main link between III and V is, typically enough, the E minor chord, IV. The stepwise line III-IV-V fits into the larger harmonic scheme; these chords take precedence over VII and I, whose function it is to make a smooth connection from one main chord to the next. In general, as in this phrase, a series of ascending 5ths consists of a rising stepwise line decorated harmonically by the upper 5ths of the main chords. In this example, consequently, the I chord before the cadential V is a I in name only, not in behavior, for it does not form part of the harmonic framework.

16-2   Bach, Chorale 265

(a)

(b) reduction of bars 2-4

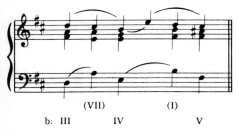

3. Bass motion by 3rds. We already know two important examples of this technique: I descending through VI to IV (or II⁶) and I rising through III to V. Progressions like I-VI-IV and I-III-V connect the beginning and goal chords by means of arpeggiation. In I-VI-IV the bass line arpeggiates the goal chord (in C major, C-A-F or IV); when the goal arrives the ear connects it with the preceding bass motion, which it sums up. In I-III-V the bass line arpeggiates the beginning chord (in C major, C-E-G or I); the V, therefore, does not sound so much like a goal. And, as we saw in Unit 15, the root of each new chord has already appeared in one (or even two) of the preceding chords, so that the chord's impact is weakened. For this reason, I-III-V does not usually occur in immediate succession without intervening chords (such as II⁶ or IV between III and V). In progressions by rising 3rds other than I-III-V, the intervening chords are usually applied dominants (Unit 25, section 18).

An interesting instance of descending 3rds occurs at the end of a Chopin mazurka (Example 16-3), where the bass moves from V through III to I; the motion as a whole arpeggiates I. III as a divider between V and I sometimes appears before reprise sections and sonata recapitulations, but its appearance at the end of a piece is quite unusual; here it emphasizes the major tonic with which this mazurka in B♭ minor ends, by bringing 3̂ into the bass.

16-3   Chopin, Mazurka, Op. 24/4

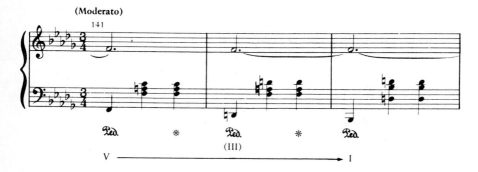

A more extended motion in descending 3rds occurs in a phrase from Chorale 101 of Bach (Example 16-4). Here the bass moves down a 9th from I to V^6. Passing tones create a completely stepwise bass line, but the organization of this stepwise motion by 3rds can be clearly heard. As the slurs connecting the roman numerals show, the motion of a 9th is subdivided by E♭ (IV) into two stages; the IV is emphasized by meter and by change of melody tone. In the first stage VI connects I and IV; in the second, II connects IV and V^6.

16-4   Bach, Chorale 101

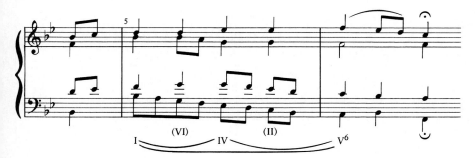

One sometimes encounters bass motions by descending 3rd leading down a 7th from I to II. Example 17-1, bars 1-2, will show such a progression in slightly elaborated form.

4. Chords built on the upper 5th. Example 16-5 shows a beautiful Chopin cadence. A literal interpretation of the first bar as V-II-V^7 would be correct as far as it goes, but it would tell us little about the meaning of the "II." This chord does not fulfill the usual function of supertonic harmony—to lead to V—for it appears *after* the cadential V has already been introduced. Furthermore this "II" does not *sound* like a harmonic entity but rather like the result of motion within the expanded V. Therefore we can best understand it as the upper 5th of V, arrived at through a bass progression down from root to 5th to root. While the bass moves down through chordal tones, the melody moves up a 3rd to introduce the 7th of dominant harmony.

16-5   Chopin, Mazurka, Op. 17/3

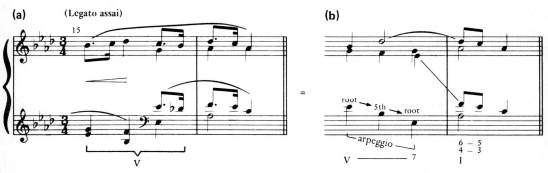

Chopin's cadence provides a good illustration of the principle that not every chord can be taken at face value as a harmonic entity. The possibility of a chord's functioning primarily as part of another, more extended, chord, as in the Chopin, is one you should bear in mind. The principle can be applied to other chords; thus "I" can function as the upper 5th of IV, "VI" as the upper 5th of II, and so on.

5. Chords built on the upper 3rd. A phrase from another Chopin mazurka (Example 16-6) shows a progression from a chord in B major to one in D♯ minor and (at the beginning of the next phrase) back to the B chord. Here, too, a literal analysis (I-III-I in B major) would fail to capture the specific meaning of the chord progression. Like the II of the preceding example, the III of this one is best understood as resulting from a motion within the governing B major chord, only this time between root and 3rd rather than between root and 5th. It helps to extend the tonic much as I⁶ might, a further instance of the connection between III and I⁶ mentioned in the preceding unit. The use of III as upper 3rd of I, of IV as upper 3rd of II, and so on, represents another important chordal function. Nineteenth-century composers sometimes wrote progressions that move back and forth between two $\frac{5}{3}$ chords with roots a 3rd apart—such as II-IV-II or IV-VI-IV. This sort of oscillating movement within a 3rd is not characteristic of eighteenth-century music.

16-6 Chopin, Mazurka, Op. 41/2

(a)

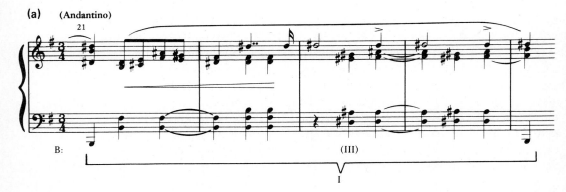

(b) reduction

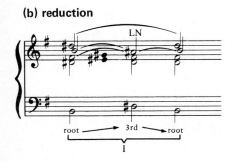

CONTRAPUNTAL CHORD FUNCTIONS

6. Chords as voice-leading correctives. Understanding that chords can act as voice-leading correctives—that is, that they can break up parallel 5ths and octaves—can help you reduce the number of errors in your written work. Much more importantly, it can also deepen your awareness of the interplay between harmony and voice leading in great music—voice leading as the composers conceived it, not narrowly, chord by chord, but comprehensively, over both small and large musical spans.

The first phrase of Bach's Chorale 280 (Example 16-7) illustrates how a chord can prevent voice-leading errors. The melody contains, in slightly decorated form, the progression $\hat{5}$-$\hat{6}$-$\hat{7}$-$\hat{8}$; the main harmonies are I, IV, V, and I. We know from Unit 9 that a motion from IV to V entails the risk of parallels unless the upper voices move down, not up as they do here. And indeed if we glance from IV to V we shall soon find the parallels: 5ths between bass and alto, octaves between tenor and soprano. We do not *hear* the parallels because of the II on the fourth beat of the first bar; this chord interpolates a 10th between the 5ths and a 5th between the octaves. In addition to permitting good voice leading, the II here also plays its characteristic harmonic role of intensifying V.

16-7   Bach, Chorale 280

*Why did Bach double the leading tone?

In this connection, look again at the beginning of Beethoven's "Spring" Sonata (Example 11-3). In addition to its harmonic function, the VI chord of bar 3 breaks up parallels between I and II (compare bars 1 and 4). The voice-leading function of VI is frequently a factor in the progression I-VI-II-V-I. Example 16-8 supplements the Bach and Beethoven excerpts by showing some other important possibilities. Voice-leading chords can be particularly useful in progressions involving chords with roots a 2nd apart (such as I-(VI)-II), but their use is not restricted to such situations. We will return to voice-leading chords later to discuss other functions they often fulfill.

16-8

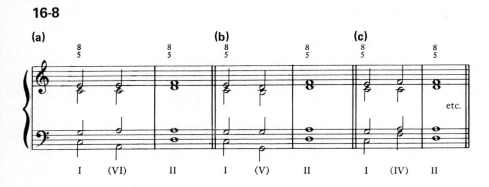

7. Chords as support for passing tones. Some chords function mainly as support for passing tones in an upper part, usually the soprano. We have already encountered this chord function, most recently in connection with III as support for $\hat{7}$ in $\frac{\hat{8}-\hat{7}-\hat{6}-\hat{5}}{\text{I-III-IV-I}}$ (Unit 15). Example 16-9 from a Brahms lied (song), demonstrates an exactly analogous use of IV. An extension of the preceding II, rather than a self-sufficient harmony, the IV gives support and a measure of emphasis to the passing tone, E, of the melody. If this chord were not there, the E would be a dissonant passing tone (7th) above the II; the IV transforms it into a consonance. Incidentally, the C♮ in the piano part is an element of E minor used in an E major context, an instance of *mixture* (see Unit 1, section 21).

16-9   Brahms, Geliebter wo zaudert, Op. 33/13

Quite often an apparent tonic—that is, a tonic in name but not in function—appears between IV and V in order to support a passing tone in the soprano. The characteristic soprano progression is $\hat{4}$-$\hat{3}$-$\hat{2}$; $\hat{3}$, of course, is the supported passing tone. This progression usually occurs when $\hat{3}$ is metrically weak; when it is strong, the cadential $\frac{6}{4}$ becomes possible. Example 16-10 illustrates.

16-10 Schubert, Piano Sonata, D. 958, I

A V interpolated between I and VI frequently supports a descending pass-ing tone in the soprano and may serve as a voice-leading corrective as well. Any bass progression of a descending 3rd can be similarly elaborated—for example, VI-(III)-IV or IV-(I)-II. We will see a very clear example of this technique in Ex-ample 16-17.

8. Chords above a bass passing tone. In small contexts $^6_3$ or $^6_4$ chords are often preferable to $^5_3$'s as passing chords, especially when moving between the root position and first inversion of a triad. In connecting I and I⁶, for instance, VII⁶ generally works better than II, whose greater stability and "weight" tend to con-tradict its transitional function. For one reason or another, however, $^5_3$'s do some-times appear as short-range passing chords. In the last phrase of Bach's Chorale 102 (Example 16-11), the chord labeled (V) passes from IV to IV⁶. A $^6_4$ chord, with B in the tenor instead of A, would produce 5ths between the inner voices and is not a possibility here. The chord at the beginning of bar 21, incidentally, is not a functional tonic; it supports the passing tone B of the soprano; the hemi-ola rhythm makes us hear the B as an unaccented passing tone.

16-11 Bach, Chorale 102

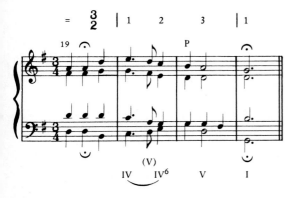

$\frac{5}{3}$ chords will more often appear above passing tones in the bass when the motion is within a seventh chord rather than a triad. A passing $\frac{5}{3}$ fits very naturally in the space between the $\frac{4}{3}$ and the $\frac{6}{5}$ positions, most typically in an expansion of V^7—also, sometimes, within II^7. Another possibility is between V^6 and V$\frac{4}{3}$ (review Example 8-15).

Stepwise bass motions can play an important part in creating continuity over longer spans; such bass progressions can be considered expanding passing motions. $\frac{5}{3}$ chords frequently appear in the course of such passing motions; thus they function as passing chords. Look again at Example 16-2: from a broad perspective the E minor (IV) chord is passing—that is, it connects the beginning of the stepwise motion, III, with the goal, V. Long-range passing motions, by their very nature, seldom proceed consecutively from one main chord to another. Subordinate tones and chords, such as the A major and B minor chords in 16-2, will appear between them.

9. Chords as support for neighboring tones. $\frac{5}{3}$ chords often support neighbors—especially upper neighbors—in the soprano, less often in one of the inner voices. Typically the root of the neighboring chord is a 5th below that of the main chord: IV supporting upper neighbors within an expanded I is the most frequent and important possibility. The same relationship can extend to other chords; in Example 16-12 we see a "I" supporting neighbors within a prolongation of V; this "I," like several others we have observed in this unit, is not a functional tonic but a detail within the expansion of V.

16-12   Mozart, Piano Sonata, K. 310, I

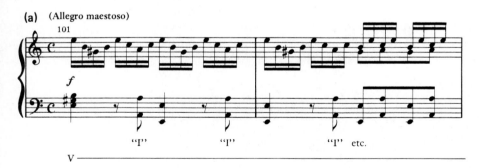

(a) (Allegro maestoso)

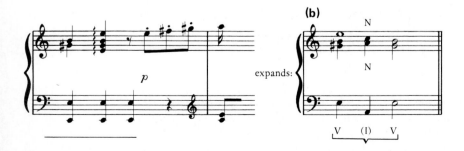

In some nineteenth-century music, starting around the time of Schubert, we now and then find neighboring chords whose root is a 3rd below that of the main chord—I-VI-I, for example. The D minor chord in Example 16-13 arises mainly as support for the D of the first violin part (upper neighbor to the 5th of I).

16-13   Brahms, String Quartet, Op. 51/1, III

10. Chords above a bass neighboring tone. These are usually easy to recognize and do not require much discussion. In immediate chord successions, neighbors in the bass tend to support $^6_3$'s rather than $^5_3$'s (such as I-VII^6-I rather than I-II-I). This is because a series of consecutive root-position chords, especially where there are no common tones, does not create an effect of flowing motion. Over longer spans (with intervening chords), neighboring $^5_3$'s become very useful. The most important possibility is VI as upper neighbor to V, an idiom that sometimes also occurs in immediate succession, as in Example 16-14. In this excerpt, VI also supports a passing tone in the soprano.

16-14   Bach, Chorale 102

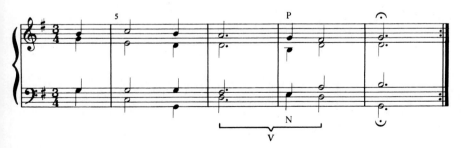

11. V as a minor triad. As we know, the natural form of minor generates a minor triad on the 5th scale step (symbol: -V). Because it lacks a leading tone, minor V does not tend very actively toward I. This makes it ineffective in immediate V-I progressions and in situations where the expectation of I becomes a factor—in half and deceptive cadences, for example. In all such cases, the major form of V (+V, with raised $\hat{7}$) helps to define the tonality much more clearly. Until now, therefore, we have employed V in minor only as a major triad.

You will learn in Unit 26 that minor V often expands into a key area and participates, sometimes very significantly, in large-scale harmonic organization. Rather like III, it functions far more typically as a structural pillar than as a decorative detail. But, again like III, minor V does have one important and characteristic small-scale function: it forms a very good support for natural $\hat{7}$, usually as a descending passing tone in a progression from I to VI (or occasionally IV⁶). As Example 16-15 indicates, the progression I-(V)-VI permits either major (16-15d) or minor V (16-15a and c). The choice depends partly on linear factors: a descent from $\hat{8}$ to $\hat{6}$ calls for minor V, to forestall the unmelodic augmented 2nd, #$\hat{7}$-b$\hat{6}$, whereas a neighbor-note motion $\hat{8}$-$\hat{7}$-$\hat{8}$ calls for raised $\hat{7}$ and, consequently, major V. Sometimes minor V might be best because the color of the minor triad is appropriate to the passage or because using it produces an expressive contrast between natural and raised $\hat{7}$.

16-15

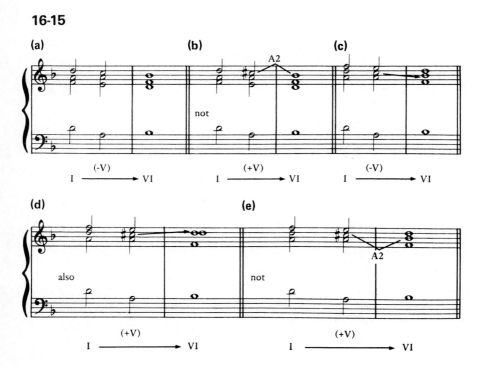

This expressive contrast is markedly in evidence in a chorale setting by Bach (Example 16-16). The alto's A♮, coming just two beats after a prominent A♯ in the bass, is most unexpected. Its use also gives a particular freshness to the

A♯ of the cadential V. In this phrase, the use of natural $\hat{7}$ and, consequently, of minor V relates directly to the motivic design. The brackets in the example point to a rising and falling 3rd, derived from the chorale tune. In connection with the alto figure, major V would be an impossibility: a line F♯-G♯-A♯ would demand a continuation to B, thus eliminating the rising 3rd. Another consequence of the motivic design is the use of IV⁶, instead of the more usual VI, to follow minor V.

16-16   Bach, Chorale 104

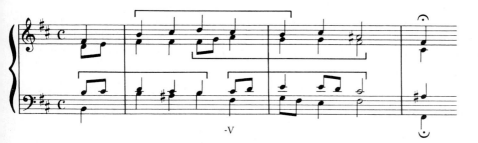

Another Bach setting of the same chorale (Example 16-17) shows the use of major V just where minor V appears in the other setting. Here major V occurs in connection with a neighbor-note motion B-A♯-B (tenor bars 1 and 2). In the opening phrase of this setting, there is no chromatic conflict between A♯ and A♮, but the chorale melody itself brings in a most unexpected A♮ at the beginning of the second phrase. The minor V that supports this note helps to prepare a tonicization of III, another important function of the minor dominant.

16-17   Bach, Chorale 62

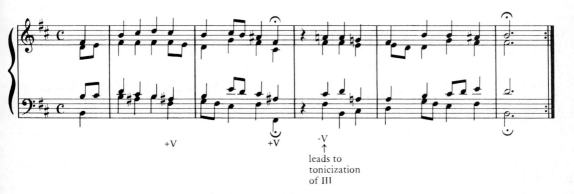

POINTS FOR REVIEW

1. In the progression of descending 5ths (I-IV-VII-III-VI-II-V-I), the bass line usually alternates descending 5ths and ascending 4ths.

2. The progression of ascending 5ths, which is much less goal-oriented than that of descending 5ths, is basically a rising stepwise line: C $\nearrow$ $\overset{(G)}{}$ D $\nearrow$ $\overset{(A)}{}$ E. The complete series I-I is virtually never used.

3. Another important type of progression is bass motion by 3rds (bass arpeggio). Motion by descending 3rds (I-VI-IV, for example) is much more goal-oriented than motion by ascending 3rds.

4. A chord can be expanded by motion to its upper 5th. For example, II can expand V and I can expand IV.

5. Similarly, a chord can be expanded by motion to its upper 3rd—IV can expand II and VI can expand IV, etc.

6. Chords can be used as voice-leading correctives (to break up parallel 5ths or octaves). Such a chord is especially useful between chords with roots a 2nd apart, for example, I-(VI)-II.

7. Chords can be used to support passing tones in the soprano. Here is an important example: $\hat{4}$ - $\hat{3}$ - $\hat{2}$

   IV-(I)-V.

8. Chords can be used above a passing tone in the bass. In a small-scale progression, $\frac{6}{3}$ and $\frac{6}{4}$ chords are most frequently used for this purpose. In a large-scale progression IV can serve as a passing chord from III to V, and so on (see Example 16-2).

9. Chords can support neighboring tones in the upper voices. Such progressions as I-(IV)-I or V-(I)-V occur very frequently.

10. Chords can occur over neighboring tones in the bass. Over small spans $\frac{6}{3}$ chords are most frequently used; over longer spans $\frac{5}{3}$ chords are more frequent. Most important is VI as upper neighbor to V.

11. An important function of –V is to support $\hat{7}$ as a descending passing tone, where it helps to avoid an augmented 2nd. Minor V also prepares for the tonicization of III.

EXERCISES

1. Preliminaries. Write progressions in different major and minor keys that illustrate the following techniques:

   a. descending 5ths—entire series
   b. descending 5ths—part of the series
   c. ascending 5ths connecting III and V in minor
   d. descending 3rds connecting III and IV in minor
   e. descending 3rds connecting I and II in major
   f. VI breaking up parallels between I and II
   g. "I" supporting $\hat{3}$ as a passing tone
   h. "IV" supporting $\hat{1}$ as a passing tone
   i. "III" supporting $\hat{7}$ as a passing tone
   j. V going twice to VI in minor, once with V as a minor triad and once with V as a major triad
   k. root-position "I" connecting V$\frac{4}{3}$ and V$\frac{6}{5}$; use two different sopranos

2. Outer voices with unfigured bass. This exercise makes use of V as a minor
   triad; sometimes you will have to decide whether major or minor V is the better choice.

*don't harmonize any of the sixteenth notes

17

Diatonic Sequences

17-1 **Bach, Well-Tempered Clavier I, Prelude 21**

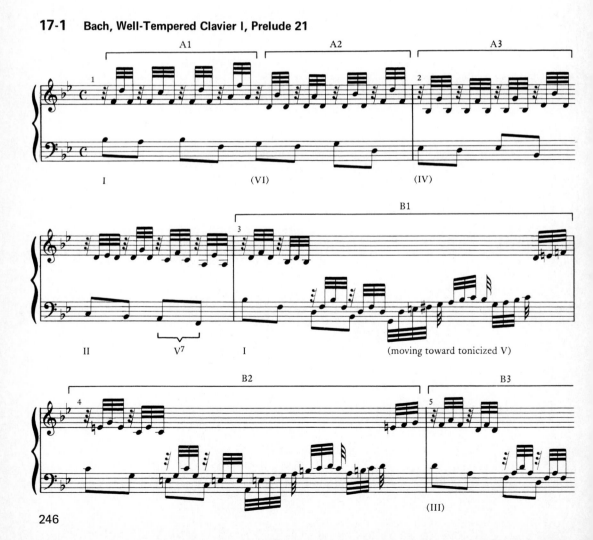

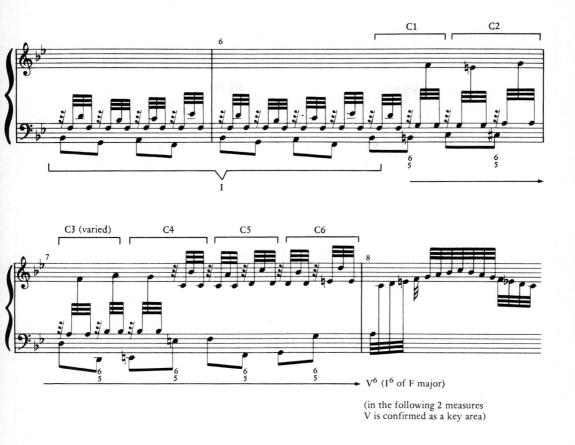

(in the following 2 measures
V is confirmed as a key area)

COMPOSITIONAL FUNCTIONS

1. Repetition. A crucial element—often, indeed, *the* crucial element—in musical design and form is repetition of a melodic or chordal pattern. If such repetitions occur on different scale degrees, the result is called a *sequence*. Maintaining the same musical idea (sometimes with slight variations) establishes a connection between the beginning and the end of the sequential passage and creates the possibility for expansions—some on quite a large scale—of many of the techniques we have already discussed.

The expansional character of sequences is very evident in Example 17-1. The passage as a whole leads from an opening tonic (bars 1-3) to a tonicized F major $^6_3$ chord (bar 8). Both the tonic and the motion from tonic to dominant $^6_3$ are expanded by sequential passages; there are three of them, labeled A, B, and C in the example. Sequence A expands the field of motion from a I to a cadential II. This motion—normally a rising 2nd—is expressed as a descending 7th; the 7th is subdivided into three 3rds (Bb-G, G-Eb, Eb-C). The material of the first half-bar repeats on G and Eb in a descending sequence that leads to a cadential II-V⁷-I.

Sequence A has helped to bring the tonic chord into a lower register (compare bar 1 and bar 3). As a natural consequence of this descent, the transition to the tonicized F chord will move up so that the goal V is in the same register as the opening I, thus helping to connect the goal to its point of origin. This process is effected in two stages (sequences B and C). Sequence B grows out of the tonic of bar 3, each pattern taking up an entire bar. The bass moves up a step with each bar until the D is reached in bar 5, where the sequence breaks off and the bass returns to the tonic and to a low register. The stepwise ascent begins once more in sequence C, but with a shorter pattern so that each step lasts only one beat. The bass moves chromatically until D is regained in bar 7. The sequential motion then continues (with varied bass) until it reaches its goal—the F major chord in bar 8. Note that the motion to the tonicized V is achieved in a much more gradual way than in the examples of Unit 14.

Like sequences A and B in the Bach, most sequences contain three statements (or two plus the beginning of a third). More than three can be tedious unless the pattern is very short and simple, as in sequence C (bars 6½-7) of the Bach.

2. Diatonic progressions. Sequences vary in many respects—some use only triads; others use seventh chords, applied dominants, and so on. In this unit we will discuss sequences using $\frac{5}{3}$ and $\frac{6}{3}$ chords only, and will confine ourselves to sequential patterns that appear frequently in composition. Some sequences are completely diatonic; others use chromatic elements. Some remain in one key; others effect a change of tonal center. We will discuss chromatic and modulating sequences in later units; here we will work with diatonic ones, like the first sequence in the Bach prelude. This passage demonstrates an important principle: when the pattern repeats in a diatonic sequence, the qualities of chords and melodic intervals will sometimes change. Thus the first statement begins with a B♭ major chord, the second with a G *minor* chord; the first melodic progression of the bass is a half step, but its repetition is a *whole* step. The lesson is clear: to keep a sequence diatonic use only tones that belong to the key; avoid accidentals (except for the customary inflections of $\hat{6}$ and $\hat{7}$ in minor).

3. Classification of sequences. Most diatonic chordal sequences fall into one of the following categories:

1. sequences with descending 5ths
2. sequences with ascending 5ths
3. sequences using ascending 5-6 technique
4. sequences falling in 3rds (descending 5-6 technique)

Example 17-2 shows these basic types in four-voice settings. You will find it helpful to compare this example both with the excerpts from the literature in this unit and with your own written work.

17-2   basic sequence types

(a) descending 5ths   **(b) ascending 5ths**

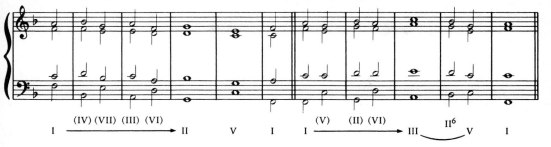

(c) rising by step (ascending 5-6)

(d) falling in 3rds (descending 5-6)

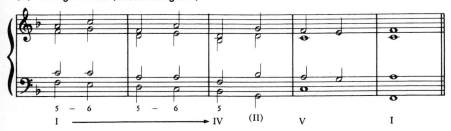

Each of these basic types of sequence can fulfill various functions in a composition, depending on how the composer uses it. The progressions of Example 17-2 illustrate, in abstract form, three important ways in which a sequence functions:

1. To form a transition between the beginning of a motion and its goal, perhaps the most frequent function. In 17-2b and d, the sequences lead from the opening tonic to III and IV, respectively.

2. To contain both the transition and the goal, as in the progression of descending 5ths in 17-2a, which moves from the initial tonic through intervening chords to the cadential II-V-I (here emphasized by the broadened rhythmic values).

3. To expand a single chord—most often the tonic. In 17-2c the sequence expands the initial tonic (moving from I to I⁶) of the progression I-II-V-I.

Sequences frequently contain a prominent scalewise line in the bass or the soprano—sometimes, in fact, in both. This scalewise component helps the sequence, the chords are grouped in twos (see the brackets in 17-3a), and each repetition of the two-chord pattern is one step lower than the preceding statement.

4. Voice-leading implications. Normally, as in the Bach prelude, *all* the voices above a sequential bass are themselves sequential. And with any repetitive patterns where all the voices participate, 5ths and octaves may become a problem. Therefore, voice-leading chords play an essential role in sequential passages. In sequence A of the Bach, the chord on the fourth eighth note prevents 5ths between successive strong beats in the bass and middle voice. And in the third sequence, the $^6_4$ chords also break up 5ths.

Keeping the upper voices sequential, as in 17-2, will occasionally produce a doubled leading tone (17-2a, third chord). As long as it does not appear before a goal tonic, this doubling is perfectly acceptable. In sequential passages based on descending 5ths or on the ascending 5-6 technique, a diminished triad in $^5_3$ position will sometimes appear. When it forms part of a repetitive pattern and when the progression as a whole conveys a sense of forward motion, the diminished triad attracts less attention than in other situations; its harshness is considerably softened. (Note the smooth effect of the third chord in 17-2a.) In sequences based on descending 5ths, a melodic augmented 4th or diminished 5th will appear in one of the voices (see the augmented 4th between IV and VII in 17-2a). However the melodic augmented 2nd can (and should) be avoided in four-part vocal writing.

SEQUENCES WITH DESCENDING 5THS

5. Harmonic and contrapuntal implications. Example 17-3a illustrates the first basic type of sequence—the one based on descending 5ths. In this type of sequence, the chords are grouped in twos (see the brackets in 17-3a), and each repetition of the two-chord pattern is one step lower than the preceding statement. The bass line reflects this grouping, for it is also arranged in groups of two—down a 5th, up a 4th (or vice versa)—so that it forms two stepwise lines, such as:

$$C \searrow \quad B \searrow \quad A \searrow \quad G \searrow$$
$$\quad F \nearrow \quad E \nearrow \quad D \nearrow \quad C$$

One of these two lines will usually predominate, such factors as rhythm and register throwing it into relief. The stepwise relationships that occur in a series of descending 5ths add a strong contrapuntal implication to this typically harmonic progression.

17-3

(a) Handel, Bourrée   (from *Royal Fireworks Music*)

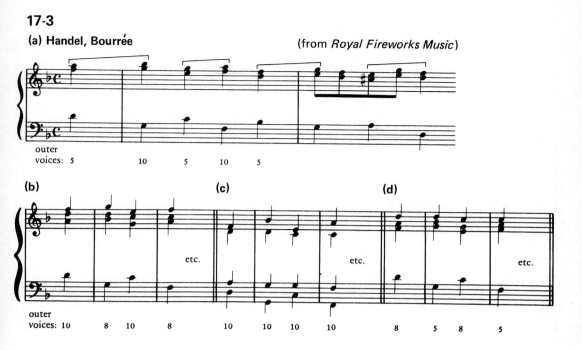

In a sequential series of descending 5ths, as in the nonsequential ones discussed in the preceding unit, some of the chords may receive more emphasis than others. The last three chords of a complete series are often important because they form a cadence II-V-I. Thus the fundamental motion of the Handel excerpt is from the opening I to IV (first strong beat, highest soprano tone) through a passing chord (III) to the cadence II⁶-V⁷-I. The VII and VI have a harmonic role as part of the series of 5ths; in addition the VII functions as a voice-leading chord that prevents parallel octaves in the stepwise descent from IV to III. Notice how the cadential II⁶ is further set off by the rhythmic change in the upper voices.

Sequential patterns are often characterized by the intervallic relationships between the outer voices. In the Handel the bass and soprano alternate 5ths and 10ths (intervallic pattern 5-10, 5-10). The progressions of 17-3b, c, and d show some other possibilities. The combinations that contain imperfect consonances (5-10, 10-8, and 10-10) are usually preferable to the 8-5 pattern, which may sound empty unless decorated.

It is by no means necessary to use the complete series of descending 5ths (I-IV-VII-III-VI-II-V-I); shorter segments may also occur, but one must be careful with diminished triads. They ought not to occur at the very beginning or end of such progressions, where they are likely to be too exposed.

6. $\frac{5}{3}$-$\frac{6}{3}$ pattern. The descending 5th pattern is often modified so that $\frac{6}{3}$ chords alternate with $\frac{5}{3}$. This procedure tends to enhance one of the stepwise bass lines. In another Handel excerpt, Example 17-4, the $\frac{5}{3}$ chords support the bass descent C-B♭-A♭; the $\frac{6}{3}$'s are clearly subordinate until the cadential II⁶ arrives in bar 88.

Notice how the register change in the top voice helps to emphasize the importance of this chord.

17-4   Handel, Musette   (from *Concerto Grosso,* Op. 6/6)

In Example 17-5, on the other hand, the series of descending 5ths *begins*
with a $\frac{6}{3}$ chord, the $\frac{5}{3}$'s coming in on the second half of the measure. This sequence leads from I^6 through V^6 to I with the $\frac{6}{3}$ chords predominating. As in the Handel Musette (17-4), the last chord of the sequence is a goal, but the two sequences function quite differently. The sequence of 17-4 connects the opening I to a cadential II^6, while the one in 17-5 moves between different positions of the same chord, I^6 to I.

17-5   Mozart, Piano Sonata, K. 545, I

SEQUENCES WITH ASCENDING 5THS

7. Harmonic and contrapuntal implications. An excerpt from Bach (Example 17-6) illustrates the second basic type of sequence—the one that contains ascending 5ths. In Unit 16, we saw that a succession of $\frac{5}{3}$ chords in rising 5ths normally grows out of an ascending stepwise line; review Example 16-2, where a stepwise motion III-IV-V in minor is expanded harmonically into a series of rising 5ths: III-(VII)-IV-(I)-V. Our present example is similar, only the progression leads from I to III in major, and it is expressed as a sequence. In the progression I-(V)-II-(VI)-III, the V and VI chords prevent parallel 5ths and octaves, and they support lower incomplete neighbors in the uppermost voice. Although the sequential progression breaks off after III, the III is not a final goal, for the ascending motion continues through another sequence to IV and on to V (see Example 26-6 for the continuation).

In sequences with ascending 5ths, each pair of chords often supports a soprano line that descends by step. In the Bach, the main top-voice notes are

E-D (bar 1), F-E (bar 2), and G (bar 3), though the many suspensions, alternating between soprano and alto, partly obscure these two-note figures. Suspensions frequently decorate sequences of this type.

17-6   Bach, Little Prelude, BWV 924

(a)

(b) reduction   **(c) reduction**

8. Omitting a step in the ascent. Like the Bach Little Prelude, an excerpt from Beethoven's "Waldstein" Sonata (Example 17-7) contains a rising sequence with ascending 5ths. In the Beethoven, however, the ascent skips over one step, the pair of chords III-VII on $\hat{3}$. In this way, a diminished triad (VII) is avoided. Omitting a step in the ascent is very frequent, usually to avoid the diminished triad; for an illustration in minor, see Example 17-22.

17-7   Beethoven, "Waldstein" Sonata, Op. 53, III

9. $\frac{5}{3}$-$\frac{6}{3}$ pattern. As with descending 5ths, $\frac{6}{3}$ chords may alternate with $\frac{5}{3}$'s (Example 17-8). As in the "Waldstein" excerpt, a step in the ascent is left out. (The chords on G♮ and C♮ are applied dominants. If the reduction [17-8b] is played *without* these accidentals it will still make sense.)

17-8   Chopin, Etude, Op. 25/9

(a)

(b) reduction

note skip
in series

(c) bass line

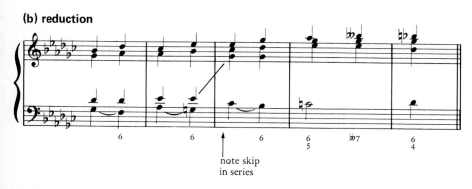

SEQUENCES USING THE ASCENDING 5-6 TECHNIQUE

10. Syncopes. Example 17-9 shows the familiar procedure whereby a $^6_3$ chord arises out of contrapuntal motion (5 to 6) over a single bass tone.

17-9

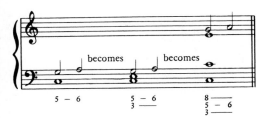

This technique can be extended over a stepwise ascending bass, producing a series of 5-6 progressions. In such a series the 6ths normally appear on weaker beats than the 5ths. The motion 5-6 emphasizes the weak beats so that the voice in which it appears sounds syncopated; for this reason, 5-6 progressions in such a series are often called *syncopes*. Example 17-10 demonstrates the 5-6 series in two and three voices. In three voices, 3rds or 10ths are added either above or below the 5-6 syncopes.

17-10

(a)   **(b)**   **(c)**

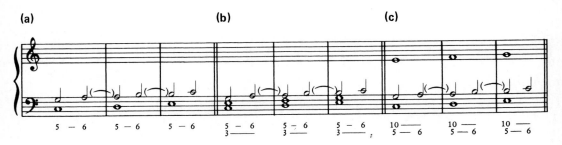

The 5-6 series occurs most naturally in a texture of three voices, but with careful attention to doubling, four voices are also possible (Example 17-11).

17-11

(a)   **(b)**

The use of 5-6 in a series is an old contrapuntal technique and one that occurs very frequently in composition. Often it serves to prevent parallel 5ths, as we can see in Example 17-12, which presents a particularly beautiful use of 5-6 technique in a fragment from an "Ave Maria" by the great Renaissance composer Josquin des Pres. Here the outer voices move by step in parallel 10ths, forming a sequence in rising 2nds. The tenor forms a 5-6 series with the bass, avoiding a series of parallel 5ths.

17-12   Josquin, Ave Maria

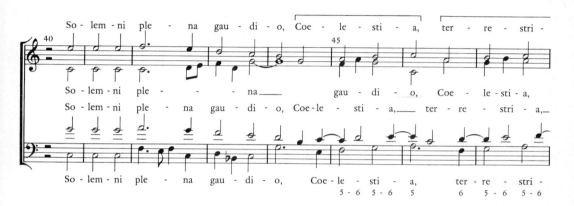

translation: [Hail to thee, whose conception] full of solemn
rejoicing, would fill heaven and earth with new joy.

In the Josquin, the 5-6's occur within a larger sequential pattern. Often, however, as in Example 17-13, the 5-6 series itself helps to form a sequence in rising 2nds; in this example, the top voice decorates the sequential pattern. The 5-6 technique lends itself easily to all kinds of sequential elaborations, ranging from the simple to the very complex. Variants using seventh chords and applied dominants (as in the third sequence of Example 17-1) occur very frequently; we will take them up in later units.

5-6 series in major often contain a diminished triad in root position (VII$^5_3$), as in bar 260 of 17-13. This diminished chord does not create a disturbing effect if the tonic follows soon after, as it does in the A major chord of bar 261. The importance of this chord as the goal of the passage is underscored—not contradicted—by the rest that precedes it.

17-13   Mozart, Piano Concerto, K. 488, I

11. Root-position variant of ascending 5-6. Example 17-14 shows an important variant of the 5-6 technique; the bass leaps down in 3rds and transforms the $\frac{6}{3}$ chords into $\frac{5}{3}$'s. Bars 3-5 of Example 17-1 also illustrate this procedure.

17-14

5-6 becomes 5-8

SEQUENCES FALLING IN 3RDS (DESCENDING 5-6)

12. Harmonic and contrapuntal implications. The fourth important type of sequence (17-2d) also alternates 5ths and 6ths, but in a very different manner. Here the 5th and 6th do not share a common bass tone. Instead, they alternate above a bass descending by step; each new interval pair (5-6) occurs a 3rd below the one before it, so that the sequence is organized in descending 3rds. Example 17-15 illustrates this very important sequential pattern. In the Mozart the descending bass line is expressed by the first and third eighth notes of the left-hand piano part; the second and fourth eighths represent an inner voice. The descending bass, supporting $\frac{5}{3}$ and $\frac{6}{3}$ chords in alternation, leads from I to the goal chord, II^6. The melody is in the right-hand part of the piano; it clearly shows the sequential repetition at the lower 3rd. The violin part—actually an "alto" voice—has a simpler line, a stepwise descent in parallel 10ths above the bass.

17-15   Mozart, Violin Sonata, K. 379, II

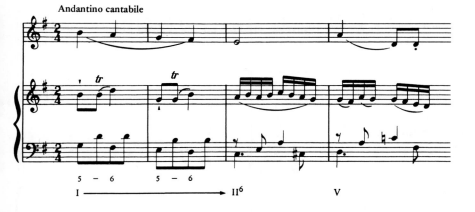

LESS FREQUENT SEQUENTIAL PATTERNS

14. Ascending by step with voice-leading $\frac{5}{3}$ chords. Example 17-20 shows another way to produce a sequence rising by step; in this respect it resembles the rising sequence with ascending 5ths and the 5-6 syncope technique. Here, the bass

Example 17-16 shows three top-voice possibilities for this progression. The first two resemble the right-hand piano part and the violin part of the Mozart excerpt.

moves alternately up a 4th and down a 3rd, all with root-position triads. The first chords of each pair are the principal ones; the second ones function as voice-leading correctives, breaking up parallel 5ths and octaves. In this excerpt the sequence forms a stepwise transition from I to V. Note that the change of rhythm and the breaking off of the sequential pattern do not occur at the same time.

17-20   Mozart, Two-Piano Sonata, K. 448, III

15. Descending sequence with 6-5 syncopes. The interval succession 6-5 over a single bass tone can occur in series thus producing a descending sequence. This procedure is the reverse of the ascending 5-6 series discussed earlier. In Example 17-21, the bass moves from I down to a cadential $\frac{6}{4}$. The bass remains sequential for three complete steps except for the chromatic A♯-A♮ in the bass. The right-hand part, at first sequential, is altered in bar 18 to allow for the chromatic bass; a leap to A would produce an ugly effect. Two neighboring chords separate the cadential $\frac{6}{4}$ from its resolution, a possibility that we shall explore in Unit 19.

17-21   **Brahms, Intermezzo, Op. 117/3**

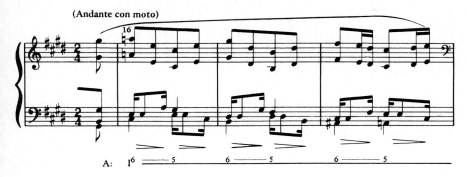

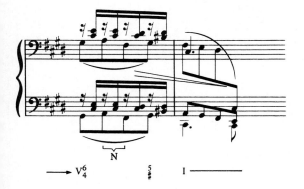

SEQUENCES IN MINOR

16. Descending motion. If you use your ear, you will soon discover that not all diatonic sequences that work well in major can be used successfully in minor. Two factors limit the possibilities for sequential treatment in minor: the diminished triad on II and possible difficulties in approaching the leading tone. Descending 5ths, the descending 5-6 succession, and their variants are the easiest to use. In the complete series of descending 5ths, from I to I, $\hat{7}$ need not be raised until the cadential V is reached (see Example 17-3a). In a sequence by descending 5ths, the diminished triad on II is good; it forms part of the cadential II-V-I and its approach from VI sounds natural. In the descending 5-6 progression, the natural form of minor will be used for the bass (Example 17-17). This progression also presents few problems in moving down from I. The approach to II, however, is less convincing than with descending 5ths; usually VII⁶ or II⁷ is used instead (thus modifying or breaking off the sequence; again see 17-17).

17. Moving up from I. In minor, moving up from I is much more difficult than moving down because of the diminished triad on II. In a rising sequence with ascending 5ths, the pair of chords II-VI can be left out to avoid this triad, a technique discussed in section 8. Example 17-22 illustrates. The bass ascends from I to IV (skipping II), the soprano moving in 10ths above the bass. In bar 4, a voice exchange between soprano and bass transforms IV to IV⁶; the IV⁶ leads to V in a Phrygian cadence. The major V in the second half of bar 1 is typical; raised $\hat{7}$ intensifies the connection with the tonic.

17-22   Corelli, Allemanda   (from *Trio Sonata,* Op. 4/8)

The ascending 5-6 series can move up from I without skipping II (Example 17-23a). The diminished triad is approached by step and is less harsh than when preceded by a leap. Moreover it "resolves" into the next $\frac{5}{3}$ chord, III (compare section 10). The tonal meaning of this progression, however, can be ambiguous; the III will tend to sound like the tonic (of the "relative major") unless followed by a progression leading to I as in 17-23b.

17-23

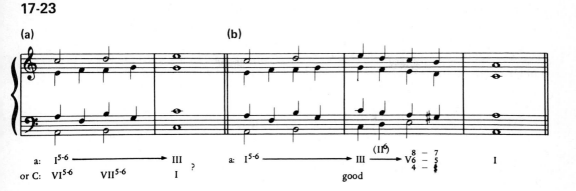

This series can be convincingly extended to the next step IV-II^6 and on to V$^{(7)}$ or V$^4_2$. Be sure to avoid the augmented 2nd in moving on to V. Example 17-24 shows several voice-leading possibilities.

17-24

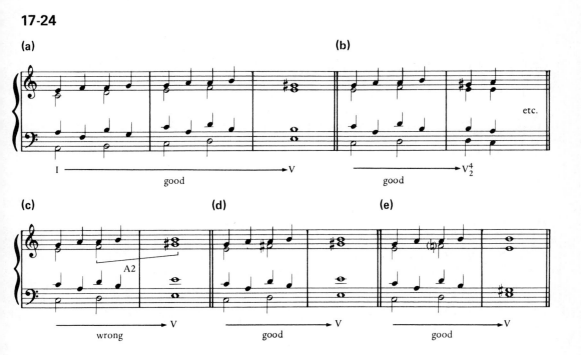

18. Moving up from III. III is the most frequent point of origin for rising sequences in minor and the easiest to use, as difficulties with the diminished triad or with the approach to the leading tone are unlikely. Because of the tendency of the minor mode to gravitate to III, this chord makes a logical beginning for a sequence. Ascending 5ths can easily move to a goal V (17-25a). Going further, however, is impossible, since the next chord would be the weak, unconvincing diminished triad on II. However, the 5-6 series can extend to VI (Example 17-25b) or even to natural VII (17-25c). The chords will be exactly the same as those contained between I and IV or V of the "relative major"; consequently a key-defining progression (leading to I or tonicizing III) must follow the VI or VII.

17-25

(a)

III ⟶ V

(b)

III ⟶ VI

(c)

III ⟶ VII

19. Moving up from V. The remainder of the minor scale—from V or VI to I—is almost unusable in a diatonic setting. $\hat{7}$ must be raised in order to move to the goal tonic, but raising $\hat{6}$ to avoid the augmented 2nd produces two diminished $\frac{5}{3}$ chords in close succession, a less than euphonious combination. Therefore, for the time being, avoid ascending sequences between V and I in minor.

POINTS FOR REVIEW

1. The following are simple four-part progressions showing the most important types of sequences in major, with typical variants.

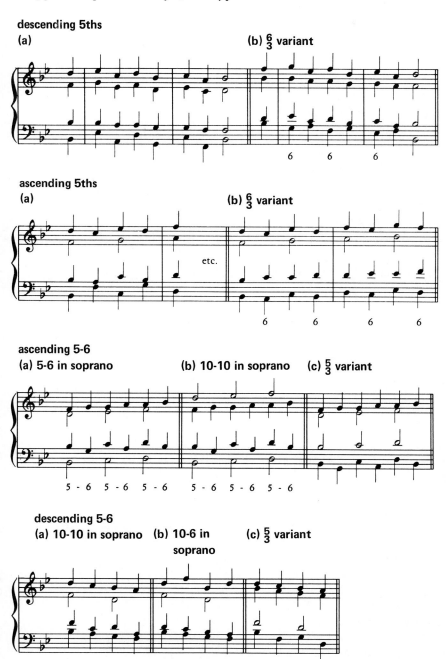

Continued

other sequences
(a) up by step with   **(b) descending 6-5**
    voice-leading chords

2. In minor, the easiest sequences to use are those that move down—the descending-5th and descending-3rd types.

3. Remember the following points when using ascending sequences in minor:

   a. When moving up from I by ascending 5ths, omit the step II-VI to avoid the diminished triad on II.

   b. When moving up from III by ascending 5ths, stop at V to avoid the diminished triad on II; using the ascending 5-6 series, however, makes it possible to continue to VI or natural VII.

   c. Moving up from V requires chromatic inflection, so avoid for the present.

EXERCISES

NOTE. From now on, you should be aware of sequential repetitions in a given melody or bass, and you should preserve the sequence in your harmonization. Remember that scale patterns in the soprano or bass can often be set sequentially, and that melodic repetition by stepwise descent in the soprano often indicates a sequence with descending 5ths (as in Example 17-3).

1. Preliminaries.

   a. Write a short progression in major using 5-6 technique over an ascending bass (in whole notes), lead to IV, and make a cadence.

   b. Using the following pattern, continue to II^7 and make a cadence. Do the same thing in the key of G♯ minor.

   c. Using the following pattern, continue to V. Extend V by a deceptive cadence before going on to I.

2. Figured bass.

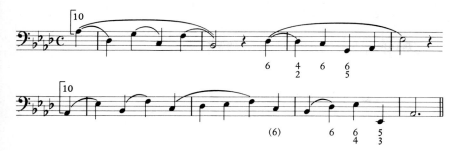

6   4 6 6
    2   5

(6)   6 6 5
         4 3

3. Melody.

4. Melody.

bass: ♩.   ♩.   etc.

*don't harmonize anticipation

18

$\frac{6}{3}$-Chord Techniques

18-1   Dufay, Ave Maris Stella

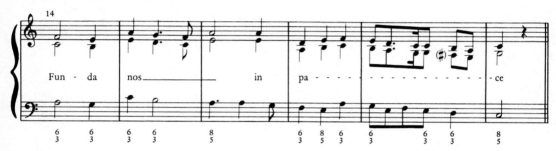

translation: Establish us in peace.

18-2   Mendelssohn, Song without Words, Op. 53/3

$\frac{6}{3}$ CHORDS IN PARALLEL MOTION

1. Transitional passages in $\frac{6}{3}$ chords. A casual glance would reveal little if any similarity between the two excerpts in Examples 18-1 and 18-2, the first from a hymn by Dufay (c. 1400-1474), the other from a piano piece by Mendelssohn (1809-1847). The pieces represent vastly different styles; they display a contrast in texture and sound that could hardly be greater. Nevertheless the two passages have one significant element in common: both are based on the use of $\frac{6}{3}$ chords in extended parallel motion. The Dufay excerpt bears witness to the fact that the use of parallel $\frac{6}{3}$ chords is a very old technique, dating back to the early Renaissance. Originally a device characteristic of both improvisational practice (*fauxbourdon,* English discant) and composition, it remained an important technique throughout the history of triadic music.

$\frac{6}{3}$ chords form perhaps the ideal sonority for extended parallel motion. In close position they do not contain the interval of the 5th; parallel 5ths, therefore, need not be a stumbling block, as they must inevitably be if a series of $\frac{5}{3}$ chords appears in parallel motion. Furthermore, in a passage of extended parallel motion, the single chords tend to lose their individual identity and merge into a continuous linear flow. Such a passage, therefore, like the sequences discussed in the last unit, can function appropriately as a transition from one stable point to another. The characteristic interval of the 6th gives the $\frac{6}{3}$ chord a more fluid, less stable sound than the $\frac{5}{3}$, a quality particularly well suited to passages of a transitional nature.

The fluid character of passages in $\frac{6}{3}$ chords is evident in both of our excerpts. In the Dufay, the $\frac{6}{3}$'s provide a sense of motion and the $\frac{8}{8}$'s (bars 16 and 19) sound like goals. In the Mendelssohn, the $\frac{6}{3}$'s form a bridge from the tonic of bar 95 to the cadential II⁶ of bar 101. This transition is a contrapuntal, not a harmonic one. Because the individual chords do not stand out, it would be misleading to describe what happens in such a series as a "harmonic" progression: for example, I-I⁶-VII⁶-VI⁶-V⁶, and so on. Only the beginning and the end of the series will .normally receive enough emphasis to form a point of articulation. In the Mendelssohn, the I⁶ that begins the series is important as an expansion of the initial tonic; the II⁶ at the end is important because of its cadential function.

2. 6ths between the outer voices. Just as consecutive or recurrent 10ths help to organize the relationship between the outer voices, so do 6ths. 6ths between the outer voices do not appear in as many kinds of progressions as 10ths, but an extended series of parallel § chords will have 6ths, not 10ths, between the bass and soprano. In the Dufay excerpt, the outer voices move in 6ths, and the two upper voices in parallel 4ths. (These parallel 4ths are absolutely correct.) The Mendelssohn does the same thing in a more elaborate manner (see reduction, Example 18-3). The soprano line is a "polyphonic melody" that implies two voices that move in parallel 4ths, as in the Dufay.

18-3

As Example 18-4 shows, a series of parallel § chords will not normally have 10ths between the outer voices because of the 5ths that would occur between the two top parts.

18-4

parallel 5ths

3. Parallel § chords in four voices. The Dufay and Mendelssohn excerpts indicate that the use of parallel § chords is essentially a three-voice technique. (The Dufay is obviously written in three voices; the reduction in 18-3 shows that the Mendelssohn, too, has only three real voices, the other tones being merely doublings.) With careful attention to doubling, a series of parallel §'s can occur in four-part writing. The main problem is avoiding parallel octaves; the solution is to allow one of the voices to forego parallel motion and to alternate doublings. Example 18-5 shows a number of possibilities. Of its ten progressions, all but 18-5e and j contain recurrent patterns of alternate doublings, and all ten are good; the choice often depends on the doubling that sounds best in the emphasized last chord. Remember not to double the leading tone if the tonic triad follows, and to avoid the melodic augmented 2nd in minor.

Series of parallel § chords can both descend (18-5a-e) and ascend (18-5f-j). However, descending progressions are much more frequent.

18-5

descending progressions

ascending progressions

4. Variants in the use of parallel $\frac{6}{3}$ chords. Quite often a passage mostly in parallel $\frac{6}{3}$ chords will contain one or more $\frac{5}{3}$ chords, will depart momentarily from parallel motion, or will show other "irregularities." Thus Example 18-6 is a variant of the progression shown in 18-5e. Instead of maintaining parallel motion, however, the soprano has a voice exchange with the bass that shifts it into a higher register and allows it to end an octave higher; this is a *double voice exchange* with two sixths and two tenths. A consequence of this voice exchange is the $\frac{5}{3}$ chord on the third beat. If nothing but $\frac{6}{3}$ chords were used, the 10ths between the outer voices would lead to parallel 5ths (Example 18-4). This danger exists even in a succession of only two chords unless one of the 5ths is diminished.

18-6

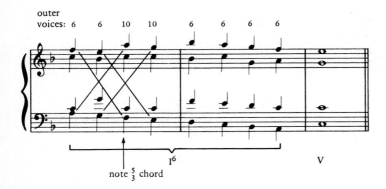

Example 18-7 shows four excerpts from the third movement of Handel's Concerto Grosso, Op. 3, No. 1, in which the use of parallel $^6_3$ chords is exceptionally clear and instructive. Note that in all the excerpts, the texture is in three voices. Composers will often change to three voices for passages using parallel $^6_3$ chords, an option not available to you in exercises in four-part vocal style, but possible when you are working in a free keyboard or other instrumental style.

18-7a, the opening of the movement, contains two phrases. The first, characterized by imitation between the outer voices, contains $^6_3$ usages familiar from previous units (such as VII⁶ passing from I⁶ to I). The second phrase, like the first, begins with imitation; however the last soprano tone of bar 3 becomes F♮ to allow a stepwise descent in parallel $^6_3$'s. The motion in $^6_3$'s continues until V⁷ arrives in bar 4. The chord just before V⁷ is IV⁶, emphasized by longer duration and by the suspension (7-6) that delays its 6th, C.

18-7b uses a variant of the same theme, but in the mediant, B♭ major. This time the descending 6ths do not continue beyond two eighth notes. Instead the soprano shifts to a higher position, forming a pair of 10ths with the bass, as in 18-6. To avoid 5ths and, at the same time, to emphasize the subdominant, a $^5_3$ chord appears on the downbeat (the continuo player would complete this chord); on the second beat the soprano moves up once more, regaining the interval of a 6th, but now an octave higher. An interesting feature of the voice leading is the continuation of the parallel 10ths in the middle part.

18-7c is in D minor, the key of the minor dominant. It contains two double voice exchanges, after which the 6ths continue. Since the first chord in bar 21 contains a diminished 5th, Handel can write two consecutive $^6_3$ chords with 10ths between the outer voices.

18-7d shows the conclusion of the movement. Like the opening statement, it consists of two phrases. Here, however, there is no imitation in the second phrase; instead the outer voices move in 10ths filled in by the descending 5-6 progression familiar to us from Unit 17.

18-7   **Handel, Concerto Grosso, Op. 3/1, III**

OTHER USES OF $^6_3$ CHORDS

Most of the techniques described in connection with $^5_3$ chords in Unit 16 can be applied to $^6_3$ chords as well. Because the techniques are mostly familiar, we will describe these $^6_3$ usages rather briefly, summing them up in the last example of this unit.

5. The neighboring $^6_3$. We are already very familiar with the most important neighboring $^6_3$ chords: V[6] as N or IN to I. Between other scale degrees, a neighbor in the bass works best when the melodic progression is a half step. Thus I[6] as N to IV is usually better in major than in minor, where I[6] is generally altered to form an applied dominant, V[6] of IV. Example 18-8 shows some possibilities.

18-8   Michael Praetorius (1571-1621), Bransle Gentil

(a)

(b)   **(c)**

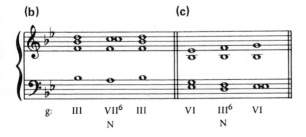

6. The passing $^6_3$. Most often a passing $^6_3$ connects a root-position triad with its first inversion, as in the familiar progressions I-VII[6]-I[6], V-IV[6]-V[6], and II-I[6]-II[6]. On other scale degrees, the passing $^6_3$ is usually altered to form an applied VII[6] unless the effect of a leading-tone chord occurs naturally as in III-II[6]-III[6] in minor, which briefly tonicizes III (Example 18-9).

18-9

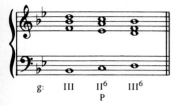

g: III   II⁶   III⁶
             P

Sometimes a $^6_3$ chord will connect two root-position triads a 3rd apart. We have already encountered this possibility in the preceding unit, in relation to sequences falling in 3rds (descending 5-6 technique). You will remember that such sequences normally begin with a motion from I down to VI, the two chords connected by a V⁶. A passing V⁶ can also introduce an applied chord as part of a descending progression from I to a tonicized V; the applied chord will be VII⁶ or V$^4_3$ of V. Example 18-10a illustrates the simplest version of this possibility. Very frequently, especially in duple time, the applied chord will be extended in order to permit the goal V to fall on a strong beat; characteristically, the lengthened chord will be animated by a suspension into the leading tone of V (18-10b and 18-10c).

18-10

(a)   **(b)**

I   (V⁶) VII⁶   V   I   (V⁶) VII⁷⁻⁶   V

(c) Bach, Well-Tempered Clavier II, Fugue 1

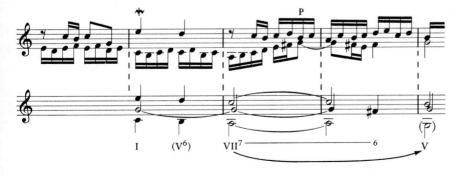

I   (V⁶)   VII⁷ —————————— 6   V

7. Motion in 3rds. Parallel $\frac{6}{3}$ chords normally occur in stepwise motion, as in the earlier examples of this unit. Parallel $\frac{6}{3}$'s can also leap in 3rds, though not very frequently and never for very long (Example 18-11a). Sometimes a stepwise progression will conceal an underlying motion in 3rds. Thus the Mendelssohn excerpt in Example 18-2 contains a two-bar pattern, repeated sequentially in descending 3rds: I-(VI^6)-(IV^6)-II^6 (Example 18-11b).

18-11

(a)

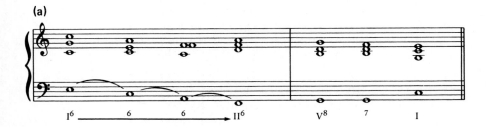

(b) bass line of Example 18-2, reduction

8. "VI^6" and "III^6" representing I and V. Excerpts from compositions by Chopin and Brahms (Examples 18-12 and 18-13) seem to feature VI^6 as their opening chord. In the Chopin, however, the 6th above the bass decorates the 5th, and in the Brahms, the 6th substitutes for the 5th; the chords function as *tonics*, not submediants (compare Example 4-10b). In the Chopin, the apparent "VI^6" results from a neighboring motion; the C♯ of the accompaniment moves directly to the B that follows; in a manner less immediately apparent, it continues the first note of the melodic line. In the Brahms, the 6th displaces the 5th entirely. However, we hear the bass tone of bar 1 as a tonic—an impression confirmed as correct by the subsequent course of the music in which the 5th, A, is implied as the point of departure for this 6th.

18-12   Chopin, Nocturne, Op. 62/2

18-13   Brahms, Piano Concerto, Op. 15, I

$\frac{6}{3}$ chords can embellish or substitute for $\frac{5}{3}$'s on any degree of the scale. These possibilities, however, are most significant in connection with the tonic and dominant degrees; $\hat{1}$ and $\hat{5}$ are such strong scale degrees that their harmonic force can be felt even when they do not support a $\frac{5}{3}$ chord. Just as "VI^6" is often a variant of I rather than an inversion of VI, so, too, "III^6" can function as a decoration of or substitute for V. In Example 18-14, bars 14 and 15 form an expansion of V. In the course of this expansion, the melody moves up from $\hat{2}$ to $\hat{4}$, the E of bar 14 functioning as a passing tone. The G in the bass that supports this passing tone functions as V; the chord, therefore, is not a III^6 but part of an expanded dominant. In Example 18-15, the top voice of bar 7 duplicates that of bar 3. The 6th above the bass makes this repetition possible without at all contradicting the impression of a V-I cadence.

18-14   Bach, Chorale 11

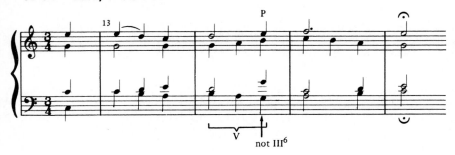

18-15   Haydn, Symphony No. 101, IV

If a 6th decorates or substitutes for a 5th over V in minor, an apparent augmented triad (in ⁶₃ position) will result. Most instances of "augmented III" in minor are examples of this usage; as far as their function is concerned, these are not III chords at all, but V's (Example 18-16).

18-16   Bach, Air   (from *Suite No. 3*)

9. Synopsis of $\frac{6}{3}$ functions. Example 18-17 lists the important contrapuntal functions of $\frac{6}{3}$ chords. All these functions have been explained in either this or a preceding unit (especially Unit 16). Thus, although a few of the progressions may be unfamiliar, you should have no difficulty in understanding their significance.

18-17

(a) neighboring   **(b) passing**   **(c) passing**   **(d) passing**

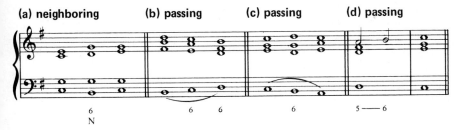

(e) expanding $\frac{5}{3}$ **(f) substituting for $\frac{5}{3}$**   **(g) substituting for $\frac{5}{3}$**

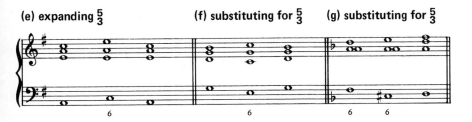

(h) voice leading   **(i) voice leading**   **(j) 6 displacing 5**   **(k) 6 displacing 5**

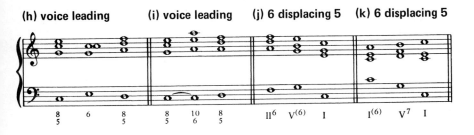

(l) moving in 3rds (from 5-6)

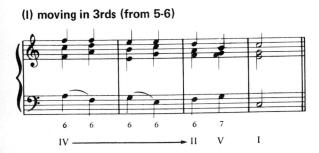

POINTS FOR REVIEW

1. Extended passages in parallel motion in which the outer voices typically move in 6ths are characteristic of $\frac{6}{3}$ chords. In four voices, careful doubling is necessary to avoid parallel octaves (Example 18-5).

2. 10ths between the outer voices are not suitable for extended motion (danger of 5ths), but brief segments may occur, often as the result of voice exchange and often involving the use of a $\frac{5}{3}$ chord (Examples 18-6 and 18-7).

3. Other contrapuntal uses of $\frac{6}{3}$ chords are as
   a. neighboring chords (Examples 18-8)
   b. passing chords (Examples 18-9 and 18-10)
   c. chords allowing motion in 3rds (Example 18-11)

4. "VI⁶" and "III⁶" usually stand for I and V (Examples 18-12, 18-13, and 18-14).

EXERCISES

NOTE. In instrumental textures, including figured-bass realizations, passages in parallel $\frac{6}{3}$ chords are often set for three voices. However, it would be a good idea for you to use four voices in these exercises to gain practice in working out the doublings.

1. Preliminaries: figured-bass fragments.

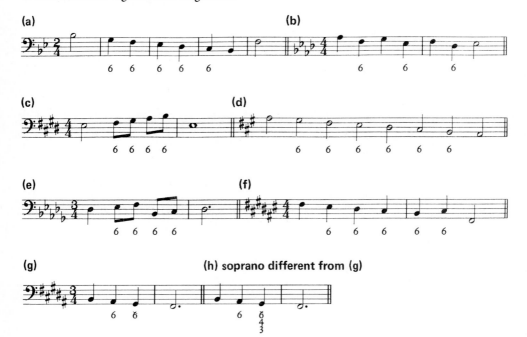

2. Figured bass (adapted from Handel). Because of the high register of Handel's
   bass, vocal ranges need not be strictly observed.

3. Figured bass (adapted from Handel).

4. Melody (adapted from Handel).

*don't harmonize

19

$\frac{6}{4}$-Chord Techniques

19-1   Beethoven, String Quartet, Op. 18/2, II

1. The double nature of the $\frac{6}{4}$ chord. The $\frac{6}{4}$ chord G-C-E occurs twice with identical spacing and doubling in the first three bars of a string quartet movement by Beethoven (Example 19-1). But although they contain the same tones, the two $\frac{6}{4}$ chords function in very different ways. The first arises out of arpeggiations within tonic harmony. It functions as an inversion of I$\frac{5}{3}$ and is treated by the composer as a consonance: both the bass tone and the 4th, C, are approached and left by leap. The second $\frac{6}{4}$, of course, is the cadential type familiar since Unit 10; in this chord the 4th is a dissonance, resolving to B by stepwise descent.

This excerpt illustrates the most striking feature of the $\frac{6}{4}$ chord; unlike any other chord, it is sometimes consonant and sometimes dissonant. Whether it is one or the other does not depend on the chord itself—as we saw, in the Beethoven the $\frac{6}{4}$'s are identical—but on how it functions *in context*. The double nature of the $\frac{6}{4}$ results from the double nature of its most characteristic interval—the perfect 4th—which itself is sometimes consonant, sometimes dissonant (Unit 2, section 11). So in order to understand the various ways in which $\frac{6}{4}$ chords can come about, let's look at some of the ways a 4th might appear in two-part texture (Example 19-2).

19-2

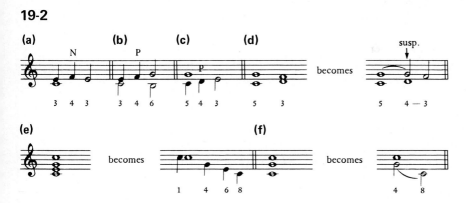

19-2a shows the 4th as a neighboring tone; in 19-2b and c the 4th is a passing tone. Note that sometimes it is the motion of the upper voice that produces the 4th (19-2a and b) while at other times (19-2c) it is the motion of the lower voice. In 19-2d the 4th is a suspension, as frequently occurs in familiar cadential $\frac{6}{4}$'s. In all four of these progressions the 4th is heard as a dissonance and is resolved by step.

In other situations, however, the 4th can be heard as consonant. If a triad (19-2e) or triadic interval (19-2f) is arpeggiated in the bass, for example, the 4th that might arise is consonant because it forms part of the unfolding of a consonant chord; the first $\frac{6}{4}$ chord of our Beethoven excerpt relates directly to the technique illustrated in 19-2e.

Example 19-3 shows the procedures described above in four-voice settings; here the 4ths of Example 19-2 become $\frac{6}{4}$ chords of various types, all of which we will discuss in the following pages.

19-3

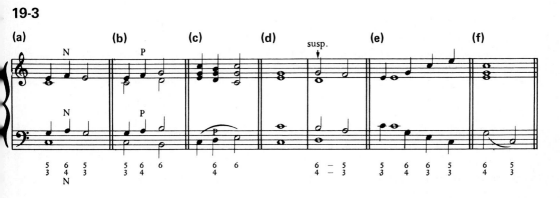

DISSONANT $\frac{6}{4}$ CHORDS

2. Three main types. Most dissonant $\frac{6}{4}$ chords belong to one of three main categories: the accented $\frac{6}{4}$ ($\frac{6-5}{4-3}$), the neighboring $\frac{6}{4}$, and the passing $\frac{6}{4}$. Since these chords derive their meaning completely from their relation to a larger context, and since even a slight difference in context can alter their significance, it is impossible (and unnecessary) to categorize every conceivable situation in which $\frac{6}{4}$ chords might appear. We will present only the most typical and important usages and a few particularly suggestive exceptional cases. If you understand the principles discussed in this unit, you will have a good basis for understanding other $\frac{6}{4}$ usages you may encounter.

3. Accented $\frac{6}{4}$ chords. Example 19-4 contains four $\frac{6}{4}$ chords. One of them (bar 2, beat 3) is a passing $\frac{6}{4}$ and will be discussed later. The other three are metrically accented relative to the chords of resolution—that is, they all resolve (over a stationary bass) from a stronger to a weaker beat. Two of these accented $\frac{6}{4}$'s are examples of the familiar cadential $\frac{6}{4}$ (bars 4 and 7). The one that begins bar 2, however, does not occur at a cadence, nor does it resolve to a dominant. But in all other respects it resembles the cadential $\frac{6}{4}$. The 6th and 4th, metrically accented, move down by step to the 5th and 3rd of the chord of resolution—in this case, VI. We use the term *accented $\frac{6}{4}$* for chords of this type—those that are metrically accented and that resolve over a stationary bass. The cadential $\frac{6}{4}$ is the most important type but, as the Mozart excerpt shows, it is by no means the only possibility. Other accented $\frac{6}{4}$'s closely resemble the cadential type. The principles of doubling and voice leading are the same (review Unit 10); so is the chord's basic function—to delay the arrival of an expected melodic or harmonic event. Accented $\frac{6}{4}$'s—including cadential ones—depend on their chords of resolution; they do not function as inversions of a root-position triad. This fact should be reflected in any chordal analysis. In bar 2 of the Mozart, therefore, the correct labeling is as shown, *not* II$\frac{6}{4}$-VI.

Accented $\frac{6}{4}$'s can occur on several scale degrees, $\hat{6}$ in major, as in the Mozart, being a particularly frequent choice. On other scale degrees, avoid a "resolution" to a diminished $\frac{5}{3}$ except in three-part texture. On $\hat{7}$ in major and raised $\hat{7}$ in minor, doubling the 6th of the $\frac{6}{4}$ and resolving to V$\frac{6}{5}$ rather than to VII$\frac{5}{3}$ will prevent such a resolution. Example 19-5a shows this possibility in major. In minor (19-5b), the $\frac{6}{4}$ contains a diminished 4th. Such a $\frac{6}{4}$ appears to be the second inversion of an augmented triad, but since the accented $\frac{6}{4}$ results from melodic motion rather than inversion, the "augmented" triad is nonfunctional here.

19-4   Mozart, Piano Sonata, K. 330, II

19-5   Schubert, Nacht und Träume

(a)

(b) in minor

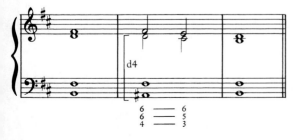

4. Neighboring ⁶₄ chords. Example 19-6 illustrates the second important type of dissonant ⁶₄, the *neighboring* ⁶₄. In this excerpt neighboring figures 5̂-6̂-5̂ and 3̂-4̂-3̂ decorate the 5th and 3rd of tonic harmony. This type of ⁶₄ arises out of neighboring motions performed above a stationary bass by two upper voices that typically move in parallel 3rds, 6ths, or 10ths.

19-6   Beethoven, Variations, Op. 34

Usually the soprano will take one of the neighboring figures—either 5̂-6̂-5̂ (as in the Beethoven) or 3̂-4̂-3̂, as in Example 19-7.

19-7   Brahms, Variations on a Theme by Haydn, Op. 56a

The bass of the neighboring ⁶₄ is generally doubled. Usually this type of ⁶₄ is unaccented, falling on a metrically weaker place than the ⁵₃ that precedes it, thus forming a kind of opposite to the accented ⁶₄. Sometimes the neighboring ⁶₄ is repeated on the next strong beat, as in bar 2 of Example 19-8, the beginning of a theory exercise written by Mozart for one of his students.

19-8   Mozart, Exercise for Barbara Ployer

As with the accented $\frac{6}{4}$, the neighboring type functions best when the $\frac{5}{3}$ chord it decorates is not diminished.

5. Passing $\frac{6}{4}$ chords (above a moving bass). Of the various types of passing $\frac{6}{4}$'s, the most important is V$\frac{6}{4}$ connecting I and I^6, as in Example 19-4 in the last half of bar 2, where V$\frac{6}{4}$ forms a stepwise connection between I^6 and I$\frac{5}{3}$ (compare VII^6 and V$\frac{4}{3}$). The passing function of this chord is obvious. In this usage the 4th above the bass is a stable tone, the 5th of the tonic chord within which the $\frac{6}{4}$ moves. The active, dissonant element in this type of $\frac{6}{4}$ chord, therefore, is not the 4th but the bass tone. When a passing $\frac{6}{4}$ is used in this way, a voice exchange frequently occurs between the bass and one of the upper voices (usually the soprano), as is evident in the Mozart excerpt. Such an exchange will often cause a doubling of the bass tone of the $\frac{6}{4}$, but the consonant 4th is also a possible doubling. Passing $\frac{6}{4}$'s can appear either on unaccented (most frequent) or accented beats or parts of beats.

Example 19-9 shows two other possibilities: expanding II and IV. The passing $\frac{6}{4}$ can also serve to expand seventh chords (Example 19-10).

19-9

(a)   **(b)**

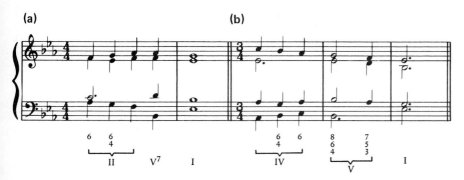

19-10   Mendelssohn, Trio, Op. 49, I

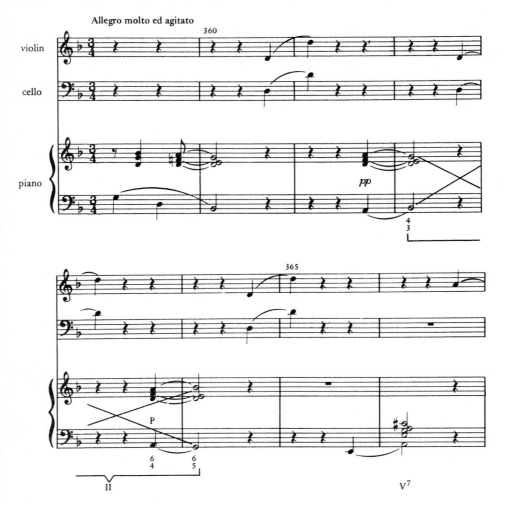

A passing $^6_4$ between IV^6 and II^6_5 (less often II^6) is *very frequent*; the outer-voice motion is usually in 6ths (Example 19-11).

19-11   Bach, Chorale   (from the motet *Jesu, meine Freude*)

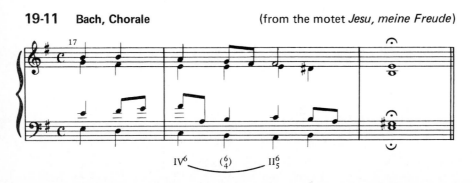

Sometimes a passing $^6_4$ occurs above a descending bass without any motion in the upper voices (Example 19-12). Because of the preponderance of common tones, we do not really hear a change of chord at the entrance of the $^6_4$; such $^6_4$'s have little vertical identity and hardly count as chords, unless the composer emphasizes them by long duration.

19-12

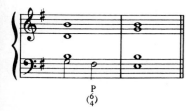

6. **Passing $^6_4$ chords (above a sustained bass).** Sometimes a $^6_4$ formation results from passing tones in parallel 3rds, 6ths, or 10ths moving up from the 5th and 3rd of a $^5_3$ chord. In this type of $^{5-6}_{3-4}$, the $^6_4$ is virtually always metrically weak (Example 19-13). In many ways this type of passing $^6_4$ resembles the neighboring $^6_4$.

19-13

(a) Bach, Geistliche Lieder, No. 47

(b)

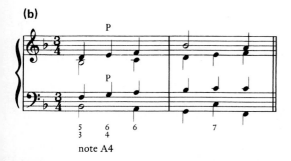

note A4

A passing $\frac{6}{4}$ above a sustained dominant can connect V^7 with V^5_3, as in Example 19-14. In such cases, the motion to the $\frac{6}{4}$ does *not* resolve the 7th of V^7, despite the downward motion. The 6th of the $\frac{6}{4}$ is a passing tone, not a goal tone; therefore it does not form an appropriate resolution of the dissonance. Normally a resolution of the 7th will follow the dominant. In the aria from which our illustration is taken, the resolution appears several bars later, transferred to another voice (bass, bars 63-64).

19-14   Mozart, Mi tradì   (from *Don Giovanni*, K. 527)

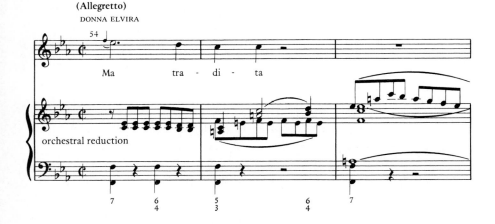

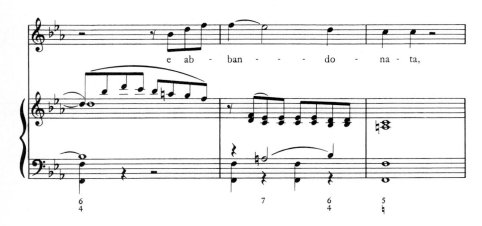

translation: But betrayed and abandoned,
[I still pity him.]

7. Elaborated $\frac{6}{4}$ chords (above a sustained bass); the progression $\frac{8\text{-}7\text{-}6\text{-}5}{6\text{-}5\text{-}4\text{-}3}$. Passing or neighboring $\frac{6}{4}$'s over a held bass can be elaborated in various ways. In Example 19-15a, the first-violin part (bar 3) is "polyphonic"; the single melodic line suggests two voices—$\hat{7}$-$\hat{8}$ and $\hat{4}$-$\hat{3}$. This creates the possibility for two $\frac{6}{4}$'s above the sustained bass.

19-15   Haydn, String Quartet, Op. 76/5, II

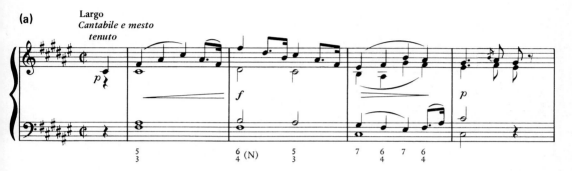

(b) reduction

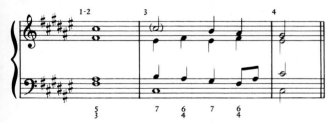

Very frequently a voice exchange accompanies a soprano line like the one in Example 19-15; Example 19-16 illustrates.

19-16

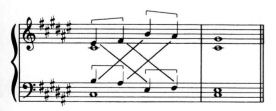

Example 19-17 illustrates another frequent possibility: two upper voices can descend in parallel 3rds, 6ths, or 10ths, creating the interval progression $^{8\text{-}7\text{-}6\text{-}5}_{6\text{-}5\text{-}4\text{-}3}$. This progression can have various meanings. Here it elaborates the resolution of a neighboring $^6_4$ over an extended I.

19-17   Mozart, Eine kleine Nachtmusik, K. 525, II

8. $^6_4$ chords as incomplete neighbors (above a sustained bass). This is similar to both the passing $^6_4$ (section 6) and the neighboring $^6_4$ (section 4); Example 19-18 illustrates. Following such a $^{5\text{-}6}_{3\text{-}4}$ by an accented $^{6\text{-}5}_{4\text{-}3}$, usually with root motion by ascending 5th, produces one of the few progressions where two $^6_4$ chords follow each other immediately (19-18b).

19-18

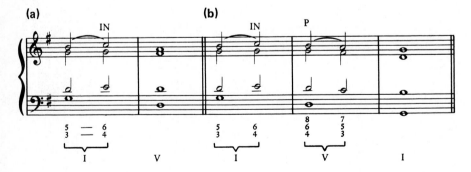

SPECIAL TREATMENT OF CADENTIAL $\frac{6}{4}$ CHORDS

9. Unprepared 4ths; transferred resolution of the 4th. In four-part vocal style, the dissonant character of the cadential $\frac{6}{4}$ imposes certain restrictions on its use—restrictions we discussed in Unit 10. In principle these restrictions hold good for instrumental music as well. However, departures from the norms of voice leading and dissonance treatment occur fairly often with cadential $\frac{6}{4}$ chords in instrumental style. Sometimes the 4th—normally a suspension or an accented passing tone—will enter by leap, as in Example 19-19. Such a leap to the 4th often results from the decoration of a stepwise line; thus the voice leading is not really as exceptional as it might at first seem. See also Example 10-3c.

19-19   Mozart, Wind Serenade, K. 388, I

Sometimes composers will treat the *resolution* of the 4th with a certain freedom. In Example 19-20, the 4th is stated in the soprano and its resolution transferred into the alto. This allows the soprano to ascend after the 4th and to express the melodic motion of a 3rd—an important element in this piece. Motion upward from the 4th (the resolution transferred to another voice) occurs quite often in music of the classical period—especially in Mozart's.

19-20   Beethoven, Bagatelle, Op. 119/11

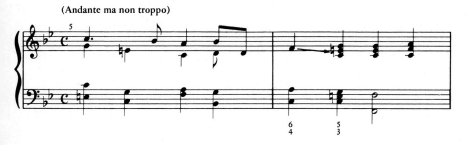

Example 19-21 shows another type of transferred resolution—into the bass, producing a V$^6_5$. Such progressions occur rather frequently, though not where a strong V-I cadence (with root-position V immediately before I) is needed.

19-21   Mozart, String Quintet, K. 516, I

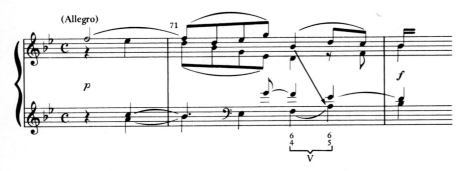

In free textures, composers will sometimes let an inner voice double a 4th that appears in the soprano (see Example 19-4, bar 7). One of these 4ths will have to move up; if both resolved down, parallel octaves would result.

10. Expanding the cadential $^6_4$. The tension created by the cadential $^6_4$ can be enhanced by expanding it. In Example 19-22, a bass arpeggio causes the expansion.

19-22   Mozart, Der Hölle Rache   (from *Die Zauberflöte*)

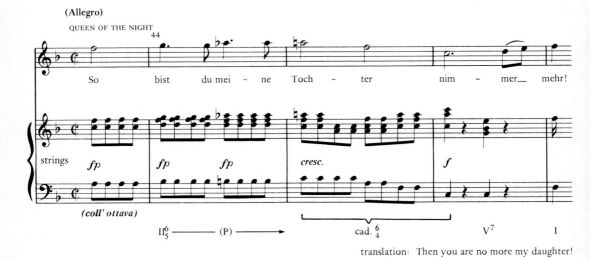

translation: Then you are no more my daughter!

At the end of Brahms' *Ein deutsches Requiem* (Example 19-23), a double neighbor prolongs the bass of the $^6_4$.

19-23   Brahms, Ein deutsches Requiem, Op. 45, VII

translation: [Blessed] are the dead, who die in the Lord.

11. Interpolations between the $\frac{6}{4}$ and its resolution. Frequently a neighboring chord separates the $\frac{6}{4}$ from its resolution (Example 19-24). Compare Example 17-21.

19-24   Bach, Chorale 220

An expansion of this same principle—interpolating material between a cadential $\frac{6}{4}$ and the dominant to which it resolves—forms the basis for the cadenza in classical concerto movements. The very word *cadenza*—which simply means "cadence" in Italian—indicates its cadential function. A cadenza from a concerto would be too long to quote here, but the principle is very well illustrated by the miniature cadenza from the first movement of Beethoven's Piano Sonata, Op. 2, No. 3, a sonata movement that is written to sound very much like a concerto (Example 19-25).

19-25 Beethoven, Piano Sonata, Op. 2/3, I

12. Metrically weak cadential $\frac{6}{4}$ chords. $\frac{6}{4}$ chords that resolve to cadential dominants are virtually always metrically strong. Occasionally, however, we encounter
such $\frac{6}{4}$'s on the weak beat preceding the dominant. Most of these "deviant" $\frac{6}{4}$
chords come about through an anticipation of V in the bass that coincides with a
passing tone in one of the upper parts. In such a case, the $\frac{6}{4}$—instead of resulting
from a delaying progression in one of the upper voices—results from a bass that
arrives at its goal just before the strong beat where it is expected. Example 19-26,
from a Schubert lied, illustrates.

19-26   Schubert, Die Liebe hat gelogen

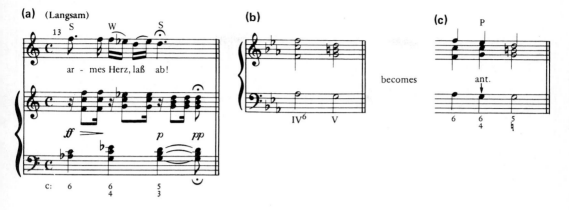

Of the great composers, Schubert and Chopin probably used these "anticipating" $^6_4$'s the most. Review Example 14-9, bars 6-7. There the metric irregularity results in part from motivic design: the repetition of the rising 4th in the bass,
D♯-G♯, G♯-C♯.

CONSONANT $^6_4$ CHORDS

13. The arpeggio $^6_4$. Review Example 19-1 and you will easily see that the first $^6_4$
chord (bar 1) has a fundamentally different meaning from any of the dissonant
$^6_4$'s we have been discussing. The obvious fact that all the voices approach and
leave the chord by leap points up this difference in meaning. The bass arpeggiates
the tonic triad; the $^6_4$ results from the arpeggiation. Because it arises out of and
derives from the root position of the triad, this $^6_4$ is heard as *consonant*. Consonant $^6_4$'s tend to occur in music with considerable rhythmic activity and where at
least some of the chords persist for a long time. Thus, such $^6_4$'s occur infrequently in chorale style, where chords change on almost every beat. Most consonant
$^6_4$'s are tonics, for the I is the chord most often expanded by arpeggiation. The
bass tone is frequently doubled; however, doubling the root or (less often) the
3rd is also possible.

14. The consonant $^{6\text{-}5}_{4\text{-}3}$. Most often the arpeggio $^6_4$ appears after the $^5_3$ chord that
makes it consonant. However in the music of some composers (Brahms in par-
ticular) the $^6_4$ will sometimes appear first; it is then stabilized "retrospectively"
by a $^5_3$ that follows it (Example 19-27). In such cases the $^6_4$ can represent the upper voices of a $^5_3$ chord whose bass is delayed.

19-27   Schumann, Albumblätter, Op. 99, V

15. The oscillating $\frac{6}{4}$ (waltz or march type). In Examples 19-1 and 19-27, the consonant $\frac{6}{4}$'s appear *above* the bass of the governing $\frac{5}{3}$ chords; in context, therefore, the bass of the $\frac{6}{4}$ functions as an inner-voice tone of the $\frac{5}{3}$. But sometimes the bass of the $\frac{6}{4}$ appears *below* that of the $\frac{5}{3}$. This is particularly frequent in instrumental accompaniment patterns, such as those in waltzes or marches, where the bass of I oscillates between $\hat{1}$ and the $\hat{5}$ below it. The $\frac{6}{4}$'s appear on weak beats; if, as in waltzes, the bass normally moves in whole bars, the $\frac{6}{4}$'s will appear on the relatively weaker bars. The descending motion from $\hat{1}$ to $\hat{5}$ emphasizes the strong-weak metric pattern—hence the popularity of this idiom for dances and marches. The repeated $\hat{5}$'s seldom form part of the main bass line; they serve to extend the governing chord and to provide a characteristic rhythmic pattern. The $\frac{6}{4}$ chords they produce are heard as consonant and dependent on the preceding $\frac{5}{3}$'s. Example 19-28 illustrates.

19-28

(a) Chopin, Valse, Op. 34/1

(b) Mozart, Piano Sonata, K. 282, Menuetto II

SOME EXCEPTIONAL CASES

16. $^6_4$ **chords by voice exchange.** $^6_4$ chords often result from a kind of double voice exchange in which two two-note figures ($\hat{4}$-$\hat{3}$ and $\hat{6}$-$\hat{5}$) are interchanged. This voice exchange usually occurs within an extended subdominant, as in Example 19-29, where the IV becomes a II⁶ (5-6 technique) before moving on to the cadential V. Here the $^6_4$ has a passing function within the extended IV.

19-29   Mozart, Piano Sonata, K. 330, III

17. $^6_4$ **chords with augmented 4th ("VII$^6_4$").** Sometimes one encounters a $^6_4$ chord with an augmented 4th, built on $\hat{4}$ as bass tone. (In major, the augmented 4th lies between $\hat{4}$ and $\hat{7}$; in minor, between $\hat{4}$ and raised $\hat{7}$.) A literal analysis of these chords as "VII$^6_4$" would be correct as far as it goes but not particularly revealing

of their function. As Example 19-30 indicates, these $^6_4$'s function as incomplete V^4_2 chords; they normally occur only in three-part texture which explains their incomplete state. In music with a figured-bass accompaniment (Baroque trio sonatas, for example) the continuo player would most probably complete the $^4_2$ chord.

19-30   Mozart, Piano Concerto, K. 453, II

18. Dissonant or consonant: V or I? The two excerpts quoted in Example 19-31 illustrate how much the meaning of a $^6_4$ chord depends on context. In the Chopin, the E♭ minor $^6_4$ "ought to" resolve to a V (the excerpt shows the final cadence of the piece). Most exceptionally, the V chord does not appear—an instance of harmonic elision. But the bass progression suggests IV-V-I so unmistakably that the cadential function of this $^6_4$ can hardly be questioned; it stands for the embellishment of a V that is not literally present but that is nonetheless strongly implied.

In the Schumann excerpt, an E♭ major $^6_4$ appears *after* the cadential V; it is, in fact, the last chord in the piece. This $^6_4$ stands for I, not for V. In order to avoid a definite conclusion that would be out of keeping with the dreamy nature of Eusebius (a character Schumann invented who represented the poetic, gentle side of his personality), Schumann lets the inconclusive I$^6_4$ substitute for a final I. This consonant $^6_4$—unlike those discussed in sections 13-15—is stabilized not by its own root position, but by the harmonic implications of the context in which it occurs.

19-31

(a) Chopin, Prelude, Op. 28/14

(b) Schumann, Eusebius (from *Carnaval,* Op. 9)

"I_4^6"

(stands for I_3^5)

POINTS FOR REVIEW

1. $_4^6$ chords are sometimes dissonant and sometimes consonant.

2. The main types of dissonant $_4^6$ chords are accented ($_{4\text{-}3}^{6\text{-}5}$), neighboring, and passing.

3. Accented $_4^6$ chords include the familiar cadential type ($V_{4\text{-}3}^{6\text{-}5}$). On other scale degrees, accented $_4^6$'s resemble the cadential type (same doubling, same metric position, same descending resolution). They are particularly frequent on $\hat{6}$ in major.

4. Neighboring $_4^6$ chords (usually unaccented) result from the progression $_{3\text{-}4\text{-}3}^{5\text{-}6\text{-}5}$ above a stationary bass. The bass is usually doubled.

5. Passing $_4^6$ chords (above a moving bass) typically connect $_3^5$ and $_3^6$ positions of the same triad, often with voice exchange between the bass and an upper voice. The most frequent progression is V_4^6 connecting I and I^6, in which V_4^6 resembles VII^6 and V_3^4.

6. Other passing $_4^6$'s connect two positions of a seventh chord or connect a triad with a seventh chord. *Important usage:* $_4^6$ passing between IV^6 and II_5^6, with the outer voices usually in 6ths.

7. Passing $_4^6$ chords (above a sustained bass) sometimes result from passing tones moving up from the 5th and 3rd of a $_3^5$ chord. Another type is the $_4^6$ that connects V^7 and V_3^5.

8. Possibilities above a sustained dominant bass include the progression $_{6\text{-}5\text{-}4\text{-}3}^{8\text{-}7\text{-}6\text{-}5}$ and the voice exchange $\hat{4}\text{-}\hat{3}$, $\hat{7}\text{-}\hat{8}$.

9. The cadential $_4^6$ is often treated irregularly in instrumental style. (See sections 9-12.)

10. Consonant $_4^6$ chords include the arpeggio type, which results from a complete or incomplete arpeggio in the bass. This chord usually prolongs tonic harmony, with I_3^5 preceding I_4^6. Another consonant $_4^6$ is the oscillating (waltz or march) type.

11. $_4^6$ chords produced by voice exchange ($\hat{4}\text{-}\hat{3}$, $\hat{6}\text{-}\hat{5}$) often help to expand IV.

12. $_4^6$ chords with an augmented 4th on $\hat{7}$ in major or raised $\hat{7}$ in minor can substitute for V_2^4 in three-voice texture.

EXERCISES

NOTE. From now on, be prepared to explain the function of every $\frac{6}{4}$ chord you use. In setting melodies, never use a $\frac{6}{4}$ chord unless you have a clear idea of how it functions; sprinkling an exercise with $\frac{6}{4}$'s unrelated to their surroundings is one of the surest ways to botch your work.

1. Preliminaries. Using a different key for each progression, write an example of each of the following $\frac{6}{4}$ usages:

   a. $\begin{smallmatrix}6\text{-}5\\4\text{-}3\end{smallmatrix}$ on $\hat{6}$ in major

   b. $\begin{smallmatrix}6\text{-}6\\6\text{-}5\\4\text{-}3\end{smallmatrix}$ in minor. Which scale degree is appropriate?

   c. Passing $\frac{6}{4}$ (bass moves) between I^6 and I in major

   d. Passing $\frac{6}{4}$ (bass moves) between II^6_5 and II^7 in minor

   e. Passing $\frac{6}{4}$ (bass moves) between IV^6 and II^6_5 in major

   f. Neighboring $\frac{6}{4}$ (upper voices move) in minor

   g. Passing $\frac{6}{4}$ (upper voices move) in major

   h. $\frac{6}{4}$ arising out of bass arpeggiation in minor

   i. $\frac{6}{4}$ resulting from voice exchange ($\hat{6}$-$\hat{5}$ and $\hat{4}$-$\hat{3}$)

   j. $\frac{6}{4}$'s resulting from voice exchange over V in bass

2. Figured bass.

*voice exchange between soprano and tenor

3. Melody. Use one neighboring $\frac{6}{4}$ and at least two passing $\frac{6}{4}$'s—one between IV^6 and II^6_5.

4. Figured bass. (Keyboard style is possible.)

*voice exchange between bass and soprano

5. Melody and bass.

*If you harmonize this B♭ as a seventh chord, you will need two quarter notes in the tenor in the first half of bar 2 to avoid 5ths. Or you can treat the B♭ as a passing tone and not harmonize it.

ELEMENTS OF FIGURATION

20

Melodic Figuration

20-1 Schumann, Vogel als Prophet, Op. 82/6

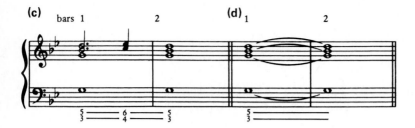

1. Figuration. A most striking aspect of Example 20-1 is Schumann's very expressive use of dissonant tones foreign to the chords against which they sound. These emphasized dissonances, together with the melody's wide range and rhythmic freedom (melodic ideas beginning before the bass and harmony) create something akin to the sound of a wild bird's song. The three successive reductions (b, c, and d) help clarify the meaning of this passage—in particular the meaning of the dissonant tones. The first reduction (20-1b) shows the melodic, rhythmic, and chordal framework of the passage. It seems almost surprisingly simple compared to the actual music, and although it reveals the tonal connections that unify the phrase, it also removes much of the music's individual flavor.

The term "figuration" refers to a melodic progression that animates a linear-harmonic substructure by means of quicker motion or rhythmic displacement. Figuration can occur in any voice, not just the soprano; it can occur in more than one voice at the same time. In the Schumann the elements or tones of figuration are the accented dissonances and quick arpeggiations that fill out the framework shown in the first reduction. The word "figuration" and the adjective form "figurated" are very old musical terms. Their derivation—from Latin *figurare,* to shape, to form—suggests the great importance of figuration as a constructive force in musical composition. The elements of figuration are part of the essential substance of music; though they are, in a sense, ornamental, they are by no means merely a decorative overlay. It would make as much sense to think of leaves and flowers as mere decorations on a tree.

Furthermore, whether or not we view a tone or group of tones as figuration depends on the perspective from which we perceive the music. Thus the first two bars of the Schumann phrase can be further reduced by eliminating the octave leaps and the melodic third G-Eb (20-1c). Even in this further reduction, however, the $^6_4$ chord of bar 1—which results from neighboring tones—can be regarded as the product of figuration at a deeper level. This would leave us with the G minor tonic chord as the ultimate reduction of the two bars (20-1d). In this unit and the next, we are going to concentrate on "surface" figurations—those of small dimension that do not produce a change of chord. Figuration varies according to medium, style, composer—even according to the character of an individual piece—far more than the chord usages of previous units. Nevertheless the elements of figuration can be classified into five fundamental types and their variants:

1. the chordal skip or arpeggio
2. the passing tone

3. the neighboring tone
4. the suspension
5. the anticipation

We will discuss each of these in turn, reserving the suspension and anticipation for Unit 21.

CHORDAL SKIPS (ARPEGGIOS)

2. Uses of the chordal skip. The terms chordal skip and arpeggio are interchangeable, although "arpeggio" tends to refer to an extended broken chord rather than to a single skip. Rapid arpeggios, as in the Schumann excerpt, are characteristic of instrumental writing; very often they serve to connect contrasting registers in a widely ranging melody. In chorale settings and in simple figured basses, arpeggiated motions tend to occur as single skips, often in a rhythm of two notes to a beat. Example 20-2 shows how they can help to intensify rhythmic activity (a) and break up parallel 5ths and octaves (b and c). In addition, they can improve melodic lines by varying a prevailing stepwise movement (d), by subdividing a large leap into smaller ones (e), or by introducing stepwise motion, especially in the bass (f).

20-2

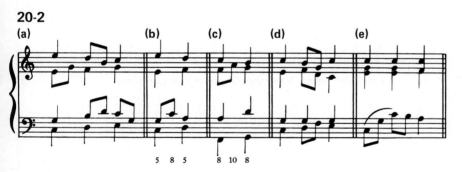

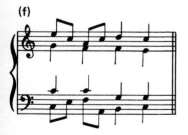

3. Polyphonic melody. Arpeggiation—moving from one to another tone of a chord—makes possible one of the basic resources of tonal melody: its ability to suggest two (or more) lines moving simultaneously. Example 20-3 provides a clear illustration. The "polyphonic" effect results from the fact that we hear important connections not just from one tone to the next but also among tones that are not immediately consecutive. Thus the D in bar 1 of the melody is heard as moving to the Eb of bar 2, an upper neighbor that returns to D in bar 3. And the Bb of bar 1 moves to the A of bar 2, a lower neighbor that, in principle, returns to Bb. However it is not always desirable (or even possible) for a composer to incorporate into a melody every tone of the implied polyphony. The Bb to which the A should move is clearly implied by the context; therefore Schubert can leave it out of the melodic line without creating a loose end (20-3b).

Polyphonically conceived melodies usually occur in the soprano. However other parts, especially the bass, can also reveal polyphonic implications, as in bars 1 and 2 of the Schubert.

20-3   Schubert, Impromptu, D. 935, Op. 142/3

(a) Andante

(b) reduction of bars 1-3

4. Chordal skips and forbidden parallels. Unless they are of very brief duration, chordal skips are effective in breaking up forbidden parallels (as in Example 20-2b and c). The pacing of the figuration, of course, will have to conform to the prevailing rhythmic structure. In his chorale settings, where eighth-note figuration is the norm, Bach often uses a chordal skip in eighth-note rhythm to break up parallels (Example 20-4).

20-4   Bach, Chorale 96

The very stability that allows chord members to break up parallels imposes upon them the obligation not to cause any. In most situations 5ths and octaves created by chordal skips count as faulty voice leading and must be avoided. Never write chordal skips without checking for forbidden parallels (Example 20-5).

20-5

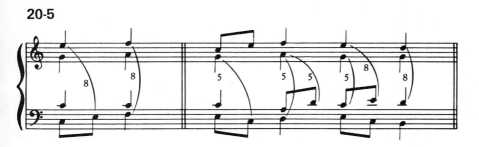

In more extended arpeggios, especially in quick note values, not every tone is necessarily part of the basic voice leading. In such situations, what might look like parallels will not necessarily sound like them, particularly if the tones in question are in a weak rhythmic position. The Bach chorale prelude excerpt of Example 20-6 illustrates.

20-6   Bach, Ich ruf' zu dir   (from *Orgelbüchlein*)

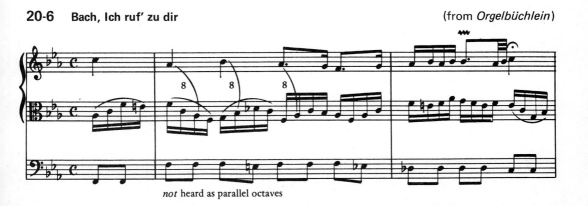

not heard as parallel octaves

PASSING AND NEIGHBORING TONES

5. Uses of the passing tone. As a detail of figuration the passing tone generally fills in the interval of a 3rd (Example 20-7) either within one chord (a) or from one chord to another (b).

20-7

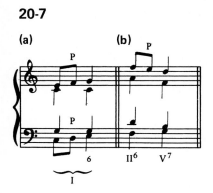

Passing tones are usually dissonant, although a 5-6 or 6-5 progression can produce a consonant passing tone. The basic function of the passing tone is a transitional one—to lead from one stable tone to another. In keeping with this transitional character, passing tones normally occur on unaccented beats or parts of the beat. Accented passing tones (section 8) occur quite frequently, but the very fact that we have to refer to them as "accented" reveals their special nature. Nobody has to call a normal passing tone "unaccented"; it is taken for granted that it is rhythmically weak.

Very often passing tones are optional. That is, whether or not to use them depends on the character and design of the place in question. In a few situations, however, passing tones are virtually obligatory in that melodic continuity depends on them. Example 20-8 shows a frequent melodic and harmonic pattern: a descending line from $\hat{5}$ to $\hat{1}$ in the soprano supported by I-IV-V-I. The passing tone A (over IV) is normally required in order to secure a stepwise motion to the goal tone, F. (On the other hand, if the last tone in the soprano were changed to A, the passing tone would be optional. Why?)

20-8

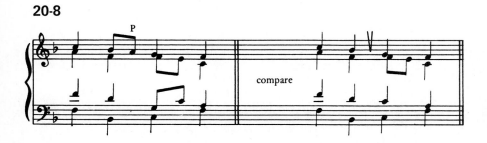

Example 20-9 shows another frequent progression, in which I^6 functions as a passing chord between II and V; a bass passing tone would usually follow I^6.

20-9

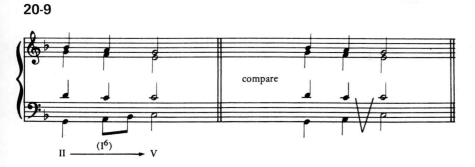

II ———— (I^6) ——→ V

Two consecutive passing tones can fill in a 4th (Example 20-10); an extended passing motion can fill in a still larger interval, in which case one or more tones will belong to the prevailing chord.

20-10   Beethoven, String Quartet, Op. 59/1, I

6. Uses of the neighboring tone. Unlike the passing tone, which connects two different tones, the neighbor decorates a stationary tone. Just like the passing tone, however, the neighboring tone can be unaccented (the norm) or accented, dissonant (the norm) or consonant. The familiar ornament known as a mordent is simply a rapid neighboring figure used to emphasize a tone. Sometimes the mordent is motivically related to other neighboring motions written in regular notation, as in Example 20-11.

20-11   Bach, Well-Tempered Clavier II, Fugue 1

Various combinations of upper and lower neighbors, including the familiar double neighbor, form idiomatic figures in many styles. Not in chorale style, however. Example 20-12a shows the double-neighbor figure in a rather unusual rhythm, emphasizing the upper neighbors. In Example 20-12b the five-note ornament consists of main tone, upper neighbor, main tone, lower neighbor, and main tone.

20-12

(a) Mozart, String Quartet, K. 465, II

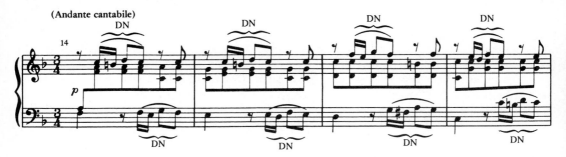

(b) Mahler, Das Lied von der Erde, VI

7. The incomplete neighbor. This figure, as we know, has only one stepwise connection with the main tone whereas the regular neighbor has two. Incomplete neighbors decorate either the preceding or the following tone. Of the two possibilities (both are illustrated in Example 20-13a), the first occurs more frequently. Sometimes called the "escape tone" or "échappée," this type of figuration is often an upper incomplete neighbor that decorates the initial tone of a descending second. It can also occur in the reverse direction as in the excerpt from Franck (20-13b).

Example 20-13c illustrates the double incomplete neighbor; the main tone is preceded by both neighbors. Example 20-13d shows figuration on two levels—the E♭ is an incomplete neighbor which decorates D♭, itself a neighbor of C.

20-13

(a)

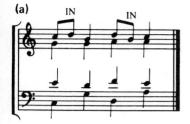

(b) Franck, Symphony in D minor, I

(c) Schubert, Piano Sonata, D. 894, IV

(d) Chopin, Etude, Op. 25/2

Especially when they are dissonant, incomplete neighbors attract a certain amount of attention; a dissonance is emphasized when it is preceded or followed by a leap. Therefore incomplete neighbors occur more often in the soprano than in the other, less prominent voices.

8. Accented passing and neighboring tones. Example 20-14 contains passing tones, neighbors, and incomplete neighbors on the strong part of the beat. As Example 20-15 indicates, accented passing and neighboring tones can be regarded as displacements of the normal, unaccented kind.

20-14   Handel, "Alexander's Feast" Concerto, IV

20-15

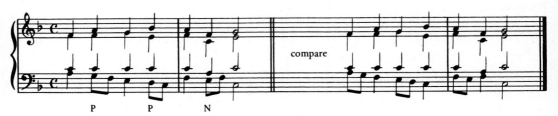

Independence of parts and rhythmic variety can benefit from the use of accented and unaccented tones of figuration in different voices; rhythms in different voices that combine into a continuous movement are termed *complementary*. Such rhythms occur in Example 20-16. Note the passing motions in parallel 10ths between the bass and alto (bar 1, beats 3 and 4). These create an excellent effect—as do parallel 3rds and 6ths used similarly—so long as they are not overdone.

20-16   complementary rhythms

An important idiom consists of an incomplete neighbor (escape tone) followed by an accented passing tone, the two tones forming the decoration of a melodic progression of a second, usually a descending one (Example 20-17).

20-17

9. Accented tones and harmonization. The presence of accented passing and neighboring tones can complicate the setting of melodies and unfigured basses. In order to harmonize a tune like the one in Example 20-14, we must be able to recognize that the chord tones do not fall on the beat; in order to do that we must perceive the large-scale organization of the melody—in particular, the rising line C-D-E that starts with the first downbeat. Example 20-18 shows a melodic fragment followed by a correct and an incorrect interpretation. In the latter the 7th of V^7 does not resolve. Another clue is the leap a^1-f^2 toward the end of the first measure. In many cases, however, trial and error—and above all, using your ear—is the only way to arrive at a correct solution.

20-18

(a)

10. Accented tones and figured basses. In figured basses, accented passing and neighboring tones are often—though not always—figured. To interpret the numbers (they are very confusing at first!), add 1 to each of them if the next bass tone is a step lower (much the most frequent) and subtract 1 if it is a step higher. If your arithmetic is correct, the result will indicate the proper chord above the following chord tone. Example 20-19 explains.

20-19

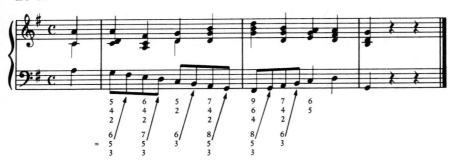

11. Accented incomplete neighbors; "appoggiaturas." Accented incomplete neighbors are metrically strong nonchord tones that are approached by leap and resolved by step, the resolution almost always *down* unless the accented neighbor happens to be a leading tone. Example 20-20 shows a familiar sequence pattern decorated with accented incomplete neighbors. This type of figuration occurs very frequently, but not in chorale style.

20-20

Accented dissonances of various types are often called *appoggiaturas* (Italian *appoggiare,* to lean). This term originated in the field of performance, not theory; its primary use is to indicate a one-note ornamental prefix, usually accented, that occurs with great frequency in Baroque and Classical music. As a theoretical term, "appoggiatura" is most usefully employed as a substitute for the more cumbersome "accented incomplete neighbor."

12. The turn. Another familiar ornament—the turn—combines an accented and an unaccented neighbor. As an embellishment, the turn is often indicated by a conventional sign (∾) but similar patterns often occur in regular notation, as in the Bach fugue subject in Example 20-21.

20-21   Bach, Well-Tempered Clavier II, Fugue 10

13. Chromatic passing and neighboring tones. A convenient and logical way to introduce the study of chromaticism is through chromatic passing and neighboring tones, for as details of figuration these can "color" the music without changing its basically diatonic character. Chromatic passing tones divide a whole step into a chromatic plus a diatonic half step. Usually the chromatic half step comes first. That is, the chromatic passing tone will usually sharp the preceding note when moving up (F-F♯-G or B♭-B♮-C) and flat it when moving down (A-A♭-G or E♭-E♭♭-D♭). Example 20-22 illustrates.

20-22

Chromatically altered neighbors occur frequently. If the diatonic neighbor is a whole step away from the main tone, bringing it a half step closer makes the two tones sound more connected. Chromatically altered neighbors are normally notated as minor 2nds, not augmented primes. Chromatic lower neighbors, which produce the melodically active effect of leading tones, occur more often than upper ones. At times, the chromatic alteration is almost obligatory in that it prevents ugly repetitions and makes for a better connection with the main tones. Play Example 20-23 as written and then with diatonic neighbors; compare the effect.

20-23

Chromatically altered neighbors often form part of compound figures such as the turn or the double neighbor (review Example 20-12a). Chromatic appoggiaturas create a particularly pungent effect, as we can hear in Example 20-1. The accented dissonances in that Schumann excerpt are, for the most part, chromatically raised lower neighbors.

14. Figurations using 6̂ and 7̂ in minor. Figurated passages in minor generally use the ascending or descending forms of the melodic minor scale depending on the direction of the line. This is not invariable, however. What goes on in the other parts and the larger harmonic context sometimes lead to the use of lowered 6̂ and 7̂ ascending and of raised 7̂ and 6̂ descending. Example 20-24 provides an interesting illustration. The descending bass line E-D♮-C♮-B brings about the use of C♮ and D♮ in the right-hand part, even though the line rises (bar 1, 1st half). At the beginning of bar 2, the V chord motivates the use of D♯ and C♯ in a descending line. Note that when the left hand takes over the eighth-note figure in bars 2 and 3, C♯ and D♯ now occur in the ascending phase of the line. Why?

20-24   Bach, Partita No. 6, Air

15. Parallels caused by passing and neighboring tones. As we mentioned earlier, the way in which composers treat figuration varies considerably depending on such factors as medium, style, tempo, and rhythm. Nowhere is this variability more evident than in connection with parallel 5ths, octaves, and unisons caused by tones of figuration. Since these tones form what one might call a surface layer of the musical texture, parallels caused by them have a different character and meaning from those caused by the more stable elements of the underlying voice leading. Sometimes—especially when the basic voice leading can be perceived clearly—"surface" parallels weaken neither the independence of voices nor the tonal coherence of a passage. They occur in the music of all the great composers. But their admissibility depends so much upon the particular character of a passage that no one can formulate "rules" to fit every conceivable situation. All we can do is indicate some very general guidelines.*

In general, unisons and octaves caused by figuration are more problematic than 5ths. (Of course we are not referring to doublings in free textures as discussed in Unit 5, section 14.) Although such unisons and octaves sometimes appear in a composition (mainly as a result of chordal skips), they do so much less often than 5ths, and you should avoid them.

Fifths—especially when produced by dissonant passing and neighboring tones (unaccented or accented)—occur much more freely than unisons or octaves. In particular when the 5ths arise out of relatively rapid figuration, the listener can easily take in the basic voice leading; the seeming parallels, then, create no ill effect whatever. In Example 20-25, an accented neighboring tone produces unobjectionable "surface" 5ths.

*Sometimes the masters themselves (Chopin is a notable example) were unsure whether to admit a particular case of "surface" parallels, as we can sometimes see from the way in which they revised their music.

20-25   Brahms, Paganini Variations, Op. 35, Book I, Finale

A consonant passing or neighboring tone forms a more stable element of the texture than a dissonant one. Therefore 5ths produced by such a consonant tone, like those produced by a chordal skip, are more problematic than those produced by dissonances, and you should avoid them.

16. Parallels averted by passing and neighboring tones. As a rule parallel octaves and unisons require a stronger tonal event than a passing or neighboring tone to preserve the effect of independent voice leading. Among tones of figuration only the chordal skip is, in principle, strong enough to avert octaves and unisons.

Unaccented passing tones and incomplete neighbors are usually too weak even to break up 5ths effectively (Example 20-26). (The normal—as distinct from incomplete—neighbor cannot break up parallels at all, for it returns to the tone that it came from.)

20-26

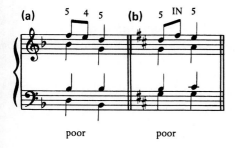

Accented passing tones and incomplete neighbors, on the other hand, displace the second 5th, causing it to be approached by oblique rather than parallel motion. For this reason they form better correctives between 5ths, especially between the upper voices. In the Mozart fragment of Example 20-27, 5ths between the first violin and viola are broken up by the accented neighbor, F♯, of the first violin. The use of accented passing and incomplete neighboring tones to break up 5ths, incidentally, is not characteristic of Bach's chorale style.

20-27   Mozart, String Quartet, K. 590, II

POINTS FOR REVIEW

1. The five fundamental types of figuration are the chordal skip (arpeggio), the passing tone, the neighboring tone, the suspension, and the anticipation.

2. The chordal skip is used to intensify rhythmic activity and to improve melodic lines. It makes polyphonic melody possible.

3. The passing tone, which is normally unaccented, usually fills in a third; sometimes it is necessary for melodic continuity. The chromatic passing tone fills in a whole step.

4. The neighboring tone, also normally unaccented, decorates a stationary tone from above (upper neighbor) or below (lower neighbor). The mordent and double neighbor are derived from the neighboring tone.

5. The chromatic neighbor is normally notated as a minor 2nd; a chromatic lower neighbor often connects better with the main tone than a diatonic one (Example 20-23).

6. The unaccented incomplete neighbor decorates the preceding tone (échappée) or the following one.

7. Accented passing and neighboring tones function as displacements of the normal, unaccented type. An accented dissonance is often called an appoggiatura.

8. Parallels caused by chordal skips are usually faulty; avoid them.

9. Parallel 5ths caused by a passing or neighboring tone are:
   a. almost always bad if the passing or neighboring tone is consonant.
   b. often good, in instrumental style, if the passing or neighboring tone is dissonant.
   c. usually avoided in chorale style.

10. Chordal skips can break up octaves, unisons, and 5ths.

11. No passing or neighboring tone can break up octaves or unisons.

12. The unaccented passing or neighboring tone is usually too weak to break up 5ths. 5ths can be averted by the accented passing or neighboring tone, but this usage is not characteristic of chorale style.

EXERCISES

1. Preliminaries.

   a. Select five sequential progressions from Unit 17. Add chordal skips, passing tones, and neighbors—not necessarily all three types in any given progression. Complete any incomplete progression with a suitable cadence. This exercise can be done at the keyboard. Optional: work out more than one version of the same sequence.

   b. Fill in the inner voices and add passing tones to the outer voices.

   c. Do the same thing in F minor.

   d. Fill in the inner voices and add neighbors, diatonic or chromatic, to the outer voices.

   e. Fill in the inner voices and add accented and normal passing tones in complementary rhythms to the outer voices.

(unfigured)

2. Melody. Continue the quarter-note rhythm in the bass through bars 2 and 3, then continue the eighth-note rhythm to the cadence in bar 7. (The 5ths in bars 4-5 are okay; why?)

bass descends in 3rds

3. Figured bass. Complete the soprano, using tones of figuration. This exercise includes chordal skips and incomplete neighbors (chromatic and diatonic). Measures 7 through 10 or 11 might be set for three voices.

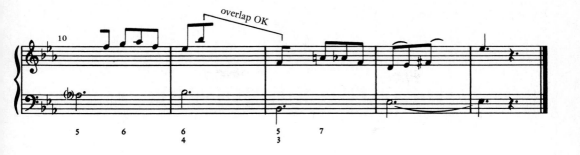

4. Add inner voices to the "Theme." Then write five or more variations, using different rhythmic patterns and as many types of figuration as possible. Label the figuration (P, N, etc.).

21

Rhythmic Figuration

21-1   **Mozart, Symphony No. 41 ("Jupiter"), K. 551, IV**

SUSPENSIONS

1. Rhythmic origin. An important purpose of figuration is to animate and individualize the voice or voices in which it appears. With the types of figuration that we have studied so far, increased rhythmic activity helps to animate the texture; arpeggios and passing and neighboring tones introduce quicker time values into melodic lines. With these types of figuration, however, the rhythmic activity, important as it is, arises mainly as a by-product of melodic motion. With the suspension, rhythm rather than melody assumes paramount importance. A suspension arises when a tone moves out of its normal position in time and continues into the segment of time that would normally belong to the next tone.

Example 21-1 shows suspensions caused by shifted (syncopated) rhythm. The tied half notes form a counterpoint to the whole notes, the main subject of the movement. The first and third tones of this counterpoint are rhythmically displaced; they are shifted over to the middle of the bar rather than appearing at the downbeat. As a consequence of this shift in position, the first and third

328

tones persist into the following bars where they form dissonances against the prevailing harmonies. And as a further consequence the second and fourth tones lose half their normal value.

A figure containing a suspension consists of *two* tones (in the Mozart there are two such figures: C-B and D-C). The first of the two tones divides into two parts, each with its own distinct function; the complete figure, therefore, contains *three* elements, two belonging to the first and one belonging to the second tone. We call these three elements the *preparation*, the *suspension*, and the *resolution* (or release). The preparation is the first part of the initial tone (in the Mozart, the half notes C and D *before* the bar lines); typically, though not invariably, the preparation is consonant. The suspension is the second part of the initial tone (in the Mozart, the half notes C and D *after* the bar lines); typically, though not invariably, the suspension is dissonant. The release is the second tone; if the suspension is dissonant, the term *resolution* is normally used instead.

In Example 21-2, the suspensions arise out of an extension rather than a shift of the initial tones. In addition the suspensions are restruck rather than tied to the preparations as in the Mozart excerpt. The difference between ordinary and restruck suspensions is not negligible, but it has much more to do with the surface texture of the music than with fundamental rhythmic and tonal relationships. In the Bach excerpt, note that suspensions appear at the same time in two voices; these are called "double suspensions" and typically occur, as in the Bach, in parallel 3rds or 6ths.

21-2   Bach, English Suite No. 2, Sarabande

2. **Metric position.** The basic rule governing the suspension is that it appears in a metrically *strong* position relative to the release or resolution. Example 21-3 shows some characteristic possibilities. Note that the preparation is metrically free and may occur either as an accented or an unaccented note; the metric rule governs only the relationship between the suspension and its release.

21-3

3. Dissonance treatment. Suspensions became part of the vocabulary of composition during the fourteenth century, a period when composers experimented a good deal with displaced rhythms and when musical notation became capable of dealing with such rhythms. By the early part of the fifteenth century, composers had learned to treat suspensions in ways that remained characteristic throughout the history of tonal music. Among the usages they established, one is of particularly far-reaching importance. It is that a dissonant suspension must resolve to a consonance by *stepwise, downward* motion. Because it is metrically accented, the suspension dissonance receives much more emphasis than most passing and neighboring tones. It follows naturally, therefore, that its resolution should sound like a relaxation, a decrease in intensity. This effect is better achieved by downward than by upward melodic motion. From the Baroque period on, upward resolutions (as in Example 21-2, bar 4), though still exceptions, occur rather frequently in one particular voice-leading situation (section 19).

A consonant suspension does not need to resolve; it can move up or down.

4. Suspensions and polyphonic textures. Suspensions—especially dissonant ones—create a much greater degree of tension than most passing and neighboring tones; consequently they bring into prominence the voice in which they occur. By bringing out first one, then another of the lines, suspensions can be very helpful in making a polyphonic texture. A glance at *The Well-Tempered Clavier* will show how frequently Bach employed suspensions in his fugues. And suspensions can be just as useful in enhancing the independence of parts in compositions not as obviously polyphonic as fugues. Example 21-4 shows suspensions first in the tenor, then in the alto (with a decorated resolution), then in the soprano, and finally in the alto again, where the suspension forms part of the cadential $^6_4$. Note in particular how much activity and prominence the suspensions bring to the inner voices. Recognizing and bringing out suspensions is of particular importance to the performer; dissonant suspensions receive something of an accent and their resolutions are softer.

21-4   Bach, Chorale 135

5. Numerical symbols. Suspensions are identified by numbers representing the intervals formed by the suspension proper and by its release or resolution. Example 21-5 shows the numerical symbols for the most important dissonant suspensions as they would occur in a two-voice texture.

21-5

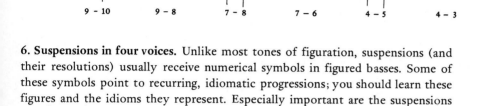

| 9 – 10 | 9 – 8 | 7 – 8 | 7 – 6 | 4 – 5 | 4 – 3 | 2 – 3 |

6. Suspensions in four voices. Unlike most tones of figuration, suspensions (and their resolutions) usually receive numerical symbols in figured basses. Some of these symbols point to recurring, idiomatic progressions; you should learn these figures and the idioms they represent. Especially important are the suspensions into $\frac{5}{3}$ and $\frac{6}{3}$ chords; you should memorize these progressions. You should then have no problems with suspensions into $\frac{6}{4}$ and seventh chords, even if these figures are not memorized.

With more than two voices, suspensions in any of the upper voices are counted from the bass; thus the first three illustrations in Example 21-6 all contain 4-3 suspensions. Suspensions in the bass usually form the interval succession 2-3 or 9-10 with one of the upper voices; in analyzing music these figures alone are often sufficient (21-6d), but more often—especially in figured basses—it is necessary to indicate a more complete set of intervals above the bass (21-6e). Horizontal lines following the figures indicate that the upper-voice tones are sustained through the bass resolution.

You have probably noticed that in the case of the upper-voice suspensions 4-3, 7-6, and 9-8, the figured bass does not indicate the tones of the remaining two voices. In addition, even with the more fully figured bass suspensions, doublings are not indicated. Thus, in order to set these suspensions properly in four voices you must learn what additional intervals are implied by the figures. This will be discussed in the following sections.

21-6

(a)   (b)   (c)   (d)   (e)

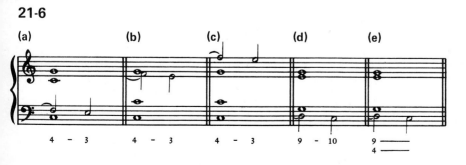

| 4 – 3 | 4 – 3 | 4 – 3 | 9 – 10 | 9 ——— |
| | | | | 4 ——— |

7. The 4-3 suspension. The 4-3 suspension is accompanied by a 5th and resolves into a $\frac{5}{3}$ chord. The complete figure (not including doubling) would be $\frac{5\,\text{—}}{4\text{-}3}$. Usually the bass tone is doubled; but the 5th is also a possibility. The 4-3 suspension appears commonly in any of the upper voices (Example 21-7).

21-7

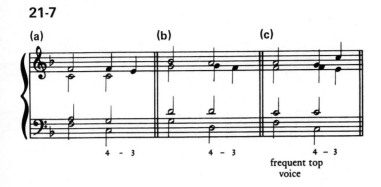

8. The cadential suspension ($V^{4\text{-}3}$). One of the most important compositional uses of the suspension is to enhance the effect of a cadence by emphasizing the leading tone. Very frequently the cadential suspension takes the form of a simple 4-3 above dominant harmony. (Review Unit 10, section 2, where this usage is discussed in connection with the cadential $\frac{6}{4}$.) Note that $V^{4\text{-}3}$ most often (though not always) occurs in the alto voice, as it does in the Bach Chorale of Example 21-8.

21-8   Bach, Chorale 172

9. The 7-6 suspension. The 7-6 suspension (Example 21-9) is accompanied by a 3rd and normally resolves into a $\frac{6}{3}$ chord. There are two possible doublings, usually depending on the soprano position. If the 7th is in the soprano (9a), the bass tone is doubled; if the 10th above the bass is in the soprano (9b), the soprano note is doubled. In Bach's chorales, a 5th will sometimes accompany a 7-6, but the 5th must move "out of the way"—usually to the 10th above the bass—so that the chord of resolution is a $\frac{6}{3}$ (21-9c). Example 21-9d shows what happens if the 5th of $\frac{7}{5}$ is held through; avoid this resolution into a $\frac{6}{5}$ chord unless the figures specify it.

21-9

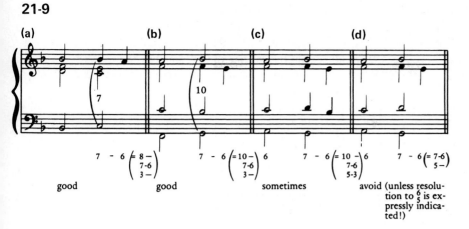

(a)	(b)	(c)	(d)
good	good	sometimes	avoid (unless resolution to ⁶₅ is expressly indicated!)

10. 9-8, $\frac{9\text{-}8}{6\text{-}}$, and $\frac{9\text{-}8}{5\text{-}6}$. The 9-8 suspension (Example 21-10) is always accompanied by a 3rd. This suspension is versatile in that either a 5th (21-10a and b) or a 6th (c) may be sustained through the dissonance and its resolution; alternatively a 5-6 succession may accompany the 9-8 (d). Most frequent soprano possibilities: the 9-8 (a, c, d), or the 10th above the bass (b).

21-10

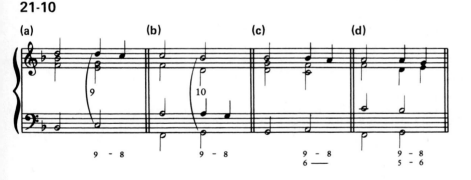

11. $\frac{6\text{-}}{5\text{-}4}$ and $\frac{7\text{-}6}{4\text{-}}$. These are suspensions into ⁶₄ chords and occur most frequently at cadences (Example 21-11).

21-11

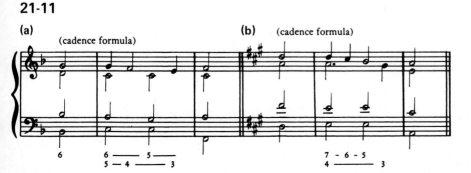

12. Anticipating the tone of resolution. In a more or less homogeneous texture (four-part choral, for example), it is usually best to avoid having the tone of resolution in another voice before the suspension actually resolves. Anticipating the tone of resolution in this way produces an unclear sound and weakens the effect of the resolution. The one situation where anticipating the resolution produces no ill effect is with a 9-8 above the bass. The function of the bass is so different from that of an upper voice that we do not hear the bass tone as a duplication of the tone of resolution (Example 21-12).

21-12

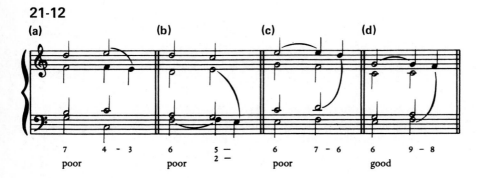

In a texture with marked contrast in rhythm, timbre, or dynamics, anticipating the tone of resolution is much less problematic. Beethoven, in particular, would sometimes allow a suspension in the top voice to sound against the tone of resolution an octave lower in one of the inner voices.*

13. Bass suspensions. The most common bass suspension is the $\frac{5}{2}$, which delays the bass of a $\frac{6}{3}$ chord (Example 21-13a). Anticipating the tone of resolution creates a poor effect, especially if, as in (b), the suspension resolves to the leading tone. Bass suspensions into $\frac{5}{3}$ chords (as shown in 21-6e) occur less often; such suspensions can be labeled $\frac{9}{4}$ or—very confusingly—$\frac{4}{2}$ (don't mix this up with the $\frac{4}{2}$ that stands for $\frac{6}{4}{2}$ and resolves to $\frac{6}{3}$). Sometimes, instead of $\frac{4}{2}$, the figure $\frac{7}{4}{2}$ is used (Example 21-13c). This indicates a doubled root and, as the example shows, an anticipated resolution.

21-13

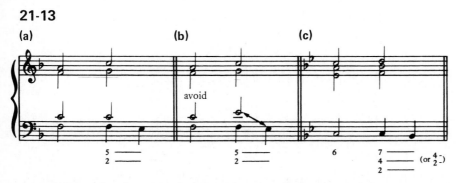

* For an example, see Beethoven's Cello Sonata, Op. 102/2, II, bar 31.

14. Suspensions with moving bass. The bass can move at the same time the suspension resolves, as Example 21-14 shows. The successions 9-6 (21-14a) and 9-(10) (21-14b) occur very frequently. The bass motion can cause either a change in the position of the same chord (a), a change of chord (b and c), or simply a passing tone without chordal significance (d).

21-14

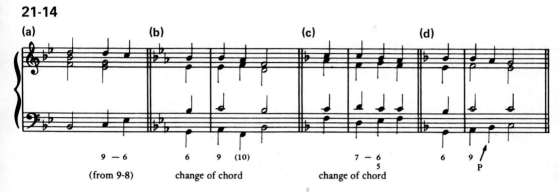

15. Suspensions into seventh chords. Example 21-15 shows a few sample possibilities and an excerpt from the literature. The $\frac{5}{4}$ shown in (c) is a very common bass suspension, closely related to the $\frac{5}{2}$. The $\frac{7}{6}$ (e) and (f) occurs rather frequently—especially in nineteenth-century music—as a delay of $\hat{2}$ over V[7]. To call it a "thirteenth chord," as some harmony books do, is most misleading; the "thirteenth" is a melodic, not a chordal element. In the Josef Strauss waltz, the $\frac{7}{6}$ forms a beautiful suspension resolving into V[7].

21-15

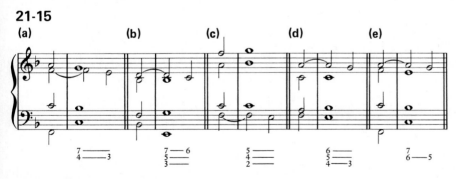

(f) Josef Strauss, Dynamiden, Op. 173, Waltz No. 1

16. Suspensions in series; sequences. Many idiomatic progressions derive from series of consonant and dissonant suspensions—especially 5-6 and 7-6. For progressions based on the 5-6 series review Unit 17, and remember that the 5-6 series produces a particularly good setting of an ascending scale in the bass.

Similarly a series of 7-6 suspensions can accompany a descending bass scale. The progression normally begins with a 5-6 in order to provide a stable chord at the opening. As with the 5-6 series, three-voice texture is the norm (Example 21-16a), but the use of chordal skips makes four voices a possibility (b and c). In (d), the tenor alternately doubles the bass at the octave and the alto at the unison; this possibility is best where the melodic augmented 4th does not appear.

21-16

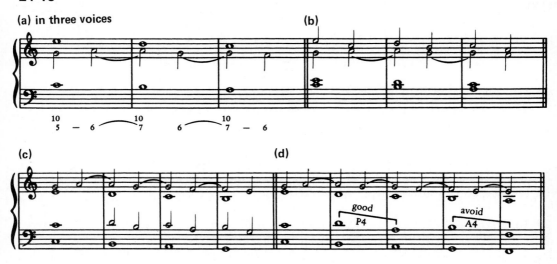

As with the 5-6 series, a chain of 7-6 suspensions often produces the effect of a sequence. In Example 21-17, note the beautiful way in which the piano and violin share the melodic line.

21-17   Mozart, Violin Sonata, K. 378, I

The descending 5-6 sequence (Example 17-16b) can be decorated by suspensions in the bass (Example 21-18a). The $\frac{5}{3}$ variant of the same basic pattern frequently has suspensions in an upper voice; the suspensions will be 4-3's and 9-8's in alternation (21-18b).

21-18

(a)   **(b)**

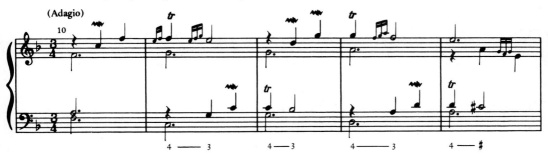

A rising sequence with ascending 5ths can be decorated by 4-3 suspensions. Frequently, the suspensions occur alternately in two voices, producing imitation (Example 21-19).

21-19   Handel, Harpsichord Suite No. 2, III

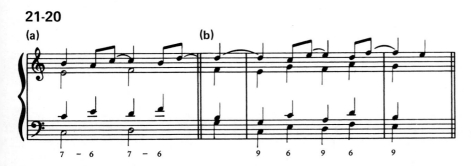

In Examples 21-19 and 21-20 the chordal skip following the resolution allows a prevailing upward direction that would be impossible otherwise. The downward resolution characteristic of dissonant suspensions normally makes it easier to use them in descending passages.

21-20

(a)   **(b)**

Upward motion can also be secured through the use of suspensions (2-3, 9-10, or 7-6) that alternate between two voices as in Example 21-21. Note that the two voices in combination produce the effect of a rising scale; also note the canonic imitation.

21-21 Pergolesi, Duetto (from *Stabat Mater*)

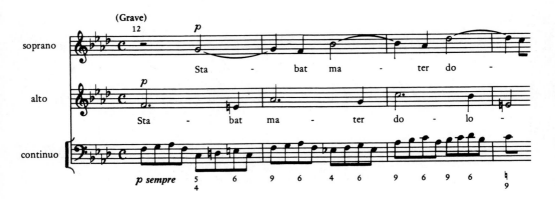

17. Indirect suspensions. In free textures, an effect similar to the alternating suspensions of the last example can come about through the use of indirect suspensions—that is, suspensions transferred from one voice to another (Example 21-22).

21-22

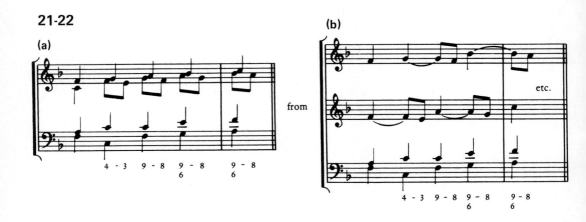

Indirect suspensions are more characteristic of instrumental than of vocal style. They occur not only in series, as in Example 21-22, but also singly.

18. Suspensions with dissonant preparation. In its simplest and most fundamental form, the suspension has a consonant preparation. Sometimes, however, the preparation is dissonant. For example, the 7th of V^7 can be suspended to form a 4-3 over I (Example 21-23a). Or neighboring and passing tones can be suspended before resolving, as in 21-23b.

21-23

(a)   (b) Bach, Chorale 19

19. Upward resolution of dissonance. The downward resolution of the dissonant suspension, established as a rule of counterpoint in the early Renaissance, remained the normal procedure throughout the entire history of triadic tonality. Starting in the Baroque period, however, one exception to this rule occurs rather frequently. When the leading tone is suspended into the I chord (or, sometimes, the VI chord)—especially at a cadence—it resolves up to $\hat{1}$. Example 21-24 illustrates. In (b) of that same example, the upper tones of V^7 are suspended into a cadential I, producing the triple-suspension formation $\begin{smallmatrix}7\\4\\2\end{smallmatrix}$. Reminder: As ill-luck would have it, there is also the bass suspension $\begin{smallmatrix}7\\4\\2\end{smallmatrix}$, discussed in section 13. Try not to confuse them.

21-24

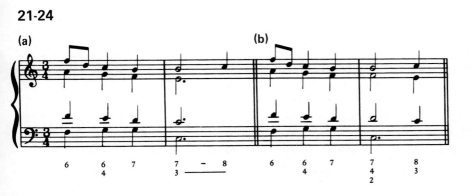

(a)   (b)

Other upward-resolving suspensions are less common. Sometimes $\hat{2}$ suspended over I resolves up to $\hat{3}$, producing a 9-10 progression. Usually this occurs in parallel 3rds or 6ths with $\hat{7}$ moving up to $\hat{8}$ (Example 21-2, bar 4). But sometimes—especially in minor—$\hat{2}$ moves up to $\hat{3}$ unaccompanied by $\hat{7}$-$\hat{8}$ (Example 21-25).

21-25 Mozart, Piano Sonata, K. 457, III

20. Decorated resolutions. Very frequently, ornamental tones decorate the resolution of a suspension. Example 21-26 shows some possibilities.

21-26

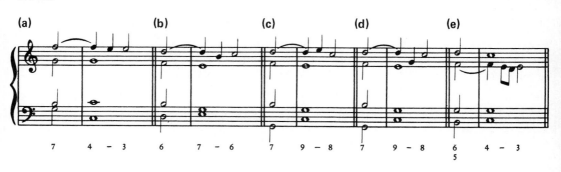

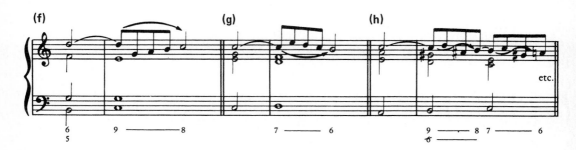

21. Delayed resolutions. A composer can build up tension by delaying the resolution of a suspension. In Example 21-27, the delay is effected by repetition. Note the imaginative way in which Scarlatti brings in the 3rd of the 4-3; it forms part of the rapid descending scale.

21-27   Scarlatti, Sonata, K. 159

(a)

(b)   (c)

22. Transferred and elided resolutions. In complex musical textures, suspensions sometimes resolve into another voice, and, perhaps, another register, as in bar 7 of Example 21-28. The abstract progressions following the Bach excerpt show the same technique in a four-part texture.

21-28

(a) Bach, Well-Tempered Clavier I, Fugue 21

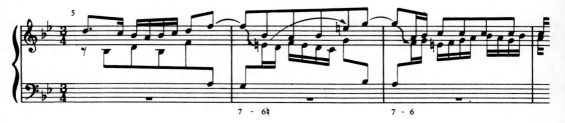

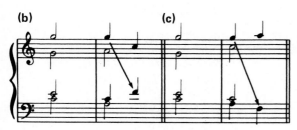

resolutions transferred.

Especially with the 9-8 suspension, where the tone of resolution is already sounding in another register, composers sometimes leave out the resolution altogether. Example 21-29 illustrates.

21-29

resolutions omitted.

23. Implied suspensions. The ability of tonal melody—especially in instrumental style—to suggest two or more lines creates the possibility for *implied* suspensions. Such suspensions are not literally present, but they would be if the implied polyphony were actually realized. Implied suspensions occur frequently in Bach's music. Performers should watch for them; they are not always easy to recognize, but bringing them out is often a necessary part of shaping Bach's complex melodic lines. Example 21-30 quotes the subject of the same fugue illustrated in Example 21-28; the reduction shows the implied suspensions.

21-30   Bach, Well-Tempered Clavier I, Fugue 21

As we know, the 7ths of seventh chords often result from suspensions. The presence of implied suspensions creates the possibility of triads that actually sound like seventh chords. This is what happens in Example 16-1, where the ear retains E♭, D, and C through the following triads, thereby transforming them into seventh chords.

24. Suspensions on weak beats. Occasionally, suspensions fall, or seem to fall, on weaker beats than their resolutions. This, of course, contradicts the basic metric rule governing the suspension. Sometimes this exception is apparent rather than real, for a composer can change the meter temporarily without indicating the change through his manner of notation. An episode in Bach's Fugue in B♭ Minor (WTC I) contains some 4-3 suspensions with the 4ths, seemingly, on weaker beats than the 3rds (Example 21-31). What actually happens here, however, is that the meter temporarily shifts to $\frac{3}{2}$; in the new meter, the suspensions are stronger than their resolutions. Note that at the entrance of the third voice, the two meters go on simultaneously for a moment.

21-31 **Bach, Well-Tempered Clavier I, Fugue 22**

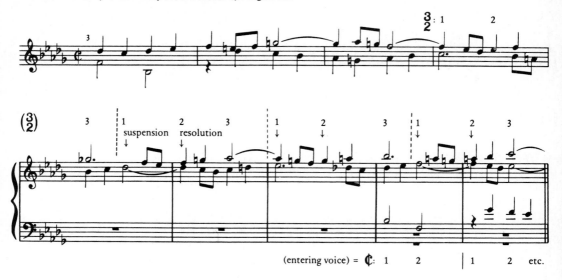

In Example 21-32, however, there is no change of meter. The 4ths of the 4-3's, therefore, really fall on metrically weaker beats than the 3rds. Within each two-bar group, there is a strong rhythmic emphasis on the second half of the first bar. The emphasis arises out of two factors in combination: the change of harmony and the long, high note in the melody. These produce a single rhythmic accent that conflicts with the meter rather than a consistent pattern of accentuation (as in the Bach) that sets up a new meter. The suspensions fall on beats that are *rhythmically* strong, though metrically weak.

21-32 **Mozart, Violin Sonata, K. 378, I**

ANTICIPATIONS

25. Rhythmic origin. The anticipation might be called the opposite of the suspension. Also a tone rhythmically displaced, it appears *prematurely* (rather than being delayed or extended, like the suspension) and it must come on a *weaker* beat or part of the beat than the tone it anticipates. The anticipation is not as important as the suspension, and it does not form the basis of so many significant compositional elaborations. It appears most characteristically in the soprano voice at cadences or other places where the next melodic tone is highly predictable. Bringing in a predictable tone earlier than expected can create a slight surprise and add to the listener's interest. Example 21-33 illustrates.

21-33   Bach, English Suite No. 3, Courante

Dissonant anticipations usually enter by step. However a traditional vocal ornament, the *portamento,* often involves a leap into an anticipation—usually a consonant one—with a slide (glissando) partly filling in the leap. Composers frequently simulated the effect of this ornament in their instrumental music, as in Example 21-34. Note that a consonant anticipation could be understood as a chordal skip. If, however, it produces the effect of a tone entering "too early," thinking of it as an anticipation is truer to its sound and meaning.

21-34   Schubert, Moment Musical, D. 780, Op. 94/1

Anticipations do not occur as often in the inner voices or bass as in the soprano. When they do, they usually form a series of two or more anticipations, as in Example 21-35. This excerpt shows another important possibility: tying the anticipation to its resolution.

21-35   Bach, Chorale 272

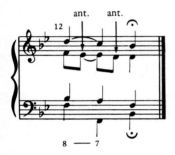

Like the suspension, the anticipation sometimes occurs in indirect form; that is, it can anticipate a tone of the next chord, but one that will appear in another voice (Example 21-36).

21-36   Bach, Chorale 149

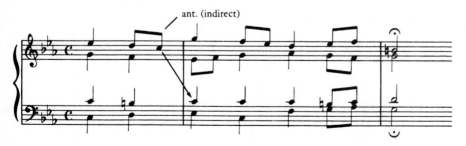

26. Entire chords suspended or anticipated. Sometimes an entire chord, not just one or more tones, appears during the span of time belonging to the following or preceding chord. The psychological effect of such chords is very much like that of suspensions and anticipations; the listener feels a need for resolution even though there is often no literal dissonance. In the Beethoven excerpt of Example 21-37, we expect tonic harmony on the last downbeat; the repeated V^7, therefore, sounds like a suspension.

21-37   Beethoven, Bagatelle, Op. 126/3

27. Forbidden parallel motion. Unless there is motion in another voice, suspensions and anticipations will not cause parallel 5ths and octaves. In his chorales, Bach frequently lets a cadential anticipation in the soprano create 5ths with a passing 7th in one of the inner voices, as in Example 21-38. Here the basic voice leading does *not* contain parallel 5ths. These 5ths involve purely decorative elements and create no ill effect whatever.

21-38   Bach, Chorale 8

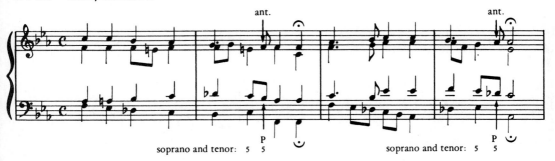

Suspensions and anticipations can be very effective in breaking up parallel 5ths. This is because they displace the underlying voice leading and convert parallel into oblique motion. Thus Example 21-39 contains a series of 7-6 suspensions in the middle voice against parallel 10ths between the outer voices. The voice leading without the suspensions would consist of a series of $\frac{6}{3}$ chords with 10ths between the outer voices—an impossible progression because of the parallel 5ths between the upper voices (review Unit 18). The suspensions transform the parallel motion into oblique motion and create perfectly good voice leading. 7-6 suspensions are very frequently used in just this way. In the Haydn, incidentally, notice how the chromatic passing tones in the bass color the suspension series.

21-39   Haydn, Piano Sonata, Hob. XVI/52, I

Example 21-40 shows an anticipation functioning as a voice-leading corrective—breaking up 5ths in a progression IV⁷-V.

21-40   Bach, Chorale 113

THE PEDAL POINT

28. Compositional function. The pedal point (or organ point) consists of a tone sustained through chord changes or contrapuntal activity (or both) in other voices. The term derives from organ playing; the organist's foot sustains a tone on one of the pedals while his hands play on the manuals. Pedal points typically occur in the bass, though top-voice or inner-voice pedals are not uncommon. Double or triple pedals (in several voices at once) are still another possibility.

In a sense the pedal point functions as the opposite of such elements of figuration as the passing and the neighboring tone. Instead of animating a slower moving substructure through relatively quick note values, the pedal point remains static while the other voices move. When it occurs in the bass, a pedal point can be one of the strongest aids to extending or prolonging a chord, for the bass tone (almost always the root of the basic chord) persists audibly through the transient, subordinate chords above it. The most important pedal points are those that prolong the most important harmonies: I and V. Tonic pedals occur frequently at beginnings and endings. Dominant pedals are almost equally frequent before a final tonic or before a tonic that comes at a recapitulation of the opening material; they can also occur at other points. Example 21-41 illustrates a cadential V and final I expanded by pedal points.

21-41   Bach, Little Fugue for Organ, No. 6, BWV 558

Sometimes a pedal point supports a single chord prolonged by figuration or imitative counterpoint. Quite often, however, the motion of the upper voices produces a succession of chords. Some of these chords may be dissonant against the bass; this is perfectly good if the chord succession and voice leading make sense. Leaps involving dissonances against the bass are also good; they need not be "resolved." Dissonances among the upper parts themselves, however, must be prepared and resolved normally. Most often a pedal point begins and ends with a statement of the chord it prolongs; the progression I-IV-V^7-I is particularly frequent over a tonic pedal. However, this is not always the case. In Example 21-42 the bass tone, at first the root of I, persists into a $\frac{4}{2}$ chord that effects a modulation to V (compare Example 14-1, bar 6).

21-42   Bach, Brandenburg Concerto No. 1, Polacca

strings

POINTS FOR REVIEW

1. Suspensions are created by syncopation or extension of the initial tone.
2. The three parts of a suspension are:
   a. the preparation, which is usually consonant.
   b. the suspension proper, which is sustained or repeated from the preparation; the suspension proper is metrically strong relative to the resolution.
   c. the resolution, which is metrically weak relative to the suspension proper; the resolution is downward by step if the suspension is dissonant and it is frequently decorated.
3. In the upper voices, the most important suspensions are:
   a. 4-3 (especially on cadential V: V$^{4-3}$).
   b. 7-6.
   c. 9-8.
4. In the bass: 2-3 or 9-10; this most frequently resolves to a $\frac{6}{3}$ chord (figured-bass $\frac{5}{2}{-}$) and sometimes to a $\frac{5}{3}$ chord (figured bass $\frac{9}{4}$, $\frac{4}{2}$, or $\frac{7}{4}$).
5. Avoid anticipating the tone of resolution, with these two exceptions:
   a. 9-8 (Example 21-12d).
   b. $\frac{7}{4}$ (Example 21-13c).
6. Upper-voice suspensions with moving bass: the most important figures are 9-6 and 9-(10).
7. The most important suspension series contains 7-6's over a descending bass. This series often begins 5-6. Outer-voice possibilities include:
   a. suspensions in soprano.
   b. parallel 10ths between outer voices.

8. Sequential progressions are frequently decorated by suspensions (Examples 21-18 through 21-21).

9. Exceptional treatment of suspensions includes:
   a. indirect suspension (Example 21-22).
   b. suspensions with dissonant preparation (21-23).
   c. upward resolution of dissonance (usually to $\hat{1}$; 21-24 and 21-25).
   d. delayed resolution (21-27).
   e. transferred resolution (21-28).
   f. elided resolution (21-29).
   g. suspension on weak beat (21-31, 21-32).

10. Anticipations usually occur in the soprano, especially at cadences. They are metrically weaker than the anticipated main tone.

11. Exceptional treatment of the anticipation is the indirect anticipation (21-36).

12. Suspensions and anticipations can break up parallel 5ths by changing parallel motion to oblique.

13. The pedal point is most commonly used in the bass to extend I or V; it usually begins and ends with the main chord.

14. Dissonant chords are possible against the pedal point if the chord succession and voice leading make sense.

EXERCISES

1. Preliminaries.

   a. Add inner voices. Include a chain or series of suspensions in *one* of them.

   b. Without adding a fourth voice, add suspensions to break up the parallel 5ths.

   c. Write the corrected progression above in four voices, adding a tenor.
   d. Write three cadences, each in a different key, decorated with anticipations.

2. Melody. The tied notes in the soprano represent suspensions. Measures 5 and 6 should contain suspensions in the bass.

*or more difficult:

3. Figured bass. An important point in this exercise is getting a good soprano line. A certain amount of trial and error may be necessary to achieve this. Occasional upward skips will very much help the line.

4. Melody. This melody is full of anticipations. Maintain a quarter-note rhythm in the bass for the most part.

5. Using the "Theme" of Exercise 4, Unit 20, write at least three additional variations that include suspensions or anticipations.

PART
V

DISSONANCE AND CHROMATICISM I

22

Mixture

22-1

(a) Mendelssohn, A Midsummer Night's Dream, Overture

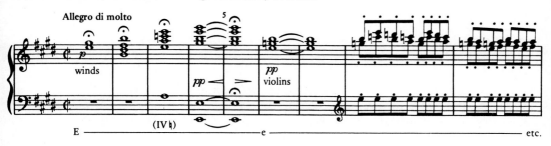

(b) Mendelssohn, bars 62-65

COMBINING MODES

1. Minor in major and vice versa. As its key signature shows, Mendelssohn's Overture to *A Midsummer Night's Dream* (Example 22-1) is in the key of E major. But it is an E major permeated by elements borrowed from the parallel minor. Thus the A minor chord of bar 3 would naturally occur on the fourth step of the E minor scale, not the E major. And, more unusually, the entire opening theme of this composition in major occurs in minor (bar 8ff). Only much later on—in bar 62—does the major reassert itself.

We use the term "mixture" to indicate the appearance of elements from minor in the context of major (as in the Mendelssohn) or the reverse—elements from major used in minor. The Mendelssohn is a rather extreme example; the extensive use of minor has a programmatic meaning, symbolizing the incursion of the supernatural into the world of everyday reality. But mixture can and frequently does occur in absolute music; it is a most important compositional resource. The major/minor duality is, of course, a basic attribute of the tonal system; using mixture enables a composer to focus on this duality within a single piece or passage. Through mixture the characteristic effects of one mode can be incorporated into the other—for instance, the active melodic progression $\hat{6}$-$\hat{5}$ in minor can occur in major. And using two different tones to represent the same scale degree (G♯ and G♮ both function as $\hat{3}$ in the Mendelssohn) provides not only variety but often the potential for dramatic juxtaposition and, even, conflict.

In this unit we shall discuss some of the most frequent and important possibilities; further applications will be discussed in Unit 30.

A NOTE ON TERMINOLOGY

The use of mixture, with its altered scale degrees, creates a few problems in terminology. In making a general statement about altered scale degrees and chords, we use the symbols ♯ and ♭ to mean raised and lowered (for unaltered scale degrees and chords we would use a ♮). But if we refer to a specific passage, we would use the accidental that occurs in the key of the passage. Thus an A♭ major chord in the key of C would be labeled ♭VI; an F major chord in the key of A would be labeled ♮VI. Note that the accidental appears *before* the roman numeral when it modifies the root of the chord; an accidental *following* the roman numeral modifies the 3rd above the bass.

---

2. ♭$\hat{6}$ in major. Mixture frequently results from the use in major of the 6th scale degree of the natural minor (such as the C♮ in bar 3 of the Mendelssohn). Using ♭$\hat{6}$ creates new forms of subdominant and supertonic harmony: IV♭, II$^{6}_{5}$, etc. Because ♭$\hat{6}$ is a "foreign" element, its introduction requires some care; improperly used it can sound arbitrary or disruptive. Chords containing ♭$\hat{6}$ require no special preparation when they come directly from tonic harmony (Example 22-2a-d); as these examples indicate, ♭$\hat{6}$ very often functions as upper neighbor to $\hat{5}$.

Another possibility is for ♭$\hat{6}$ to come about as an inflection of ♮$\hat{6}$. In 22-2e, the F♭ is a passing tone, but one unlike any passing tone we have encountered thus far, for it can also be construed as the 3rd of the chord. We still hear a D♭ chord, but one of minor rather than major quality. In the piano accompaniment of Example 22-2f, ♭$\hat{6}$ also comes from ♮$\hat{6}$, but the leap in the voice part up to A♭ emphasizes the contrast with ♮$\hat{6}$ and highlights the key word "Herz."

As you can hear in the progressions and excerpts of Example 22-2, $b\hat{6}$ is strongly active in the direction of $\hat{5}$. Once introduced it tends to move to $\hat{5}$; it will not normally be replaced by $\natural\hat{6}$ before $\hat{5}$ is reached. Example 22-2g shows you what to avoid.

22-2

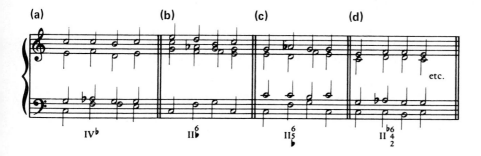

(a)   (b)   (c)   (d)

IV♭   II♭⁶   II⁶₅♭   II♭⁶₄₂

(e) Chopin, Nocturne, Op. 32/2

Lento

(f) Schumann, Dichterliebe, Op. 48/7

Nicht zu schnell

Ich grol - le nicht,   und wenn das Herz _____ auch bricht,

II♭⁷₅

translation: I bear no grudge although my heart is breaking.

(g)

The melodic tension and expressive power of ♭$\hat{6}$ can be evident even when it functions as a dissonant tone of figuration, especially if it contrasts with ♮$\hat{6}$, as in Example 22-3.

22-3 Chopin, Prelude, Op. 28/5

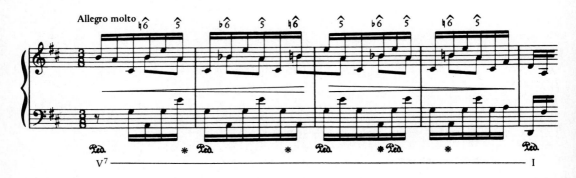

3. ♭$\hat{3}$ in major. Using ♭$\hat{3}$ in major, as in the Mendelssohn example, can produce a minor tonic harmony and a beautifully expressive contrast with the normal, major tonic. Like ♭$\hat{6}$, ♭$\hat{3}$ often originates as an inflection of the natural scale degree. In Example 22-4, the melodic progression ♮$\hat{3}$-♭$\hat{3}$ occurs over a cadential $^6_4$. The ♭$\hat{3}$ functions as a large-scale chromatic passing tone on the way to $\hat{2}$. Note the appearance of B♭ as upper neighbor to $\hat{5}$ in bar 17. The use of ♭$\hat{6}$ as a tone of figuration continues the minor color introduced by the F♮ of the preceding bar.

Note: When a composer introduces an emphasized tone that belongs to minor, the accompanying details of figuration will usually follow the minor scale.

22-4

(a) Schubert, Im Dorfe

(from *Winterreise,* D. 911)

Gu - ten und Ar - gen er - la - ben

und mor - gen früh _____ ist al - les zer -

translation: [Dreaming, they] refresh themselves with good
and bad. And in the morning, it's all gone away.

flos - sen.

(b) reduction

Combining ♭3̂ and ♭6̂ permits the introduction into major of ♭VI—the VI of the parallel minor—one of the most important and frequently used chords created by mixture. In Example 22-5, ♭VI marks the beginning of a brief passage in minor, culminating in a plagal cadence IV♭-I—a very characteristic use of mixture.

22-5

(a) Brahms, Symphony No. 3, Op. 90, II

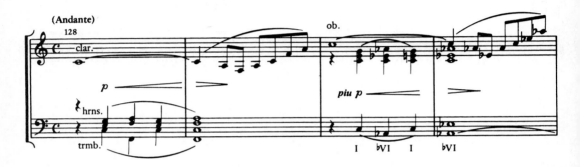

Using ♭VI in place of ♮VI as the goal chord of a deceptive cadence in major greatly increases the tonal contrast and, consequently, the deceptive effect. In Example 22-6, ♭VI initiates a brief passage in minor; a passing D minor $\frac{6}{4}$ chord leads to the II$^6_5$ borrowed from D minor which moves on through an applied dominant (Unit 25) to V, the principal goal of the phrase.

22-6   Mozart, Madamina   (from *Don Giovanni*, K. 527)

translation: [He seduces older ladies] for the pleasure of adding them to his list.
But his predominant passion is for those who are new to the game.

4. ♯3̂ in minor. Using the major form of 3̂ in minor produces a major tonic; this
is one of the most frequent instances of mixture. Its use at the end of a piece (or
section) creates the well-known "Picardy 3rd." Familiar as this device may be, it
can create effects of startling power, as in Example 22-7.

22-7 Mozart, Don Giovanni, Finale

There is no need to discuss at this point the use of $\sharp\hat{6}$ and $\sharp\hat{7}$ in minor; you are already familiar with these scale degrees through working with the harmonic and melodic forms of minor.

5. More extended uses of mixture. Sometimes an entire phrase or group of phrases is cast in the parallel minor or major. The contrast is particularly vivid when the change of mode varies what otherwise would be a repetition (Example 22-8, bars 79-80 and 83-84).

22-8   Mozart, Piano Sonata, K. 311, I

6. Secondary mixture. We use the term "secondary mixture" to denote the alteration of the 3rd of a triad where such alteration does not result from normal mixture. A very frequent example is the use of III in major as a major triad (for example, an E major triad as III in C major). This alteration makes for more contrast of sonority between III and I or V than is possible in a purely diatonic setting; consequently III is very much emphasized and can serve as a temporary goal (Example 22-9).

22-9   Chopin, Etude, Op. 10/5

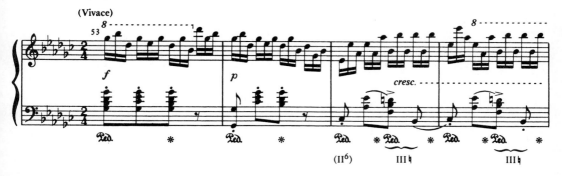

In moving from I to III♯ and from III♯ on to V, composers generally avoid the direct chromatic progression ♮$\hat{5}$-♯$\hat{5}$ (in C major, G♮-G♯). In Example 22-9 the II⁶ chord preceding the III♯ prevents such a direct chromatic progression and helps to integrate the III♯ into a smooth musical flow. In the Chopin note that the approach to III♯ produces the effect of a Phrygian cadence.

III♯ can fulfill a variety of functions of which three are particularly characteristic. In the Chopin excerpt, it is an element of motion leading to an important cadential II⁶ that eventually reaches a final V-I. At other times, III♯ forms part of a large-scale arpeggiation I-III♯-V. (Beethoven used this plan for some of his sonata movements in major, for example the first movement of Op. 53, where the exposition moves from C major to E major, and the development leads to V.) A third possibility is for III♯ to divide the progression V-I, as in Example 22-10. As a divider between V and I, III♯ typically appears before reprise sections, as it does in this example, and sonata-allegro recapitulations. It would not normally lead from a cadential V to the final tonic of a phrase.

22-10   Beethoven, Violin Sonata, Op. 24, III

7. **The cross relation.** Mixture creates numerous possibilities for the cross relation —that problematic aspect of voice leading we encountered in Unit 15, section 4, third paragraph. You will remember that a chromatic succession can sound disagreeable if it is split between two voices, especially when the two outer voices are involved (Example 22-11a). If, as in 22-11b, a direct chromatic succession occurs in one voice, the doubling of one of the tones does not constitute a cross relation and is unobjectionable.

22-11

(a)   (b)

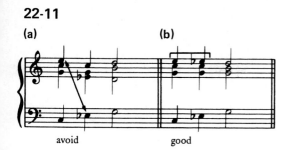

avoid   good

Composers sometimes have compelling reasons for writing cross relations—even harsh ones—between outer voices. The first movement of Brahms's Symphony No. 3, for example, opens with the motto F-A♭-F (Example 22-12). This motto then appears in the bass (bars 3-5) creating a cross relation (A♮-A♭) with the melody. The drastic confrontation between major and minor expressed by this cross relation is an important feature of this movement.

22-12   Brahms, Symphony No. 3, Op. 90, I   ART

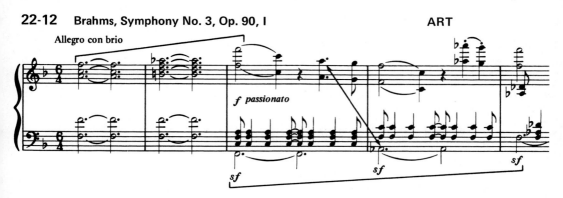

POINTS FOR REVIEW

1. Mixture means using tones from the parallel minor in a major key or the reverse.
2. The following are frequent uses of $b\hat{6}$ and $b\hat{3}$ in major:
   a. $b\hat{6}$ to color and intensify IV, II⁶, II⁷, etc.
   b. a combination of $b\hat{6}$ and $b\hat{3}$ to produce bVI.
   c. $b\hat{3}$ to produce minor tonic.
3. Once introduced, $b\hat{6}$ tends to move to $\hat{5}$. Thus, $\natural\hat{6}$-$b\hat{6}$-$\hat{5}$ is good; $b\hat{6}$-$\natural\hat{6}$-$\hat{5}$ is poor.
4. $\sharp\hat{3}$ in minor yields major tonic ("Picardy 3rd").
5. III♯ in major is a frequent example of secondary mixture. Three characteristic uses are:
   a. leading to II⁶ (or perhaps IV).
   b. as part of the arpeggiation I-III♯-V.
   c. as part of the arpeggiation V-III♯-I.
6. III♯ is often approached by II⁶, thus avoiding the direct chromatic succession $\natural\hat{5}$-$\sharp\hat{5}$.
7. Cross relations occur where a chromatic succession is split between two voices. They are usually avoided between outer voices, but the apparent cross relation produced by doubling is unobjectionable (Example 22-11b).

EXERCISES

1. Preliminaries. Write brief progressions, each in a different key, showing typical usages of the following:

   a. IV♭, II$_♭^6$, II$^6_{5♭}$, II$^7_{5♭}$ (major)
   b. ♭VI (major)
   c. III♯ (major)
   d. I♯ (Picardy third-minor)

2. Figured bass.

3. Melody. A special feature of this exercise is the contrast between ♯$\hat6$ and ♮$\hat6$. Don't overlook opportunities to use ♮$\hat6$ in the inner voices. Except where indicated, the rhythm of the bass mostly follows the soprano.

4. Melody. This exercise provides opportunities for using III♯. Except where indicated, the rhythm of the bass mostly follows the soprano.

*octaves by contrary motion OK.

23
Leading-Tone Seventh Chords

23-1   Beethoven, Piano Sonata, Op. 10/1, I

THE DIMINISHED SEVENTH CHORD

1. VII⁰⁷ in minor. Example 23-1, the beginning of a Beethoven piano sonata, provides an excellent illustration for the leading-tone seventh chord in minor. This chord is based on the characteristic tones—$\sharp\hat{7}$ and $\flat\hat{6}$—of the harmonic form of the minor scale (in the Beethoven, B♮ and A♭). The interval between these tones is a diminished 7th; the chord, therefore, is called a *diminished seventh chord* (convenient symbol °7). The leading-tone seventh chord in minor (VII⁰⁷) is a particularly intense and unstable sonority, strongly directed toward I. $\sharp\hat{7}$ and $\flat\hat{6}$ are active in the direction of $\hat{1}$ and $\hat{5}$—both elements of tonic harmony. And the chord contains an unusually large number of dissonant intervals: a diminished 7th and diminished 5th from the bass, and a diminished 5th or augmented 4th between the 3rd and 7th ($\hat{2}$ and $\hat{6}$). All these dissonances tend to resolve to intervals belonging to the tonic chord.

As the figures below the bass indicate, the Beethoven excerpt contains three different positions of this chord: °$\frac{6}{5}$, °$\frac{4}{3}$, and °7. These chords are closely related to the inversions of V⁷, differing by only a single tone; we can transform V$\frac{6}{5}$ into VII⁰⁷ merely by replacing $\hat{5}$ with $\hat{6}$. Despite these similarities, the various positions of VII⁰⁷ *sound* very different from the inversions of V⁷, as you can hear by playing 23-1 and substituting inversions of V⁷ for the diminished seventh chords.

A NOTE ON SYMBOLS AND FIGURED BASS

For the sake of convenience in analyses, we will often use the symbol ° or ∅ combined with figured-bass numerals to indicate diminished or half-diminished seventh chords. In such cases (as in Example 23-1), the accidentals that would be required to produce the specified quality of the chord are *not* given. In a figured bass—or in a figured-bass exercise—where the symbol ° or ∅ is not used, the figures would have to be modified by the appropriate accidentals if °7 or ∅7 is in inversion. Thus, in the Beethoven excerpt, the $\frac{6}{5}$ of bar 5 would be figured ♮$\frac{6}{5}$, and the $\frac{4}{3}$ of bar 10 would be figured ♮$\frac{4}{3}$; on the other hand, the figure for the root-position °7 of bar 17 would not require accidentals since it is the bass tone itself that is modified.

2. Contrapuntal functions. The easiest way to understand how the various positions of the diminished seventh chord function is to relate them to the inversions of V^7 that they resemble. You can see some typical functions in the Beethoven excerpt. Thus VII^{O7}, like V^6_5, is based on the lower neighbor of I (bar 17). VII^{O6}_5, like V^4_3, is a passing chord connecting I and I^6 (bars 4-8). And VII^{O4}_3, like V^4_2, is built on the upper neighbor of I^6 (bars 10 and 12). The $^4_2$ position, not present in the Beethoven and to be discussed later, is the only one that does not correspond to an inversion of V^7.

3. Dissonance treatment. As in other seventh chords, the 7th resolves by stepwise descent (to the 5th of I). The leading tone moves up to the tonic. Therefore the interval of the diminished 7th resolves inward to a perfect 5th; the augmented 2nd (which often occurs in inverted positions) resolves outward to a perfect 4th (Example 23-2).

23-2

VII^{O7} contains two diminished 5ths—one between $\sharp\hat{7}$ and $\hat{4}$ and another between $\hat{2}$ and $\hat{6}$; depending on inversion and voicing, either or both of these diminished 5ths might be expressed as an augmented 4th. In all positions of VII^{O7}, a diminished 5th or augmented 4th *that involves the bass* resolves regularly (the diminished 5th inward to a 3rd, the augmented 4th outward to a 6th). Between upper voices, diminished 5ths also tend to resolve normally, but augmented 4ths often resolve irregularly, usually in similar motion to a perfect 4th.

4. Resolving VII^{O7}. Example 23-3 shows some voice-leading possibilities for the root position. In (a) all the dissonant intervals resolve regularly, producing a tonic chord with doubled 3rd. In (b) a doubled root is achieved by resolving irregularly the augmented 4th between soprano and alto; both voices go in similar motion to a perfect 4th. This strategy permits the soprano progression $\hat{2}$-$\hat{1}$ and is also useful where the doubled 3rd might sound out of place. The "improper" resolution of the upper-voice dissonance is hardly noticeable. But if the upper dissonance forms a diminished 5th (c), the similar motion that follows creates an obtrusive set of hidden 5ths; avoid this voice leading. *Note:* The treatment of upper-voice diminished 5ths and augmented 4ths relates to the discussion of VII^6 in Unit 7, section 12. Review!

23-3

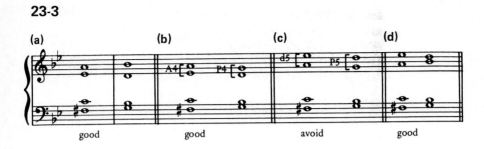

5. **Resolving VII$^{o6}_5$.** Example 23-4 illustrates the resolution of $^{o6}_5$. The bass tone, $\hat{2}$, ascends to $\hat{3}$ if the lower diminished 5th resolves regularly; as a consequence VII$^{o6}_5$ normally moves to I^6 rather than to I$^5_3$ (23-4a and b). 23-4c and d show two frequent exceptions to normal dissonance treatment. In (c), where the outer voices move in parallel 10ths, the upper diminished 5th moves to a perfect 5th, just as with V$^4_3$. 23-4d shows a possibility for moving to I$^5_3$ rather than the usual I^6; the VII$^{o6}_5$ functions as a neighboring chord. This progression works best with the soprano motion $\hat{8}$-$\hat{7}$-$\hat{8}$ and in *close position;* the hidden 5ths are softened by the parallel 3rds above the bass and the contrary motion of the outer voices.

23-4

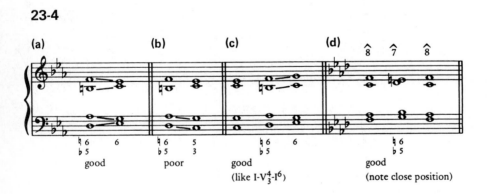

The complexities of instrumental figuration can provide additional opportunities for leading VII$^{o6}_5$ effectively to I$^5_3$. In a passage from a Beethoven string quartet (Example 23-5), the downward resolution of the first violin's $\hat{6}$ (D♭) is taken over by the second violin, allowing the top voice to move up to $\hat{8}$ and forestalling hidden 5ths with the bass line. (This progression carries almost to an extreme the technique of the transferred resolution—there are two in addition to the one mentioned above. Can you identify them?)

23-5   **Beethoven, String Quartet, Op. 95, III**

(Allegro assai vivace ma serioso)

6. **Resolving VII$^{o4}_{3}$.** Example 23-6 illustrates the resolution of VII$^{o4}_{3}$. It closely resembles that of its analogue, V$^{4}_{2}$; $\hat{4}$ in the bass descends to $\hat{3}$, producing a resolution to I^{6}. As in the other positions, the dissonance between $\hat{2}$ and $\hat{6}$ will resolve normally if it forms a diminished 5th (a). If it forms an augmented 4th, $\hat{2}$ may move up to $\hat{3}$ or down to $\hat{1}$ (c) or up to $\hat{5}$ (d); this last possibility is as characteristic of VII$^{o4}_{3}$ as it is of V$^{4}_{2}$.

23-6

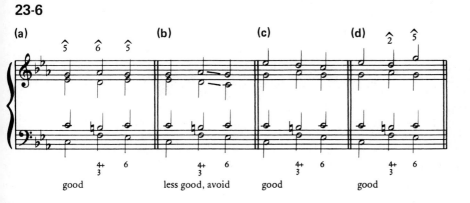

7. **Approaching VII^{o7}.** The 7th of ^{o7} is best introduced in one of three ways: as a neighbor, as a common tone, or as a passing tone. If VII^{o7} comes from a tonic chord, as in Examples 23-1 and 23-6, the 7th will function as an upper neighbor to $\hat{5}$. In fact, harmonizing $\hat{6}$ in the soprano progression $\hat{5}$-$\hat{6}$-$\hat{5}$ is a particularly characteristic and important function of the diminished seventh chord (23-6a). If VII^{o7} comes from a position of IV, II, or VI (Example 23-7a-c), the 7th is prepared as a common tone. Coming from III or $\natural$VII the 7th enters as a passing tone (23-7d-f). As with V^{7}, the 7th will sometimes enter unprepared as an incomplete neighbor (g). Sometimes an embellishing $\natural\hat{7}$ decorates $\hat{6}$, creating a transitory clash with $\sharp\hat{7}$. Coming on the strong part of the beat, this powerful dissonance can produce a very intense and poignant effect (23-7h).

23-7

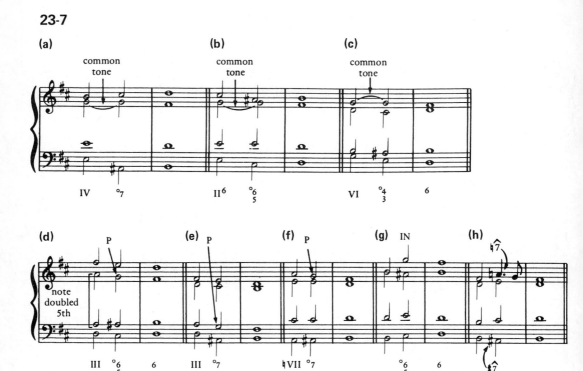

8. The $\frac{4}{2}$ position. Unlike the other positions of VII^{o7}, VII$^{o4}_{2}$ does not relate closely to an inversion of V^7. Resolving the augmented 2nd (or 9th) from the bass to a perfect 4th produces a $\frac{6}{4}$ chord. Example 23-8a shows resolution to a stable $\frac{6}{4}$. In 23-8b the $^{o4}_{2}$ comes about through passing and neighboring motion in the upper voices leading to a *cadential* $\frac{6}{4}$. Strictly speaking, in this situation it is the upper voices that cause the dissonance, not the chordal 7th ($\hat{6}$). This type of seventh chord will be discussed more fully in Unit 24. Owing to the problematic nature of the $\frac{6}{4}$ as "goal," the $\frac{4}{2}$ position occurs much less frequently than any of the others.

9. VII^{o7} associated with V^7. Sometimes $^{o}7$ results from a neighbor or suspension resolving to the root of V^7 (Example 23-9). In such cases one does not hear a real change of harmony; V^7 is the functional chord and $^{o}7$ a contrapuntally derived embellishment. This is so even if $^{o}7$ lasts for a very long time.* Many seeming examples of $^{o4}_{2}$ are really embellishments of V^7 (23-9b).

---

*As, for example, in the development section of the first movement of Beethoven's "Appassionata" Sonata, bars 123-31.

23-8

(a)   **(b)**

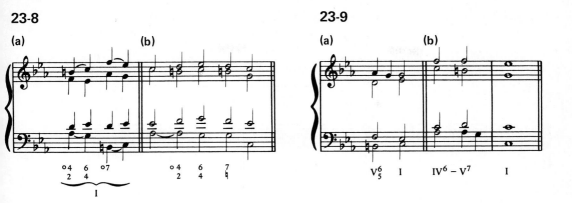

$$\underbrace{{}^{\circ}\!\!\begin{smallmatrix}4\\2\end{smallmatrix} \quad 6 \quad {}^{\circ}7}_{I}$$ $${}^{\circ}\!\!\begin{smallmatrix}4\\2\end{smallmatrix} \quad 6 \quad 7\!\!\begin{smallmatrix}\\4\end{smallmatrix}$$

23-9

(a)   **(b)**

$$V^6_5 \quad I \quad\quad IV^6 - V^7 \quad I$$

10. VII$^{\circ 7}$ over a tonic pedal. VII$^{\circ 7}$ often appears over a tonic pedal, usually taking the place of V^7 in the progression I-IV-VII$^{\circ 7}$(= V^7)-I (Example 23-10).

23-10   Bach, Well-Tempered Clavier I, Prelude 2

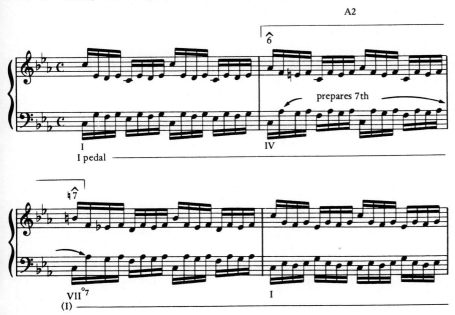

11. The melodic augmented 2nd. Passages including VII$^{\circ 7}$ sometimes contain a *melodic augmented 2nd,* usually in the soprano. The presence of this interval in the chord makes its melodic use sound less awkward. The A2 can result from an arpeggiation within VII$^{\circ 7}$; it can also appear in the course of a motion from II, IV, or VI to VII$^{\circ 7}$, as in 23-10.

12. VII°7 extended through voice exchange. A diminished seventh chord can be extended by means of the technique of voice exchange. Often, passing chords will appear between two different positions of °7 as shown in Example 23-11.

23-11

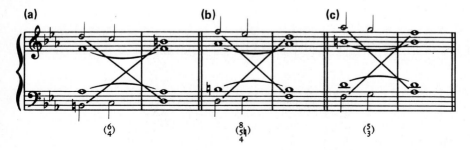

13. VII°7 in major. In the preceding unit, we saw that the use of ♭6̂ in major is one of the most important possibilities of mixture. Using ♭6̂ instead of ♮6̂ in VII7 makes it possible to introduce the diminished seventh chord into a composition in major. This happens very frequently. Using VII°7 in major creates no new problems; the contrapuntal functions and the details of dissonance treatment are the same as in minor. Example 23-12 is the beginning of a Chopin Mazurka in A♭ major that contains the diminished seventh chord as a prominent feature. In this piece the opening upbeat (which represents tonic harmony) is not supported by a chord; VII°7 is the first actual chord heard. In a literal sense, therefore, the 7th enters without preparation; what happens later, however, clarifies the function of F♭ as upper neighbor to E♭.

23-12   Chopin, Mazurka, Op. 17/3

14. Enharmonic relationships. In close position, °7 consists of minor 3rds between adjacent voices. Adding an octave above the bass makes an augmented 2nd, enharmonically the same as a minor 3rd (Example 23-13).

23-13

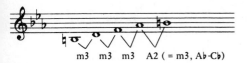

m3   m3   m3   A2 (= m3, A♭-C♭)

The diminished seventh chord, therefore, divides the octave into equal, or enharmonically equivalent, intervals. As a result, the inversions of °7 sound like one another and like the root position, and each position of °7 is, out of context, indistinguishable from a different position in some other key. This ambiguity is very important in chromatic textures and, especially, in modulation, as we shall see later. Example 23-14 shows how a diminished seventh chord can be reinterpreted enharmonically.

23-14

c: °7   =   a: °6/5   =   f♯ °4/3   =   e♭ °4/2

THE HALF-DIMINISHED SEVENTH CHORD

15. VII^{ø7} in major. In the major mode (without mixture) VII⁷ is a half-diminished seventh chord (minor 3rd, diminished 5th, minor 7th—like II⁷ in minor). The symbol ᵠ7 is used to indicate its quality. VII^{ø7} typically occurs as a neighboring chord to I (or embellishment of V⁶/₅), often with a soprano progression $\hat{5}$-$\hat{6}$-$\hat{5}$. VII^{ø7} cannot occur in minor, for the downward resolution of its 7th contradicts the upward tendency of ♯$\hat{6}$. Example 23-15 shows VII^{ø7} in a free piano setting.

23-15   Schubert, Piano Sonata, D. 845, Op. 42, III

(Allegro vivace)   11

VII^{ø7} _____

Moving between I and VII$^{\phi 7}$ can easily lead to parallel 5ths, especially if the 7th is in the soprano, by far the most frequent disposition (Example 23-16a). Example 23-16b shows how to solve this problem: double the 3rd of I. If the 7th is not in the soprano (c and d) the problem of 5ths need not arise.

23-16

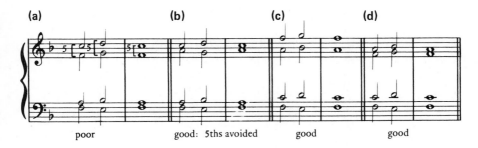

poor   good: 5ths avoided   good   good

16. Inversions of VII$^{\phi 7}$. Except for the $\frac{4}{3}$ position, $^{\phi}7$ occurs much less often in inversion than does $^{o}7$. VII$^{\phi\frac{4}{3}}$ functions as a variant (or embellishment) of V$^{4}_{2}$ and leads to I^{6}, usually with $\hat{6}$ in the soprano. Example 23-17 illustrates.

23-17

(c) Schubert, Moment Musical, D. 780, Op. 94/6

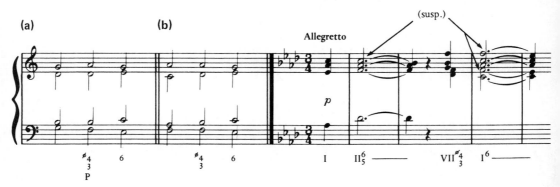

POINTS FOR REVIEW

1. VII^7 is built on the raised seventh step of minor and resolves to I. Its first three positions correspond to inversions of V^7:

position		typical function
VII^{o7} = V$^6_5$		LN to I
VII$^{o6}_5$ = V$^4_3$		P between I and I^6
VII$^{o4}_3$ = V$^4_2$		UN to I^6

2. In resolving all positions of VII^{o7}, keep the following general principles in mind:
   a. The d7 must resolve to P5 (A2 to P4).
   b. All dissonances involving the bass must resolve.
   c. Between upper voices, d5 tends to resolve normally, but A4 may resolve irregularly, usually to P4.

3. The $^{o4}_2$ position is the least frequently used; it resolves to either a stable or an unstable $^6_4$ (Example 23-8).

4. The seventh of VII^{o7} or its inversions is usually introduced as a neighboring tone ($\hat{5}$-$\hat{6}$-$\hat{5}$), common tone, passing tone, or incomplete neighbor.

5. VII^{o7} may result from a neighbor or suspension resolving to the root of V^7 (Example 23-9), may occur over a tonic pedal (Example 23-10), and may be extended by voice exchange (Example 23-11).

6. In major, VII^{o7} is frequently used to support $\flat\hat{6}$.

7. VII$^{\emptyset7}$ is used in major only, usually as a neighbor to I (soprano $\hat{5}$-$\hat{6}$-$\hat{5}$). Its most frequent inversion is $^{o4}_3$, with $\hat{6}$ in the soprano. Example 23-16 shows typical ways of avoiding 5ths when resolving VII$^{\emptyset7}$.

EXERCISES

1. Preliminaries. Write at least ten of the following progressions. Use a different key for each one.

   a. minor key: I-VII^{o7}-I. Begin with $\hat{5}$ in the soprano.

   b. major key: I^6-VII^{o7}-I. Begin with $\hat{1}$ in the soprano.

   c. minor key: I-IV-VII^{o7}-I

   d. major key: I^6-II-VII^{o7}-I

   e. minor key: I-II^6-VII^{o7}-I

   f. minor key: I-III-VII^{o7}-I

   g. minor key: I-III-$\natural$VII-VII^{o7}-I

   h. minor key: I-V$^6_5$-VII^{o7}-I

   i. major key: I-VII$^{o6}_5$-I^6. Begin with $\hat{1}$ in the soprano.

   j. minor key: I-VII$^{o6}_5$-I^6. Include parallel 10ths in the outer voices.

   k. major key: IV-VII$^{o6}_5$-I^6

   l. minor key: II^6-VII$^{o6}_5$-I^6. Begin with $\hat{2}$ in the soprano.

   m. minor key: V-VII$^{o4}_3$-I^6

   n. major key: I-VII$^{o4}_3$-I^6

    o. minor key: ♮VII-VII$^{o4}_{2}$-V$^{6-5}_{4}$$_{♯}$-I

    p. major key: I-VII^{ø7}-I. Begin with $\hat{5}$ in the soprano.

    q. major key: I-VII$^{ø4}_{3}$-I^6

2. Set Exercise 4 from Unit 13, using VII^{o7} wherever practical.

3. Figured bass.

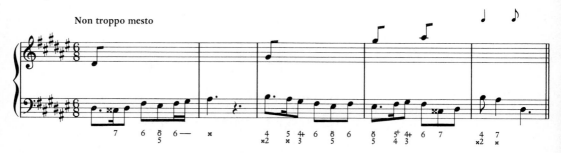

4. Melody. Set for string quartet. Use VII^{o7} where appropriate. In certain places an overlap between soprano and alto is unavoidable.

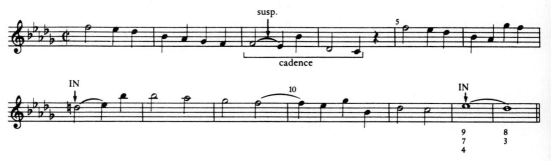

5. Melody. Set for string quartet, using VII^{ø7} wherever appropriate.

In bars 7(end)-8 unusually wide spacing is almost inevitable. The soprano and alto could be a 10th apart.

24

Remaining Uses of
Seventh Chords

24-1 Mozart, Piano Concerto, K. 491, I

Continued

SEVENTH CHORDS IN SEQUENCE

1. Some new techniques. You will quickly recognize the similarity between Example 24-1 and the examples in Unit 17. Clear sequential patterns occur in the piano part and in the bass and upper voices of the orchestral reduction. The underlying bass motion is in descending 5ths: E♭-A♭-D-G-C-F-B♭-E♭—a procedure by now very familiar to us. What is different from the Unit 17 examples is that the bass tones support seventh chords instead of triads; in fact every chord, except for the initial and closing tonics, is a seventh chord. In this unit, we shall first discuss how seventh chords can be used in connection with techniques studied earlier—especially sequential techniques, like the descending 5ths of the Mozart. The second part of the unit will deal with more complex uses of dissonance, and the third with chords that outwardly resemble seventh chords but function differently.

2. Possibilities for chord succession. Progressions in which seventh chords occur must accommodate the descending resolution of the 7th; this is as true for I^7, III^7, and VI^7 as for the seventh chords already familiar to us. By far the most frequent possibility is root motion by descending 5th; another is root motion by ascending 2nd (Example 24-2). As a consequence, seventh chords can substitute for triads in such progressions: for instance, VI^7-II (descending 5th) and III^7-IV (ascending 2nd). The resolution of the dissonance intensifies the motion to the second chord. Such progressions occur frequently in sequential, as well as in nonsequential, passages.

24-2

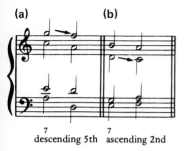

<table>
<tr><td>(a)</td><td>(b)</td></tr>
</table>

7   7
descending 5th   ascending 2nd

3. Descending 5ths with root-position seventh chords. As Example 24-1 illustrates, sequential descending 5ths can easily incorporate *interlocking seventh chords*—that is, those that resolve into other seventh chords. With this pattern, each chordal 3rd prepares the 7th of the following chord as a common tone. In four-part vocal writing every other seventh chord must be incomplete if the dissonance is to resolve correctly; this is shown in Example 24-3a. To have every seventh chord complete requires a free texture (as in the Mozart) or five voices (24-3b).

24-3

(a) reduction of 24-1   **(b) in five voices**

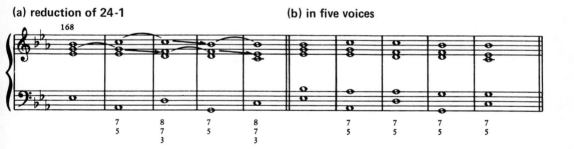

The contrast in appearance between Examples 24-1 and 24-3 indicates that, like other sequences with descending 5ths, those with seventh chords lend themselves to considerable elaboration. Example 24-4a shows the elaborations that occur in the orchestral part of the Mozart. The bass motion of an ascending 4th is filled in by step, while the flute and oboe alternate in connecting the 3rds of each chord. 24-4b, a reduction of the piano part, shows a most important technique: the decorated resolution of the chord 7th. Note that canonic imitation occurs both in (a) and in (b).

24-4

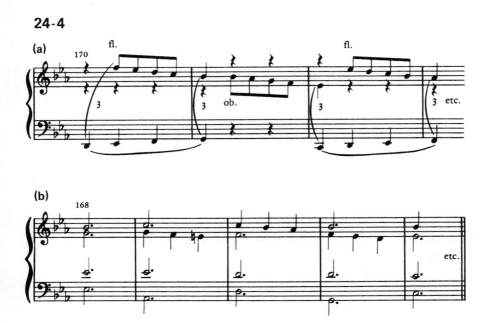

4. Descending 5ths and 7-6 suspensions. In Unit 17, section 5, we saw how a bass descending in 5ths often stands for the elaboration of a stepwise descending line. Example 24-5 shows how the series of seventh chords in the Mozart is derived from a 7-6 suspension series over such a descending bass. Thus the series combines a contrapuntal (stepwise) motion with harmonic progression by 5th. The disjunct bass of 24-5b gives more emphasis to each chord and makes for a denser texture because of the added dissonance caused by the new bass tones.

24-5

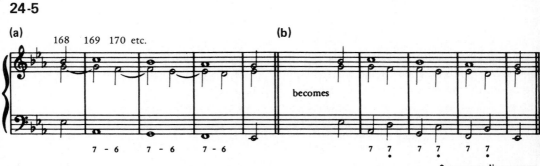

*note new dissonances

5. Descending 5ths alternating $\frac{5}{3}$ and ^{7}. A bass descending in 5ths may support $\frac{5}{3}$ chords alternating with seventh chords. In Example 24-6, the outer voices move in parallel 10ths from downbeat to downbeat. Besides adding variety and dissonance, the seventh chords serve to break up the 5ths that occur on the first beat of each measure.

24-6

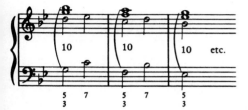

6. Descending 5ths with inversions of seventh chords. The patterns shown above may be varied by using inversions of seventh chords. A Bach excerpt (Example 24-7) closely resembles 24-6 except that $\frac{6}{5}$ chords take the place of root-position sevenths.

24-7 Bach, Gamba Sonata, BWV 1029, I

(a) (Vivace)

(b) reduction

Sequences with $\frac{4}{2}$ chords occur frequently, sometimes resolving to $\frac{6}{3}$ chords (Example 24-8), sometimes to $\frac{6}{5}$'s. In the Corelli, the descending, stepwise bass, which results naturally from the resolution of the $\frac{4}{2}$ chords, fills in the 6th between I and I^6.

24-8   Corelli, Concerto Grosso, Op. 6/8, Pastorale

Example 24-9 illustrates some variants using $\frac{4}{3}$'s.

24-9

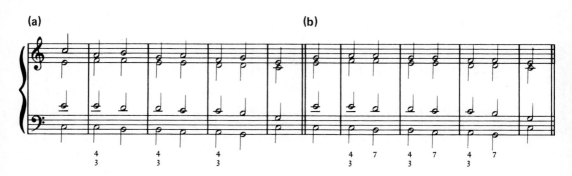

7. Descending 3rds. In the previous examples, the 7th is prepared as a common tone, but it may also come about as a passing tone; this makes possible motion in descending 3rds, as in Example 24-10.

24-10

(a)   (b)

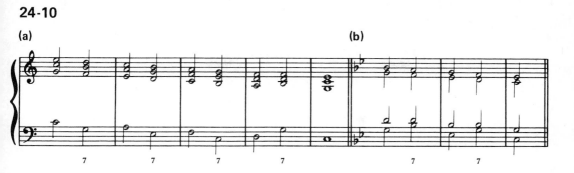

7   7   7   7   7   7

8. Ascending 5-6 technique. In instrumental style, an important variant of the 5-6 technique becomes possible—the $^6_3$'s are transformed into $^6_5$'s. In such progressions, the dissonant tone in each $^6_5$ is prepared indirectly in a lower voice. In Example 24-11 the dissonance is prepared in the tenor and shifted into the soprano. For an illustration from the literature, review Example 17-1, bars 6½-8.

24-11

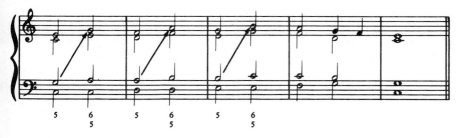

5   6   5   6   5   6
       5   5   5

EXPANDED TREATMENT OF SEVENTH CHORDS

9. Transferred resolutions. The vast majority of seventh chords resolve according to the principles already familiar to us. Exceptions to the norms of dissonance treatment occur for the most part in complex instrumental textures. Sometimes, as with suspensions (review Unit 21, section 22) and with the 4ths of $^6_4$ chords (Unit 19, section 9), the resolution of the 7th will be transferred into a different voice. Examples 24-12 and 24-13 show typical ways in which this may occur. In Example 24-12, the soprano must move up in order to arrive at a theme that begins on $\hat{5}$. The tone of resolution appears in the same register in the alto voice. In the Mozart (Example 24-13), the 7th resolves into the bass (hence the I⁶), a voice sufficiently exposed to make the tone of resolution prominent. In general, a transfer will be most successful if the resolution occurs in the next lower voice and in the same register, as in the Beethoven; or if it occurs in the bass, as in the Mozart, or in the familiar progression I-V$^4_3$-I⁶ with parallel 10ths in the outer voices.

24-12   Beethoven, Piano Sonata, Op. 14/2, I

24-13   Mozart, Piano Sonata, K. 280, II

A type of transferred resolution that occurs mainly in recitatives is one where the bass tone of a dominant $\frac{4}{2}$ skips down to the root of tonic harmony. When this happens, there is a marked tendency for the tone of resolution to appear in the top voice, as in Example 24-14.

24-14   Bach, Cantata 18, recitative

(a)

translation: Thus also should be the word that goes forth from my mouth.

(b)   **(c)**

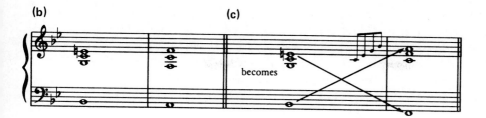

becomes

Do not confuse the transferred *resolution* of the 7th with the much more frequent and simpler technique of transferring the 7th itself from one voice to another (Example 24-15).

24-15

(a)   **(b)**

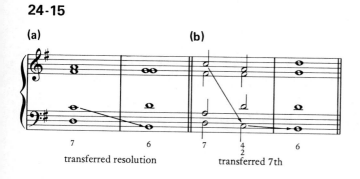

7   6   7   4   6
                                2
transferred resolution   transferred 7th

10. Delayed resolutions. Particularly if the 7th is in the soprano, a transferred resolution may not in itself be sufficient to resolve the tension created by the original dissonance. In Example 24-16, the listener does not hear a convincing resolution of the F♮ until the E arrives in bar 87. This technique—the delayed resolution of a 7th—occurs frequently, sometimes over much longer spans of time than in this example.

24-16   Mozart, Piano Concerto, K. 467, I

11. Extended 7ths. We already know that a seventh chord may be extended before it resolves (for example, V⁷-IV⁶-V⁶₅), or that a chord may be interpolated between a 7th and its resolution (for example, II⁶₅-cadential ⁶₄-V). In both cases the 7th eventually resolves down by step. Sometimes these techniques form the basis for further compositional elaboration, as Example 24-17 illustrates. Here the 7th of the V⁷ chord in the last beat of bar 17 does not resolve until the tonic chord of bar 19.

24-17   Handel, Flute Sonata, Op. 1/5, Bourrée

Note the difference between the delayed resolution of a 7th and the extended seventh chord. With the former the chord of resolution is extended, while in the latter the seventh chord itself is extended (Example 24-18).

24-18

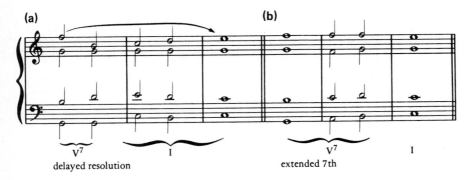

12. Subtonic 7th leads to V⁷. Related to the extended seventh chord is the use of the seventh chord on ♮7̂ in minor to prepare a position of V⁷, usually V⁶₅. As we know from Unit 15, section 9 (Example 15-17), ♮VII can move into a V⁶₅ that leads to I. The Handel excerpt of Example 24-19 illustrates a variant of this progression in which ♮VII is expressed as a seventh chord. Adding a 7th to ♮VII transforms the triad into a dissonant sonority that we might expect to resolve to III, since ♮VII^7 is also V^7 of III. In the Handel this expectation is particularly strong: ♮VII^7 comes from a G minor chord, suggesting II-V^7 in F; in addition, it extends for three bars, expanded by a passing F major $^6_4$ chord, which further enhances the suggestion of a resolution to III. When the ♮VII^7 continues on to V$^6_5$, the effect is surprising and dramatic. Creating an association between ♮VII^7 and V^7 gives a valuable alternative to extending dominant harmony through changes within V^7 itself, for the ultimate destination of the progression initiated by the ♮VII is much less predictable.

24-19   Handel, Harpsichord Suite No. 3, I

(a)

(b) reduction

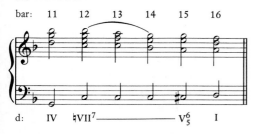

APPARENT SEVENTH CHORDS

13. Upward-resolving dissonance. The beginning of Act III of Wagner's *Tristan und Isolde* (Example 24-20a) includes a chord that appears to be the familiar II$^6_5$ of F minor. However, this chord does not progress to V, nor does the 5th above the bass resolve down by step. A closer look at the music explains why. The "II$^6_5$" continues the IV chord that begins the phrase; the dissonance is caused by the passing tone G, not by the F, as would be the case with a true II$^6_5$. Example 24-20(b-d) illustrates.

24-20   **Wagner, Tristan und Isolde, Act III, Introduction**

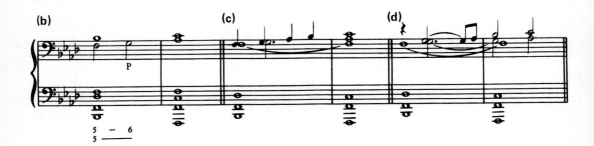

We use the term *apparent seventh chord* to indicate complexes of tones that appear to be seventh chords but that in fact are not, since the dissonance is not caused by a 7th above the root. They are less important than real seventh chords, but there are certain idiomatic progressions involving apparent sevenths that you need to know. The most characteristic possibilities are discussed in the following sections.

14. Triads with added 6th. As we saw in the excerpt from *Tristan*, the apparent $^6_5$ occurs where a 6th is added to a $^5_3$ chord. This happens most often with IV (as in the Wagner). In such cases the "II$^6_5$" is really a IV with added 6th. Such IV chords occur frequently at plagal cadences, especially where an ascent to $\hat{3}$ is wanted, as in Example 24-21 where the consonant origin of the passing tone is omitted through contraction. (Compare this usage with that of the "II⁶" in Example 13-4.)

24-21   Chopin, Etude, Op. 25/6

A similar technique can be applied to $\frac{6}{3}$ chords. Example 24-22 shows how the addition of a 4th turns a $\frac{6}{3}$ chord (here a passing I⁶) into an apparent $\frac{4}{3}$. Note that the 4th above the bass is the active element, not the 3rd, as would be the case with a real $\frac{4}{3}$.

24-22   Bach, Chorale 142

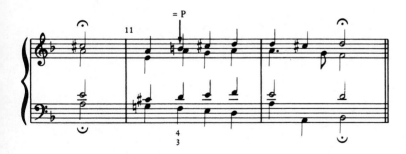

15. Apparent $\frac{4}{2}$ and $^{\circ}\frac{4}{3}$ over a stationary bass. Neighboring or, sometimes, passing motion over a sustained bass can produce an apparent $\frac{4}{2}$. In Example 24-23, the bass of the "II$\frac{4}{2}$" is consonant; the chord functions as an embellishment of I. This chord is therefore similar in its function to the neighboring $\frac{6}{4}$ (Examples 19-6 and 19-7). It contains the same tones as the neighboring $\frac{6}{4}$ plus a neighboring or passing 2nd or 9th.

24-23 Chopin, Scherzo, Op. 31

(a)

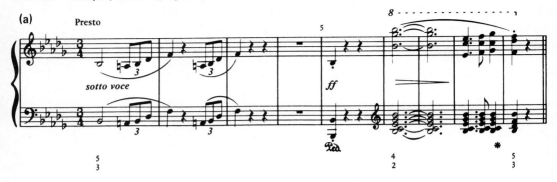

(b) reduction

Quite often one encounters what seems to be a diminished seventh chord (in $^o4_3$ position) that moves to a tonic over $\hat{4}$-$\hat{1}$ in the bass. Usually, as in Example 24-24, this is an apparent $^o4_3$, caused by neighbors and passing tones that decorate the IV-I progression. The special feature of this technique is that it adds the intensity of a leading-tone sonority to what is basically a IV-I or plagal progression. (Because the diminished seventh chord contains both $\hat{4}$ and $\hat{6}$, it can sometimes stand for subdominant or supertonic harmony. For an additional illustration, see Example 31-15.)

24-24 Schumann, Kreisleriana, Op. 16/5

16. Pedal points in an upper voice. In Example 24-25, bars 6-7, a tonic pedal is held in the top voice. Against this pedal, a complex of passing tones produces an apparent II$_3^7$. Unlike the examples quoted thus far, this "chord" does not consist of a complete triad plus an added tone, but instead merely results from a contrapuntal motion against the sustained d^2. Therefore, it is not really a chord. In the following bars, IV and V^7 are expanded by means of exactly the same technique; the C♮'s in bar 8 effect a momentary tonicization of the IV. (The B♯ and D♯'s of bar 11 are chromatic passing tones that intensify the motion to the 3rd and 5th of V^7 and, at the same time, delay their arrival.) This kind of apparent 7th—a "II" produced by a passing motion in 3rds or 10ths against a sustained $\hat{1}$—occurs rather frequently as a means of expanding tonic harmony.

24-25   Beethoven, Missa Solemnis, Op. 123, I

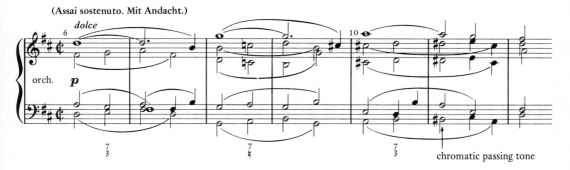

Example 24-26, by contrast, shows a much more unusual apparent 7th, though it too results from contrapuntal motion against an upper-voice pedal. The final tonic chord contains a Picardy 3rd, E♮, in the soprano. The major 3rd is sustained as a pedal, while the lower voices decorate the tonic with a plagal progression, IV-I. The coincidence of the F minor chord and the held E♮ produces an apparent minor-major $\overset{7}{\underset{3}{5}}$.

24-26   Chopin, Mazurka, Op. 56/3

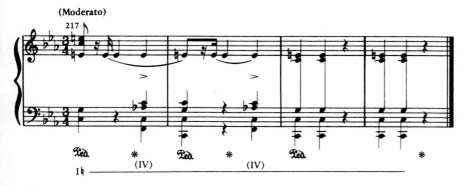

POINTS FOR REVIEW

1. Seventh chords often occur in sequence. Those based on descending 5ths are the most frequent.

2. Possibilities with roots descending by 5th include:

   a. $7\text{-}7$ e. $\frac{4\text{-}7}{3\text{-}5}$

   b. $7\text{-}\frac{5}{3}$ f. $\frac{4\text{-}6}{2\text{-}3}$

   c. $\frac{6\text{-}5}{5\text{-}3}$ g. $\frac{4\text{-}6}{2\text{-}5}$

   d. $\frac{4\text{-}5}{3\text{-}3}$

3. Sequences based on descending 3rds are less frequent but possible.

4. $5\text{-}\frac{6}{5}$ is an important variant of the ascending 5-6 series; the 5th of $\frac{6}{5}$, often in the soprano, is prepared indirectly in a lower voice.

5. Nonsequential applications of these voice-leading techniques may occur.

6. More complex treatment of the 7th and its resolution may occur in instrumental style:

   a. the resolution of the 7th may be transferred into another voice.

   b. the resolution of the 7th may be delayed.

   c. the 7th may be extended.

7. A larger harmonic complex can consist of $\natural\text{VII}^7$ leading to $\text{V}\frac{6}{5}$.

8. Apparent seventh chords resemble real seventh chords but function differently. Some frequent examples:

   a. $\frac{5}{3}$ plus added 6th becomes apparent $\frac{6}{5}$

   b. $\frac{6}{3}$ plus added 4th becomes apparent $\frac{4}{3}$

   c. $\frac{5\text{-}4\text{-}5}{3\text{-}2\text{-}3}$ over stationary bass

   d. $^{\text{o}}\frac{4}{3}$ decorating IV-I progression

   e. pedal points in the upper voice

EXERCISES

1. Preliminaries. Write short sequential progressions, each in a different key, that illustrate the techniques of sections 2 and 4 of the Points for Review in this unit.

2. Figured bass. Keyboard style possible.

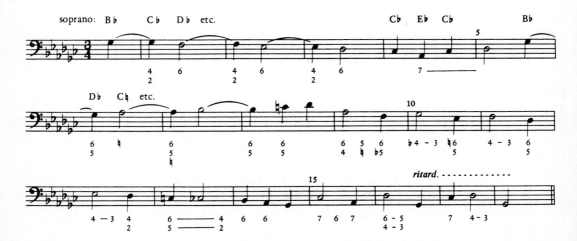

3. Melody. Add a keyboard accompaniment.

4. Figured bass using apparent 7ths. In this exercise, you may use long sustained tones in the soprano.

25

Applied V and VII

25-1 Beethoven, Piano Sonata, Op. 14/2, II

APPLIED CHORDS

1. New usages. Example 25-1, the theme from a variation movement by Beethoven, contains many applied-chord usages, only some of which we know from Unit 14. In bar 3, the soprano G♯ functions as a leading tone to A; the chord forms V_3^4 of II (V_3^4 ⌐II). In bar 7, the applied chord tonicizes V, but it is a diminished 7th (VII^{o7} ⌐V), a chord not presented in Unit 14. In this unit, then, we shall discuss some new kinds of applied chords as well as new goals and new voice-leading techniques. But before you go on, review Unit 14, sections 3 and 4.

The possibilities for applied chords include V and its inversions, V^7 and its inversions, VII and its inversions, and VII^7 and its inversions (diminished moving to either minor or major triads, half-diminished moving to major only). Example 25-2 shows some of these possibilities. Note that procedures of voice leading and chord construction follow those for normal V and VII. In particular, remember that the temporary leading tone is *not* doubled.

25-2

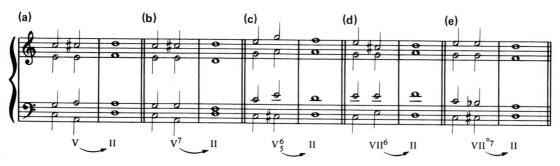

Sometimes an applied chord connects two statements of its "tonic." In our Beethoven theme, the chord on the second beat of bar 10 passes from IV^6 to IV in the same way that V_3^4 passes from I^6 to I. Similarly the fourth beat of bar 11 contains VII^6 of II passing between II and II^6; again the voice leading is exactly the same as if the D minor chord were really a tonic.

2. Cross relations. The chromaticism associated with applied chords can easily lead to cross relations (Unit 15, section 4 and Unit 22, section 7). In simpler textures it is usually best to keep the chromatic progression in a single voice (Example 25-3a). Try to avoid the harshest cross relations—those between the outer voices (25-3b).

25-3

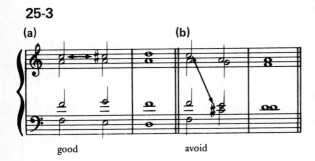

good   avoid

Sometimes, however, cross relations are quite tolerable. In progressions containing applied V_5^6 or VII^{o7}, the active character of the leading tone in the bass makes up for any slight harshness. Example 25-4 illustrates the two conditions for success:

1. Keep the cross relation between an inner voice and the bass—don't involve the top voice.
2. Avoid unnecessary leaps in the upper voices.

25-4

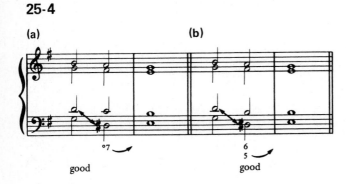

good   good

Cross relations in the same register and between adjacent upper voices have a mild effect and occur frequently, especially in keyboard style (Example 25-5).

25-5

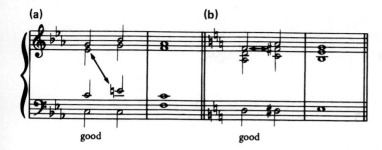

Passing tones (or passing chords) soften the effect of cross relations. Compare Example 25-6a, from a Bach chorale, with 25-6b, a version from which we have removed the passing tones.

25-6

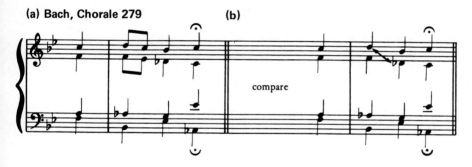

A cross relation—even between outer voices—can be logical and beautiful when it results from a *chromaticized voice exchange,* as in Example 25-7.

25-7

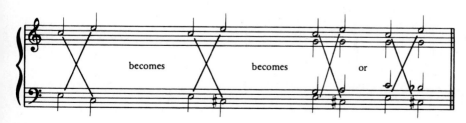

Its harshness can be further softened if the chords are connected by a passing chord. The most frequent possibility is a $^6_4$ (Example 25-8a), but a $^5_3$ (as in 25-8b) is also possible.

25-8

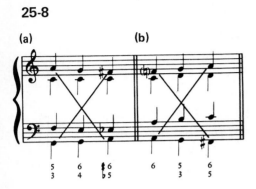

3. Applied chords as altered diatonic chords. Sometimes applied chords function as altered forms of the triads and seventh chords that normally occur within a key. Example 25-9 shows two analytic notations for the same progression, one as applied chords related to the V that follows and the other as altered functions of the tonic key. Either label is correct; one points to a local meaning of the chord, the other to a longer-range meaning. Only the larger context can help us determine which meaning is the more pertinent to a particular case. In general, chords that serve mainly to lead into broader harmonic connections—for example, replacing II or IV in an important cadence—might well be heard primarily as altered harmonies within the main key and only secondarily as applied chords.

25-9

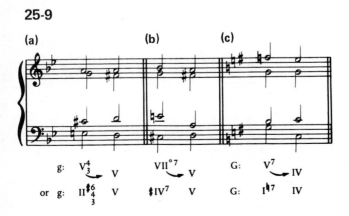

CHORDS APPLIED TO V

4. Altered II and IV. The most important applied chords are those that lead into and intensify dominant harmony. All chords applied to V are alterations of II or IV; all contain $\sharp\hat{4}$—probably the most frequent chromatically altered tone. The chromaticism and the tonicizing character of these applied chords make them much more unstable than the corresponding diatonic forms of II and IV and very much increase their drive to the dominant.

5. $\sharp\hat{4}$ in an upper voice. VII^6 of V often supports $\sharp\hat{4}$ in a rising soprano line, $\hat{3}$-$\sharp\hat{4}$-$\hat{5}$. Review Example 14-4 and the accompanying text (Unit 14, section 5). If a root-position V is not needed for $\hat{5}$, V$^4_2$ of V makes a good support for $\sharp\hat{4}$ (Example 25-10).

25-10

$$V^4_2 \quad V^6$$

   VII^6 (or V$^4_3$) of V can be very useful in harmonizing $\hat{6}$ in a bass line that descends by step from I to V (Example 25-11; see also Example 18-10).

25-11   Bach, Goldberg Variations, Aria

6. $\sharp\hat{4}$ in the bass. Perhaps the most important function of chords applied to V is to emphasize dominant harmony (usually at a cadence) by means of a rising half-step progression in the bass ($\sharp\hat{4}$-$\hat{5}$). The typical chords are V$^6_5$ of V (already presented in Unit 14, section 5) and VII^7 of V. As in Example 25-12, $\sharp\hat{4}$ is most often a chromatic passing tone leading from IV, II^6, or II$^6_5$ to V, possibly embellished by $^6_4$.

25-12

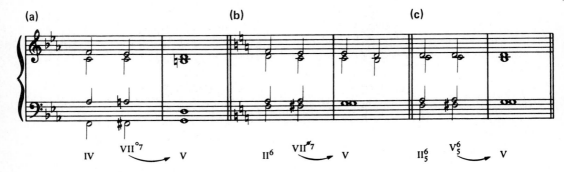

Sometimes, #$\hat{4}$ in the bass replaces ♮$\hat{4}$ altogether as in Example 25-13.

25-13   Mozart, Adagio, K. 540

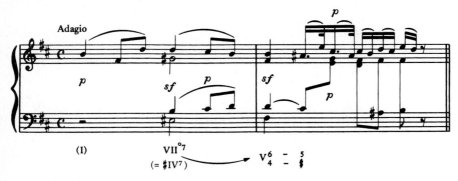

Moving directly to V, applied VII°⁷, and VII⁰⁷ create difficulties in voice leading when they support $\hat{3}$ (or ♭$\hat{3}$) in the soprano, just as with diatonic IV⁷ (review Example 12-18). Parallel 5ths (with ⁰⁷) and rather obtrusive hidden 5ths (°⁷) are the unpleasant consequences of bringing all the upper voices down by step (Example 25-14a-b). And what is a possibility with VII⁷ moving to I—doubling the 3rd of the chord of resolution—turns out to create still another difficulty—a doubled leading tone (25-14c). Bach's solutions of this problem are shown in 25-14d-f.

25-14

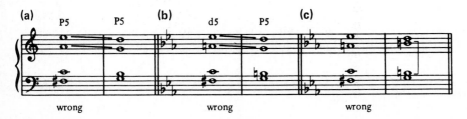

(d) Bach, Chorale 237   **(e) Bach, Chorale 336**   **(f) Bach, Chorale 146**

(tenor skip prevents hidden 5ths; compare diatonic IV⁷-V)

(The skip 1-5 in tenor prevents doubled leading tone.)

(Ant. prevents hidden 5ths.)

7. Chromaticized voice exchanges preceding V. Chromaticized voice exchanges, sometimes with #$\hat{4}$ in the bass and sometimes with #$\hat{4}$ in an upper voice, are particularly frequent in passages that connect IV with V (Example 25-15).

25-15

(a) Haydn, String Quartet, Op. 74/1, I

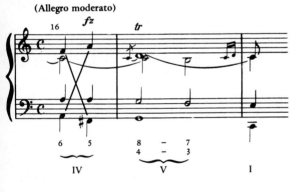

(b) Bach, Chorale 108   **(c) Haydn, String Quartet, Op. 54/1, IV**

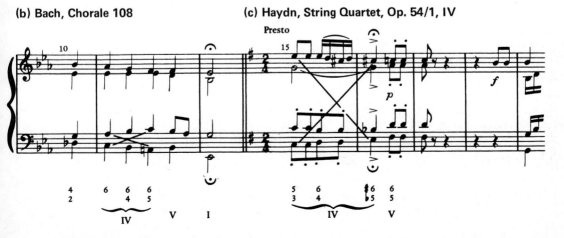

(d) Mozart, String Quartet, K. 428, II

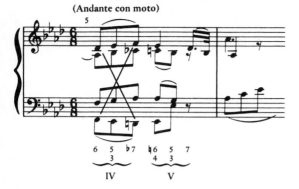

8. Deceptive cadences. Sometimes a chord applied to V appears where one would expect a cadential tonic; the applied chord, therefore, participates in a kind of deceptive cadence (Example 25-16). The soprano normally leads to $\hat{1}$ over the applied chord; the bass moves by step, either down to $\sharp\hat{4}$ (VII^{o7} or V$^6_5$ of V) or up to $\hat{6}$ (V$^4_3$ or VII^6 of V—major only). As we know, deceptive cadences usually lead on to authentic ones, their function being to delay rather than to cancel a harmonic resolution. In these progressions, therefore, the applied chord will lead on to a restatement of the cadential V and on to an authentic cadence made stronger by the immediately preceding tension.

25-16

(a) Mozart, Kyrie, final bars   (from *Requiem*, K. 626)

(b) Mozart, String Quintet, K. 515, III

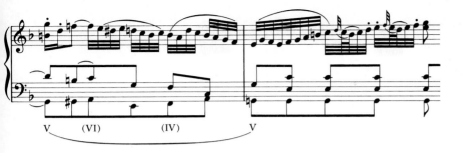

V   (VI)   (IV)   V

OTHER APPLIED CHORDS

9. Chords applied to IV. In major, V of IV is the tonic triad itself. To identify the chord as an applied dominant, we must add $\flat\hat{7}$ (Example 25-17b). In minor it is necessary to raise $\hat{3}$ in order to transform I into V of IV (25-17c).

25-17

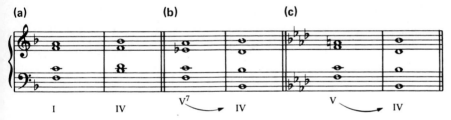

(a)   (b)   (c)

I   IV V^7 → IV   V → IV

Sometimes a tonic chord becomes V of IV as in the progression over a tonic pedal shown in Example 25-18. V of IV frequently helps to expand a I-IV-V^7 (or VII^{O7})-I progression over a tonic pedal.

25-18   Bach, Little Prelude, BWV 939

V^7 of IV can also function as $I^{\flat 7}$—as a modification of tonic harmony. The celebrated opening of Beethoven's Symphony No. 1 (Example 25-19) most certainly does *not* begin in F major. But it is only partially correct to state that the first chord is V^7 of IV in the key of C. To be sure, that is its function in relation to the next chord. However, once we begin to realize that C must be the tonic, we reinterpret the opening chord and understand it as the tonic. (A perceptive listener will begin to feel C as the tonic in the second bar.)

25-19   Beethoven, Symphony No. 1, Op. 21, I

10. Chords applied to III. III in minor is unique in the tonal system in that its applied V, V^7 and VII are present as diatonic chords in the key. As was explained in Unit 15, this is one of the reasons why the minor mode tends to gravitate to III. Example 25-20a-b illustrates. To produce V of III in major, we must raise $\hat{2}$ and $\hat{4}$ (25-20c).

25-20

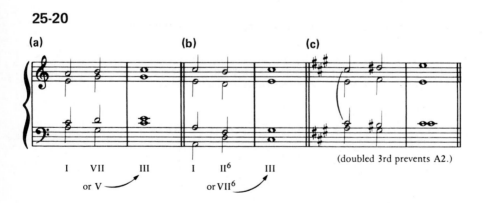

(doubled 3rd prevents A2.)

11. Chords applied to II in major. V of II and VII of II are possible only in major, for the diminished quality of II in minor prevents it from simulating a tonic. These applied chords frequently connect I and II, usually with the melodic progression $\hat{1}$-#$\hat{1}$-$\hat{2}$ in the soprano or bass (Example 25-2). Any progression from I through an applied dominant to II has as its basis the familiar 5-6 technique, as you can see in Example 25-21a. This technique is also inherent in 25-21b and c where an 8-7 passing motion over I introduces the 6th of the applied $^6_5$, a rather frequent substitution for the direct 5-6 progression. (The idiom shown here resembles the progression VII^7-V$^6_5$-I in minor discussed in the preceding unit; this resemblance relates to the fact that the progression G^7-G$\sharp^6_5$-A could also occur in A minor as VII^7-V$^6_5$-I.)

25-21

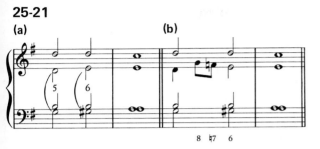

(c) Bach, Gamba Sonata, BWV 1027, IV

In major, VII of II is an altered I (VII^7 of II is an altered I^7), a relationship that makes it possible to introduce VII of II where we would expect to hear a tonic. This happens in bar 36 of Example 25-22; the diminished seventh chord replaces the expected tonic.

25-22   Schubert, Horch, horch! die Lerch, D. 889

translation: my lady sweet, arise.

12. Chords applied to VI. In minor, V of VI is identical with III; V^7 of VI and the various forms of VII of VI, however, require at least one accidental, $\flat\hat{2}$. In major, V^6_5 (less often V^6) and VII^7 of VI permit a chromatically embellished deceptive cadence (Example 25-23). Why is this not possible in minor?

25-23   Mozart, Fantasy, K. 475

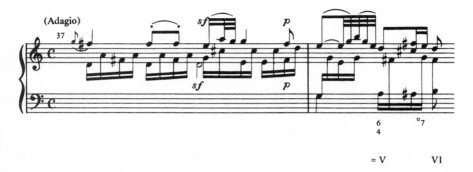

13. Chords applied to VII. As a diminished triad, VII in major (like II in minor) cannot be tonicized. On the other hand, $\natural$VII in minor can attract applied chords (Example 25-24). In this excerpt $\natural$VII functions as a neighboring chord to I, returning to it through V^6.

25-24   Bach, Chorale 23

14. Irregular resolutions of applied chords. In a passage from a Schubert waltz (Example 25-25), a chord occurs that seems to function as V^7 of IV. However, it resolves not to IV but to II^6, decorated by a suspension. In view of the close connection between IV and II^6, it would not be wrong to regard the dominant seventh on A as a chord that suggests a motion to IV but that moves irregularly to II^6.

25-25   Schubert, Valse Sentimentale, Op. 50/13

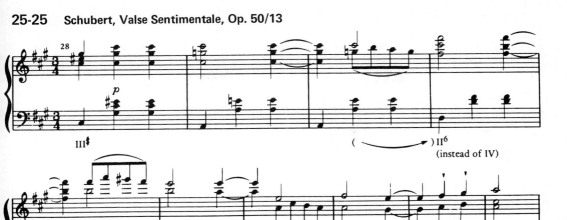

15. Apparent applied chords. Not all chords that appear to function as applied dominants actually do so. Rather frequently a chord that appears to be V (or V⁷) of VI moves to IV rather than to VI. The progression is a varied form of I-(III)-IV as you can see by comparing Example 25-26 with Example 15-11, a quotation from the beginning of the same song. Only if the larger context strongly suggests VI as a temporary center (and here it does not) ought we to think of such a progression as V of VI moving deceptively to VI of VI. Similarly, III♯, as in Example 25-25, does not function as an applied dominant.*

25-26 Schubert, Im Frühling

translation: . . . deep in the dark mountain spring [I saw] the beautiful sky, blue and bright.

*Nor is it an applied dominant in Examples 22-9 and 22-10.

APPLIED CHORDS IN SEQUENCE

16. Descending 5ths. Progressions by descending 5th (or those derived from descending 5ths) contain numerous possibilities for incorporating applied chords, since the motion from an applied V to its "tonic" is, of course, by descending 5th. Sometimes, in fact, an extended progression (usually sequential) is chromatically inflected so that each chord (triad or seventh chord) becomes the dominant of the next one. Thus, in Example 25-27, III# proceeds to I⁶ through a chain of triads, each the dominant of the next.

25-27   Beethoven, Piano Concerto, Op. 58, I

In a complete series of descending 5ths, I ⟶ I, the inevitable diminished 5th or augmented 4th (major: $\hat{4}$-$\hat{7}$, minor: $\hat{6}$-$\hat{2}$) will prevent the use of an applied dominant, for the dominant-tonic relationship is based on the perfect 5th, not the diminished 5th (Example 25-28). There is nothing incorrect, however, about a progression that mixes successive dominants with other types of motion by descending 5th.

25-28

Brief or extended chains of successive applied dominants often contain interlocking seventh chords, as discussed in Unit 24. In Example 25-29a, applied $\frac{4}{2}$ chords alternate with a $\frac{6}{5}$. Several elements of this excerpt are of interest. Brief descending chromatic lines occur in the bass and between the most prominent tones of the soprano (25-29b); such chromatic descents are the almost inevitable result of successive applied V⁷'s. The two chromatic lines produce a series of consecutive tritone dissonances: A4, d5, A4. These dissonances may look as if they don't resolve, but they don't *sound* unresolved. The reason is that the underlying voice leading (as shown in the reduction) contains the proper resolutions. In the actual progression, the resolutions are modified by contraction, but they are strongly enough implied by context to be sensed as the "background" of the progression.

25-29   Beethoven, Piano Sonata, Op. 2/3, I

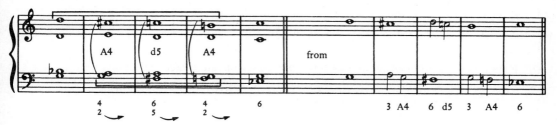

Successions of applied V^7's often contain alternating $\frac{4}{2}$'s and $\frac{6}{5}$'s, as in Example 25-29. Another frequent possibility is a series of root-position seventh chords (Example 25-30).

25-30   Chopin, Ballade, Op. 23

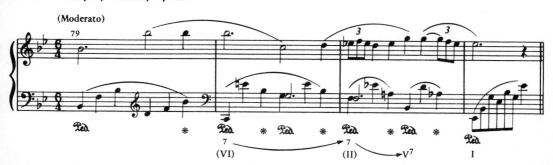

Sometimes a diminished 7th can substitute for the corresponding position of a dominant seventh (Example 25-15c, bar 16).

As we know, a progression by descending 5ths often decorates a descending stepwise line. Applied dominants are easily incorporated into such a progression. In Example 25-31, the basic idea is a stepwise motion down from I to V; the dominant seventh chords applied to VII and VI add to the directional quality and fulfill a voice-leading function as well—they prevent the 5ths and octaves that would otherwise occur between the main chords. In this excerpt, triads alternate with seventh chords (compare Example 24-6).

25-31   Chopin, Ballade, Op. 38

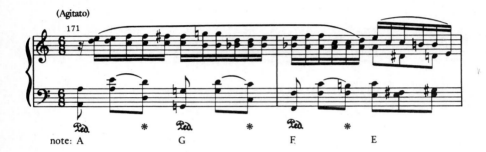

17. Sequences based on 5-6. Stepwise sequential passages based on the ascending 5-6 progression are frequently intensified by chromatic passing tones that produce applied chords of various kinds. As we can see in Example 25-32, ascending chromatic lines become a possibility; they produce the strongest effect when they are in the bass or top voice. In all these progressions, the applied chords break up parallel 5ths and octaves.

25-32

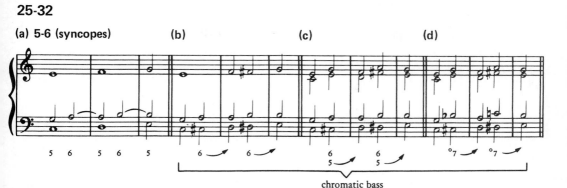

chromatic bass

chromatic soprano

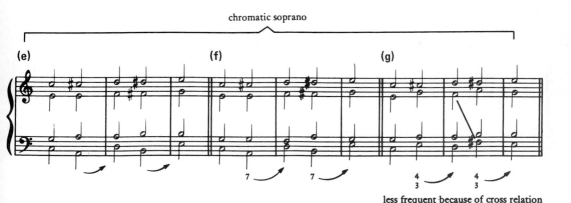

less frequent because of cross relation

Examples from the literature abound. Review, for example, two previously cited excerpts that use this technique: Example 17-1, bar 6, and Example 25-1, bars 17-18. In the latter, two points require comment. Beethoven places the applied dominants on the metrically strong beats and the "tonics" on weak beats —the reverse of what would normally occur. The rhythm implied by the harmony, therefore, contradicts the meter—a conflict humorously underscored by the *sf* signs. Moreover, the 7ths of the applied chords ascend instead of resolving down, with the resolutions transferred into the next lower voice (review Unit 24, section 9).

Until now, sequences rising from V to I in minor have been unavailable to you. With applied dominant chords added to your vocabulary, such passages become unproblematic. They can be used in connection with a deceptive cadence, the VI forming part of a passing motion from V up to I, as in Example 25-33. Note how the chromatic bass line is summarized in diminution (eighth notes) in bar 81. (Review Example 13-15, which contains a similar chromatic passing motion.)

25-33   Mozart, Piano Concerto, K. 491, I

(a)

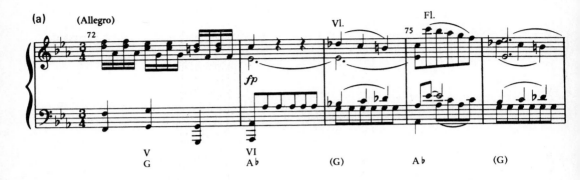

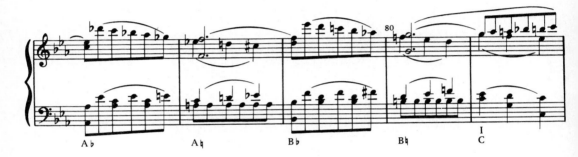

(b) reduction

18. Sequences rising in 3rds. Because of the nondirectional nature of immediate root progression by ascending 3rd, sequential passages moving up in 3rds normally require interpolated chords to contribute a feeling of forward motion. Applied dominants, usually $\frac{5}{3}$, ^{7}, or $\frac{6}{5}$, are the most useful chords for this purpose. These sequential passages usually begin on I and, most often, lead to V (sometimes, in minor, to ♮VII). In Example 25-34, the applied dominants are decorated by $\frac{6}{4}$'s.

25-34   Beethoven, String Trio, Op. 9/3, III

19. Sequences falling in 3rds. These are variants of the 5-6 progression with descending bass shown in Examples 17-15 through 17-19. In Example 25-35, $\frac{4}{3}$'s function as passing chords within a motion in 3rds from VI down a 9th to V, thus: VI-(IV-II-VII)-V. All the $\frac{4}{3}$'s are applied dominants except the one before VII (why isn't it?). In this example (and in others using $\frac{4}{3}$'s) the bass line is completely stepwise and diatonic. As a result the applied $\frac{4}{3}$'s attract very little special attention; their contrapuntal meaning as passing chords outweighs in importance the rather weak harmonic implication of V^7-I. Incidentally this sequence is unusual in that it persists through five statements of the initial idea, with only minimal variation. The reason here is a dramatic one—this is a moment of great comic suspense, as reference to the libretto and score will reveal.

25-35   Mozart, The Marriage of Figaro, K. 492, Act I

(a)

ed   al - zan - do,   pian, pia - ni - no,   il   tap - pe - to   al

ta - vo - li - no,   ve - do il   pag - gio.

translation: And gently, gently raising the
table cloth, I see the page.

(b) compare

etc.

5 - 6   5 - 6   5 - 6   5 - 6   5

A frequent variant of this sequence replaces the $\frac{4}{3}$'s with $\frac{6}{5}$ or ^{o7} chords, as in Example 25-36. Applied dominants in root position ($\frac{5}{3}$ or ^{7}) can also occur (Example 25-36b); without figuration, however, the completely disjunct bass produces a choppy effect.

25-36

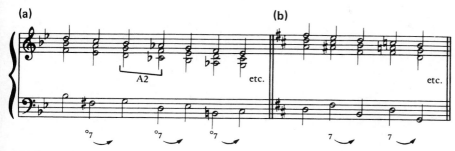

A2 OK. See Unit 23, section 11.

20. Applied dominants after main chords. Sometimes—especially in a rising progression with ascending 5ths—a chromatic alteration produces the effect of an applied chord *following* its main chord. Thus in Example 25-37, bar 12, the D♯ turns the B chord into a V of the preceding II. Such "back-relating" applied dominants are usually triads: $\frac{5}{3}$'s as in this example, or $\frac{6}{3}$'s as in Example 17-8, which contains a similar underlying progression.

25-37   Schubert, Mein!   (from *Die schöne Müllerin*, D. 795)

translation: Brook, stop your murmuring! Millwheels, stop your roaring!

POINTS FOR REVIEW

1. Any major or minor triad may be preceded by an applied V or VII (triad or seventh chord). Sometimes an applied chord connects two statements of its own "tonic." Much less frequently, an applied chord follows its tonic without leading into another statement of it.
2. Possible applied chords are:
   a. V or V^7 and their inversions.
   b. VII^6 (less often VII^5_3).
   c. VII^{o7} and its inversions.
   d. $VII^{\emptyset 7}$ and its inversions, applied to major triads only.
3. Rule of doubling: Don't double the temporary leading tone or the 7th.
4. Cross relations are generally avoided in simple textures. Possible exceptions:

   a. when the bass has the leading tone of the applied chord (V^6_5 or VII^7).
   b. when the cross relation is between adjacent upper voices *in the same register.*
   c. when the cross relation is broken up by passing tones or a passing chord.
   d. when there is a chromaticized voice exchange.
5. Avoid doubled leading tone resolving VII^{o7} of V and $VII^{\emptyset 7}$ of V. See Example 25-14 for solutions.
6. Applied V and VII often function as passing chords, particularly in sequences.
7. In sequences with descending 5ths, a chain of applied chords is possible, each sounding like the dominant of the next.

EXERCISES

1. Preliminaries (without sequences). Write a series of chords, beginning and ending with I, as described below.

	key	progression
a.	g	II^6_5 through an applied ^{o7} to $V^{6\text{-}5}_{4\text{-}3}$
b.	Ab	tonic pedal using I^{b7} as V of IV
c.	E	V^4_2 moves to VII^{o6} of II
d.	B	chromatically embellished deceptive cadence using an applied dominant to VI
e.	f	applied V to bVII followed by a convincing motion to I

2. Preliminaries (with sequences). Write sequential progressions as described below.

	key	progression
a.	g	V ⟶ I, up by 2nds using $^6_5$ chords
b.	F♯	rising 3rds to V using ^{o7} followed by deceptive cadence chromatically embellished
c.	f♯	rising 3rds to ♮VII followed by motion to I
d.	d	descending 3rds with $^4_3$ chords I ⟶ IV followed by a cadence
e.	Eb	descending 3rds with dominant 7th I ⟶ II followed by a cadence

f. f   descending 5ths with interlocking 7ths. I——▸VI followed by a cadence

g. e   I, followed by a progression of interlocking applied $\frac{4}{2}$ and $\frac{6}{5}$ chords leading to a cadence

3. Outer voices given (adapted from Chopin). Fill in the inner voices in keyboard style.

4. Figured bass.

5. Melody. Harmonize each starred note with an applied chord.

26

Diatonic Modulation

MODULATORY TECHNIQUES

1. New goals of modulation. Example 26-1 contains a modulation from G minor to D minor. Both the goal and the path leading to it differ from those discussed in Units 14 and 15. The goal—minor V—is a frequent one in pieces in minor; the path leads through a sequence in descending 5ths and includes a prominent applied chord (bar 6). In this unit you will continue the work on modulation begun in Units 14 and 15.* You will learn the remaining diatonic goals—those other than V in major and III in minor. You will learn techniques for arriving at these goals. And you will learn how these new goals function within the tonal plans of large sections and of entire compositions.

2. Related and remote keys. The majority of modulations—especially those where the new key persists for a long time—are to closely related rather than to remote keys. Two keys are closely related if the tonic of the new key functions as a diatonic chord in the old one. Two keys are more or less remote from each other if they are not so related. There are degrees of remoteness. Thus, F♯ major is more remote from C major than is A♭ major, which functions as VI in C minor and can therefore relate indirectly to C major through mixture. This unit concerns itself only with modulation to closely related keys; other modulations will be reserved for later work in chromaticism.

The keys closely related to C major are:

D minor (II)
E minor (III)
F major (IV)
G major (V)
A minor (VI)

The keys closely related to C minor are:

E♭ major (III)
F minor (IV)
G minor (V)
A♭ major (VI)
B♭ major (VII)

In each case, note that the family of closely related keys comprises all the major and minor triads that belong to the main key—the same triads, in fact, that can generate applied V's or VII's. Also note that the signatures of the related keys either are the same as that of the main key or differ by only a single accidental. One further observation: as a key area, V in minor is, in principle, *minor* (Example 26-1) rather than major; a tonicized V in C minor is usually G minor rather than G major. This is because the large-scale organization of pieces in minor tends to follow the natural form of the scale.

3. Introducing and confirming the new key. The principles that govern modulation to V, as explained in Unit 14, apply just as well to other modulations. To summarize them briefly: the new key is most often introduced by a pivot chord (sometimes by more than one); it is confirmed by a cadential progression, usually containing some form of II or IV. The pivot can be any chord that belongs to both keys; the cadence can include the pivot chord, it can follow immediately

---

*Reviewing Units 14 and 15—especially 14, sections 7-10—will make your work in this unit easier.

after the pivot, or it can appear after intervening material. Example 26-2 demonstrates modulations to IV, II, and VI in major. Note that the techniques of modulation in no way differ from those you learned in Unit 14. Of course, some of the techniques we have discussed since Unit 14 enrich the possibilities for modulation. In particular, applied chords and sequential passages can help in introducing the new key. In Example 26-3, the pivot chord follows an applied °7—a good illustration of how applied chords can help to intensify a modulation.

26-2

(a) Bach, Chorale 222

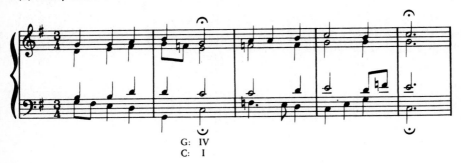

G: IV
C: I

(b) Bach, Chorale 209

Bb: IV
c: III ——— (VI) ———→ II⁶₅ V   I

(c) Bach, Chorale 137

G: V
e: ♮VII   V⁶₅   I

26-3   Bach, Chorale 207

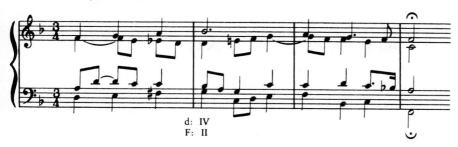

d: IV
F: II

Sometimes a sequential passage will form a more or less extended transition between two key areas. In Example 26-1, Mendelssohn achieves the modulation by means of a sequence in descending 5ths—C-F-Bb-E♮—that leads from the main tonic, G, to A, V of D minor. (From bar 4½ to the D minor tonic, the bass moves entirely by descending 5th, but only bars 5 and 6 are sequential.) It would be pointless to search for a pivot chord in this quotation. The likeliest candidate —the seventh chord on Bb (bar 6)—is in the middle of a sequence and hardly sounds like a pivotal event. The sequence as a whole forms the transition here. However, one element in the sequence—the augmented 4th in the bass of bar 6— helps to orient the listener toward D as tonic.

Sequences other than those based on descending 5ths can also prove useful in modulations. In this connection, review Example 17-1, where the second and third sequential passages lead from Bb major to F. Sequences using applied V's and VII's, as discussed in the preceding unit, appear frequently as modulatory transitions.

4. Applications to written work. Students confronted with the possibility of modulating to six different keys are often bewildered by the seemingly endless array of approaches to the new key. It is helpful (and perhaps comforting) to realize that you have already learned most of the information you need to accomplish these modulations. You will have no need to memorize the available pivot chords for any particular modulation—a formidable and wholly unnecessary task. All you need to do is to recall the way each diatonic triad functions within its key and then apply this knowledge to the new situation.

For instance, suppose you are writing an exercise in C minor and a modulation to Ab major is called for. You can reinterpret the C minor tonic chord as III of Ab. But of course you will have to know what to do with the III chord. Since establishing a temporary key area requires a strong dominant in the new key, your III will have to move convincingly to a V. You could do this fairly quickly by means of a motion through IV or II⁶ to a cadential dominant. Or you could move a bit less directly through a progression of descending 5ths: III-VI-II-V, perhaps expressed as a sequence. In either case, don't forget to insert the appropriate accidentals or your modulation will be shipwrecked. And for a strong sense of arrival, you will want to approach the new tonic with a melodic line that gravitates to its $\hat{1}$ and reaches it with a sense of rhythmic resolution. Example 26-4 illustrates. (For a review of the basic diatonic progressions as applied to modulation, see the keyboard progressions for this unit in the Appendix.)

26-4

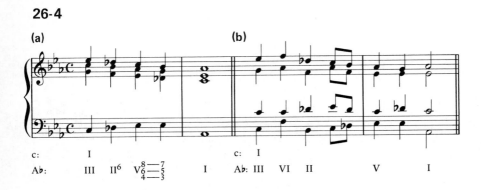

5. New techniques of tonicization. As we know, compositions can incorporate not only large-scale departures from the tonic but also smaller-scale tonicizations. The least emphatic tonicizations are those produced by the play of melodic figuration alone, without the participation of chords. In textures where the changes of chord occur more slowly than the melodic rhythms, the melodic lines (especially the top voice) will often borrow tones from the key in which the supporting chord would be the tonic. The first example in this book (Example 1-1) can serve as an illustration; the C♯'s in bar 9 produce a D minor scale and—very faintly—hint at D as tonic.

Stronger tonicizations arise out of a combination of melodic and chordal activity, as with the applied chords discussed in Unit 25. The principle of the applied chord can be extended to include brief progressions. In Example 26-5 both VI and III (the goal of the phrase) are expanded by the progression IV-V⁶-I. Any progression that expands a tonic can be used to tonicize other major or minor triads.

26-5   Bach, Chorale 201

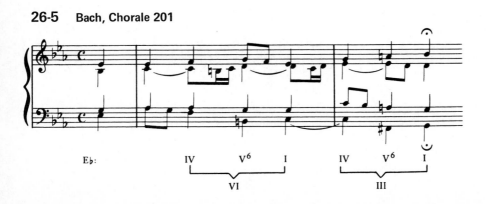

Sometimes a series of tonicized chords forms a sequence. In Example 26-6 the familiar sequence by descending 3rds is expanded by chords that suggest IV$^6_5$-V$^6_5$-I in C major, A minor, and F major. The sequential passage leads from E to F, expressed as a descending 7th rather than as the simpler ascending 2nd. (Compare Example 17-1, bars 1-2.)

26-6

(a) Bach, Little Prelude, BWV 924

(b) reduction

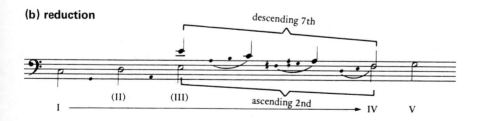

Note: The reduction shown in Example 26-6b uses in simplified form the technique of graphic music analysis developed by the great Austrian theorist Heinrich Schenker (1868-1935). In these graphs, note values mostly show structural importance rather than rhythmic relationships. In our reduction, for example, half notes depict the ascending line from I to V, which forms the harmonic/ voice-leading framework of the bass. Quarters are used to show the sequence by descending 3rds, which expands one segment of that line. And stemless noteheads refer to bass tones whose chords function locally, without entering into large-scale connections.

6. Transient modulations. Quite frequently what seems to be a newly established key area turns out to be the springboard for a more important goal. In Example 26-7, from the exposition of a Mozart trio, the main tonic, E♭ major, gives way to a C minor that persists for some three bars. The C minor "tonic," however, becomes a kind of pivot chord in a larger modulation from I to V. Such transient modulations that connect two more stable key areas are often called "passing modulations." In the Mozart, note how the twice-stated progression V$^6_5$___VI in bars 16-19 foreshadows the larger tonicization of C minor that follows immediately. (And, indeed, even the applied dominant is foreshadowed by the B♮ to C in the melody of the preceding phrase, as you can see by looking back to Example 13-14, which quotes this phrase.)

26-7   Mozart, Trio for Clarinet, Viola, and Piano, K. 498, I

MODULATION, LARGE-SCALE MOTION, AND FORM

7. Tonal plans. In a unified composition, the succession of key areas is no more haphazard than the succession of chords in a single well-composed phrase. The great composers had the marvelous ability to convey a sense of purposeful motion over large as well as small musical spans. The large-scale plan of a piece involves more than key areas, but within such a plan, modulation can play a most important role; it is this aspect of composition that we shall begin to investigate in the remaining sections of this unit. Or, better, we shall begin to begin to investigate it. The subject is exceedingly complicated and the possibilities are virtually endless, so we can present only some of the most important and typical ones. Even experienced musicians can encounter great difficulties in trying to understand the unifying principle of a complex piece. In this respect, as in others, the study of music is a lifetime's work—and more.

8. I-III-V in minor; modulation to III. By far the most frequent modulation in minor is from I to tonicized III. A modulation to III often helps to articulate the form of a piece in minor, much as a modulation to V might do in major. Thus sonata-form movements in minor normally move to III for the second key area of the exposition; Baroque pieces in binary form often arrive at a tonicization of III before the central double bar. Of all modulations, the one to III in minor is the easiest to accomplish and the most natural sounding. This is partly because no accidentals are required, partly because of the inherent tendency of minor to gravitate to its mediant (Unit 15, section 2).

Despite the importance of modulation to III in minor, the III itself is not a final goal. Instead it usually forms the midpoint of a bass-arpeggio motion from I to V, often expanded by a passing IV between III and V. The III fulfills the same function, therefore, as in the smaller progressions discussed at the beginning of Unit 15; only the scope is expanded—sometimes considerably. The importance of I-V-I as the basic harmonic progression is reflected in the fact that even modulations to areas other than V—to III, for example—normally function within a larger framework of tonic-dominant.

Example 26-8 shows the basic harmonic plan of the exposition and development of the first movement of Mozart's Piano Sonata in C minor, which moves from III through a passing IV to V. The goal V appears first as a *minor* chord. The minor V, of course, does not lead forcefully to I; before the recapitulation, therefore, the leading tone must appear. Mozart introduces it prominently in the bass, supporting V$^6_5$. One other feature deserves mention. The development section begins with a quotation of the opening idea—but, startlingly, in C major. Subsequent events clarify the meaning of this C major; it does not function as a tonic, but rather as V of IV (F minor). On a very large scale, tonicized IV fulfills its familiar function of leading from III to V.

26-8   Mozart, Piano Sonata, K. 457, I (sketch)

From this point on, we shall be showing the large-scale harmonic plans of many of the pieces discussed by means of voice-leading reductions (as, for instance, in Example 26-8). You *must* consult the scores when you study these reductions if they are to be at all meaningful.

9. Modulation to III in major. Modulation to III has much less importance in major than in minor; the major mode has no inherent tendency to move to III, as has minor. Especially in the Classical period, diatonic III occurs rather infrequently as an abiding key area in major-mode pieces. Both in the Baroque period and in the nineteenth century, however, tonicized III does sometimes form part of large-scale harmonic progressions. Nineteenth-century composers would occasionally introduce into major the characteristic I-tonicized III-V pattern of minor, as in Example 26-9.

26-9   Brahms, Intermezzo, Op. 117/1

10. Modulation to the minor V. A frequent goal of modulation for pieces in minor is the natural, minor V. In fugal expositions in minor, for example, where the alternation of subject and answer creates movement between tonic and dominant, tonicizations of the minor dominant will naturally occur. If the fugue has a long subject, the tonicization may be substantial and may even create the impression of a brief modulation, as in Example 26-10. Note how Bach introduces the leading tone (bar 12) to prepare for the next entrance in the tonic—exactly the same principle as in 26-8.

26-10   Bach, Organ Fugue in G Minor, BWV 578

Modulations to the minor V can also occur at the midpoint of binary movements and—much less often—in sonata expositions (Beethoven, Op. 90, first movement).

11. Modulation to IV. If it occurs early in the piece, a modulation to IV in major can disorient the listener. This is because the tonic in major is also V of IV (Unit 25, section 9); too much emphasis on IV as a "key" can upset our sense of tonality, making us hear IV as I and I as V. Composers have generally avoided modulating to IV early on, though brief tonicizations frequently occur even at the very beginning.

Modulation to IV in major creates no problems of tonal balance if it occurs later in the piece, as in the middle section of a three-part form. The tonicized IV usually moves on to V of the home key in order to prepare the return of I. This procedure is sketched in Example 26-11. A similar use of tonicized IV often characterizes the C section of rondo forms. When tonicized IV occurs in ABA and rondo forms, it frequently—and typically—enters right at the beginning of the new section without a transition.

26-11   Mozart, Violin Sonata, K. 377, III

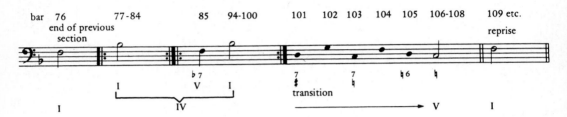

Early modulations to IV are not as problematic in minor as in major, for the minor tonic cannot sound like V of IV unless its 3rd is raised. Nevertheless such early modulations are quite rare. The main theme of Chopin's F minor Ballade contains a modulation to a considerably emphasized and extended IV. Example 26-12 sketches the tonal plan, in which a briefly tonicized III (Ab major) leads from the opening F minor to its subdominant, Bb minor. Note the difference between this tonal plan and Example 26-8. In the earlier excerpt, the IV forms a transition between III and V. In the Ballade, on the other hand, IV functions as a goal; this time it is the III that forms a transition—between I and IV. Eventually, of course, the IV itself moves on to V and I.

26-12   Chopin, Ballade, Op. 52

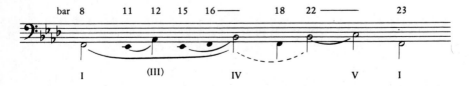

Tonicized III can lead to a goal IV in major as well as in minor.

12. Modulation to VI. Modulation to VI occurs frequently in both major and minor. In major, VI is the easiest *minor* triad to tonicize. This is because the two scales have seven common tones; only one accidental is needed to effect the modulation—the leading tone of VI (G♯ in a modulation from C major to A minor). In minor, VI is also quite easy to tonicize, since its dominant occurs naturally (without chromatic alteration) on the third scale degree.

A most important function of tonicized VI is to lead down in 3rds from I to IV. The progression that results represents the expansion of the descending bass arpeggio discussed at the beginning of Unit 11. Example 26-13 shows the small-scale application of this technique.

26-13   Beethoven, Violin Sonata, Op. 30/1, II

The same plan frequently occurs over much larger musical spans. Mozart sometimes uses it in the C sections of his rondo movements. Example 26-14 shows a reduction from a substantial part of the last movement of his Piano Concerto, K. 488. (The expanded and tonicized IV moves to V through an "augmented 6th chord"—a type of chromatic chord to be discussed in Unit 29.)

26-14   Mozart, Piano Concerto, K. 488, III (sketch)

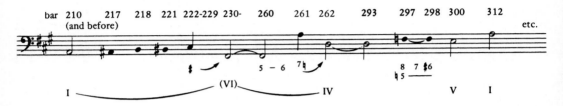

Beethoven—especially in his later works—sometimes used a similar plan for movements in sonata form, thus:

For illustrations, see the first movements of the Piano Sonata, Op. 111 and the Ninth Symphony.

13. Modulation to II in major. II occurs infrequently as an enduring key area, partly because of its strong tendency to move to V. However, tonicizations lasting a few measures are quite common, especially at the beginning of a piece, where repeating the opening idea one step higher can be most effective. As one would expect, the tonicized II will normally move on to V. Example 26-15 illustrates.

26-15 Bellini, Casta Diva (from *Norma*)

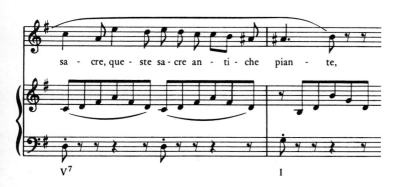

translation: Goddess, chaste and silvery,
these ancient, sacred plants . . .

14. Modulation to VII in minor. Brief tonicizations of VII in minor occur fairly often, especially in Baroque music. Usually the VII leads to V, as in Example 26-16, where it serves as the connecting link in a III-V progression.

26-16   Bach, Chorale 149

Large-scale tonicizations of VII—as in the Scherzo from Beethoven's Ninth Symphony—are rare and unusual occurrences.

15. Modulation within a prolonged dominant. Compositions in which the main modulation is to V often extend the V through one or more subordinate modulations before returning to I. Such sections often gravitate to a tonicized VI as upper neighbor to V. When the V comes back, it is often preceded by a II or IV and often supports a 7th in order to lead convincingly to I. Example 26-17 shows a sketch of the tonal plan of the Gavotte from Bach's French Suite No. 5. The piece is in binary form; the tonicized V arrives before the first double bar. The V is extended by a tonicization of VI (upper neighbor) and a briefer one of IV (lower neighbor). Development sections of movements in sonata form often show similar tonal plans, but usually on a much larger scale.

26-17   Bach, French Suite No. 5, Gavotte (sketch)

16. Large-scale expansions of contrapuntal chords. All the tonal plans we have discussed so far may be thought of as expansions of basic progressions leading to V and eventually to I. Although these form what is undoubtedly the most important category of modulation in tonal music, other possibilities exist, especially in sectionalized compositions. For example, in *da capo* arias of the Baroque period and in nineteenth-century ABA forms, the middle section might expand IV, VI, or III; the composition might then return to the tonic at the reprise of the A section without an intervening dominant, thus expanding the contrapuntal progressions discussed in Units 13 and 16.*

POINTS FOR REVIEW

1. Most modulations are to related keys—those whose tonics occur as diatonic triads in the main key and whose key signatures are the same as or differ by only one accidental from that of the main key.

2. Modulations to related keys are usually introduced by a pivot chord and confirmed by a cadence that includes some form of II or IV as well as V.

3. Instead of a pivot chord, a sequence can lead to the new key.

4. A transient, or passing, modulation can connect two more stable key areas.

5. Tonicizations can be produced by:
   a. figurated melody.
   b. chord progressions—most often including an applied dominant.

6. Tonicized chords can occur within sequences, frequently those descending by 3rds.

7. In I-tonicized III-V-I in minor, a passing IV (often tonicized) usually connects III V. This is the most frequent tonal plan in minor. Occasionally, the same plan occurs in major.

8. Another frequent possibility in minor: I-V♭-V♮-I.

9. A possibility both in major and minor is I-tonicized IV-V-I. Beware of modulating to IV *early* in the piece, especially in major.

10. Tonicized VI leading down in 3rds from I to IV is frequent in both major and minor.

11. I-tonicized II-V-I (possible in major only) is a frequent progression in opening themes; II is usually of brief duration.

12. Tonicized VI often functions as upper neighbor to V within a large-scale expansion of dominant harmony.

*A simple example, too long to quote, is Chopin's Mazurka, Op. 17, No. 1, which expands I-IV-I, the most important of these possibilities.

EXERCISES

1. Preliminaries. Write the following progressions. Each should consist of about 8-12 chords and should be in a definite meter. For illustration, see the Appendix, Example *l* in the progressions for this unit.

   a. Establish F♯ minor; modulate to A major, using IV of F♯ minor as a pivot.
   b. Establish A♭ major; modulate to C minor, using V of A♭ major as a pivot.
   c. Establish F minor; modulate to B♭ minor, using VI of F minor as a pivot.
   d. Establish E major; modulate to A major, using II of E major as a pivot.
   e. Establish D minor; modulate to A minor, using III of D minor as a pivot.
   f. Establish D♭ major; modulate to B♭ minor, using V of D♭ major as a pivot.
   g. Establish B minor; modulate to G major, using IV of B minor as a pivot.
   h. Establish E♭ minor; modulate to D♭ major, using I of E♭ minor as a pivot.

2. Select three progressions from Exercise 1; expand them into more extended phrases that return to the original tonic. For illustration, see the Appendix, Example *m* in the progressions for this unit.

3. Figured bass. Set for strings. Vocal ranges need not be strictly observed. Where the figure 7 occurs, you will have to decide whether it stands for a seventh chord or a suspended 7th resolving into a $\frac{6}{3}$.

Corelli

4. Unfigured bass.

    a. Make a simple four-part setting, paying particular attention to tonicized areas.

    b. Optional. Make a more elaborate figurated setting of the same bass.

Fenaroli (adapted)

5. Melody. Set for strings. Measures 9-12 could be in three parts. Analyze carefully for figuration.

6. Chorale melody. Set for four voices.

7. Melody. Set in four-part chorale style.

Bach

8. Menuetto. Set for piano or strings with free texture.

VI

DISSONANCE AND CHROMATICISM II

9th and 7th resolve by parallel motion into the 9th and 3rd of tonic harmony.
Since the 9th appears mostly in the soprano, the parallel motion will usually be in
3rds or 10ths; if the 9th appears in an inner voice, parallel 6ths become possible.

27-2

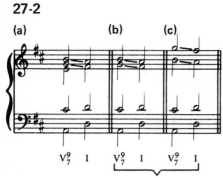

in five voices   5th omitted in four voices

In major, the 9th between $\hat{5}$ and $\hat{6}$ is major; in minor, it is minor. As we know, $\flat\hat{6}$ frequently appears in major through mixture; $V^{9\flat}_7$, consequently, occurs readily in major (Example 27-3).

27-3   Beethoven, Piano Sonata, Op. 31/1, I

2. Melodic functions of the 9th. The 9th above the dominant—like the 7th—functions as an element of melodic figuration. Most often, as in the Schubert, the 9th is a neighbor. As we know, the most characteristic function of $\hat{6}$ is to form an upper neighbor to $\hat{5}$; using V^9_7 gives us a new way to harmonize $\hat{5}$-$\hat{6}$-$\hat{5}$. If it follows a chord that contains $\hat{6}$ (mainly IV or II), the 9th can appear as a common tone (suspension if accented). If V^9_7 follows III or $\natural$VII in minor, the 9th can function as a descending passing tone; this usage is by far the least frequent. Example 27-4 illustrates.

27-4

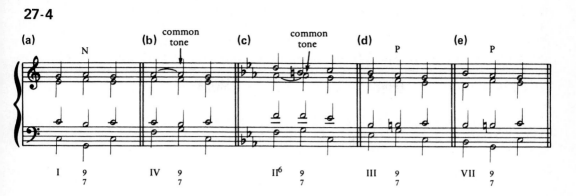

Compared to seventh chords, ninths play a decidedly secondary role in composition. The reason lies in the different ways the resolution of the dissonance relates to chord progression. Adding a 7th to a triad produces a dissonance *that cannot resolve within the chord.* Thus F in the seventh chord G-B-D-F resolves to E, a tone foreign to the G chord. Using the 7th, therefore, promotes progression to a new chord—one that contains the tone of resolution. Because the dissonance so powerfully influences harmonic direction, it is useful—indeed necessary—to think of seventh chords as a special category, bearing in mind the fact that they are really triads plus a dissonant passing tone or suspension.

With ninths, the situation is completely different. If we add a 9th to a seventh chord, we produce a dissonance that can easily resolve within the chord —that resolves, in fact, to a tone already present in the bass. Thus A in the ninth chord G-B-D-F-A resolves to G, a chord tone already present in a lower voice and register. And very frequently, in fact, a 9th above V resolves to an octave within dominant harmony. Example 27-5 illustrates this possibility; in such cases it is best to think of the 9th as an ordinary neighbor or suspension.

27-5   Schubert, Trauer-Walzer, Op. 9/2

Because the 9th can—and frequently does—resolve without a change of chord, it cannot intensify chord progression in the way the 7th does. What it *can* do is intensify the dissonant character of the dominant—the harmony that more than any other tends to attract dissonant formations. And the added dissonance helps to create a rich sonority, a feature that was attractive to many composers— especially those of the nineteenth century. For the most part, you can get along very well without thinking of "ninth chords" as a separate category; think of them simply as seventh chords that support an emphasized tone of figuration. However, dominant ninths *in root position* often reveal seeming irregularities in dissonance treatment; the label V_7^9 makes it easier to discuss such cases. Non-dominant ninths occur infrequently except in sequences; inverted ninth chords are also infrequent, for reasons that we shall discuss in section 7. You do not need to learn them as individual chords.

3. Unresolved 9ths. Undoubtedly the most unusual feature of V_7^9 is the fact that the dissonance, seemingly, is often left unresolved. In principle, as we have learned, the 9th of V_7^9 resolves by stepwise descent. However, if the 9th accompanies a 7th that *does* resolve, composers will frequently omit the resolution of the 9th. The converse, by the way, is not true; unresolved 7ths occur most infrequently, whether or not they accompany 9ths. Example 27-6 contains two unresolved 9ths, both from works of Beethoven. In the first excerpt, the 9th appears in the course of a florid melodic line as a kind of embellishing tone above the 7th. (The 7th does not resolve in the melodic line, but it is transferred into the accompaniment where it resolves.) In the second excerpt, the 9th is followed by a passing octave (*not* a resolution) that leads down to the 7th, which resolves in the soprano line.

27-6

(a) Beethoven, Violin Sonata, Op. 24, II

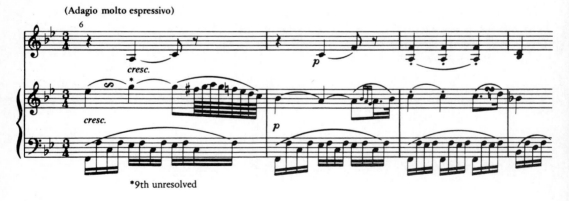

*9th unresolved

(b) Beethoven, Piano Sonata, Op. 10/1, I

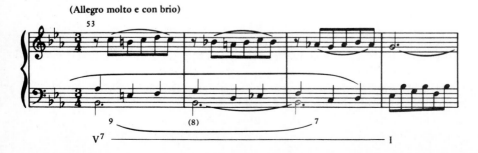

However they may look on paper, such 9ths do not *sound* unresolved—hence the unusual freedom in dissonance treatment. Because $\hat{5}$, the tone of resolution, is present as a common tone in both V (the chord that contains the dissonance) and I (the following chord), the listener does not require a literal resolution as strongly as with the 7th. If an unresolved 9th receives a great deal of emphasis, a composer might incorporate a stepwise descent from the same pitch into a later part of the piece. This happens, in fact, in the Beethoven violin sonata of Example 27-6 where the G returns in bar 18 and initiates a stepwise descending line, perhaps as a compensation for its having been left in the air earlier in the piece.

4. Unprepared 9ths. Unprepared dominant 9ths, as in the two excerpts of Example 27-6, appear rather frequently, especially if the 9th enters in the soprano *after* dominant harmony has begun to sound.

5. 9ths in applied dominant chords. 9ths occur as freely in applied dominant chords as in the true dominant of the key. In Example 27-7, $^9_7$'s are applied to IV and V. Note that the 9ths are transferred into an inner voice, where they resolve.

27-7   Chopin, Barcarolle, Op. 60

6. 9ths in sequences by descending 5th. Because the resolution of the 9th goes very well with root progression by descending 5th (as in V^9_7-I), 9ths are easily incorporated into sequential progressions by descending 5th. If the sequence is diatonic, as in Example 27-8, such 9ths are always suspensions. Most nondominant 9ths that appear in music before the latter part of the nineteenth century form part of such sequential progressions. In four-part writing—and, for the most part, in free textures as well—the sequence will alternate $^9_7$'s and $^7_5$'s (Example 27-8a);* a five-part texture permits a series of interlocking $^9_7$'s (27-8b).

*See also Mozart's Piano Concerto, K. 467/I, bars 147-53.

27-8

(a)   **(b)**

Chromatic textures sometimes contain sequences of applied V_7^9's in descending 5ths; each applied chord sounds like the dominant of the next. In Example 27-9, an excerpt from Dvořák's G major Symphony, the 9ths are all minor. Note the curious simultaneous use of E♭ in the winds and D♯ in the strings; this enharmonic conflict arises because the winds play a melodic figure that requires the E♭.

27-9   Dvořák, Symphony, Op. 88, IV

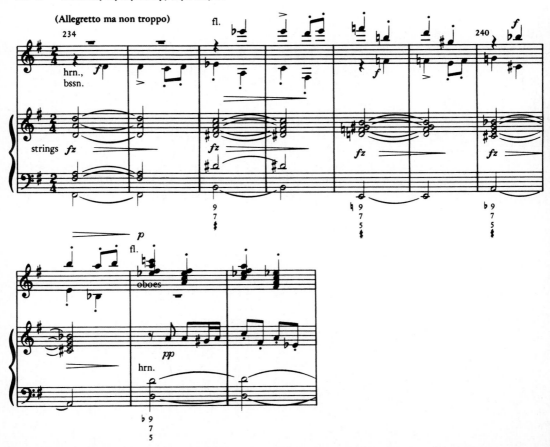

7. Inversions of V⁹₇. V⁹₇ appears most often in root position, not in inversion. Where a seeming inversion of V⁹₇ occurs, it can always be regarded simply as an inversion of V⁷ supporting a neighbor or suspension. In Example 27-10, for instance, the chord applied to III is easily understood as a ⁶₅ that supports a suspension in the soprano. Dissonant formations like the one in this excerpt are not very frequent, owing to the simultaneous presence of a dissonant suspension in the soprano and the tone to which it will resolve in the "tenor." You will remember (Unit 21, section 12) that suspensions are most effective if the tone of resolution is not anticipated in a voice other than the bass. With inverted ninth chords the dissonance always appears at the same time as the tone of resolution, which is never in the bass. The result is usually an unclear sonority and an ineffective resolution of the dissonance. In the Chopin excerpt, the contrast in register caused by the unusually wide space between melody and accompaniment helps to maintain a clear texture.

27-10   Chopin, Mazurka, Op. 63/2

*See Unit 28.

8. Relationship between V⁹₇ and VII⁷. Perhaps you have already noticed that the four upper notes of V⁹₇ form a leading-tone seventh chord, diminished or half-diminished depending on whether the 9th is minor or major (Example 27-11).

27-11

In free textures a composer can exploit this relationship by adding V in the bass below a leading-tone seventh chord, thus creating a $\frac{9}{7}$, as in Example 27-12.

27-12   Schumann, "Spring" Symphony, Op. 38, I

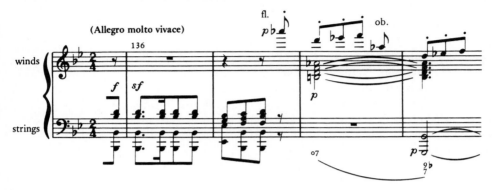

9. 9ths above a pedal point. We have seen that the initial tonic over a pedal point may be expressed as V^7 of IV (Example 25-18). Adding another dissonance creates the possibility of expressing the tonic as V^9_7 of IV, as in Example 27-13, where the chords above the pedal suggest I-IV-V-I, the initial I transformed into V^9_7 of IV.

27-13   Schumann, Das ist ein Flöten und Geigen   (from *Dichterliebe,* Op. 48)

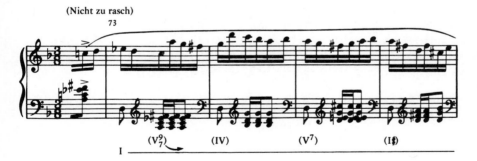

Example 27-14, also from a Schumann lied, contains a 9th that has a very different meaning. Note that the opening sonority does not contain the leading tone (the D♯ on the last sixteenth of bar 1 is simply a neighbor, not a chord tone). Because $\hat{7}$ is missing, the opening chord does not sound like a normal dominant ninth but, rather, like a II above a dominant pedal. The underlying sense of bars 1 and 2 is a progression leading from II to V over V as a pedal point. Quite often, the 5th, 7th, and 9th above V seem to form a II chord, especially when the leading tone—such an important feature of V—does not sound.

27-14   Schumann, Mondnacht   (from *Liederkreis,* Op. 39)

"ELEVENTHS" AND "THIRTEENTHS"

10. **V⁷ with unresolved 4ths and 6ths ("dominant eleventh and thirteenth chords").** As we know, 4ths and 6ths can appear over V^7 as suspensions or incomplete neighbors; they will normally resolve to 3rds and 5ths (Example 27-15a and b). Sometimes, especially in nineteenth-century music, such dissonances are left unresolved, the resolutions being supplied mentally by the listener (27-15c and d).

27-15

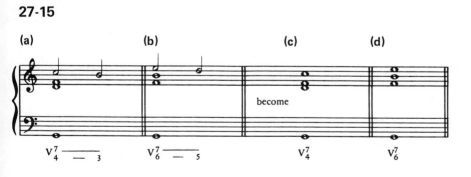

An excerpt from a Schumann Novellette (Example 27-16), contains an unresolved 4th over V^7 and, in a sequential repetition, over V^7 of II. Leaving the 4ths unresolved makes them sound like anticipations of the following chord tones, $\hat{1}$ and $\hat{2}$.

27-16 **Schumann, Novellette, Op. 21/8**

The end of the first section of Chopin's Ballade, Op. 38 (Example 27-17) contains an unresolved 6th. By leaving out the tone of resolution, Chopin creates the effect of a pedal point in the soprano; the A seems to float above the alternating tonic and dominant chords. By writing as he does, Chopin achieves a wonderful dramatic preparation for the Presto con fuoco in A minor that follows; the association of E and F under A is a common element that connects these two contrasting sections.

27-17 **Chopin, Ballade, Op. 38**

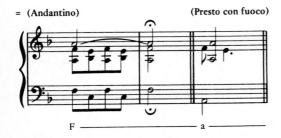

Unless the listener hears an unresolved dissonance clearly, it will create a mess rather than the expressive effect the composer intended. As a consequence, such dissonances must appear in a prominent part, almost always the soprano. Therefore the unresolved 4th or 6th will appear *above* rather than below the 7th. Partly because these tones typically appear in the highest voice, some theorists refer to such 4ths and 6ths as "11ths" and "13ths." These terms also result from the erroneous idea that such dissonances are chordal in origin, that "9ths," "11ths," and "13ths" result from adding 3rds above seventh chords. In some twentieth-century music, dissonant chords might really result from the piling up of 3rds. In Example 27-18, for instance, a II^7 chord is sustained while first a 9th and then an 11th are added to it; eventually all six tones sound at once.

27-18 Ravel, Valses Nobles et Sentimentales, I

But in earlier music, dissonant chords originate in melodic motion, not in the piling up of vertical intervals. There is no reason, therefore, to regard "11ths" and "13ths" as anything but 4ths and 6ths that replace, rather than resolve to, 3rds and 5ths belonging to seventh chords. Some passages in music of the late nineteenth century might, perhaps, form an intermediate category. The excerpt quoted in Example 27-19 contains a melodic sequence rising in 3rds over a pedal point; the rising melodic progression produces three unresolved dissonances with the bass or inner voices: a 9th, a 4th (11th), and a 6th (13th). The cumulative effect is less dissonant than in the Ravel, for the 3rd and 5th are not retained throughout the passage. Yet in some ways—the manner in which the dissonances enter and their lack of clear contrapuntal function—the passage seems closer to the Ravel than to the Chopin and Schumann excerpts quoted earlier.

27-19   Bruckner, Symphony No. 8, III

*sounds one octave lower than written

Elevenths and thirteenths, like ninths, can result from a progression of chords above a pedal point. The remarkable opening of Schumann's Fantasy (Example 27-20) contains a II^7 over a dominant pedal. The II^7 moves to a V in bar 7; note, however, that the F and A of the left-hand part move to G and B only in bar 8 so that for a moment the two chords are blurred together. You might compare this excerpt with Example 27-14, also a quotation from Schumann, to see how a great composer can use very similar voice-leading and harmonic techniques to achieve vastly different expressive results.

27-20   Schumann, Fantasy, Op. 17, I

POINTS FOR REVIEW

1. The dominant ninth (V_7^9) results from adding $\hat{6}$ to V^7. $\hat{6}$ almost always appears in the soprano and functions as a suspension or a neighbor, less often as a passing tone. Through mixture, $V_7^{9\flat}$ can appear in major.

2. Except, perhaps, for V_7^9 in root position, ninth chords are best understood as seventh chords that support an additional dissonant tone of figuration.

3. In principle, 9ths resolve down by step. If they accompany 7ths that resolve, however, 9ths are frequently left unresolved.

4. 9ths are normally prepared as suspensions or neighbors; unprepared 9ths, however, are frequent.

5. 9ths often appear in applied dominant chords and (as suspensions) in sequences by descending 5th. In four voices such sequences must alternate $\frac{9}{7}$'s and $\frac{7}{5}$'s.

6. 9ths in inversion occur infrequently and are best regarded as inversions of V^7 accompanied by a tone of figuration.

7. The four upper tones of V_7^9 form a leading-tone seventh chord; in free textures it is possible to introduce $\hat{5}$ in the bass below VII^7, thus producing a $\frac{9}{7}$.

8. 9ths can appear over pedal points.

9. So-called dominant eleventh and thirteenth chords are merely dominant sevenths with unresolved 4ths and 6ths (suspensions or neighbors), almost always in the soprano, that replace the 3rd or 5th of V^7.

EXERCISES

1. Preliminaries. Write progressions which contain the chords described below. Use a different key for each progression.

   a. the 9th of V_7^9 treated as a neighbor

   b. the 9th of V_7^9 treated as a suspension

   c. the 9th of V_7^9 treated as a passing tone

   d. the 9th of V_7^9 not resolved

   e. 9th chords in a diatonic sequence of descending 5ths ($\frac{9-7}{7-5}$)

   f. applied dominant 9ths in sequence

   g. VII^7 becomes V_7^9

   h. V^7 with an unresolved 4th

   i. V^7 with an unresolved 6th

2. Figured bass. Beginning with bar 11, the 9ths are incomplete neighbors.

soprano: c♯²

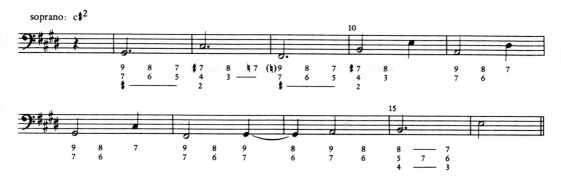

3. Melody. The bass will be mostly half and whole notes, with some quarters.

Slow

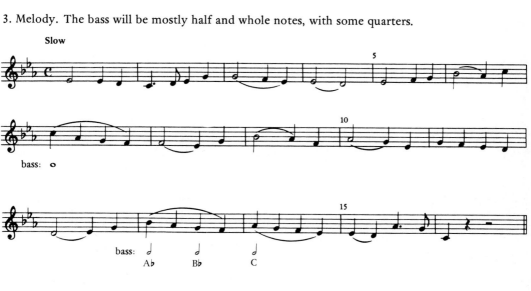

bass: o

bass: ♩   ♩   ♩
      A♭ B♭ C

4. Waltz. Set in free keyboard style, one chord per measure. ($\frac{6}{4}$ chords may occur on "weak" measures).

bass: G —————————— G♯ ——————————

28

The Phrygian II (Neapolitan)

A CHORD LEADING TO V

1. The Phrygian II and the Neapolitan 6th. Example 28-1, an excerpt from Mozart's well-known Fantasia in D minor, illustrates a most important chromatic procedure. The climax of the piece (bar 52) is marked by the statement, in a sudden and dramatic forte, of an E♭ major chord in $\frac{6}{3}$ position. This chord results neither from tonicization nor from the mixture of major and minor—the two

456

sources of chromaticism that we have already encountered. What, then, is the "foreign" E♭ triad doing in a composition in D minor? Playing the passage with E♮'s instead of Mozart's E♭'s gives us at least a partial answer. The E♮'s produce a diminished triad—the normal II chord of D minor. Even in $^6_3$ position, this diminished chord has a sound that is too meager and harsh for the extended duration and strong emphasis indicated by the composer. Mozart's E♭ triad, therefore, is a chromatic variant of II^6 with $\hat{2}$ lowered to $♭\hat{2}$; the alteration produces a major triad that replaces the normal diminished triad where the latter might give an unsatisfactory effect.

♭II in minor is often called the *Phrygian II,* for like II in the Phrygian mode, it is a major triad whose root lies a minor 2nd above the tonic. In using this term we do not imply that the composition has changed—even temporarily—from minor to Phrygian; we simply indicate the presence in minor of a sound normally characteristic of Phrygian. (In a genuine Phrygian piece, the chord would *function* quite differently than it typically does in minor.)

In the Mozart Fantasia, ♭II appears in $^6_3$ position. This is normal; the root position occurs much less frequently. Most musicians refer to ♭II^6 as the *Neapolitan 6th*—supposedly in reference to the school of composers active in Naples in the latter part of the seventeenth century and the beginning of the eighteenth. The Neapolitan composers did indeed use the chord, but so did some of their contemporaries located elsewhere—Henry Purcell among others. The symbol N^6 (N for Neapolitan) sometimes appears in harmonic analyses; we do not recommend using it, for it fails to convey the relation of the chord to diatonic II^6.

2. Harmonic and melodic functions. Just like diatonic II^6, the Neapolitan 6th typically moves to V or V^7, most often at a cadence. Sometimes the V follows immediately. At other times, as in the Mozart, the bass passes chromatically through $\sharp\hat{4}$ with an applied $^o7$ (or $^6_5$) connecting the Neapolitan chord and V; the rising chromatic line of the bass and the descending chromatic line of the soprano make for a beautiful and expressive contrast. Very frequently (again, Example 28-1), a cadential $^6_4$ expands V. Placing $♭\hat{2}$ in the soprano creates the greatest intensity; therefore, that arrangement is the most usual, especially at cadences. But $\hat{4}$ and $\hat{6}$ can also occur in the soprano. In the Mozart, the melodic figuration touches upon all three chord tones, but we hear $♭\hat{2}$ as the main one.

Example 28-2 shows some typical progressions in a four-part texture without figuration. The main point to remember is that $♭\hat{2}$ tends to move *down.* If the Neapolitan 6th goes directly to V (or V^7), $♭\hat{2}$ skips down to the leading tone; the melodic line will contain a diminished 3rd (28-2a and b). If there is a $^6_4$ (c), a passing applied chord (d), or both (e), the diminished 3rd is filled in by a passing tone. The diminished 3rd often makes for a peculiarly intense melodic line, especially when it occurs in the soprano.

In general, the bass ($\hat{4}$) is the best tone to double. This doubling allows one to prepare the 7th of V^7 (28-2b); note that V^7 will be incomplete. One further point: $♭\hat{2}$ and $♮\hat{2}$ form a cross relation when ♭II^6 moves directly to V$^5_3$ (a). The cross relation is softened if a $^6_4$ or applied chord decorates the progression, but it does not create a bad effect even in immediate succession. You may use it freely.

28-2

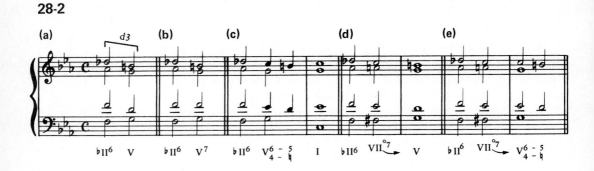

The Neapolitan chord has a characteristically individual quality that is unmistakable, though very difficult to describe in words. In part, this quality results from a tension between melodic and harmonic tendencies. $\flat\hat{2}$ is melodically active in the direction of $\hat{1}$, just like all tones situated a minor second from a stable degree of the scale. If melody were the only consideration, $\flat\hat{2}$ would proceed immediately to $\hat{1}$ as its goal. But the chord it belongs to represents supertonic harmony and tends to move to V. When V appears, $\flat\hat{2}$ must be replaced by $\natural\hat{2}$—usually in another voice; harmonic necessities prevent the immediate progression of $\flat\hat{2}$ to $\hat{1}$. ($\flat\hat{2}$ might seem to move directly to $\hat{1}$ if a cadential $\frac{6}{4}$ or an applied chord follows $\flat$II^6, but this "$\hat{1}$" functions as a passing tone, not a melodic goal.) Only if V moves on to I, does $\hat{1}$ appear as a goal. The chromatic adjustment of $\flat\hat{2}$ to $\natural\hat{2}$ and the impossibility, in normal circumstances, of an immediate motion from $\flat\hat{2}$ to a goal $\hat{1}$ can give a great deal of intensity to progressions involving $\flat$II^6. This is often a compelling reason for using $\flat$II^6 even in places where diatonic II^6 would not be incorrect. It also accounts for the frequent use of $\flat$II^6 at climactic moments, at fermatas, before rhetorical silences, and so forth.

3. Melodic contrast between $\flat\hat{2}$ and $\natural\hat{2}$. The contrast between "dark" $\flat\hat{2}$ and "bright" $\natural\hat{2}$ can have great expressive power, especially when both tones appear in the soprano. Composers often use this contrast as an important compositional feature. One possibility is to state a musical idea twice with diatonic II^6 (or $\frac{6}{5}$) in one statement and the Neapolitan chord in the other. A remarkable instance occurs at the end of the Menuetto from Mozart's G minor Quintet (Example 28-3), where the varied repetition sounds like a despairing answer to the "questioning" deceptive cadence before it. And the third statement—in major—of the same idea, at the beginning of the Trio, takes on added significance through its contrast with the dark color of the preceding phrase—a color to which the Neapolitan chord contributes so much.

28-3 Mozart, String Quintet, K. 516, II

Another way to contrast $\flat\hat{2}$ and $\natural\hat{2}$ is to feature the latter as the soprano tone of V. In Example 28-4, the A♭ of the Neapolitan sets off and emphasizes both the A♮ of V and the passing A♮ over the cadential $^6_4$.

28-4 Mendelssohn, Song without Words, Op. 102/4

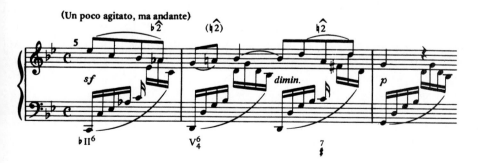

4. Avoiding the direct progression ♭$\hat{2}$-♮$\hat{2}$. Although the contrast between ♭$\hat{2}$ and ♮$\hat{2}$ is an important resource, especially when it occurs in the soprano, composers usually avoid the *direct* chromatic progression ♭$\hat{2}$ (over ♭II) to ♮$\hat{2}$ (over V). The melodic motion seldom sounds convincing; also, it can result in bad voice leading —a melodic augmented 2nd and, possibly, parallel octaves (Example 28-5a, b, and c). (If ♭$\hat{2}$ is doubled in an inner voice, it may go to ♮$\hat{2}$, as in d.)

28-5

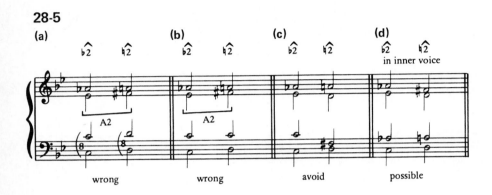

A soprano progression ♭$\hat{2}$ to ♮$\hat{2}$, therefore, will usually occur *indirectly*; other tones will be interpolated between the variant forms of $\hat{2}$. Example 28-6 shows the most important possibilities; all of them involve ascending chordal skips. (Also compare Example 28-3, bars 41-43.)

28-6

5. Leading to the Neapolitan 6th. Any chord that leads to II⁶ in minor can also precede ♭II⁶. VI (as in Example 28-1) is a very frequent possibility; so is I. Using I⁶ or III allows a stepwise ascent in the bass; Example 28-3 shows I⁶ while Example 27-10 shows a similar use of III. Very frequently ♭II⁶—just like diatonic II⁶—comes from IV through a 5-6 progression, as in Example 28-7.

28-7   **Handel, Harpsichord Suite No. 3, I**

(Presto)

(IV) ——— ♭II⁶

(♪♪ in original)

Adagio

VII°⁷ ———→ V⁶₄ ———————————— ⁷ I
                  ⁸   ⁵
                               ♮

The Neapolitan 6th can form an excellent goal for a series of ⁶₃ chords in parallel motion, as in Example 28-8. In this excerpt the ⁶₃'s lead from a tonic to the cadential Neapolitan chord. In bar 28 a seeming tonic is interpolated between ♭II⁶ and V; this "I" supports a passing tone in the soprano and is not part of the harmonic framework.

28-8   **Mozart, Dies Irae**   (from *Requiem,* K. 626)

(Allegro assai)

sol - vet sae - clum   in fa - vil - la te - ste Da - vid cum Sy - bil - la.

a: I ——————————————————————————→ ♭II⁶   ("I")   V⁶ - ⁵
                                                        ₄   ♮

translation: All shall crumble into ashes, as David and the Sybil prophesied.

6. Moving to V$^4_2$ or VII$^{o4}_3$. Like diatonic II^6 or IV, the Neapolitan 6th can move to an inverted dominant (or to a diminished 7th) in places where a strong cadential V is not needed. Of the several possibilities, the most important is moving over a sustained bass to V$^4_2$ (Example 28-9) or to VII$^{o4}_3$.

28-9   Bach, Well-Tempered Clavier II, Prelude 14

7. The Phrygian II in $^5_3$ position. The $^5_3$ position of ♭II occurs much less often than the $^6_3$. An immediate motion to V, as at a cadence, creates a dissonant leap —a diminished 5th or an augmented 4th—in the bass. As a result, the root position of ♭II sounds somewhat disconnected from V and does not lead to it as naturally and convincingly as does the Neapolitan 6th. As a cadential chord, therefore, ♭II$^5_3$ will usually occur for a specific compositional reason. In Example 28-10, using it allows Chopin to state an important motivic element—a descending 5th in the bass.

28-10   Chopin, Prelude, Op. 28/20

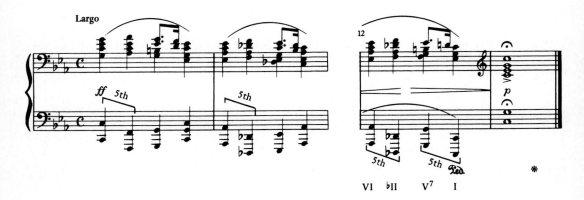

The Phrygian II in root position moves very convincingly to V^6, V$^6_5$, or VII^{o7}. Example 28-11 illustrates; note that the characteristic diminished 3rd now occurs in the bass. Usually, as in our example, a passing tone fills in the diminished 3rd; the passing tone often supports a $^6_3$ or $^6_4$ chord.

28-11   **Schubert, Die Krähe**   (from *Winterreise,* D. 911)

$\flat$II   V^6_____7_____ VI $\flat$II^6 V$^6_4$ $^7_\natural$ I

If $\flat\hat{2}$ is doubled in an inner voice (the most usual disposition), it may move directly to $\natural\hat{2}$. But remember to avoid this melodic progression in the soprano (Example 28-12).

28-12

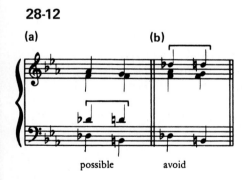

possible   avoid

8. $\flat$II in major; enharmonic notation. The real home of $\flat$II is the minor mode; the chord occurs much less readily in major. The fact that II in major is not a diminished triad eliminates one reason for introducing $\flat\hat{2}$. In addition, the intense, "dark" character of $\flat$II makes it more generally suited to minor than to major. Finally, producing the chord in major requires two chromatic alterations: $\natural\hat{2}$ to $\flat\hat{2}$ and $\natural\hat{6}$ to $\flat\hat{6}$. Both alterations create augmented 2nds (with $\hat{3}$ and $\hat{7}$), a feature that can make for awkward melodic lines. In eighteenth-century music, $\flat$II usually appears in major as part of a larger mixture with minor. Thus in Example 28-13, the introduction of A$\flat$ minor in bar 73 prepares the Neapolitan chord of bar 74. The main bass tone of this chord is D♭; the chord, therefore, is in $\frac{6}{3}$ position. At its onset, however, the chord is a $\frac{6}{4}$—a stable one, since it moves immediately to the $\frac{6}{3}$ position.

28-13

(a) Bach, Well-Tempered Clavier II, Prelude 17

(b) reduction

In Example 28-14, lowered VI precedes ♭II and acts as its dominant. The expressive power of the Phrygian II is used to beautiful effect in this excerpt. It occurs at the end of a movement in major; the unexpectedly dark color of ♭VI-♭II gives a peculiarly inward quality to these last exclamations of "Christe, Christe."

28-14   Verdi, Kyrie   (from *Requiem*)

translation: Christ, have mercy.

Sometimes, especially in nineteenth-century music, ♭II will come directly from a chord that belongs to major rather than from one that results from mixture with minor. Use your ears if you attempt this procedure; progressions that lead convincingly to ♭II in minor can sound unnatural in major. In most situations, the best strategy is to approach ♭II⁶ from I⁶.

In major keys with four or more flats in the signature, ♭II will require one or two double flats as accidentals. Especially in figurated textures, this can complicate reading the music (as some of you surely observed in studying Example 28-13). Composers, therefore, will sometimes adopt an *enharmonic notation* for ♭II: in G♭ major, for instance, they might write it as G♮-B♮-D♮ instead of A♭♭-C♭-E♭♭. To understand such passages you must be guided by the sound, not the visual pattern.

9. The $^6_4$ position. An enharmonic notation occurs in Example 28-15, where the D major chord stands for E♭♭ major—the Phrygian II of D♭ major. This excerpt shows the most unusual position of ♭II—the "Neapolitan $^6_4$." The bass moves by stepwise descent to the root of V⁷, thus inverting the typical ascending bass motion of the Neapolitan 6th. Here, the $^6_4$ has a linear function—its bass is upper neighbor to V. At the same time it has a harmonic meaning, for the root progression ♭II-V is heard quite clearly. Because of the harmonic meaning, this is a stable $^6_4$—stabilized not by its own root position (or $^6_3$) but by the associations evoked by its progression to V.

28-15

(a) Liszt, Waldesrauschen

(b) reduction

10. Tonicizing ♭II. Tonicizations of ♭II occur frequently—especially those in which the chord is preceded or expanded by its own dominant. The expansions—though they may be fairly long—do not impede the eventual progression from ♭II to V, as we can see in Example 28-16. In this excerpt, note how the expressive effect of the Phrygian chord is enhanced by the suddenly low register of the melodic line.

28-16   Chopin, Mazurka, Op. 33/4

A thematic idea first presented on I in minor can be convincingly repeated, a half step higher, on ♭II. In such situations, ♭II is often briefly tonicized, as in Example 28-17 where it is followed by an applied dominant. In this example, the large-scale progression is I (bars 1-4)-♭II (5-8)-V (9ff). Using ♭II makes possible in minor a design you learned in major in Unit 26 (review Example 26-15). The diminished chord on ♮II would be impossible here, as you can prove by playing Example 28-17 with G♮'s instead of G♭'s.

28-17   Beethoven, Piano Sonata, Op. 57, I

11. ♭II in figurated textures. Figuration—especially scalewise figuration—against ♭II can occur in one of two ways. Sometimes it follows the scale of which ♭II is the tonic. Thus in Example 28-13, the 32nd-note figuration follows the B♭♭ major scale and hints at a very brief tonicization of ♭II. More often, though, composers follow the tonic scale when they figurate ♭II. In Example 28-1, bar 53, for instance, Mozart uses A♮ rather than A♭ in the soprano. This latter option is often the better one, especially when ♭II moves fairly directly to a cadential V; the figuration can then help to prepare the listener for the subsequent course of the music. But if ♭II is tonicized for a long time (as in Example 28-16), the elements of figuration should be drawn from its own scale.

OTHER USES OF ♭II

12. ♭II in sequential passages. ♭II can improve the effect of sequences in minor—particularly those that rise by step from I. (You will perhaps remember from Unit 17 that the diminished triad on II makes it difficult to use such sequences in minor.) In Example 28-18, note that Verdi uses a C major triad instead of diatonic II (C♯ diminished); since this passage includes applied chords, an alteration of II is required—a diminished triad cannot generate an applied V.

28-18   Verdi, Son giunta!   (from *La Forza del Destino*, Act II)

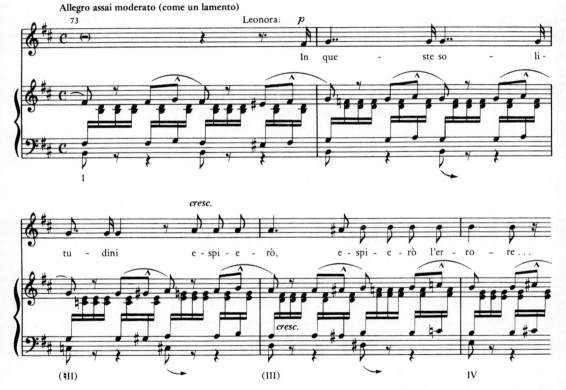

translation: In this solitude, I will atone my sin.

13. ♭II as a pivot chord. In the modulations that we have dealt with so far, the pivot chord (if there is one) occurs diatonically in both keys. In general, diatonic pivots tend to produce a smooth, unobtrusive change of key. Since ♭II is not a diatonic chord, its use as a pivot can create a feeling of surprise that attracts attention to the key change. The very unexpectedness of such a modulation can enhance the expressive character of the passage. In Example 28-19, the reprise of the opening idea owes much of its unusual charm to the way the D major $^6_3$ chord changes its meaning. This excerpt illustrates what is probably the most frequent use of ♭II as pivot: the Neapolitan 6th of a minor key becomes IV^6 in the major key a 3rd lower.

28-19   Schubert, Piano Sonata, D. 959, III

The term *chromatic modulation* is often used to describe a key change in which the pivot is a chromatically altered chord in one or both of the keys. Any modulation in which ♭II serves as pivot would be a chromatic one.

14. "♭II" as a passing or neighboring chord. As you have seen, ♭II characteristically leads to and intensifies V within the framework of the harmonic progression I-V-I. In addition, though much less frequently, "♭II" can result from a linear progression in which $\hat{2}$ is lowered for expressive, coloristic, or motivic reasons. Most often this will happen within an expansion of I. An excerpt from Chopin (Example 28-20) shows "♭II" formed by a passing and by neighboring tones within the final tonic of the piece. Because it occurs during the coda, the "♭II" functions much like a IV used at a plagal cadence. Note the pedal points—typical for a coda—in the tenor (bars 61-62) and the bass (bars 63-64).

28-20   Chopin, Etude, Op. 25/4

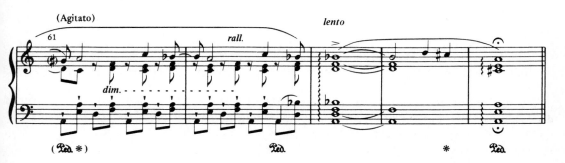

15. The apparent Neapolitan ⁶₅. ♭II rarely supports true seventh chords. A progression from a "Neapolitan seventh" to V could produce difficulties in voice leading, for both the 7th and ♭$\hat{2}$ tend to have the same goal of motion, #$\hat{7}$. The majority of "Neapolitan sevenths," therefore, are apparent, rather than real seventh chords. Mostly, as in Example 28-21, they are apparent ⁶₅'s and result from a combination of a minor triad on IV and a minor 6th above the bass. This minor 6th is ♭$\hat{2}$; as in our example, it functions as an ascending chromatic passing tone similar, in principle, to the diatonic "added 6ths" that we discussed in Unit 24, section 14.

28-21

(a) Schumann, Anfangs wollt'ich fast verzagen
(from *Liederkreis,* Op. 24)

translation: And I believed I would never bear it.

(b) basic plan   **(c) with chromatic passing tones**

CHROMATIC NOTATION

16. Why chromatic notation sometimes varies. Some of you have probably noticed that similar chromatic elements are sometimes notated differently. For example, a passing tone that rises from $\hat{1}$ to $\hat{2}$ in A minor might be an A# in one piece and a B♭ in another; indeed, the two notations might coexist in the same piece. This variability reflects the fact that the structure of tonal music is basically diatonic and that chromatic elements function within a diatonic framework.

It does not signify that chromatic notation is entirely arbitrary, that there are no principles or conventions governing its use. In fact there are a number of such principles, and following one of them might make it necessary to set aside another. This is the main reason for the variations in "spelling" chromatic elements.

17. Notating chromatic neighbors. One principle that is almost always followed deals with the notation of chromatically altered neighbors. They are notated as minor 2nds (thus on a *neighboring* part of the staff) and not as augmented unisons (on the same line or space). The preferred notation gives a better visual image and also conveys the "leading-tone" quality often associated with chromatic neighbors. This principle applies to incomplete as well as to complete neighbors. Example 28-22 illustrates.

28-22   chromatic neighbors

(a)   **(b)**

18. Showing the direction of passing tones. With chromatic passing tones, notate the passing tone and its goal as a minor 2nd, thus: C-C♯-D, not C-D♭-D♮. The first notation gives a better sense of direction than the second, for the resolution of the passing tone coincides with a change to a new line or space on the staff. And just as with the neighboring notes, the preferred notation conveys leading-tone implications. Remember, then, that we use raised notes ascending and lowered ones descending, as Example 28-23 illustrates.

28-23   chromatic passing tones

(a)

(b)

19. Avoiding "remote" accidentals. Sometimes, however, chromatic passing tones are notated in a way that contradicts their direction. Thus, as in Example 28-24, a chromatic descent from $\hat{5}$ to $\hat{3}$ in C major might be written with an F♯ instead of a G♭. And one rising from $\hat{5}$ to $\hat{8}$ might have a B♭ instead of an A♯. Composers have tended to avoid accidentals that suggest remote keys and to prefer those that are closely connected with the home key. In C major, F♯ and B♭ (which belong to the closely related keys of G and F) fit in more smoothly than G♭ and A♯ (which belong to the remote keys of D♭ and B).

28-24

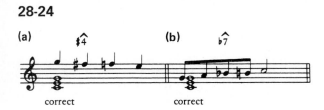

(a) $\sharp\hat{4}$ (b) $\flat\hat{7}$

correct   correct

The chromatics that are preferred because of their close relation to the key are: in major, ♯$\hat{4}$ and ♭$\hat{7}$; in minor ♯$\hat{4}$ and ♯$\hat{3}$. These normally occur as passing tones both ascending and descending. (Remember that this rule applies only to passing tones, not to chromatically altered neighbors.) The alternative forms should be avoided as passing tones unless using them gives a clearer picture of how the music goes. In Example 28-25, for instance, the G♭ is unquestionably correct. The soprano's F♮ and the F major chord that supports it are goals; using F♯ (which does not suggest F as a goal) would obscure the tonal direction.

28-25

G♭, not F♯

20. Notating chromatic scales. The information in sections 18 and 19 forms the basis for notating chromatic scales. The conventional procedure is as follows:

In major: The scale degrees that belong to the key *must* be represented in the chromatic scale, both ascending and descending. In A major, for example, *always* use C♯, F♯, and G♯ rather than D♭, G♭, and A♭. The chromatic steps are raised notes going up the scale and lowered notes descending (section 18), *except* that #4̂ and ♭7̂ are used both ascending and descending (section 19). Example 28-26 shows the completed scale.

28-26

(a) ascending

(b) descending

In minor: The diatonic scale degrees will occur both ascending and descending. In addition, the raised forms of 6̂ and 7̂ will be used in both directions. #3̂ and #4̂ will also occur in both directions (section 19). This means that a chromatic scale in minor is the same up and down *except* that #1̂ will occur ascending and ♭2̂ descending (Example 28-27).

28-27

(a) ascending

(b) descending

And even this lone distinction sometimes disappears. Composers (Mozart, for example) will sometimes use ♭2̂ in the ascending scale; as the "Neapolitan" note, ♭2̂ bears a sufficiently close connection to the key to count as a preferred chromatic.

POINTS FOR REVIEW

1. ♭II (Phrygian II) in minor is a major triad built on lowered $\hat{2}$.

2. ♭II typically occurs in $\frac{6}{3}$ position; it is generally called the Neapolitan 6th. Its usual goal is $V^{(7)}$, mostly, though not always, at a cadence. ♭II⁶ and $V^{(7)}$ may be connected by a passing applied chord built on $\sharp\hat{4}$; a cadential $\frac{6}{4}$ may expand the V.

3. ♭$\hat{2}$ tends to move down. If ♭II⁶ goes directly to $V^{(7)}$, a melodic diminished 3rd (♭$\hat{2}$-$\sharp\hat{7}$) will normally result; the melodic succession ♭$\hat{2}$-♮$\hat{2}$ is best avoided, especially in the soprano. The melodic diminished 3rd is often filled in with a passing tone, thus: ♭$\hat{2}$-$\hat{1}$-$\sharp\hat{7}$.

4. The best doubling in ♭II⁶ is the bass ($\hat{4}$); the other doublings are possible.

5. In minor, any chord that leads convincingly to ♮II⁶ can also lead to ♭II⁶; a series of parallel $\frac{6}{3}$'s can culminate in ♭II⁶.

6. In non-cadential situations, ♭II⁶ can lead to inversions of $V^{(7)}$ and to various positions of VII°⁷. Typical possibilities are V^4_2 and VII°$^4_3$.

7. ♭II$^5_3$ occurs much less often than ♭II⁶, largely because of the diminished 5th or augmented 4th in the bass when moving to V. Sometimes ♭II$^5_3$ moves to V⁶, V$^6_5$, or VII°⁷ with a bass motion by diminished 3rd, frequently filled in by a passing tone.

8. ♭II$^{(6)}$ sometimes occurs in major, though it is less frequent than in minor, and more difficult to use convincingly. It is most easily approached through ♭VI and through I⁶. For convenience in reading, ♭II is sometimes notated enharmonically, especially in keys with four or more flats.

9. The $\frac{6}{4}$ position is the least frequent; sometimes it arises out of a bass arpeggiation within ♭II, sometimes the bass acts as upper neighbor to V.

10. ♭II may be tonicized.

11. ♭II may be a pivot chord in a chromatic modulation; a typical use is ♭II⁶ of a minor key reinterpreted as IV⁶ of the new (major) key.

12. ♭II makes possible a convincing sequential progression rising by step from I in minor.

13. ♭II may function as a passing or neighboring chord—often within an expansion of I, sometimes over a tonic pedal at the end of a piece.

EXERCISES

1. Preliminaries. Using a different key for each, write brief phrases or progressions that demonstrate the techniques listed below. In some of the progressions ♭II⁶ should follow a chord other than I or I⁶. Use minor except where major is indicated.

   a. ♭II⁶-V

   b. ♭II⁶-V$^4_2$

   c. ♭II⁶-VII°$^4_3$

d. $\flat$II^6-applied chord on $\sharp\hat{4}$-cadential $^6_4$

e. $\flat$II^6 preceded by parallel $^6_3$ chords

f. $\flat$II$^5_3$-V$^6_5$ or VII^{o7}

g. $\flat$VI-$\flat$II^6 in major

h. $\flat$II briefly tonicized

i. $\flat$II in a sequence rising from I

j. Modulation from G minor to E$\flat$ major using $\flat$II^6 of G minor as a pivot

2. More preliminaries. Write one-octave chromatic scales: B major, G$\flat$ major, D$\sharp$ minor, F minor.

3. Melody.

* = appoggiaturas

4. Melody. Don't harmonize the sixteenth notes.

5. Figured bass.

29

Augmented Sixth Chords

29-1   Mozart, Piano Sonata, K. 310, I

A CHROMATIC PREPARATION FOR V

1. Leading-tone chromaticism. The interval of the augmented 6th characterizes an important group of chromatic chords called, naturally enough, *augmented 6th chords*. They are featured prominently in Example 29-1, an excerpt from the development section of a sonata movement by Mozart. This part of the development contains the climactic dominant that forms the goal of the entire section. The first augmented 6th (bar 73) ushers in this culminating dominant; the later ones (bar 78) intensify the dominant immediately before the onset of tonic harmony at the beginning of the recapitulation.

In the Mozart, the augmented 6th chords contain F in the bass and D♯ (together with other tones) in the right-hand part. The augmented 6th, F-D♯, resolves by opening out into an octave on E; this octave E forms part of a V chord (Example 29-2). To generalize, the bass of an augmented 6th chord is a half step above $\hat{5}$ ($\hat{6}$ in minor or $♭\hat{6}$ in major), one of the upper voices is a half step below $\hat{5}$, and the resolution is to an octave on $\hat{5}$ as part of dominant harmony.

29-2

The presence of an augmented 6th chord is a sure indication of chromaticism, for the augmented 6th cannot occur diatonically; no diatonic scale contains, for example, both F♮ and D♯. The resolution of an augmented 6th to an octave sounds like nothing else in tonal music. With its half-step progressions by contrary motion, it intensifies the following chord in a unique way. As a consequence, augmented 6th chords often occur just before important structural points; composers can use them to signal the beginning or end of a phase in the tonal movement or the form.

Like applied V and VII chords, augmented 6ths exemplify a fundamental type of chromaticism: *leading-tone chromaticism*. In the Mozart, for example, the D♯'s—the chromatically altered tones—are leading tones to E.* However, the augmented 6ths differ from applied chords in at least one crucial respect. The temporary leading tone, taken by itself, is an agent of tonicization, but the chord as a whole does not belong to the "key" of the chord to which it resolves. In the Mozart, D♯ sounds like $\hat{7}$ of E, but F♮, the bass tone, does *not* belong to the key of E. Unless there is strong evidence to the contrary, therefore, the resolution of an augmented 6th will not sound like a tonic, one reason why augmented 6ths function so well as preparations for important dominant chords.

*The sonata begins with a grace-note figure D♯-E. The augmented 6ths and their resolutions embody this figure; they recall the opening of the movement to the listener's mind and help to prepare the recapitulation motivically as well as harmonically.

2. Contrapuntal origin. As we know (Unit 25), $\sharp\hat{4}$ is one of the most frequently used chromatic tones, often functioning as a passing tone, as in a bass line rising from IV to V. As Example 29-3a indicates, augmented 6th chords originate in a similar use of $\sharp\hat{4}$ as a chromatic passing tone, but in an upper voice; the chordal background is the familiar Phrygian cadence in minor. If $\natural\hat{4}$ is omitted, through the technique of contraction, the interval of the augmented 6th will occupy the full duration of the chord (29-3b). This certainly gives greater emphasis to the augmented 6th but does not change its essentially passing function.

29-3

The augmented 6th chord shown in Example 29-3 is the simplest type, a $\frac{6}{3}$ chord. Adding a 5th, as in Example 29-4a produces an augmented $\frac{6}{5}$. Starting with $II\frac{4}{3}$—a chord very closely related to IV^6—gives us an augmented $\frac{4}{3}$ (29-4b).

29-4

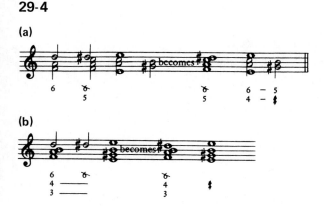

3. Geographical names. Musicians frequently refer to the augmented $\frac{6}{3}$ as the "Italian 6th," to the augmented $\frac{6}{5}$ as the "German 6th" (or "German $\frac{6}{5}$"), and to the augmented $\frac{4}{3}$ as the "French 6th" (or "French $\frac{4}{3}$"). The geography is meaningless, but the names are convenient and are in very wide use; learn them. Example 29-5 shows the three important types of augmented 6th chord.

29-5

Italian $\frac{6}{3}$ German $\frac{6}{5}$ French $\frac{4}{3}$

Introducing ♭$\hat{6}$ through mixture makes it possible to use augmented 6th chords in major (Example 29-6).

29-6

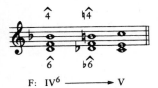

F: IV⁶ ⟶ V

4. The Italian 6th. Example 29-7 illustrates the solution for the main problem posed by this simplest of the augmented 6ths: what to double in four-part texture. Beethoven doubles the 3rd—the only good strategy, for any other doubling will lead to a poor sonority, awkward melodic lines, or parallel octaves.

29-7   Beethoven, Piano Sonata, Op. 78, II

Very often, the Italian 6th appears as a three-note chord without doubling, either in a three-part texture or in a free setting where the number of parts changes. It is usually the best of the augmented 6ths for places that need a thin, transparent sonority.

5. The German $\frac{6}{5}$. By contrast, the German 6th—probably the most frequently used augmented 6th chord—has a fuller sound and is appropriate to thicker, more complex textures. Unlike the Italian 6th, which usually moves directly to V, the German 6th typically moves to a V expanded by a cadential $\frac{6}{4}$. In minor, the German 6th and the $\frac{6}{4}$ share two common tones (Example 29-8); in major, there is a common tone and a motion by chromatic half step (Example 29-13). The progression to the $\frac{6}{4}$ is smooth and convincing in either mode.

29-8 Beethoven, Piano Sonata, Op. 13, III

Moving directly to V (without a $^6_4$) is also possible and, in fact, is rather frequent. But there is a problem. In a setting without figuration and with normal, stepwise voice leading, parallel 5ths are inevitable (Example 29-9).

29-9

Composers have developed various strategies for dealing with these 5ths. But since motion to a cadential $^6_4$ (which breaks up the 5ths) is by far the most frequent possibility, we shall reserve discussion of these more specialized techniques for a later section.

6. The French $^4_3$. Unlike the other augmented 6th chords, the French 6th contains two dissonances above the bass: an augmented 6th and an augmented 4th. There are also dissonances among the upper voices: another augmented 4th (or diminished 5th) and a major 2nd (or minor 7th). This high concentration of dissonances gives the French 6th a sharp, pungent sonority. When it is emphasized by rhythm, texture or accentuation, the effect can be rather biting, as in Example 29-10.

29-10 Brahms, Variations on a theme by Paganini, Op. 35, Theme

Moving to V, either plain or embellished by a cadential $^6_4$, offers no difficulties in voice leading. The presence of $\hat{2}$ as a common tone removes the threat of parallels. The French 6th is a very effective neighboring chord of V as in Example 29-1, bar 78.

Sometimes an anticipation of $\hat{2}$ over a German 6th can produce the momentary impression of a French 6th (Example 29-11). This is a very frequent way of avoiding 5ths with the German 6th.

29-11 Mozart, Pamina's aria (from *The Magic Flute,* K. 620)

translation: The joy of love forever gone.

7. **The augmented 6th chord with doubly augmented 4th (German $^4_3$).** Sometimes one encounters an augmented 6th chord that sounds exactly like a German $^6_5$ but is notated as a $^4_3$ with #$\hat{2}$ in place of b$\hat{3}$ (in C major, D# instead of Eb). This variation in spelling produces the curious interval of a doubly augmented 4th above the bass (in C major, Ab—D#). There is only one common situation that might call for using this notation: moving to a *major* $^6_4$ chord. Especially in the middle and late nineteenth century, composers sometimes liked to emphasize $\hat{3}$ as a goal by using #$\hat{2}$, its leading tone. In Example 29-12, the progression #$\hat{2}$-$\hat{3}$ is in an inner voice.

29-12 Schumann, Novellette, Op. 21/4

In most cases, the regular German 6th serves just as well, for the basic progression is to the dominant, not the $^6_4$. You needn't try to learn the "chord of the doubly augmented 4th" as a separate entity but merely as a notational variant of the German 6th.

APPROACHING AUGMENTED SIXTH CHORDS

8. Approaching from IV and II. Augmented 6th chords occur in many different contexts and in connection with many different types of bass and soprano lines. Occasionally they enter without preparation at the very beginning of a piece or movement, as in Example 29-7. Starting with an augmented 6th is not very common and probably does not happen at all in music before Beethoven. The most frequent immediate preparation for augmented 6th chords of all types is some form of IV; in such cases the augmented 6ths continue subdominant harmony; they are chromaticized subdominants that have become active in the direction of V. Very often, the point of departure is IV⁶, minor or major, and #$\hat{4}$ is a simple chromatic passing tone, just as in Examples 29-3 and 29-4. Example 29-13 illustrates. Note that in major the bass of IV⁶ is inflected to produce b$\hat{6}$.

29-13   Beethoven, String Quartet, Op. 18/2, II

Augmented 6ths, like applied V and VII of V, often result from a chromaticized voice exchange from IV and sometimes II⁶ or II$^6_5$ (Example 29-14). #$\hat{4}$ still represents a passing tone, but one shifted into a new voice and register. Very frequently the voice exchange is filled in by a passing $^6_4$. Sometimes, as we shall see, this progression can be expanded to unify broad musical spans.

29-14   Haydn, String Quartet, Op. 64/5 ("Lark"), II

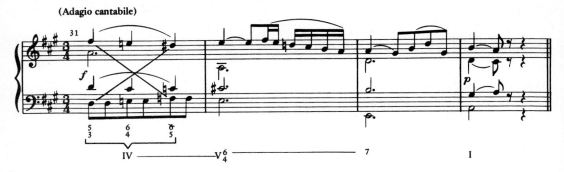

Sometimes II forms the diatonic preparation for an augmented 6th, so that the harmonic framework is II-V, the II intensified chromatically by the augmented 6th (Example 29-15). According to an old harmonic theory, all normal augmented 6ths have $\hat{2}$ as their root. As a generalization, this theory is farfetched and unconvincing: Why should we hear the "root" of Ab-C-Eb-F♯ as a D when that note virtually never sounds together with the chord it supposedly generates? But in a context where the last stable harmony before the augmented 6th is a II, it does make sense to hear that II as the diatonic harmony that gives rise to the augmented 6th. In that case, $\hat{2}$ is indeed the root of the chord, but by a kind of "remote control."

In general, the chromaticism of the augmented 6ths gives them an intensely linear character and weakens the impression that they are vertical structures generated from a root. The impression of root will then arise out of the larger context rather than within the chord itself. If the augmented 6th follows a strong IV, $\hat{4}$ will carry over as root (altered, of course, to $\sharp\hat{4}$); if the augmented 6th follows II, then it will continue supertonic harmony.

29-15   Haydn, String Quartet, Op. 76/1, II

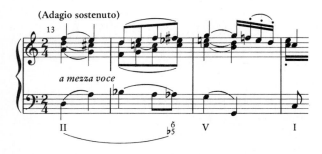

9. Approaching from altered IV and II. Applied   dominant and leading-tone chords to V, like augmented 6th chords, are chromatically altered forms of IV and II. In one sense, all these chords form a related group: they share the same diatonic origin and the presence of $\sharp\hat{4}$ as a chromatically altered tone. On the other hand, the presence of $\flat\hat{6}$ and the interval of the augmented 6th give the augmented 6th chords a distinct individual character as well as imparting a particular intensity to the resolution to V.

Very frequently augmented 6th chords originate in a chord applied to V with $\flat\hat{6}$ introduced as a passing tone in the bass (Example 29-16a) or through voice exchange (29-16b).

29-16

(a) Chopin, Etude, Op. 10/3

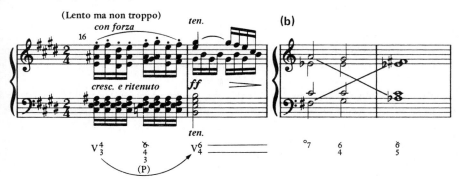

10. Approaching from I. Very often—especially in minor—augmented 6ths follow I^5_3 without any intervening chords (Example 29-17). Another possibility is a leap from I^6, as in 29-8.

29-17   Mozart, Crudel! perchè finora

(from *The Marriage of Figaro*, K. 492)

In the quotation from *Figaro*, the bass skips from $\hat{1}$ down to $\hat{6}$. Using a passing V^6 makes possible a stepwise bass. Especially characteristic is the completely chromatic bass shown in 29-18. This chromatic bass often occurs in music of a programmatic character as a symbol for death, suffering, or some other kind of tragic destiny; the opening of the *Don Giovanni* overture is a classic example.

29-18   Mozart, Fantasy, K. 397

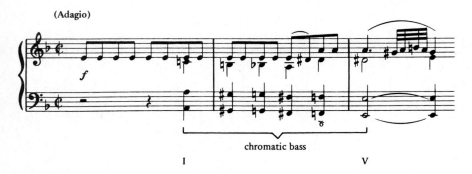

chromatic bass

29-19   Mozart, Violin Sonata, K. 304

Sometimes an augmented 6th chord that comes immediately from IV⁶ has a tonic chord as a prior point of origin, as in Example 29-13, where the bass line as a whole fills in, partly chromatically, the 4th from I down to V.

Since all augmented 6th chords contain $\hat{1}$ and the German 6th contains $\hat{3}$ as well, augmented 6ths can be used to harmonize part of a tonic arpeggio in the soprano. In Example 29-19, the German 6th arrives with striking effect at the culmination of the broken chord.

Another important possibility for the soprano is a rising line, wholly or partly chromatic, that leads to $\hat{5}$; the augmented 6th, of course, would harmonize $\sharp\hat{4}$. An unforgettable example is the tremendous passage where Mozart depicts the dead rising from their graves to the seat of judgment (Example 29-20). The soprano rises a full 12th, supported at first by a sequence in ascending 3rds. The C minor chord that forms the goal of the sequence is an example of secondary mixture (see the following unit); after the C minor chord the soprano line is wholly chromatic.

29-20   Mozart, Lacrymosa   (from *Requiem,* K. 626)

translation: [Most sorrowful of days,] when the world rises from the ashes,
full of sin and ripe for judgment.

11. Approaching from VI. Another frequent point of departure for augmented 6ths is VI (in major, ♭VI). Very often, as in Example 29-21, a VI (♭VI) that has been extended through tonicization returns to the home dominant and, eventually, the tonic, through an augmented 6th. All that is needed is to add ♯4̂ to VI (♭VI); often, as in our example, the doubled root of VI moves down a diminished 3rd to the augmented 6th.

29-21   Schubert, Piano Sonata, D. 960, I

Another possibility for the soprano is the rising chromatic line discussed in section 10. The chromatic line will produce the intervals of a perfect 5th, augmented 5th, major 6th, and, finally, augmented 6th. (The augmented triad produced by the passing augmented 5th will be discussed in Unit 30.) Example 29-22 illustrates.

29-22   Haydn, Symphony No. 104, III

Augmented 6ths frequently follow deceptive cadences to VI (in major, to ♭VI), because they form a convincing transition to V.

12. Augmented 6ths as neighbors of V. Very often, augmented 6th chords originate in the use of ♭$\hat{6}$ as upper neighbor to V in the bass, as in Example 29-1, bar 78, or to the cadential $^6_4$ before it resolves into V. Because it contains $\hat{2}$ as a common tone with V, the French $^4_3$ is particularly well suited to this function, but the Italian and German 6ths are also possible (see Example 29-11).

13. Augmented 6ths as agents of modulation. Because of their striking sonority, and because their goals are normally identified as dominants, augmented 6th chords play an important role in modulation, especially in the large, structural modulations that help to determine the basic plan of a piece. Two possibilities are of particular importance: modulations from I to V (as in sonata expositions) and modulations that return to I (as at the end of development sections).

Example 29-23 illustrates, in several stages, a frequent way of effecting the second of these possibilities: a motion from a tonicized IV through an augmented 6th to the home dominant. In (a), the IV is transformed into an augmented 6th through a chromaticized voice exchange. In (b), a "I" supports a passing tone in the soprano and also introduces two tones of the augmented 6th. In (c), the progression is expanded by a sequential passing motion (from D to A in the bass) followed by a chromatic descent to V. If you refer to the opening example in this unit, you will see that Example 29-23 depicts the plan that governs this excerpt.

A modulation from I to V in major follows a very similar procedure. In Example 29-24, (a) shows the basic plan, again a chromaticized voice exchange. In (b) we again find a transitional chord that supports a descending passing tone.

29-23

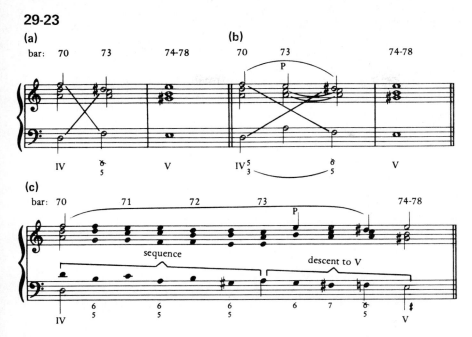

Although the modulation is from E♭ major to B♭ major, the passing chord is a B♭ minor triad; the D♭ of this triad prepares the 5th of the German $\frac{6}{5}$. 29-24c shows the transition from the E♭ major tonic to the B♭ minor chord. This plan is drawn from an actual piece—the first movement of Beethoven's Violin Sonata, Op. 12, No. 3, bars 17-23; very similar plans govern many other modulations to be found in the literature.

29-24

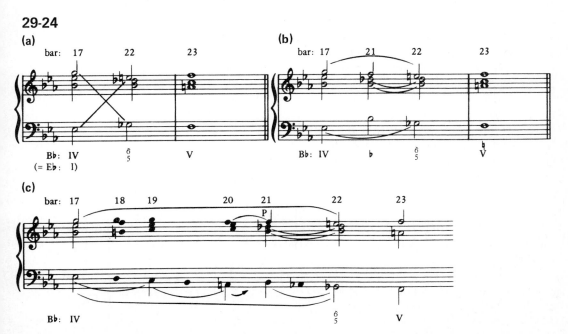

Example 29-25 contains four progressions, each the outline of a modulation from I to V in major. In (a) the modulation is effected by a 5-6 motion, as explained in Unit 14, section 8. In (b), an applied $\frac{6}{5}$, derived from the 6th of the 5-6, leads to the V of the dominant key area. In (c), an applied °7 substitutes for the $\frac{6}{5}$; except for one note, the progression is the same as the one in (b). The progression of (d) is very similar to (c), though now we find an augmented 6th in place of °7. The chromaticized voice exchange complicates the voice leading slightly, but three of the notes are the same as those of the °7, and the only different one is merely a chromatic variant, G♭ instead of G. These progressions, then, form a related group; they are presented here in an order of increasingly complex chromaticism. All of them occur frequently in modulations to V, especially in modulations (like those in many sonata expositions) where the new key area is introduced by an emphasized preparatory dominant.

29-25

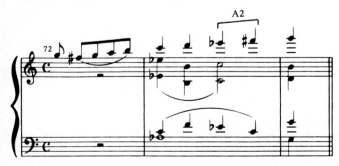

14. Melodic augmented 2nds. Melodic augmented 2nds frequently appear above an augmented 6th chord, or in the progression from another chord (usually I in minor) to an augmented 6th. In free textures, such augmented 2nds can be most beautiful and appropriate (Example 29-26).

29-26   Mozart, Piano Concerto, K. 467, I

15. The German ⁶₅ and parallel 5ths. As we know (section 5), direct progression from a German ⁶₅ to a dominant produces the threat of parallel 5ths. Such 5ths occur frequently in figurated keyboard textures that contain arpeggiated instead of block chords. Look again at Example 29-1, bars 73-74. Had the passage been written in block chords, the 5ths would have been very evident. The broken-chord setting, with the 5ths in weak rhythmic positions, separates the tones enough to offset the impression of parallels.

Another frequent possibility is to skip from the 5th to another tone of the German 6th before moving on to V. Such chordal skips can occur in any of the upper voices and are particularly effective in the soprano (Example 29-17).

Example 29-27 shows another possibility: a leap up from the 5th of the German ⁶₅ to the root of V.

29-27   **Haydn, String Quartet, Op. 76/6, I**

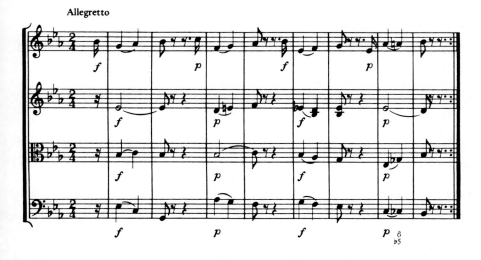

Occasionally composers will simply write consecutive 5ths, though not between outer voices (Example 29-28). In trying to evaluate such cases, bear in mind the fact that the 5th of the German ⁶₅ represents a passing tone. In a deep sense, therefore, it is an element of figuration. In Example 29-28, the passing function of the E♭ (between the F of IV⁶ and the D of V) is clearly evident. Therefore these 5ths fall into the category of parallels caused by figuration, as discussed in Units 20 and 21. In addition, the resolution of the augmented 6th—the dissonant interval that characterizes the chord—holds the listener's attention; the other tones recede into the background and become less important.

29-28   Mozart, Symphony No. 39, K. 543, I (strings only)

16. **Moving to V^7.** Turn again to Example 29-19. Note that the augmented 6th chord of bar 113 moves directly to V^7 instead of V$^8_5$. As we know, the 7th of ^{3} V^7 represents a passing tone whose consonant point of origin (an octave) is elided. In our example, the dissonant interval of the augmented 6th appears not to resolve—it moves to a 7th rather than an octave—but the resolution is so strongly implied by context that we do not hear the dissonance as unresolved. Direct motion from an augmented 6th to a V^7 occurs rather often, especially if the 7th is in an inner voice.

17. **Moving up from the bass.** Sometimes the bass of an augmented 6th (usually a German $^6_5$) moves up a chromatic half step before the resolution to V occurs (Example 29-29). In such cases upward motion is merely a momentary inflection; the goal of motion remains the same.

29-29   Mozart, Piano Sonata, K. 280, II

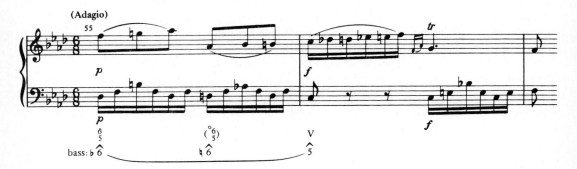

In our next quotation, however (Example 29-30), the bass ascends chromatically from $\hat{6}$ to $\hat{1}$, bypassing root-position V altogether; the diminished
seventh chord on B♮ substitutes for V here. In this example, $\hat{5}$, normally the goal
of motion, is elided and the bass moves into the 3rd of dominant harmony (♮$\hat{7}$),
normally an inner-voice tone. This procedure, though far from unique, is certainly unusual. In this case, the rising bass has an important motivic purpose; in this
connection, review Example 25-33, another excerpt from the same movement,
and note the use of a similar rising chromatic line.

29-30   Mozart, Piano Concerto, K. 491, I

"INVERSIONS" OF AUGMENTED SIXTH CHORDS

18. Diminished 3rd chords. Chords containing the same tones as the Italian, German, and French 6ths but with scale degrees other than ♭$\hat{6}$ in the bass occur
comparatively infrequently. Of these possibilities, the only ones that would
normally move to root-position V are those with ♯$\hat{4}$ in the bass; they contain a
diminished 3rd (or 10th) between the bass and one of the upper voices. As we
know, ♯$\hat{4}$ supports a variety of dissonant chords that lead effectively to V, whereas ♭$\hat{6}$ does not. Furthermore the augmented 6th (on ♭$\hat{6}$), which expands into an
octave, gives greater emphasis to the interval of resolution than do the diminished
3rd and 10th, which contract. For these reasons, chords based on the diminished
3rd occur much less often than those containing augmented 6ths. Mozart, who
favored augmented 6th chords, and who used them with incomparable mastery,
avoided diminished 3rd chords altogether. They were used, however, by other
great masters—by Chopin, in particular—to wonderful advantage.

By far the most frequently used chord of the diminished 3rd is ♯IV^7, which
contains the same scale degrees as the German $^6_5$. Example 29-31 shows usual
contrapuntal origin of the diminished 3rd; like the augmented 6th, it results
from the use of ♯$\hat{4}$ as a chromatic passing tone, only now in the bass rather than
in an upper voice. Note the similarity to VII^{o7} of V.

29-31

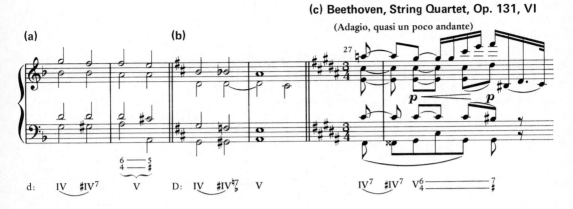

(a)   (b)   (c) Beethoven, String Quartet, Op. 131, VI
(Adagio, quasi un poco andante)

d: IV   ♯IV⁷   V   D: IV   ♯IV⁴⁷♭   V   IV⁷   ♯IV⁷   V⁶₄————⁷♯

♯IV⁷ can also occur more independently; it can replace a diatonic subdominant before a cadential V (Example 29-32).

29-32   Chopin, Prelude, Op. 28/22

♯IV⁷   V⁶₄⁻⁷   I

In addition, ♯IV⁷ occurs appropriately in many of the situations where the German 6th is used: as neighbor to V (or the cadential ⁶₄), in a voice exchange from a diatonic subdominant (IV⁶-♯IV⁷), and so on. You have have no difficulty understanding these usages when you encounter them.

19. Other positions. If tones other than ♭$\hat{6}$ or ♯$\hat{4}$ occur in the bass, the chord will not move by stepwise bass to root-position V.* Therefore such chords tend not to possess any long-range structural importance in music before the late nineteenth century—a time when composers sought alternatives to the frequent use of root-position V at cadences. In an excerpt from Tchaikovsky (Example 29-33),

*The root-position equivalent of the French 6th has $\hat{2}$ in the bass and moves by leap to root-position V. It functions as V⁷ of V with a diminished 5th replacing the normal 5th. Altered V⁷ chords will be taken up in Unit 30, sections 10 and 11.

V_3^4 functions as the goal of a semicadence. Tchaikovsky strengthens this normally weak inversion of V^7 by resolving into it from the $\frac{4}{2}$ equivalent of the German $\frac{6}{5}$.

29-33   Tchaikovsky, Symphony No. 5, Op. 64, I

Musicians sometimes refer to altered chords like those in Examples 29-31 through 29-33 as "inverted augmented 6ths." Though not literally correct—the augmented 6ths are not root-position chords—the expression nonetheless conveys a truth. The linear forces that govern the origin and resolution of this family of chords are usually most effectively expressed when the bass and an upper voice form an augmented 6th.

MOTION TO GOALS OTHER THAN V

20. Augmented 6ths in sequential passages. Most augmented 6ths move to dominants, but not necessarily to the main dominant of the key. Very often they serve to intensify applied dominant chords. This possibility is especially useful in sequential passages. Example 29-34 contains a sequence rising in 3rds in which each new step is tonicized by an applied dominant. The applied dominants, in turn, are preceded by augmented 6ths.

29-34   Chopin, Ballade, Op. 47

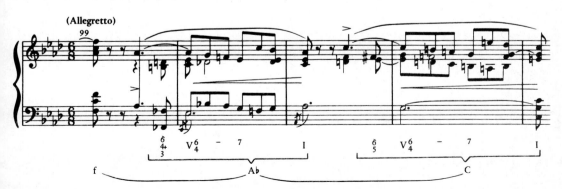

21. Resolving to I. Augmented 6th chords can result from chromatic neighbors that expand a tonic—virtually always a major one, and frequently a final tonic near the very end of a piece. The bass of the augmented 6th is $\flat\hat{2}$; one of the upper voices takes $\hat{7}$. Because it is based on $\flat\hat{2}$, this type of augmented 6th chord has a "Neapolitan" flavor, a flavor strongly evident in Example 29-35, where the chord begins as an arpeggiated $\frac{5}{3}$ with the augmented 6th added later.

29-35   Schubert, Piano Sonata, D. 959, I

V_3^4 chords are sometimes inflected to become French 6ths that resolve into tonics. In the excerpt shown in Example 29-36, Tchaikovsky uses a V_3^4 to lead into a goal tonic—a situation where most other composers would have used a root-position V. (Compare the very different use of V_3^4 in Example 29-33.) In this excerpt the V_3^4 is modified by chromatic inflection and becomes a French 6th; the E$\flat$ in the bass functions as a passing tone, but one very much emphasized by repetition and duration.

29-36   Tchaikovsky, Symphony No. 5, Op. 64, II

GERMAN SIXTH AND DOMINANT SEVENTH

22. An enharmonic relationship. You have doubtless noticed that the German $\frac{6}{5}$ is enharmonically equivalent to a dominant seventh chord—specifically, V^7 of $\flat II$. These two chords—so divergent in function but so similar in sonority—provide wonderful opportunities for composers, especially for those with a dramatic conception of musical structure. Example 29-37 shows two excerpts from Chopin's Prelude in G minor. $\sharp IV^7$ (the diminished-3rd equivalent of the German $\frac{6}{5}$) is a prominent feature of the first. The second tonicizes $\flat II^6$ largely through an applied V^4_2—enharmonically equivalent to the earlier chord of the diminished 3rd. Chopin uses the enharmonic relationship to connect two contrasting sections of the piece. The C$\sharp$ early in the piece also helps to prepare the very prominent D$\flat$ chord (IV of $\flat II$) in bar 17. And finally, the C$\sharp$'s and D$\flat$'s of the first part of the piece add to the effect of the wonderful climax on $\sharp IV^7$ at the very end (Example 29-32). Here the enharmonic equivalency helps to give coherence to the piece, for it forms the most striking element in its design.

29-37   Chopin, Prelude, Op. 28/22

(a)

(b)

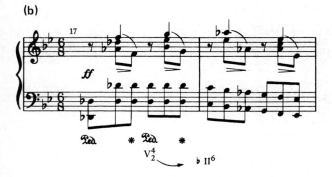

As we shall see in Unit 32, the enharmonic connection between the German $^6_5$ and the dominant seventh can be of considerable help in modulation.

Note: Some composers—Chopin in particular—occasionally notate an augmented 6th chord as a dominant seventh. In such cases the context will always clarify the function of the chord. The reasons for such enharmonic notation can vary: ease in reading and motivic connections with other parts of the piece are probably the most frequent. The phrase that follows the excerpt shown in Example 29-38 tonicizes C major, and Chopin's "incorrect" notation points to this later development.

29-38   Chopin, Nocturne, Op. 72/1

23. The "Neapolitan $\frac{6}{4}$" as an embellishment of the German $\frac{6}{5}$. Composers often use a "Neapolitan $\frac{6}{4}$" as if it were a cadential $\frac{6}{4}$ resolving to a V or V^7. They might then transform the supposed dominant into its enharmonic equivalent, the German $\frac{6}{5}$. Schubert demonstrates this possibility most movingly in the excerpt quoted in Example 29-39. Note that the chord of resolution is first notated as a V^7, as if the piece were going to gravitate to C major. Only at the second statement of the passage does Schubert's notation make it clear that the C major is an impossible hope, that the piece will subside into B minor.

29-39   Schubert, Einsamkeit   (from *Winterreise,* D. 911)

translation: While the storms still raged, I was not so wretched.

POINTS FOR REVIEW

1. Augmented 6th chords contain the interval of an augmented 6th above the bass, resolving to an octave, usually on $\hat{5}$. They normally proceed to V or V^7, possibly embellished by a cadential $^6_4$. Through contraction, the interval of the augmented 6th can move directly to the 7th of V^7.

2. The three main types are:
   a. The Italian $^6_3$ (augmented 6th plus major 3rd above bass). In four-part texture, double the 3rd above the bass.
   b. The German $^6_5$ (Italian 6th plus perfect 5th above the bass). It usually resolves to a cadential $^6_4$ to avoid 5ths that would occur if it proceeded directly to V. 5ths are sometimes tolerable in this progression, if not between outer voices.
   c. The French $^4_3$ (Italian 6th plus augmented 4th above bass).

   An alternative possibility to (b) is:

   d. The German $^4_3$ (Italian 6th plus doubly augmented 4th above bass). Occasionally replaces German $^6_5$ when resolution is to *major* $^6_4$.

3. Augmented 6th chords frequently represent a chromatically inflected IV or II on the way to V. Important possibilities include the chromatic inflection $\natural\hat{4}$-$\sharp\hat{4}$, usually from IV^6, and chromaticized voice exchange, usually from IV, but also from II^6_5, etc. Augmented 6th chords can also result from the chromatic inflection $\natural\hat{6}$-$\flat\hat{6}$ in the bass, often from altered II or IV (V or VII of V). Voice exchange between augmented 6th and diminished or half-diminished 7th applied to V is also possible.

4. Augmented 6th chords come frequently from I, often in connection with a chromatically descending bass, a chromatically rising soprano, or both. Motion from VI, over a sustained bass is another important possibility.

5. Augmented 6th chords often function as neighbors of V.

6. Long-range functions include preparing modulations to V in major and preparing return modulations to I, both in major and minor. The underlying plan of such a modulation might include a large-scale voice exchange.

7. Positions with scale degrees other than $\flat\hat{6}$ in the bass occur less frequently. Most of the important possibilities are built on $\sharp\hat{4}$ and resolve to root-position V; these are frequently called diminished 3rd chords, for they contain that interval above the bass. $\sharp IV^7$ (corresponding to German $^6_5$) is the most frequently used.

8. Augmented 6th chords can move to chords other than V. They occur effectively in sequences, often preceding applied dominants. Augmented 6ths on $\flat\hat{2}$ sometimes occur; they resolve to I (almost always major), often at the very end of the piece.

9. The enharmonic relationship between the German $^6_5$ and the dominant seventh chord can play an important part in composition. Sometimes a "Neapolitan $^6_4$" decorates the German $^6_5$ in the manner of a cadential $^6_4$ chord.

EXERCISES

1. Preliminaries. Write each of the following progressions in four different minor and four different major keys. Use four-part texture.

a. Italian 6th—V

b. German $\frac{6}{5}$—V$^{6\text{-}5}_{4\text{-}3}$

c. French $\frac{4}{3}$—V

d. German $\frac{4}{3}$ (doubly augmented 4th)—V$^{6\text{-}5}_{4\text{-}3}$ (major only)

2. Write more extended four-part progressions that illustrate the following:

a. IV^6 in minor becomes Italian 6th.

b. IV in major becomes German $\frac{6}{5}$ through a chromaticized voice exchange.

c. V$^4_3$ of V in major becomes French $\frac{4}{3}$.

d. VI in minor becomes German $\frac{6}{5}$.

e. I in minor leads to a German $\frac{6}{5}$ through a chromatically descending bass.

f. A French $\frac{4}{3}$ in minor acts as a neighboring chord to V.

3. Write a phrase (in four-part or free texture) in which an augmented 6th chord intensifies a modulation to V in major.

4. Less frequent usages. Write four-part progressions showing:

a. ♯IV^7 leading from IV to V in minor.

b. A German $\frac{6}{5}$ as a neighboring chord of I in major.

c. The "Neapolitan $\frac{6}{4}$" embellishing a German $\frac{6}{5}$ in minor.

5. Unfigured bass.

soprano: f♯^{1} b^1

6. Melody (* = ^{o}7).

7. Figured bass.

8. Melody. Set for keyboard. Carry through the march rhythm in the lower voices, using repeated chords where appropriate. In this exercise the harmonic rhythm will vary—sometimes moving only in half notes, sometimes following the rhythm of the soprano voice. Look for opportunities to use augmented 6th chords.

30

Other Chromatic Chords

30-1

(a) Chopin, Prelude, Op. 28/9

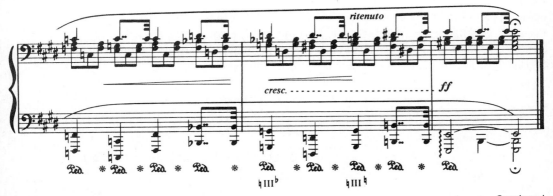

Continued

(b) reduction

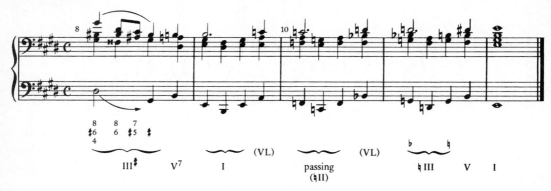

III♯   V⁷   I   passing   ♮III   V   I
                      (♮II)

ADVANCED USES OF MIXTURE

1. Simple mixture, secondary mixture, and double mixture. Example 30-1 shows the last five bars of a brief but highly chromatic piece by Chopin. These few bars contain many chromatic chords—in fact, a large majority. After a climactic authentic cadence in A♭, we find the following "foreign" triads: A minor, F major, C major, B♭ major, G minor, D major, and G major. How do these elements function so convincingly within a larger context in E major?

To answer this question, we must first distinguish between chords that have a purely local function and those that enter into larger tonal relationships. Obviously, the A♭ chord of bar 8 represents an important event. And, since it is followed immediately by a V-I progression in E, it must have some relation to the main tonic. That relation is easy to understand once we realize that the A♭ major is merely an enharmonic respelling of G♯ major—III in E, part of the harmonic progression III♯-V-I. As you learned in Unit 22, the use of III♯ in major is an example of *secondary mixture*.

The final cadence of the piece also shows the use of mixture, but mixture of a different kind. The G major triad of bar 11 is another type of altered III; it is the III chord borrowed from the parallel minor. A most striking feature of this piece, therefore, is the close juxtaposition of, and strong contrast between, two forms of the progression III-V-I: G♯(A♭)-B-E, and G♮-B-E. Moreover, there is yet a third altered form of III in this excerpt. At the beginning of bar 11 we find a G *minor* triad that connects, through an applied dominant, to the cadential G major triad.

Our example demonstrates three different types of mixture. They are:

1. Simple mixture, borrowing an element from the parallel mode—in the Chopin, the G major chord.
2. Secondary mixture, altering the quality of a triad without using scale degrees from the parallel mode—in the Chopin, the G♯ (A♭) major chord.

3. Double mixture, applying secondary mixture to a triad achieved through simple mixture. In the Chopin, the G major chord, a product of simple mixture, is altered to become a G minor chord.

Once we understand the function and origins of the A♭ major, G minor and G major chords, the rest of the passage becomes much more accessible. As the reduction (30-1b) indicates, the F major chord of bar 10 (♮II) makes possible a passing motion from I to ♮III. The A minor and B♭ major chords of bars 9 and 10, fourth beats, break up parallels between the main chords of these measures. And the C and D chords of bars 10 and 11 are, of course, applied dominants.

2. Simple mixture. Example 30-2 shows the major and minor triads that can be introduced into C major and minor through simple mixture; some of them are already familiar to us from Units 22 and 28 (we count ♭II as part of minor). It is interesting to note that mixture tends to create the effect of a special device more in major than in minor. This is because $\sharp\hat{6}$ and $\sharp\hat{7}$—themselves products of mixture—are necessary for the normal functioning of the minor mode; a certain amount of mixture, therefore, is already built into the structure of pieces in minor.

30-2   simple mixture

(a) in C major

(b) in C minor

The most important chords produced by mixture are those presented in Unit 22. The others occur much less often, and usually follow from the particular expressive or structural character of a given passage. Of the remaining possibilities, the most important are ♭III, V♭, and ♭VII in major. We saw an example of ♭III in the Chopin excerpt that begins this unit; in that piece, the use of contrasting forms of III constitutes a kind of motivic element. Example 30-3 shows a beautiful use of the minor V in major; the unexpected minor quality underlines the words "cool" and "shady." Note that V immediately reverts to its normal, major quality to prepare the eventual return of I.

30-3   Purcell, Dido and Aeneas, Chorus

to the rocks and the moun-tains, To the mu - si - cal

groves, and the cool sha - dy foun-tains,

V^b $V^\natural$

Sometimes bVII in major—like natural VII in minor (Unit 15, section 9)—leads to V⁷. In Example 30-4, bVII connects with V⁷, the 5th of bVII preparing the 7th of V⁷.

30-4   Schubert, Piano Sonata, D. 958, I

(Allegro)

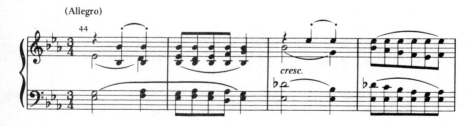

cresc.

bVII ——————————————————— V⁷ ——————————————— I

3. Secondary mixture. As we saw in Unit 22, by far the most important product of secondary mixture is III♯ in major. Example 30-5 also shows other possibilities in both major and minor.

30-5   secondary mixture

(a) in C major

II ♯   III ♯   VI ♯   VII♯5   VII♯5♯

(b) in C minor

♭II♭   III♭   VI♭   VII♭

An important possibility is VI♯ in major. Example 30-6 contains an A major chord as VI in C major. Note that this chord does *not* function as we might expect—as V of II. Instead it fulfills another basic function of the submediant triad: to lead down in 3rds from I to IV. Raising C to C♯ gives emphasis to the chord and intensifies the "searching" quality of these bars.

30-6   Schumann, Fantasy, Op. 17, III

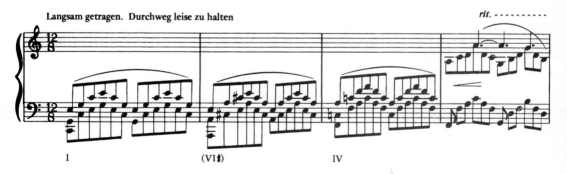

Leading-tone triads are sometimes altered so that they become major or minor triads. This gives them a momentary stability that would be impossible with their normal diminished quality. In Example 30-7, VII♯5♯ first appears as V of a briefly tonicized III, but then functions as the upper 3rd of an important cadential V⁷. Note the beautiful chromatic descent in the upper voices as altered VII melts into V⁷.

30-7 Schubert, Symphony No. 9 ("The Great"), D. 944, I

4. **Double mixture.** Example 30-8 shows double mixture. The G minor chord in bar 11 of Example 30-1 is ♮III♭ of E major and, consequently, an instance of double mixture. Example 30-9 provides an even more dramatic illustration, for here the altered chord is the climactic event of the phrase. The chord in question is the Phrygian II, normally an element of minor, used in major and altered to become a minor triad. Note that the chord following ♭II♭ has a double meaning; at first, it sounds like V⁷ of the preceding F minor but turns out to be a German 6th leading into V of E.

30-8 double mixture

(a) in C major

(b) in C minor

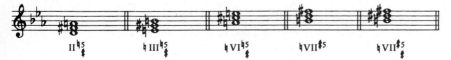

30-9   Schubert, String Quintet, D. 956, II

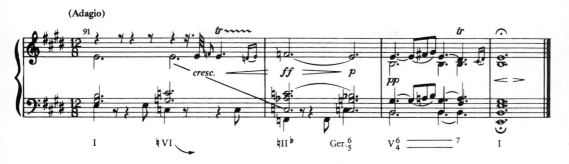

(Adagio)

I   ♮VI   ♮II♭   Ger.$^6_5$ V$^6_4$ ———— 7   I

5. Preparing chromatic chords. Some of the altered chords produced by the various kinds of mixture occur easily and require little or no special preparation. This is particularly true of the ones presented in Unit 22. Some of the others—especially those resulting from double mixture—can sound forced and unconvincing if they occur in an otherwise diatonic context. An E♭ minor chord abruptly introduced into a phrase in C major will sound like an intruder, not a variant of III. The more drastic alterations, therefore, require preparation in order to function effectively as representatives of their scale degrees.

Such preparation can be of various kinds. In Example 30-4, bar 46, the use of D♭ as part of an applied dominant to IV prepares the listener for the subsequent D♭ chord (bar 48) and helps to integrate it into the passage as a whole. Or to generalize, the unusual use of an altered scale degree will sound less odd if the listener can associate it with a prior statement of the same scale degree used in a simpler, more normal fashion.

In Example 30-3, the preparation of the G minor chord is different, but equally convincing. Note that an applied dominant lasting a full bar precedes the chord. Most listeners, surely, would expect this applied dominant to move to a G major chord. But G major and G minor share the same dominant; therefore, the minor chord, though unexpected, appears logical in retrospect. Preceding a chromatic chord by its own V or VII can be one of the simplest and most effective ways to prepare it.

The F minor chord of Example 30-9 also follows its own dominant, but it has another sort of preparation as well. The middle section of the movement (bars 29-63) begins with a long and stormy passage in F minor; the strange altered chord at the end of the piece is a recollection of this earlier episode, whose turbulent character is reflected in the crescendo and fortissimo of bars 91-92.

Of the many chromatic chords in Example 30-1, the G minor triad of bar 11 is the most foreign sounding. Several features of this chromatic passage help to prepare the G minor chord. First, the passage is sequential; chords that belong to a repeated pattern tend to stand out less than those that do not. Second, the preceding bar centers on the F major triad—♭II functioning as a passing chord. Since the G minor triad occurs in the key of F, it grows naturally out of what comes just before it. Third, and perhaps most important, the alto line of bars 9-12 is based on the chromatic ascent G♯-A-B♭-B♮. The G minor chord and the G major one that follows it result from this chromatic linear progression.* If the altered tone of a chromatic chord forms part of a chromatic melodic progression, the chord will create a less disruptive effect than in a more diatonic context.

In Unit 32 we shall discuss how expansions of altered triads can occur within large-scale tonal progression. Some of the more drastic alterations—those requiring a fairly extensive preparation—often function more effectively within a large structure than as details.

6. Seventh chords through mixture. Seventh chords, as well as triads, can be modified by mixture. Among the obvious examples are $II^6_{5♭}$, VII^{o7}, and the German and French 6ths—all of these in major. When the altered chord is directed to some other harmony as goal, the combination of chromaticism and dissonance can intensify the motion. But if the chord arrived at through mixture is to form a focal point, adding a dissonance may well neutralize its coloristic effect.

AUGMENTED TRIADS

7. The augmented 5th as an upper-voice passing tone. Augmented triads—unlike major, minor, and diminished triads—cannot be derived from major and natural minor scales without the use of accidentals. Sometimes (Unit 18) they come about when a 6th displaces the 5th of V in minor. Most of the other augmented triads that occur in tonal music are the product of chromaticism. In all cases the augmented quality results from voice-leading activity: the augmented triad expands or represents a major or minor triad; it does not function as a self-sufficient harmonic entity.

Example 30-10 shows the most frequent origin of the augmented triad as a chromatic chord. The augmented 5th is a chromatic passing tone moving up from the perfect 5th of a major triad. Usually, as in our example, the augmented 5th moves up to the 3rd of another major chord, this melodic progression supported by a descending 5th in the bass. Here the underlying progression is I-IV; V-I in major is another important possibility. Note how the augmented 5th creates a tension that makes the tonic sound like V of IV.

*Compare the C minor chord—VII♭—of Example 29-20 in which the E♭ similarly forms part of a rising chromatic line, this time in the soprano.

30-10   Bizet, Carmen, final bars

translation: It is I who killed her! Ah, Carmen!

In Example 30-11, the augmented 5th replaces the perfect 5th altogether through the familiar technique of contraction. But we hear the augmented 5th as a variant of the perfect 5th (which, incidentally, appears in the original statement of the passage).

30-11   Mendelssohn, Piano Trio, Op. 49, IV

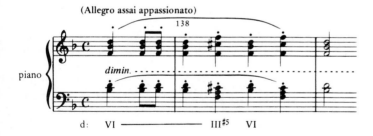

Example 30-12 is most unusual in that it contains an augmented triad at the very beginning of the piece. In this excerpt, the augmented chord is in $\frac{6}{3}$ position; it represents an altered I^6 leading to IV. The stepwise voice leading produced by the $\frac{6}{3}$ position creates a particularly smooth progression into the following chord. Augmented triads frequently appear as altered $\frac{6}{3}$'s—probably more often than as $\frac{5}{3}$'s.

30-12   Schumann, Humoreske, Op. 20, I

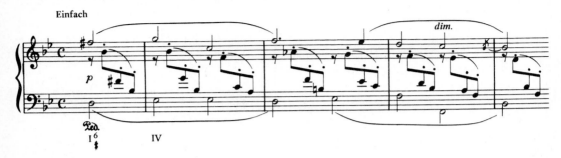

Sometimes an augmented 5th decorates a 5-6 progression above a sustained bass, thus: 5-5♯-6. Continuing the chromatic progression will produce an augmented 6th. This can be a most attractive way of moving from VI to a German $\frac{6}{5}$ as in Example 29-22.

For the most part, augmented triads result from momentary inflections of voice leading and tend to have a purely local function. In this respect they differ from some other chromatic chords—applied chords and augmented 6ths, for example—that can enter into long-range progression. In the later part of the nineteenth century, however, some composers began to give a larger role to augmented triads. In Example 30-13 an augmented chord substitutes for the goal tonic of an authentic cadence in D♭ and leads to a new section in F♯ (enharmonically, G♭: hence, an expanded IV). In this excerpt, as in Examples 30-11 and 30-12, the augmented 5th represents a passing tone that, through contraction, replaces the 5th of a major chord.*

30-13   Wagner, Götterdämmerung, Act III, Scene III

*Interestingly enough, the opera ends in D♭ major a few pages later. Thus, The D♭ tonic avoided in our excerpt is ultimately achieved. In this way, Wagner indicates, through musical means, that the end of the drama is not Brünnhilde's death, but the end of the gods and beginning of a new world order made possible by her self-sacrifice.

grüsst _____ dich   dein   Weib.

Die Viertel bedeutend schneller wie vorher.

I⁵♮ (=D♭ F A♮)

translation: See! Your wife greets you blissfully!

8. The augmented 5th as a bass passing tone. Sometimes an augmented triad results from a chromatic passing tone that descends from the root of a minor triad, as in Example 30-14.

30-14   Schubert, Piano Sonata, D. 960, I

(Molto moderato)

9. Augmented triads from 5-6-5 neighboring progression. In the two excerpts of Example 30-15 momentary augmented triads—they don't really function as chords—result from very different procedures than those in earlier examples. They are not based on chromatic passing tones. Instead both excerpts have as an important feature a neighboring motion that produces the interval succession 5-6-5. In 30-15a, the succession results from motion in an upper voice against a major triad; in 30-15b, it is the bass that moves, and the triad is minor.

30-15

(a) Brahms, Capriccio, Op. 76/1

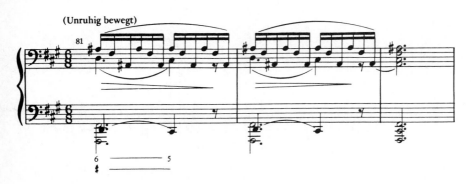

(b) Schubert, Der Atlas

Augmented triads can appear in other contexts—especially in chromatic sequences, as we shall see in the following unit.

ALTERED DOMINANT SEVENTH CHORDS

10. V^7 with augmented 5th. The same voice leading that produces most augmented triads—an augmented 5th as an upper-voice chromatic passing tone—can produce an altered V^7 if the chord contains a 7th. In Example 30-16a, the augmented 5th is literally a passing tone. Note that the bass contains both the 3rd and root of the dominant chord, the 3rd emphasized rhythmically.

In Example 30-16b, the natural 5th of V^7 is omitted and replaced by the augmented 5th.

The augmented 5th of altered V^7 normally occurs in the soprano, as in Examples 30-16a and b. In Example 30-16c, however, through an extended voice exchange, the altered tone appears in an inner voice as well as in the soprano. In this excerpt, the augmented V^7 is applied to IV, as frequent a possibility for this chord as for the augmented triad.

30-16
(a) Chopin, Sonata, Op. 35, I   **(b) Franck, Symphonic Variations**

(c) Beethoven, Diabelli Variations, Op. 120, Var. 28

11. V⁷ with diminished 5th. Much less frequently root-position V^7 appears with a diminished 5th ($\flat\hat{2}$), as in Example 30-17. Chopin was perhaps the first composer to use this alteration, which lends to dominant harmony the characteristic tension of the Phrygian scale degree, $\flat\hat{2}$. $V^7_{5\flat}$ appears far more often in $\frac{4}{3}$ than in root position; as a $\frac{4}{3}$ chord, it functions as a French 6th resolving to I (review Example 29-36).

30-17   Richard Strauss, Salome, Op. 54

translation: The red fanfares of the trumpets are not as red [as your mouth.]

COMMON-TONE DIMINISHED SEVENTH CHORDS

12. A chromatic embellishment of I in major. In Example 30-18, the tonic of E major is expanded by a diminished seventh chord of neighboring function. Clearly, this is not the familiar leading-tone chord, VII^{o7}; it does not even contain the leading tone. Because it contains a common tone ($\hat{1}$) with the expanded tonic, this diminished seventh chord is called a *common-tone diminished seventh*. In addition to the sustained $\hat{1}$ it contains three tones of contrapuntal origin: $\sharp\hat{2}$ as chromatic neighbor of $\hat{3}$, $\sharp\hat{4}$ as chromatic neighbor of $\hat{5}$, and $\hat{6}$ as diatonic neighbor of $\hat{5}$.

30-18   Mendelssohn, Rondo Capriccioso, Op. 14

Common-tone diminished sevenths are apparent, rather than true, seventh chords; they are similar to the diatonic apparent sevenths discussed in Unit 24 (review Example 24-23), but they are chromatically altered. In the Mendelssohn, the diminished seventh is in $\frac{4}{2}$ position. In a real $\frac{4}{2}$ the bass would function as the dissonant element, but in our excerpt, the bass is clearly a stable tone; the dissonances are created by the neighboring $\sharp\hat{2}$ and $\sharp\hat{4}$ in the upper voices. The two half-step progressions ($\sharp\hat{2}$-$\hat{3}$ and $\sharp\hat{4}$-$\hat{5}$) create a powerful resolution into the tonic, one reason why the common-tone $^{o}7$ is one of the most frequently used chromatic embellishments of major triads. Example 30-19 shows some typical voice leadings. Note the possible use of $\sharp\hat{4}$ as a passing tone between $\hat{3}$ and $\hat{5}$; also note that placing $\sharp\hat{2}$ in the bass permits resolution to I^6.

30-19

13. Notation. To construct a common-tone °7 simply build a $\frac{4}{2}$ on the root of the chord to which it resolves and raise the 2nd and 4th. This gives the usual notation, with the upper voices an augmented 2nd, an augmented 4th, and a major 6th above the bass. Quite frequently, however, as in Example 30-20, a minor 3rd substitutes for the augmented 2nd. The basis of this notation is mixture between ♭$\hat{3}$ and ♮$\hat{3}$; composers often use it when mixture is an important feature of the piece. In the Brahms, the immediately preceding movement is a Scherzo in C minor; the E♭ carries some of the minor quality into the Finale.

30-20   Brahms, Trio, Op. 87, IV

14. Moving to a cadential $\frac{6}{4}$. Example 30-21 shows two possible ways to notate a diminished seventh chord on ♯$\hat{4}$ leading to a major cadential $\frac{6}{4}$. In 30-21a, the °7 is notated as an applied leading-tone chord to V; in 30-21b, it is notated as a common-tone chord with the $\frac{6}{4}$—a nuance of notation that composers occasionally use when they wish to indicate an emphasis on the $\frac{6}{4}$.

30-21

(a)   (b)

15. Embellishing a minor triad. Common-tone diminished sevenths rarely embellish minor triads. There are two common tones, $\hat{1}$ and $\hat{3}$, which weaken the contrast between the two sonorities. In addition, $\sharp\hat{6}$ does not normally function as upper neighbor to $\hat{5}$ in minor. For these reasons, common-tone °7 will decorate a minor chord only where its use fits the particular character of a passage or piece. For a most remarkable example, see Schubert's great song *Die Stadt*, in which a common-tone °7 over the tonic forms part of the basic plan of the piece.

16. Embellishing V and V⁷. Common-tone diminished sevenths can embellish V. A particularly important possibility is moving to V⁷, with all of the upper tones ascending a half step. Example 30-22 illustrates resolution to V⁷ and shows as well possibilities of moving to inversions of V⁷.

30-22

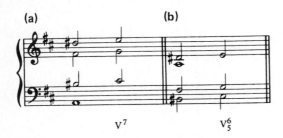

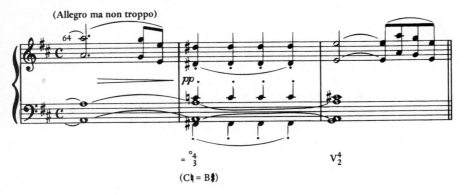

(c) Beethoven, Violin Concerto, Op. 61, I

Example 30-23 contains two common-tone °7's. The first passes between I and V$_3^4$, the second between V$_3^4$ and I⁶. The progression as a whole is a chromaticized version of the familiar I-V$_3^4$-I⁶; it occurs frequently in nineteenth-century music.

30-23   Tchaikovsky, Symphony No. 5, Op. 64, III

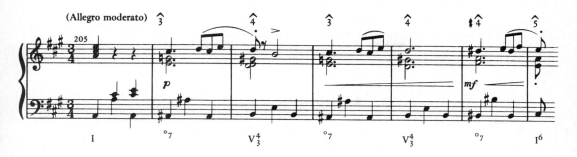

OTHER CHROMATIC EMBELLISHING CHORDS

17. Common-tone augmented 6th chords. From around the time of Schubert on, one frequently finds chromatic embellishing chords containing an augmented 6th or diminished 3rd. As Example 30-24 demonstrates, a common-tone augmented sixth resembles a common-tone °7 in structure and function, though it has its own characteristic sound. Also note that the interval of the augmented 6th resolves normally by expanding into an octave. But its resolution is to the 5th of tonic harmony rather than to the root of V.

30-24   Schubert, Am Meer

(from *Schwanengesang,* D. 957)

In the later nineteenth century, composers sometimes emphasized a common-tone augmented 6th (or °7) by allowing the bass to leap. Thus, in Example 30-25, the bass does not remain on E, but moves to C♮. This procedure disguises (but does not obliterate) the contrapuntal connection between the common-tone augmented 6th and the chord it decorates.

30-25   Wolf, Morgenstimmung (1896)

18. Apparent dominant sevenths. Very occasionally, a chromaticized common-tone chord appears in the guise of a dominant seventh. Mostly, as in Example 30-26, they are apparent $^4_2$'s over a sustained tonic bass. Of all the chromatic common-tone embellishments, this one creates the most unusual effect, especially if it is emphasized by duration or accent. This is because its resolution—though governed by perfectly logical voice leading—is so greatly at variance with the expectations produced by its sound. In the Schubert, the logic of voice leading is underscored by the fact that this passage is a variation of an earlier one that uses a diatonic embellishment (we quoted the earlier passage in the Workbook, Unit 24). The unexpectedness of the apparent V$^4_2$ gives a most expressive emphasis to the word "stören" (interrupt).

30-26   Schubert, Gute nacht!   (from *Winterreise*, D. 911)

translation: I will not interrupt your dream; it would be a shame to disturb your rest.

POINTS FOR REVIEW

1. The three types of mixture are simple mixture, secondary mixture, and double mixture. Simple mixture results from borrowing elements from the parallel minor or major. An example is an A♭ major triad as VI in C major. Secondary mixture is modal alteration other than that produced by simple mixture. An example is an A major triad as VI in C major. Double mixture is the application of secondary mixture to a chord resulting from simple mixture. An example is an A♭ minor triad as VI in C major.

2. The three types of mixture produce major and minor triads on every degree of the chromatic scale except #$\hat{4}$. Thus the possibilities for C major and C minor are the following triads, each in both major and minor qualities:

I	II	III	IV
C	D♭, D	E♭, E	F

V	VI	VII	
G	A♭-A	B♭-B	

3. The more remote products of mixture—especially those resulting from double mixture—require preparation in order to function effectively. Possible types of preparation include applied chords and asso-ciation with a more normal use of the altered tone.

4. Augmented triads do not function as independent harmonic entities in tonal music. Mostly they represent major triads whose 5th is displaced by an upward-moving chromatic passing tone. They often occur over root movement by descending 5th (such as V$^{5\sharp}$-I); they also decorate a 5-6 over a sustained bass, often leading to an augmented 6th. A less frequent possibility is for the augmented chord to result from a *bass* passing tone that leads down from a minor triad.

5. Dominant seventh chords frequently have an augmented 5th leading to the 3rd of a major tonic. V^7 with diminished 5th is much less frequent.

6. Common-tone diminished seventh chords are a frequent contrapuntal decoration of major triads and dominant seventh chords, especially I, V and V^7. The upper tones generally function as neighbors to the 3rd and 5th (also to 7th of V^7), with the root of the main chord as the common tone.

7. Other chromatic embellishing chords include common-tone augmented 6ths and apparent dominant sevenths. They usually embellish tonic triads, with $\hat{1}$ as common tone.

EXERCISES

1. Preliminaries. Write short progressions, each in a different key, that contain the following chromatically altered chords:

a. ♭VII in major

b. VI♯ in major

c. VII$^{5\sharp}_{\sharp}$ in major

d. an augmented triad as V of IV in major

e. V$^7_{5\sharp}$ in major

f. V$^7_{5♭}$ in minor

g. common-tone °7 decorating I in major

h. common-tone °7 decorating V$^4_3$ in major

i. common-tone augmented 6th decorating I in minor

2. Figured bass (for mixture).

3. Figured bass. Use augmented triads. (Keyboard style is possible.)

4. Melody. Use common-tone °7 chords.

31

Chromatic Voice-Leading Techniques

31-1

(a) Chopin, Impromptu, Op. 29

(b) reduction

CHROMATICISM BASED ON PARALLEL MOTION

1. Chromatic parallel $\frac{6}{3}$ chords. In previous units, we have observed that chromatic techniques—especially mixture, tonicization, and the use of chromatic passing tones—produce altered chords of various kinds. Applied to larger contexts, these same techniques can give rise to entire chromatic passages. Many of these passages can be understood as chromatic transformations of familiar diatonic procedures. Thus we might encounter chromatic parallel $\frac{6}{3}$ chords, chromaticized 7-6 suspensions, chromatic 5-6 syncopes, and so forth. To begin to understand such passages we must be able to perceive both the underlying diatonic progression and the chromatic elements that modify it.

In Example 31-1, for instance, the harmonic framework is the simple diatonic progression I-II^6-V^7. Filling in the space between the I and the II^6 is a series of descending parallel $\frac{6}{3}$'s. The passage is similar to those discussed in Unit 18 in all respects except a most important one—it is chromatic instead of diatonic. The reduction following the excerpt (31-1b) show its diatonic basis (half notes) and its chromatic elaboration (black noteheads). We can readily see that the chromaticism of this passage involves procedures already familiar to us: specifically, the use of mixture and of chromatic passing tones. The 5-6 motion that introduces the descending $\frac{6}{3}$'s is altered by mixture so that the first $\frac{6}{3}$ is expressed as an F♭ major chord instead of a F minor one. And the other chromatics can be understood as passing tones.

One other aspect of this excerpt deserves attention, for it is characteristic of all sorts of chromatic passages—not just those based on parallel $\frac{6}{3}$'s. Note that all the $\frac{6}{3}$ chords are *major* except for the goal II^6. Obviously, if a succession of chords is parallel and chromatic, all the chords will have the same quality. Since the major triad represents a preferred sonority, composers have tended to favor it in such passages.

2. Chromaticized 7-6 suspension series. A frequent diatonic elaboration of parallel $\frac{6}{3}$'s is a chain of 7-6 suspensions. Such a suspension series can be further elaborated chromatically, mostly by means of chromatic passing tones. The two excerpts of Example 31-2 show different applications of this technique. In the Bach, chromatic passing tones in the bass coincide with the suspended 7ths; in the Haydn, both the middle voice and the bass are inflected chromatically. The full texture of the Bach allows the 7ths to be reinforced by 5ths above the bass; the Haydn is written in three voices. In the Bach, the descending bass moves chromatically from I to V—a favorite device of Baroque composers, especially if the *affect* (mood or emotion) of the piece is one of grief. You might remember for your own written work that using 7-6 suspensions can be a most effective way of harmonizing a descending chromatic bass.

In passages like the Bach and Haydn, the 7ths are suspensions decorating $\frac{6}{3}$'s; they are *not* seventh chords. This means that the lower tone of the 7th does not function as a root. Realizing this fact can prevent serious misunderstandings about the harmonic direction of such passages. In bar 11 of the Haydn, for example, it would be nonsensical to interpret the 3rd beat as containing a V^7 of F moving "irregularly" to an Ab_3^6; the 7th on C arises out of voice leading alone and has no harmonic function whatever.

31-2

(a) Bach, Crucifixus   (from Mass in B Minor, BWV 232)

(b) Haydn, Piano Sonata, Hob. XVI/52, I

3. Chromaticized ascending 5-6 series. A number of different chromatic passages can be derived from the familiar ascending 5-6 progression (Example 31-3a). For example, we can insert chromatic passing tones in the bass, transforming the 6's into applied chords (31-3b); in keeping with the preference for major triads in chromatic textures we can express the $\frac{5}{3}$'s on D and E as major chords. Adding chromatic passing tones alternately to the middle voice and the soprano (31-3c) creates momentary augmented triads on the weak beats. Using the same tones (or their enharmonic equivalents), but aligning them differently (31-3d) gives us a new progression—one in which each step of the chromatic scale in the bass supports a 5-6 motion. In this new progression, the 6's are augmented triads that serve as leading-tone chords to the major $\frac{5}{3}$'s. Here—and in any progression that contains two leading-tone chromatics within each whole step—enharmonic transformation is required. In 31-3d, bar 2, Db is transformed to C♯ in order to make it a leading tone to the following D♮. Other notations might be possible—for example, C♮-B♯-C♯ in bars 1-2. Even if one did not notate the enharmonic at all, perhaps writing the bass line as C♮-C♯-Db-Db-D♮ (bars 1-3), the enharmonic relationship would still be inherent in the progression, though not expressed in its notation.

31-3   ascending 5-6 series

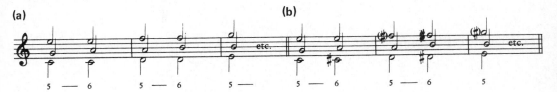

Examples 31-4 and 31-5 contain excerpts from the literature based on chromaticized 5-6's. The Liszt resembles 31-3c except that it moves within dominant harmony—between V and V⁶ of F♯ minor. The Chopin is very much like 31-3d except for the use of a minor triad as goal chord. In the Chopin, note the parallel 10ths between the bass and the emphasized soprano tones; parallel 10ths are as important an organizing element in chromatic textures as in diatonic ones.

31-4

(a) Liszt, Gnomenreigen

(Presto scherzando)

(b) reduction

31-5   Chopin, Nouvelle Etude No. 2

(Allegretto)

Another derivation from the ascending 5-6 progression is shown in Example 31-6. As in the Chopin excerpt and in 31-3d, 5-6's occur on each chromatic step, only now the 6's are expressed as root-position applied dominants.

31-6

etc.

4. Chromaticized descending 5-6 series. We are familiar with the 5-6 progression, repeated sequentially in 3rds over a descending diatonic scale (Example 31-7a). Sometimes one encounters a 5-6 progression repeated sequentially in whole steps over a descending *chromatic* scale (Example 31-7b). In this progression, the chromaticism results, in part, from tonicization, for the $^6_3$'s are applied dominants to the chords that precede them. If the progression begins on I in major (its usual starting point), there is a strong impression of mixture as well, for the emphasized chords following the tonic belong to the parallel minor.

31-7

(a) diatonic descending 5-6   **(b) chromatic descending 5-6**

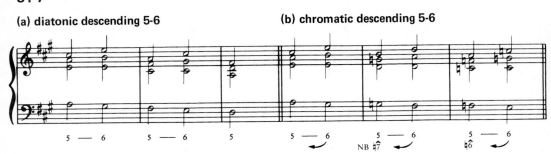

The feeling of mixture is very strong in Example 31-8, an excerpt drawn from a piece that mixes major and minor in a particularly dramatic way. This excerpt and 31-7b demonstrate a curious feature of descending chromatic 5-6's. A progression descending from I would normally have V as its first goal. But with this progression, V cannot be reached without breaking the sequence, for the third statement arrives at $\hat{5}$ in the bass with a $^6_3$ chord above it. Note that Schubert stops the sequence on ♭VI (bar 19) and moves on to a $^6_4$, the function of which is not altogether easy to determine. We regard it as a consonant $^6_4$ that continues the tonic harmony at the beginning of the phrase, and is connected with the initial I by the melodic figure D-E-D, which recalls the opening motive.*

*Were it not for the fact that the first violin brings in an important melodic idea with the d2 of bar 20, one would be inclined to read the $^6_4$ as passing to IV.

31-8   Schubert, String Quartet, D. 887, I

5. Descending sequences with augmented 6ths. Example 31-9 illustrates a sequential technique that occurs frequently in nineteenth-century music. Augmented 6th chords connect major triads over a descending chromatic scale-segment. Parallel 10ths, usually between outer voices, are often a feature of such progressions and they occur prominently here. Note that we have interpreted the first chord of bar 24 as an E major triad that becomes an augmented 6th; the reason is that the V of bar 23 leads the listener to hear an E major tonic at the downbeat. The chords that begin bars 25 and 26 receive no such preparation, and are heard solely as augmented 6ths. Incidentally, the triads to which the first two augmented 6ths resolve function as passing chords; they have no harmonic meaning as dominants. But the cumulative effect adds to the power of the final resolution, which, this time, *is* to a dominant. Note that this progression would contain consecutive 5ths if it were written in block chords; the piano setting eliminates the 5ths by displacing the tones rhythmically.

31-9

(a) Chopin, Prelude, Op. 28/17

(b) reduction

6. Consecutive diminished sevenths—descending. A series of consecutive diminished seventh chords can form a passing motion between the beginning and goal chords of a larger progression. Because of their instability, diminished sevenths impart a far greater degree of tension than do parallel $\frac{6}{3}$ chords. In Example 31-10, the $^\circ$7's help to connect a tonicized III with a goal V. Note that some of the bass tones are written as grace notes; they are, nonetheless, main tones, not decorations.

31-10   **Beethoven, Piano Sonata, Op. 101, III**

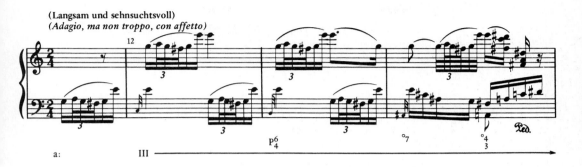

In writing consecutive °7's—especially if the larger context is diatonic—composers tend to avoid using accidentals that are remote from the key. This means that such a passage will not normally contain just a single position of °7. If Beethoven had continued to write root-position diminished sevenths, the resulting chord progression would be like that of Example 31-11—a most unsightly notation for a progression in A minor.

31-11

But there is also a deeper reason for Beethoven's notation. As Example 31-12 shows, the alternation of °7 and °$^4_3$ permits the 7th of each chord to resolve normally. It also conveys the connection between such a series of consecutive °7's and a passage of interlocking applied dominant $^6_5$'s and $^4_2$'s (Example 25-29)—a connection based on the relationship between positions of °7 and inversions of V^7. The pairing of °7 and °$^4_3$ also reflects the articulation of the passage into groups of two chords each. In bar 16 Beethoven changes the notation in order to point to the coming dominant: he uses a D♯ rather than an E♭ and a G♯ instead of an A♭. These changes produce the succession °$^6_5$-°$^4_2$.

31-12

The two successions that occur in the Beethoven—alternating °7's and °$^4_3$'s or °$^6_5$'s and °$^4_2$'s—represent the normal notation for such passages.

7. Consecutive diminished sevenths—ascending. Extended passages of consecutive ascending °7's occur comparatively infrequently. A progression rising chromatically does not permit a normal downward resolution of each 7th. In addition, the rising progression lacks the association with interlocking applied dominants that adds to the directional quality of the descending progression. There are two reasons for the fact that ascending °7's appear at all in tonal music. First, the diminished 7th interval is enharmonically equivalent to a major 6th; furthermore, if the surroundings are not diatonic, the listener cannot know whether a given interval is in fact d7 or M6. This ambiguity makes it possible to postpone resolution until the end of the series is reached. Second, as the arrows in Example 31-13 demonstrate, the progression gives the impression that the diminished 5ths above the bass resolve. In this example, the rising bass develops a cumulative leading-tone tension that is not dispelled until the final °7 resolves to I. Bach's notation in this passage follows two principles. He avoids accidentals remote from G major/E minor, and he always writes the uppermost interval of each chord as a minor 3rd (rather than an augmented 2nd) to permit the interpolation of a passing tone.

31-13   Bach, Toccata (from Partita No. 6, BWV 830)

8. ♮4̂-♯4̂ supporting °7's. An applied °7 on ♯4̂—one of the most important intensifications of V—is itself often preceded and intensified by another °7 on ♮4̂. This represents by far the most frequent and characteristic usage of consecutive rising °7's. The first °7 is in $\frac{4}{3}$ position and usually comes from a IV or a II in first inversion (Example 31-14). As the example demonstrates, the °7 on ♮4̂ is an apparent $\frac{4}{3}$, rather than a true seventh chord; it results from tones of figuration leading from the IV (or II) to the applied chord.

31-14

In Example 31-15, the °7 on B♮ does not literally come from IV or II. Nevertheless, the contour of the bass line, with its characteristic leap from 1̂ down to 4̂ strongly suggests that the latter has a cadential function (supporting IV or II) and that B♮ is a passing tone. And, as the reduction points out, the chord on B♭ represents a II$^6_5$ with the 5th above the bass—F—displaced by the neighboring E♮. Progressions like this one—with $^{o}\frac{4}{3}$ standing for IV or II—are by no means rare.

31-15

(a) Schubert, Moment Musical No. 3, D. 780

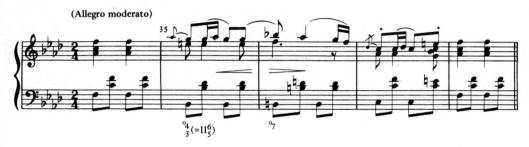

(b) from

9. Consecutive augmented triads. Like the diminished seventh chord, the augmented triad is a tonally ambiguous formation. Its inversions sound the same as the root position, owing to the fact that its tones divide the octave into equal, or enharmonically equivalent intervals—two major 3rds and a diminished 4th. Outside of a diatonic context, therefore, the listener cannot determine which tone of the chord is dissonant and cannot assign a specific direction to the chord. In the later nineteenth century, some composers—especially Liszt—took advantage of the ambiguity of this sonority and made it the basis of transitional passages in parallel motion. Such passages occur in both ascending and descending direction, but the former predominates, probably because the upper tone of an augmented 5th tends to move up. In Example 31-16, Liszt avoids accidentals too remote from the key of F♯ minor. The passage as a whole serves to expand V.

31-16   Liszt, Gnomenreigen (compare Example 31-4)

CHROMATICISM BASED ON CONTRARY MOTION

10. Motion within a single voice exchange. Contrary motion within the voice exchange 6-10 (or 10-6) forms the basis for a number of important chromatic progressions. Example 31-17 has, as a very prominent feature, contrary motion between the bass and the soprano. The harmonic framework is I-IV-V-I, with the IV extended by a voice exchange. Within the expanded IV, we hear the following sonorities: IV⁶ (on ♮6̂), a German $\frac{6}{5}$ (on ♭6̂), a C minor $\frac{6}{4}$ (on 5̂), and IV$\frac{5}{♭}$ (on 4̂). To see how these sonorities function, look at 31-17b, which relates the chromatic passage to its diatonic basis. The kernel of the expanded IV is a progression from IV⁶ through a passing $\frac{6}{4}$ to IV$\frac{5}{3}$—a technique familiar to us from Unit 19. The major IV⁶ (on A♮) and the augmented 6th (on A♭) result from chromatic passing tones in the outer voices.

31-17

(a) Beethoven, Thirty-Two Variations, Theme

(b) reduction

You will note from bars 5 and 6 of the Beethoven that the voice leading of the German $^6_5$ through the passing $^6_4$ is identical with that of a German 6th to a cadential $^6_4$. In order to understand passages like the Beethoven theme, you have to look beyond the progression from one chord to the next and try to grasp the larger direction. The same is true in Example 31-18, where another progression from a German $^6_5$ to a $^6_4$ might seem to indicate an imminent cadence in B minor. But the context is one of D major, not B minor, and the German $^6_5$ is part of a most unusual and beautiful voice exchange within II^7 of D.

31-18   Mendelssohn, Song without Words, Op. 85/4

11. The 6-10 voice exchange: some writing techniques. The possibilities for chromatic progressions within the 6-10 (or 10-6) voice exchange are far too numerous to catalog here, but we shall demonstrate some of the most important. The *minor 6th* and *major 10th* form the most favorable framework for chromatic motion because the succession m6, P8, M10 can be completely filled in with chromatic passing tones (Example 31-19a). Usually this motion is deployed between V$^6_5$ and the root-position V^7 or its enharmonic equivalent—the German 6th (31-19b). Note that the inner voices remain stationary.

31-19

(a)   **(b)**

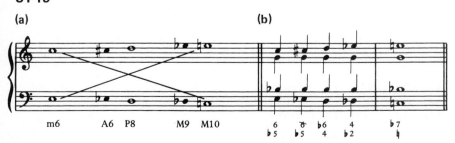

A segment of the above progression—one that moves between A6 and M10 is another possibility (Example 31-20a). Starting on the 10th permits an elaboration of the IV/German $^6_5$ (or $^4_3$) voice exchange in major (31-20b).

31-20

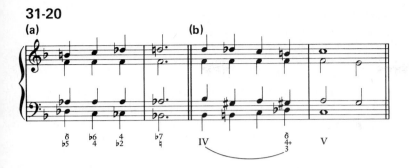

Between a *major 6th* (or its enharmonic equivalent, a diminished 7th) and a *minor 10th,* note-against-note motion in the outer voices is scarcely possible, because of the poor sonorities produced (Example 31-21a). But introducing some oblique motion and, sometimes, omitting a chromatic step, permits a number of interesting possibilities, including motion within an expanded diminished seventh chord (31-21b, c, d).

31-21

Note: In progressions of this type (Examples 31-17 through 31-21), a passing $^6_4$ usually occurs at the point where the voice exchange brings about an octave.

12. The m7-M10 voice exchange. The progression shown in Example 31-20a often occurs with a minor 7th instead of an augmented 6th in the initial chord. This notational variation permits a kind of chromaticized voice exchange between ♮VII⁷ and V⁷ in minor or ♭VII♭⁷ and V⁷ in major (Example 31-22). This usage elaborates the progression of a subtonic 7th to V⁷ as described in Unit 24, section 12.

31-22

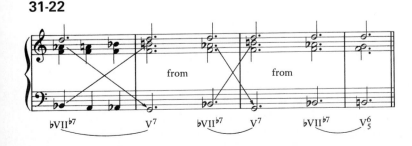

A remarkable excerpt from Schumann (Example 31-23) makes use of the technique shown in the preceding example. Bars 1 and 2 elaborate V^7 of C major through a $\flat VII^{\flat 7}$-V^7 voice exchange. The very prominent $c\sharp^2$ of the melody is an accented neighbor of d^2. Is it not rather amazing that a V^7-I progression in C major forms the basis of such an unusual—even bizarre—passage?

31-23

(a) Schumann, Davidsbündler Tänze, Op. 6/9

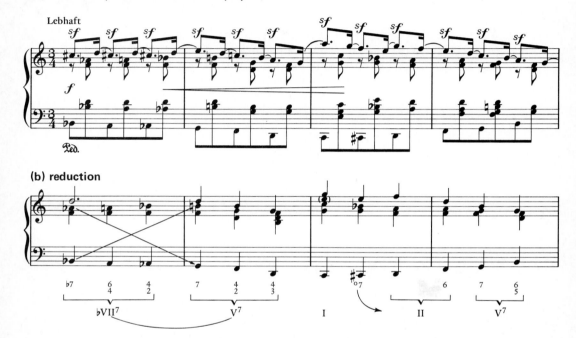

(b) reduction

13. Extended passages with voice exchanges. In the music of some late eighteenth- and nineteenth-century composers—especially Beethoven, Schubert, and Chopin—one encounters extended passages containing a number of 6-10 (or 10-6) voice exchanges; these passages often form the transitional element in a modulation. Example 31-24 shows a remarkable passage from the same Chopin Prelude we quoted in Example 30-1. This excerpt moves from E, the tonic, to the cadence of A♭ that began our earlier quotation; you will recall that the A♭ major stands for G♯, III♯ of E. As the first reduction (31-24b) reveals, the passage contains four voice exchanges; the total effect is highly chromatic, though no single voice exchange contains chromatic passing tones like those in Examples 31-19 through 31-23. In addition to effecting changes in register, their purpose is to gradually transform the C major $^6_3$ first into a dominant-type seventh chord, and eventually a diminished seventh resolving into the A♭ (G♯) $^6_4$. The A major triad and the B♭ minor $^6_4$ function as emphasized passing chords within the voice exchanges. Though they add considerably to the richness and color of the passage, they are products of voice leading and have no independent harmonic status.

31-24

(a) Chopin, Prelude, Op. 28/9

(b) reduction 1

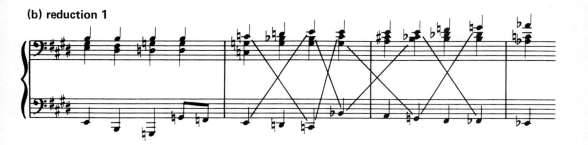

(c) reduction 2

Example 31-25 is equally remarkable and very different. In the first place, the passage as a whole does not modulate. In the second place, the voice exchanges are 10-6's within a diminished seventh chord—VII^{o7} of V. There are three of them, the third incomplete, so that the diminished seventh becomes an applied V^7. In a 10-6 exchange, the voices come closer together. An extended series, therefore, carries with it the danger of collision, unless the progression begins with improbably wide spacing. That danger is obviated here by the leap in the bass (bar 62) and, more importantly, by the upward leaps in the vocal part whereby inner-voice tones of the preceding chord are shifted to the top voice.

31-25

(a) Schubert, Wegweiser   (from *Winterreise*, D. 911)

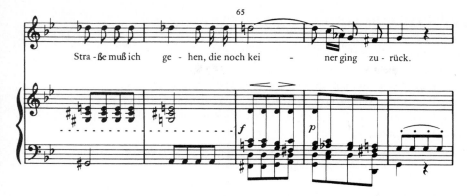

translation: I see a signpost standing firmly in my path; it points a road
               I must travel, a road from which no one has ever returned.

(b) reduction

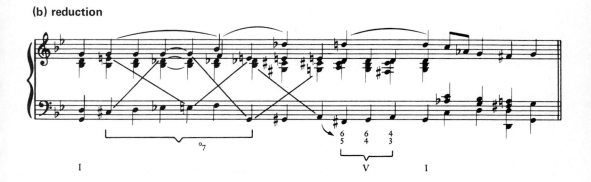

The B♭ minor and the C♯ minor $^6_4$'s receive considerable emphasis from their rhythmic position and from the upward leaps in the vocal part. This emphasis contradicts their passing function; for a moment the listener might mistakenly believe that a new key area is being prepared. The contradiction between emphasis and function creates a temporary uncertainty as to the larger direction that wonderfully expresses the sense of the text. The words are also reflected in a breathtakingly original quirk of notation. In bars 63-64, Schubert writes D♭ in the vocal part, in contradiction to the C♯ of the accompaniment and the drive to D, the dominant. The vocal line, of course, has been arpeggiating a diminished seventh chord. Now an arpeggio through °7 will traverse one or more octaves—will return, therefore, to the initial scale degree—only if an augmented 2nd occurs in each octave, thus: G-B♭-C♯-E-G. If it consists only of minor 3rds—G-B♭-D♭-F♭-A♭♭ and so on, through an infinite series—it will never return to its origin, no matter how long it goes on. Schubert's strange notation, therefore, embodies a musical symbol for "a road from which no one has ever returned."

EQUAL SUBDIVISIONS OF THE OCTAVE

14. The chromatic necessity of equal divisions. Using diatonic elements alone, we cannot articulate the musical space within an octave into equal subdivisions. If we wished to divide the space between the tonic and its upper octave into two segments, the closest we could come to equality would be a 5th and 4th (in C major, C-G-C or C-F-C). If we wished to divide it into three parts, the most nearly equal possibility would be a major 3rd, minor 3rd, and perfect 4th (in C major, C-E-G-C, C-E-A-C, or C-F-A-C). Some important elements of the diatonic system are symmetric: that is, they are based on the equal segmentation of musical space. Among these are the division (in all modern tuning systems) of the major 3rd into two whole steps and the balance between the 5ths from $\hat{1}$ up to $\hat{5}$ and from $\hat{1}$ down to $\hat{4}$. But many of the most important relationships are asymmetric, and it is partly the lack of uniformity in the divisions of the octave that makes each scale degree sound different from the others and that gives to tonal music the possibility of directed, goal-oriented motion.

Using chromatics makes it possible to divide the octave into segments that are equal or enharmonically equivalent. There are four possible divisions of the chromatic scale's twelve semitones; since twelve can be divided by two, three, four, and six, the possibilities are: into two tritones (A4 and d5), into three major 3rds (one written as a d4), into four minor 3rds (one written as an A2), and into six whole tones (one written as a d3). As Example 31-26 shows, the four subdivisions intersect with one another at various points. The tritone appears midway through the subdivisions into six whole tones and into four minor 3rds, and one of the major 3rds coincides with every other whole tone. These intersections represent structural connections among the subdivisions. Note that the use of enharmonic equivalents is necessary if the motion is to span an octave. Without the enharmonics we would be in the position of the character in Schubert's *Wegweiser* and would arrive at an augmented 7th or a diminished 9th, but never at an octave. (In that case, the progression would still contain an enharmonic, but this time between the beginning and the final tones.)

31-26   **equal divisions of the octave**

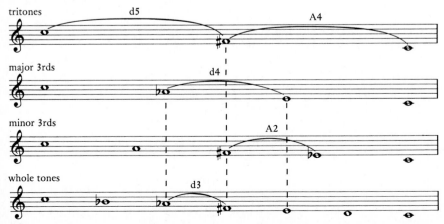

Starting in the late eighteenth century, composers began to explore the possibilities resulting from equal division. The resultant progressions represent one relatively minor aspect of nineteenth-century compositional technique. A predominance of equal division would weaken the gravitational attraction of the tonic that is the central feature of tonality. Such passages can be interesting for several reasons. One is to observe how composers—especially great composers—integrated them into compositions mainly based on very different procedures. Another is to observe in them one of the nineteenth-century sources of a basic premise of much twentieth-century music: that all twelve tones of the chromatic scale are available to the composer as elements of potentially equal status.

15. The octave divided into major 3rds. The most important equal division of the octave is into three major 3rds. Such passages usually serve to extend a major triad, often though not always the tonic, appearing at the beginning and end of the progression (Example 31-27). Of all the equal divisions, this one is the most closely related to diatonic procedures. In major, the only bass tone foreign to the scale is $\flat\hat{6}$—a very frequent product of mixture. Usually $\flat\hat{6}$ also occurs in an upper part, where it functions normally as neighbor to $\hat{5}$; consequently the foreign tone, $\flat\hat{6}$, is not left unresolved. Before it resolves, $\flat\hat{6}$ will probably be transformed to $\sharp\hat{5}$ at the point where the diminished 4th occurs in the bass (Example 31-27a). Most often the diminished 4th is notated between $\flat\hat{6}$ and $\hat{3}$, for that is the way the passage sounds. For ease of reading, however, other notations will sometimes occur in keys with many accidentals in their signature (31-27b). Sometimes each new triad is introduced by an applied chord.

31-27

(a)   **(b)**

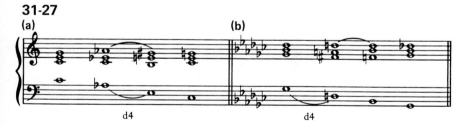

In Example 31-28, the bass line first moves down a major 3rd from G to E♭ (I-♭VI). The E♭ chord is then extended by a continuation of the motion in 3rds; eventually it becomes a German $^6_5$ resolving to V. Two aspects of this passage are typical of chromatic motions in major 3rds. First, the progression descends; 3rds descend more often than they ascend in both chromatic and diatonic textures. Second, the progression in 3rds uses only major triads—a feature typical, as we have seen, of many chromatic techniques. A third aspect is more special, though by no means unique: a whole-tone scale is formed by the passing tones between chord roots (see the relation between whole-tone and major 3rd subdivisions in Example 31-26). The descending bass in this excerpt relates to the bass in Example 31-8, drawn from an earlier passage in the same movement. You may recall from the earlier excerpt that $\flat\hat{6}$ in the bass did not lead directly to dominant harmony. Here, $\flat\hat{6}$—extended by the chromatic motion in 3rds—does, in fact, lead to V in a culminating moment near the very end of the movement.

31-28

(a) Schubert, String Quartet, D. 887, I

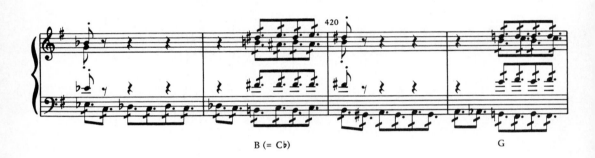

(b) reduction

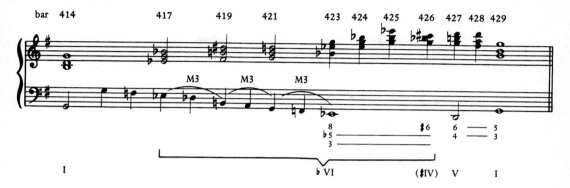

16. **The octave divided into tritones and into minor 3rds.** These divisions are related in that the sum of two minor 3rds is a d5; thus, the progression C-E♭-F♯-A-C
contains the progression C-F♯-C. Both of them tend to be less satisfactory expansions of the tonic than a motion in major 3rds because they are in conflict with
the strong tendency of ♯$\hat{4}$ to resolve into $\hat{5}$. The conflict is particularly drastic if
the motion is simply $\hat{1}$-♯$\hat{4}$-$\hat{1}$. If the tritone is embedded in a series of minor 3rds,
its effect is considerably softened, especially if the passage is sequential. But
sequential repetition brings other problems, for the number of steps needed to
fill the octave can sound excessive. Example 31-29, based on minor 3rds, is, indeed, more than usually repetitious, but it is not without a certain fascination.
A curious feature is the use of common-tone °7's, which lead into applied dominants. There are four °7's, all enharmonic equivalents of each other.

31-29   Rossini, Crucifixus   (from *Messe Solenne*)

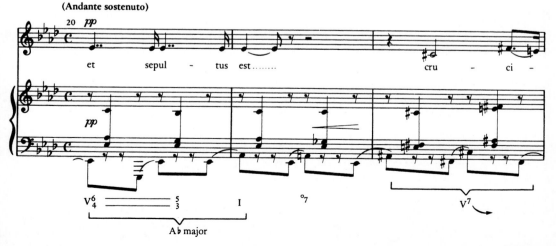

Continued

translation: He was crucified and was buried.

17. Extending seventh chords through division into minor 3rds. Dividing the octave into minor 3rds often works more effectively within the expansion of a seventh chord than within a triad, especially a tonic triad. Let us begin with a diminished seventh chord. Since °7 divides the octave into minor 3rds, extending it through changes of position can easily produce a minor 3rd subdivision of the octave, as in Example 31-30a. We can express each of these positions of °7 by an enharmonic equivalent, producing four different notations (31-30b). And since each °7 differs by only one note from a dominant seventh chord, we can derive from the four °7's a chain of dominant sevenths whose roots divide the octave in minor 3rds, just like the °7's (31-30c). That is what happens in a passage from Schumann (31-30d), whose basis is an extended V⁷ of D. This fundamental harmony receives a most colorful elaboration through a cycle of minor 3rds, with a different seventh chord (of "dominant" type) built on each new bass tone: A, C, E♭, F♯, A. Only the A seventh functions harmonically as a dominant; the others are subordinated to the governing A⁷ chord. Each "dominant" seventh is preceded by a diminished seventh whose bass tone forms an appoggiatura, and it is the fleeting °7's that form the connective threads of this passage, integrating its disparate tonal elements into a unified fabric of sound.

31-30

(a)   (b)   (c)

m3   etc.   m3   etc.

= D: V⁷

(d) Schumann, Novellette, Op. 21/2

(Äusserst rasch und mit Bravour)

m3   etc.

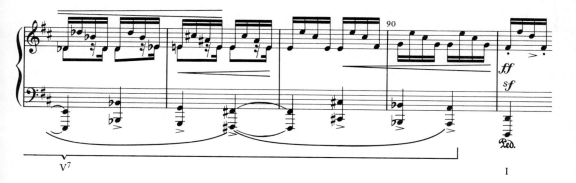

V⁷   I

If you look at the lower line of the right hand of the Schumann (the part with the downward stems), you will see that it consists of a stepwise line that alternates whole tones and semitones—a formation known as an *octatonic* (eight-note) scale. In fact, the entire passage contains only these same eight notes. The scale exists in two forms: starting with the whole tone (as in the Schumann) or with the semitone (Example 31-31). In Classical and early Romantic music, the scale usually arises as a by-product of extended °7's and has no functional importance, but some composers in the late nineteenth century—especially Rimsky-Korsakov—began to cultivate it for its own sake. Together with other symmetrical tonal structures, it forms a bridge into the music of the twentieth century (Stravinsky, a pupil of Rimsky-Korsakov, used it).

31-31   octatonic scale

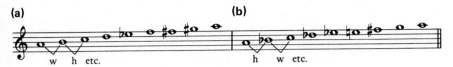

(a)   (b)

w   h etc.   h   w   etc.

A minor 3rd cycle of "dominant" sevenths can form the basis of an extended voice-exchange passage; the voice exchange is of the m7/A6-M10 type discussed in section 12. As Example 31-32a shows, the cycle can extend through an entire octave, forming the expansion of a V^7. The chord progression resembles the one in the Schumann excerpt of Example 31-30d, but the cycle of 3rds descends, and the extended chromatic lines by contrary motion integrate the "dominant" sevenths more easily into the chromatic passing motions so that individual chords stand out less.

The C. P. E. Bach excerpt that follows (31-32b) is much the same except at the beginning and end, which depart from the pattern so that the passage expands $^o7$ (VII^7 of a) instead of V^7. This passage is unusual in many ways, not least of them the great length of time it takes for an intensely dissonant sonority to resolve. The excerpt is the final statement of an opening rondo theme that has been varied and expanded in its subsequent appearances; our excerpt shows the most spectacular of these variations. In its initial form, the theme contains a diminished seventh in bar 2 that resolves to I in bar 3, just as in the opening four bars of Example 31-32b. When this idea is repeated, however, the bar with the diminished seventh chord expands to thirteen bars (!) of highly chromatic passing motions within the very same $^o7$; only at the fourteenth bar does I finally appear so that the theme can proceed as before. Written in 1780, this is an early example of a kind of writing that we mainly associate with the nineteenth century.

31-32

(a) extended voice-exchange passage

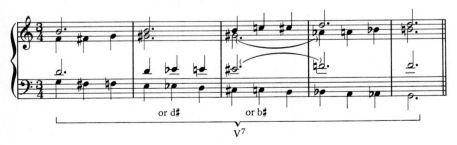

or d♯   or b♯

V^7

(b) C. P. E. Bach, Rondo, W56/5

18. The octave divided into whole steps. Whole-tone scales in the bass or in an upper part can arise as a by-product of a motion in major 3rds (Example 31-28). However, placing a major or minor triad over each step of a whole-tone scale in the bass, as happens with major and minor 3rds, is a most unlikely possibility in tonal music. In Example 31-33, a whole-tone progression of major triads does in fact appear, but each triad follows an applied dominant seventh so that the whole-tone scale appears embedded in a *chromatic cycle of descending 5ths*—all twelve notes of the chromatic scale arranged by 5th. The 5th progressions add an element of direction to the passage that would be lacking in the whole-tone progression by itself.

31-33   Chopin, Piano Concerto, Op. 21, III

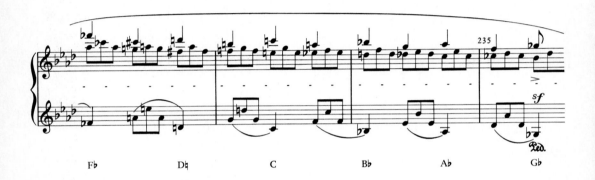

The Chopin excerpt illustrates the relation between whole-tone and tritone subdivisions presented in Example 31-26, for the passage continues beyond the octave and stops on Gb, midway through a second octave and a tritone below the C triad on which the first phase of the passage is based. In a fascinating and amusing musical pun, Chopin leads into the first C chord through the augmented 6th Db-B, and he uses an enharmonic equivalent of this augmented 6th (Db-Cb) to form the applied dominant to the Gb that ends the passage.

Example 31-34 also subdivides an octave into six whole tones, (filled in by chromatic passing tones), but the chords above the whole-tone steps are diminished sevenths, not triads. As a consequence, symmetrical subdivisions not only determine the bass line but also can be inferred from the chordal structures above the bass. Although the passage occurs in a more or less tonal context (it can be regarded as the expansion of a leading-tone chord applied to the F♯ triad), its internal organization is very close to that of some twentieth-century music.

31-34   Liszt, Piano Concerto No. 1

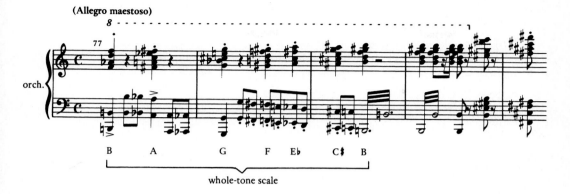

whole-tone scale

POINTS FOR REVIEW

1. Some chromatic techniques are directly related to diatonic ones. Among these are passages in parallel $^6_3$ chords, usually major. Another possibility is 7-6 suspensions altered by chromatic passing tones; in full textures, the 7ths are often accompanied by 5ths. Also important are chromaticized ascending 5-6's, often with augmented triads produced by chromatic passing tones: parallel 10ths between outer voices are frequent.

2. Descending 5-6's occur over a chromatic bass. They are used sequentially, often starting on I. They cannot reach V without breaking the sequence.

3. Augmented 6th chords often serve as connectives in passages usually descending in parallel major 10ths.

4. Consecutive °7's frequently appear in descending chromatic progressions of a transitional nature. They are usually notated as $^{6-4}_{5-2}$ or $^{7-4}_{3}$, and are related to passages of interlocking applied dominants. Ascending consecutive °7's are less frequent except for the progression on ♮$\hat{4}$-♯$\hat{4}$.

5. In some nineteenth-century music, passages in consecutive augmented triads (usually ascending) occur.

6. Chromatic passages in contrary motion are often organized within a 6-10 or 10-6 voice exchange. Such passages can expand a V^7, a diminished seventh chord, an augmented 6th chord, or a triad. The most characteristic possibility is a voice exchange between a minor 6th and a major 10th. Outer voices produce the following intervals: m6, A6, P8, M9 (or d10), and M10. A passing $^6_4$ normally fills in the octave; the other sonorities are usually positions of German $^6_5$ or V^7. Extended passages containing several voice exchanges are possible.

7. The most important of the equal subdivisions of the octave is into three major 3rds (one of them expressed as a diminished 4th). They usually descend and usually consist of major triads, possibly introduced by applied dominants. Passages in minor 3rds (one expressed as an augmented 2nd) are a less frequent possibility.

EXERCISES

1. Preliminaries.

   a. Write five brief progressions, each in a different key, with basses descending chromatically from I to V. Include: chromatic parallel $^6_3$'s (in major), chromaticized 7-6's (in major and minor), chromatic descending 5-6's (in major) and parallel °7's (in minor). Sometimes you may find it convenient to change to three-part texture.

   b. Write three brief progressions, each in a different *major* key, with basses rising chromatically from I to III♯. Include: chromaticized ascending 5-6's (2 different versions), and parallel augmented triads. Lead III♯ to a cadence each time.

   c. Write three progressions containing chromatically filled-in voice exchanges between: V^6_5 and V^7 (major), two positions of °7 (minor), *major* IV^6 and IV (minor).

   d. Write two progressions, both in major, based on the equal division of the octave into M3's and m3's.

2. Figured bass.

3. Melody.

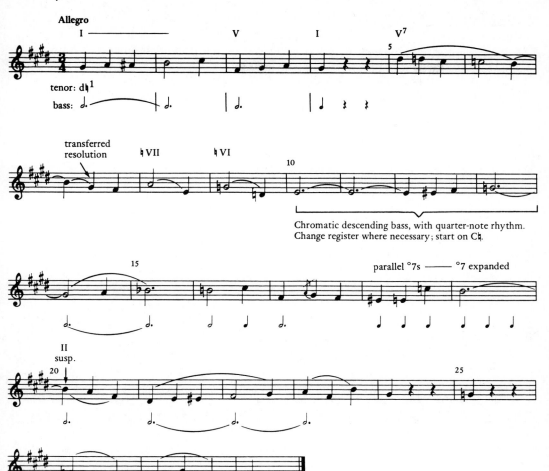

Chromatic descending bass, with quarter-note rhythm.
Change register where necessary; start on C♮.

4. Melody. Set as a three-voice piece for keyboard; add a bass and complete the middle voice. The middle voice should contain the same kinds of rhythmic values as the soprano, but mostly in a complementary rhythm so that quick notes coincide with a long note in the soprano and vice versa. The bass, on the other hand, should be simpler rhythmically and should mostly use longer notes; you might begin with a dotted half followed by a quarter. The bass should be very chromatic.

32

Chromaticism in
Larger Contexts

32-1 Beethoven, "Hammerklavier" Sonata, Op. 106, I

NEW MODULATORY TECHNIQUES

1. Modulation by chromatic inflection. Example 32-1 shows the beginning of the bridge passage from the first-movement exposition of Beethoven's "Hammerklavier" Sonata. This movement exemplifies an important tendency in music of the Classical and Romantic periods: the large-scale use of chromaticism. The exposition moves from B♭ major to G major—from I to VI♮; our excerpt contains the passage where the change of key occurs. A most striking aspect of this modulation is the chromatic progression F♮-F♯ in bar 37. The F♯ is an inner-voice tone of the pivotal D major triad, III♯ of B♭ and V of G. Since the pivot is a chromatically altered chord in one of the keys (the first), this is a *chromatic modulation*, like those discussed in Unit 28, section 13. But this modulation, unlike those discussed earlier, contains a direct chromatic inflection (F♮-F♯), which juxtaposes the two tonal areas in a rather drastic, uncompromising way.

A composition cannot move from B♭ major to G major through a diatonic pivot chord, for the two keys have no chords in common. But it would be easy to effect a smoother chromatic modulation than Beethoven's by avoiding the direct chromatic progression F♮-F♯, as in Example 32-2. Why Beethoven did not choose to avoid it—why he wrote an abrupt rather than a smooth modulation—has to do with the motivic design of the piece. The contrast between F♮ and F♯ (together with a related one between B♭ and B♮) is a most important feature of the movement and, indeed, of the entire sonata.* To have softened this first confrontation would have weakened the compositional fabric.

32-2

instead
of   F♮   F♯

Not all modulations by chromatic inflection are brusque; some are quite gentle—for instance, the Schubert excerpt quoted in Example 30-7, bars 27-28. Rhythm, texture and dynamics can all influence the effect of a modulation. So can the quality of the chromatic inflection—whether it is one of increasing intensity, like the F♮-F♯ ($\hat{5}$-#$\hat{5}$) of the Beethoven, or of decreasing intensity, like the D♯-D♮ (#$\hat{2}$-♮$\hat{2}$) of the Schubert. But whether abrupt or gentle, modulations by chromatic inflection tend to attract the listener's attention to the key change much more than diatonic modulations.

Modulation by chromatic inflection is one of the techniques that accompany the extended application of chromatic procedures. In this final unit we shall first study some of these new modulatory techniques. We shall then investigate compositional plans that embody large-scale chromaticism.

---

*See especially bars 227-77 of the first movement. Also see the Scherzo, bars 160-72 and the connection of the Adagio—in F♯ minor!—to the Finale. These are just a few instances.

2. Modulation by common tone. The A section of Schumann's *Widmung* stays in
Ab major, the tonic. Most of the B section is in ♭VI, really F♭ major, but written
in E to make it easier to read. Example 32-3 shows the transition from one key
area to the other. As in the Beethoven excerpt, the immediate chord progression
is by 3rd, but descending rather than ascending. And there is also a chromatic
inflection, though it is disguised by the enharmonic notation; if you think of the
E major as F♭, you will see that the inner-voice progression C-B♮ (bars 13-14)
stands for C-C♭. An important difference between this modulation and Beethoven's is that this one lacks a real pivot chord. The E (F♭) triad so obviously
marks the beginning of a section that we hear it immediately as a new local tonic
rather than as part of the previous key area. Owing to the lack of a pivot chord,
this modulation looks abrupt on paper. Yet it does not *sound* abrupt, for an
important common element helps to integrate the two tonal regions. It is the
melody tone Ab/G♯, sustained in the vocal part above the chord progression
Ab-E (F♭).

32-3   Schumann, Widmung, Op. 25/1

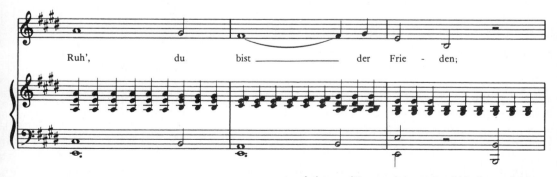

translation: [You are the grave in which, forever,] I have
buried my grief. You are rest, you are peace;

Modulations where the main connecting element is a common tone rather than a common chord are often called *common-tone modulations*. (If there is a pivot chord, as in the Beethoven, this term is not usually applied, even though there might be a prominent common tone.) The common tone will appear in an exposed position, usually in the soprano. Common-tone modulations are particularly effective when the immediate chord progression is from a major triad down a 3rd to another major triad. The typical possibilities are I to ♭VI in major (as in the Schumann) and III♯ to I, also in major. If, as is usual, both the triads connected by the common tone are major, the modulation will also contain a chromatic inflection.

Common-tone modulations can create surprising effects, as in the astonishing recapitulation of the Finale of Schubert's C major Symphony (Example 32-4). The development culminates in a long pedal point on G, V of C major, setting the stage, one thinks, for the return of the tonic. Instead, the V chord thins down to an octave G, against which a passing F moves to an E♭ (32-4a). At first, this E♭ sounds like another passing tone within V, leading down to D. But suddenly the full orchestra enters fortissimo with the recapitulation—not in C at all, but in the remote key of E♭ major (32-4b).

As in the Schumann, the connecting link is a common tone (G), and the chord progression is down a major 3rd with major triads. What is so startling about the Schubert is that the E♭ chord supplants an expected tonic and that a seeming element of melodic figuration—the tone E♭ of bar 592—becomes the basis of a whole section. Interestingly, the section in E♭ (♭III) is one phase of an elaborate progression from the V at the end of the development to a delayed C major much later in the recapitulation.

32-4   Schubert, Symphony in C Major ("The Great"), D. 944, IV

(a)

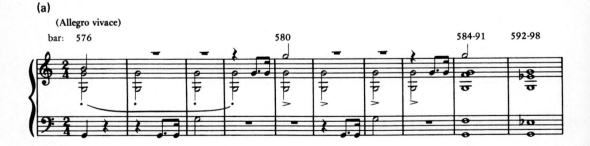

(b) recapitulation

3. Modulation by chromatic sequence. You know from Unit 26 that sequential transitions can connect two key areas. Such passages can have a chromatic character, sometimes, even, when they move between diatonically related areas. Example 32-5 shows, in reduction, the transition between a movement in A minor and one in D minor. The motion from A down to D divides into two 3rds, A-F and F-D; the one from A to F is filled in chromatically by a sequential progression. Each chromatic step between A and F—Ab, G, and Gb—is tonicized by an applied V^7. Note that the sequence changes as it approaches Gb; the pattern is compressed and the Gb triad occurs in $\frac{6}{4}$ position. This change forestalls excessive repetition and helps to emphasize the immediate goal, F. A curious feature of this passage is the prevalence of minor triads. They undoubtedly reflect the penitential character of the text, as do the augmented-4th leaps in the bass line and the large-scale chromatic descent. The common-tone $^o7$'s produce a most extraordinary effect here; it will be discussed in section 5.

32-5   Mozart, Confutatis (reduction)   (from *Requiem*, K. 626)

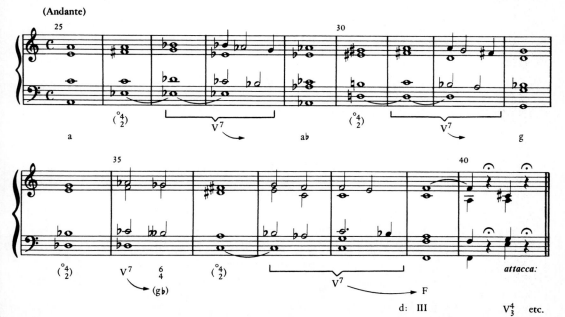

4. Enharmonic modulations; true versus notational enharmonics. Among the most interesting modulations are those in which the pivot chord is reinterpreted enharmonically. But before we can begin to deal with these *enharmonic modulations,* we must distinguish between two kinds of enharmonic. One is purely notational; a composer uses an enharmonic spelling for ease in reading or to convey some expressive nuance. Thus in Schumann's *Widmung* (Example 32-3), the B section is in E rather than F♭ purely for convenience in reading; notating the whole section in F♭ would certainly be possible, though unkind to the performers. True enharmonics, on the other hand, are inherent in the musical structure; no change in notation could possibly eliminate them, for they would be heard even if they were not expressed in the notation. We have already encountered true enharmonic relationships in connection with the chromaticized ascending 5-6 progression and the equal subdivisions of the octave (Unit 31).

5. Enharmonic modulation based on the diminished seventh chord. Enharmonic modulations involve true, rather than merely notational, enharmonics. Thus Example 32-3 does *not* contain an enharmonic modulation. In Example 32-6, however, the modulation is truly enharmonic. A diminished seventh chord belonging to G minor is reinterpreted so that it leads to E minor; the E♭ is enharmonically transformed into a D♯. In its new notation, and with its new orientation, the °7 embellishes the V⁷ that ushers in the E minor tonic.

32-6   Beethoven, "Pathétique" Sonata, Op. 13, I

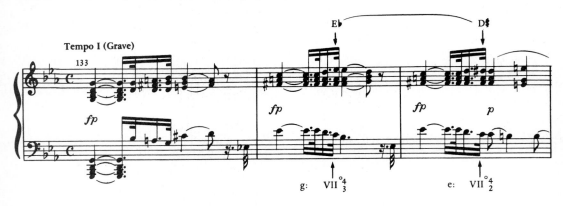

No other chord has so great an enharmonic versatility as the diminished seventh. Any °7 can be so notated that it functions as VII⁷ of four different minor keys (Example 32-7). Through mixture, each of these keys can become major. In addition, VII°⁷ can function as an applied chord; its resolution need not be to a tonic. And, finally, °7 can act as a common-tone embellishment rather than as a leading-tone chord. Bruckner used to say that the diminished seventh was like the Orient Express; it could take you rapidly to the most distant places!

32-7

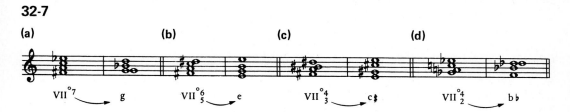

Composers often exploit the enharmonic ambiguity of the diminished seventh in sequential passages. In the Mozart Requiem excerpt (Example 32-5), the first diminished seventh (bar 26) sounds at first like an applied chord to V of A minor, but it turns out to be a common-tone °7 embellishing V⁷ of A♭ minor. The unexpected lowering of pitch resulting from the change in meaning partly accounts for the strangely moving effect of the °7's in this passage.

6. Enharmonic modulations based on dominant seventh and augmented 6th chords. The enharmonic connection between the dominant seventh and German $^6_5$ (Unit 29, section 22) can be the basis of a modulation. A V⁷ can be reinterpreted as an augmented 6th belonging to a different key; less often, a chord first heard as an augmented 6th can turn into a V⁷. Example 32-8 demonstrates the first possibility. In bar 45, an applied dominant seventh on F (V⁷ of V in E♭) is reinterpreted as a German $^6_5$ and resolves to V of A minor. The first violin's E♭ becomes a D♯; as often happens, the enharmonic change is not notated. In this excerpt, the resolution of the augmented 6th involves an indirect anticipation (Unit 21, section 25): the D♯/E♭ of bar 45 resolves on the last eighth note of the bar, before the rest of the chord changes. Also note the use of mixture; between bars 42 and 45, the bass line and most of the chords are borrowed from E♭ minor.

Knowing how the modulation works in detail makes it possible to study the larger context in which it occurs. As the reductions following the excerpt demonstrate, the framework is a motion from F major (an expanded III of D minor) to A minor (an expanded V). The F major chord becomes a German $^6_5$ in order to lead to V of A minor (32-8b). The transitional tonicization of E♭ permits a consonant preparation for the dissonance; what is surprising is that this dissonance is prepared as a minor 7th but resolved as an augmented 6th (32-8c). This enharmonic procedure allows Mozart to suggest a vast expanse of musical space in the course of a simple harmonic motion from III to V. What listener could predict that E♭ major would turn out to be a stop on the way from F major to A minor?

In Example 32-9, we see the opposite enharmonic transformation; a chord that begins as an Italian 6th in G major is turned into a V^7 of A♭ (bar 234). This introduces a brief tonicization of ♭II in place of an expected tonic. As it happens, the tonic is simply delayed, and not for very long. As the example shows, the amusing return to G depends on an enharmonically reinterpreted °7.

32-8

(a) Mozart, String Quartet, K. 421, I

(b) V^7 becomes Ger. $\frac{6}{5}$

(c)

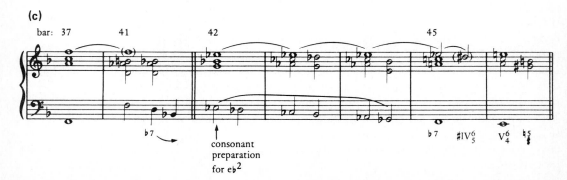

32-9   Beethoven, String Quartet, Op. 18/2, IV

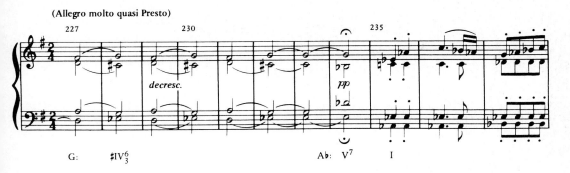

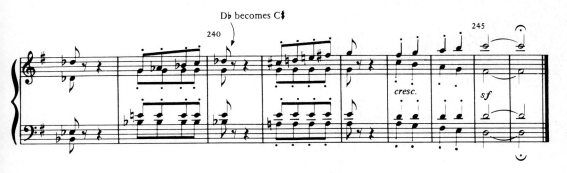

In using the enharmonic connection between the German $^6_5$ and V^7, keep the following in mind: A change from V^7 to augmented 6th occurs most simply in a modulation *down* a half step (Example 32-10a). The reverse—changing the augmented 6th into a V^7—produces a modulation *up* a half step (32-10b). These modulations are possible with major, as well as minor, keys.

32-10

(a) V^7 becomes Ger. $^6_5$

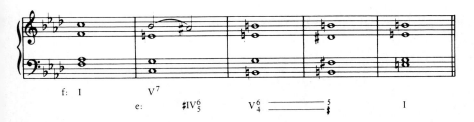

Continued

(b) Ger. $^6_5$ becomes V^7

f: I

$\natural$IV$^6_5$

f$\sharp$:   V^7 —— $^6_4$ —————— 7   I

CHROMATIC TONAL AREAS

7. Large-scale uses of mixture. The expansion of chromatically altered triads into key areas makes possible a large-scale application of chromaticism. This technique sometimes occurs in pieces of the Baroque period—most impressively, perhaps, in some of Domenico Scarlatti's harpsichord sonatas. But it was the masters of the Classical and Romantic eras who fully realized the expressive and structural possibilities of large-scale chromaticism. A most remarkable feature of their work is their ability to exploit the greatest variety of tonal areas without sacrificing the underlying diatonicism that gives unity and a sense of directed, goal-oriented progression to their compositions.

All the consonant triads that result from the three kinds of mixture can be expanded; these include major and minor triads on every degree of the chromatic scale except $\sharp\hat{4}$ (Unit 30, Points for Review). Tonal plans that involve these chromaticized key areas frequently resemble those that include expanded diatonic chords; however, the aural effect and the compositional meaning can differ greatly—especially with the more remote alterations. Thus a section in C minor might represent an expanded III in A major; like diatonic III, the C minor might subdivide the motion from I to V. But unlike diatonic III, the C minor will create tonal conflicts that the composer must somehow work out in the composition. How a great composer resolves such conflicts depends largely on the individual character of the piece—on such factors as length, rhythm, tempo, form, and motivic design. Given the number of chromatic tonal areas and the number of ways a great composer can deal with them, no textbook can provide more than a sampling of the possibilities. The examples and techniques discussed here will give you an orientation to this complex material and, we hope, a basis for your own further study.

8. ♭VI in major. As one of the most important products of mixture, ♭VI frequently expands into a key area. The approach to expanded ♭VI can vary. Often, as in Schumann's *Widmung* (Example 32-3), ♭VI comes directly from I through a common-tone modulation. In Chopin's Impromptu in F♯ major, however, a large expansion of ♭VI is introduced by a deceptive cadence (Example 32-11).

32-11   Chopin, Impromptu, Op. 36

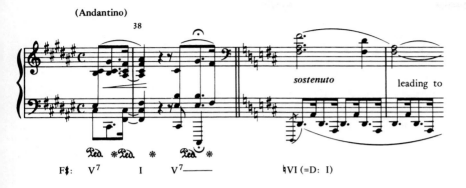

The usual goal of ♭VI is a cadential V that moves on to I; the half-step progression in the bass helps to intensify the V. A most natural way of leading ♭VI to V is to transform it into an augmented 6th chord. In the Chopin, after a fantastic digression, the D chord returns as an augmented 6th leading to a V. Turning ♭VI into an augmented 6th chord is not the only way to approach V, though it is the most frequent one. In the Schumann song, ♭VI moves to V⁷ through ♭II.

9. III♯ in major. If the quality of a modulation were determined only by the distance in 5ths, a modulation from I to III♯ would create exactly as much contrast as one to ♭VI, for the distance is the same—four 5ths up as against four 5ths down. However, the contrast is much greater with III♯ than with ♭VI, where $\hat{1}$ of the main key is available as a common tone. For this reason, a modulation to III♯ often requires a more elaborate preparation than one to ♭VI. An effective way to achieve such a preparation is to transform the main tonic into an augmented 6th chord leading to V of III♯. The bridge section of Beethoven's "Waldstein" Sonata is based on this procedure; Example 32-12 presents a synopsis of the modulation. Incidentally, Beethoven was the first to use III♯ as the second key area in sonata-allegro movements in major.

32-12   Beethoven, "Waldstein" Sonata, plan of exposition (to second theme)

As part of a basic harmonic structure, III♯ moves on to V, usually through a passing IV. This, in fact, happens in the gigantic development section of the "Waldstein," which begins in F major (bar 90), changes to F minor (bar 104) and, after a long transition, finally arrives at V (bar 136). Thus the plan of this exposition and development—containing 155 bars—is essentially the same as that of the first four bars of Example 15-1—the example where we first demonstrated the function of III as divider between I and V.

10. VI♯ in major. VI♯ and III♯ relate to I in similar ways. Both roots lie a 3rd away from $\hat{1}$; both chords contain a chromatically altered factor of tonic harmony—♯$\hat{1}$ in VI♯, and ♯$\hat{5}$ in III♯. Perhaps because of these similarities, Beethoven incorporated a tonicization of VI♯ into the recapitulation of the "Waldstein's" first movement. The second theme begins in A major, changes to A minor, and moves to V of C.

Like expanded diatonic VI, expanded VI♯ most characteristically forms part of a large-scale arpeggio leading down from I to IV. This is what happens in bars 213-277 of the last movement of Mozart's Piano Concerto, K. 467; the IV, as one would expect, leads on to V and I. Example 32-13 contains the very interesting sequential passage that prepares the V of A. The sequence descends in 3rds and reaches as its goal the D minor triad, II of C and IV of A minor. A voice exchange introduces an augmented 6th that leads to the new V.

32-13   Mozart, Piano Concerto, K. 467, III

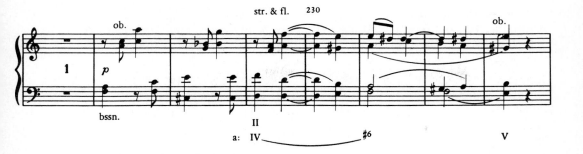

To arrive at the expanded IV (F major), Mozart simply changes the A major to minor (III of F) and moves through V_3^4 to I of F.

As you saw in Example 32-1, the first-movement exposition of Beethoven's "Hammerklavier" Sonata moves from I to VI♯ (B♭ to G). The development section contains E♭ major as a first goal. Thus the progression I-VI♯-IV—used by Mozart for the central part of a rondo (Example 32-13)—spans the exposition and beginning of the development of a Beethoven sonata-allegro movement; compare Beethoven's use of large-scale I-VI-IV in minor (Unit 26, section 12).

11. ♭III in major. The relation of ♭III to V is the same as that of ♭VI to I. As we might expect, therefore, ♭III often follows a common-tone modulation from V. This is what happens in a Brahms Waltz, the tonal plan of which appears in Example 32-14. The D♭'s in the right-hand part before the double bar help to prepare the listener for the arrival of D♭ as a key area. As the sketch indicates, ♭III moves through an applied dominant to a strong IV that precedes the final V and I.

32-14   Brahms, Waltz, Op. 39/8, sketch

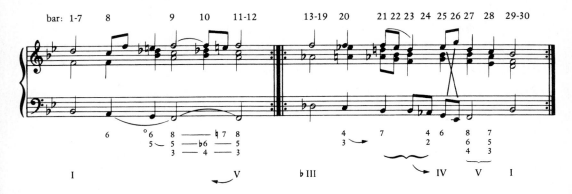

Look again at the Schubert excerpt of Example 32-4, where a common-tone modulation from V to ♭III occurs in an entirely different context.

12. Altered triads in minor. The minor mode is the normal home of ♭II—a particularly important altered chord, and one that can be expanded into a key area (Unit 28). And, as we know, pieces in minor often expand the major form of tonic harmony. Aside from these two possibilities, expansions of altered triads occur less often in minor than in major. There are several reasons for this. Altered triads containing $\sharp\hat{6}$ and $\sharp\hat{7}$ are difficult to stabilize, for these scale degrees create the expectation of a quick resolution to $\hat{1}$. This means that the major forms of IV and V will not normally expand into key areas; it also limits the effectiveness of ♯III and ♯VI. A second consideration is the tendency of composers to avoid an unrelieved succession of minor chords, the sonority of the minor triad creating more tension than that of the major. Therefore, such products of secondary mixture as III♭ and VI♭ are less generally useful than the corresponding alterations in major.

The exposition of the first movement of Beethoven's "Appassionata" Sonata (sketched in Example 32-15) shows the most frequent way of stabilizing such chords as III♭ and VI♭. The second key area of the exposition is A♭ major (diatonic III); the A♭ major is then inflected so that it becomes minor (III♭). The exposition closes in A♭ minor; as we shall see, the expansion of A♭ continues into the development section (section 15 below).

32-15   Beethoven, "Appassionata" Sonata, I, plan of exposition

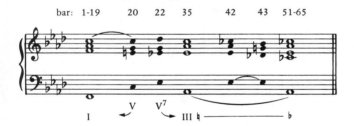

13. An example of double mixture: ♭III♭ expanded. Among the most difficult triads to expand convincingly into key areas are the products of double mixture, for these can create an extreme contrast with the main key. One way of dealing with this difficulty might be to approach the altered chord in stages. Thus, a composer who wanted to express III of A major as a C minor chord might first change A major to A minor. Moving to C major would be easy; the C major might then be inflected to minor. At times, however, an immediate confrontation between the two contrasting key areas becomes a compositional necessity.

In the second number of *The Creation*, Haydn had to depict both the freshness of the newly created world and the flight to Hell of the defeated forces of chaos and darkness. These two opposing ideas are represented by sections in A major (the main tonic) and C minor (♭III♭). As Example 32-16 makes clear, Haydn does not at all attempt to soften the contrast between A major and C minor. On the contrary, the music moves abruptly from one to the other, plunging immediately into V⁷ of C minor.

32-16   Haydn, The Creation, No. 2, aria

translation: Terrified, the evil spirits of Hell retreat.

How is it that Haydn is able to achieve an integrated composition in the face of so disruptive a contrast? It is because of a most subtle connection that he establishes among the main pitches of the uppermost voice. As the sketch of Example 32-17 shows, the main top-voice tone of the C minor section is E♭, which comes from E♮; the return to A major (and to E♮ in the soprano) is effected by an augmented 6th chord whose soprano tone, D♯, is an enharmonic transformation of E♭. Thus the integration of C minor into the piece as a whole results in part from the enharmonic connection between E♭ and D♯. Furthermore, Haydn took great pains to emphasize D♯ as leading tone to E in the first, A major, section; Example 32-17b shows one of the many prominent D♯-E progressions. In this way the E♭ belonging to C minor is prepared by the repeated use, in A major, of its enharmonic equivalent, D♯.*

*The contrast between E♭ (C minor) and E♮ (A major) also relates to the opening number of the oratorio, which depicts the overthrow of chaos (C minor, E♭) by God's creation of light (C major, E♮).

32-17

(a) Haydn, The Creation, No. 2

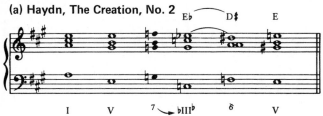

I V ^{7} ↘ bIII♭ δ V

(b) (Andante)

14. ♯IV as a goal. Unlike the altered chords we have been discussing so far in this unit, major and minor triads built on ♯$\hat{4}$ do not result from mixture. Mostly they function as emphasized leading-tone chords to V; they can be expanded into key areas, usually of brief duration. A particularly interesting way of getting to ♯IV is to move up in two minor 3rds from I. Since the sum of two minor 3rds is a diminished 5th, not an augmented 4th, the point of arrival will be bV, not ♯IV. If it is to act as a leading tone to V, the chord—or at least its bass tone— must be reinterpreted enharmonically. This is what happens in Example 32-18, where a motion in minor 3rds leads from G through Bb to Db. But in bar 46, the Db returns as C♯; it supports an °7 and resolves to V.

A fascinating feature of this excerpt is the enharmonic transformation of diminished seventh chords. The °7 of bar 37 is on ♯$\hat{4}$ and "ought to" resolve to V. But with enharmonic reinterpretation and some transferred resolutions (see the arrows in the example), the °7 arrives at the "wrong" dominant—at V of Bb instead. Note that the final diminished seventh (bar 46) is also on C♯—♯$\hat{4}$—but this time it resolves as expected. It is as if the music took the wrong turn at the diminished seventh of bar 37 and found its way only where the °7 on C♯ returns in bar 46.

32-18

(a) Haydn, String Quartet, Op. 54/1, II

(b) bass plan

15. **Equal subdivisions of the octave.** In some nineteenth-century music, equally divided octaves (Unit 31, sections 14-18) form the basis of extensive passages in which each intermediate chord is expanded. A famous example occurs in the development section of the first movement of Beethoven's "Appassionata." You may recall that the exposition closes in A♭ minor (Example 32-15). At the beginning of the development, the A♭ changes to G♯ and moves (common-tone progression) to E major. The E major turns to minor; then the motion continues in major 3rds to C minor and, again, to A♭, but A♭ major. Thus the A♭ chord is expanded by the motion in major 3rds. As Example 32-19 shows, A♭ becomes V^7 of D♭, the first main goal of the development.

32-19   **Beethoven, "Appassionata" Sonata, I, plan of first half of development**

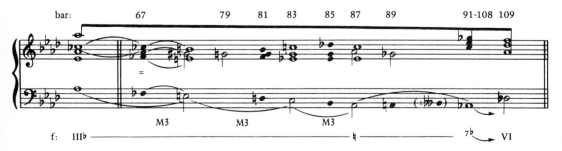

A particularly ambitious application of equal subdivisions occurs in the first movement of Tchaikovsky's Fourth Symphony. The exposition contains three main themes, each in a different key area: F minor, A♭ minor, and B major. The recapitulation resumes the motion in minor 3rds, the first theme sounding over a dominant pedal in D minor and the second and third in D minor and F major; the coda restores F minor. Example 32-20 shows the plan; in its avoidance —even contradiction—of a large-scale tonic-dominant relationship, it is scarcely tonal, at least in a traditional sense.

32-20   Tchaikovsky, Symphony No. 4, Op. 36, I, plan

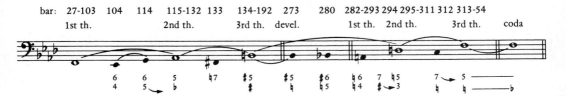

bar: 27-103   104   114   115-132 133   134-192 273   280   282-293 294 295-311 312 313-54
      1st th.   2nd th.   3rd th. devel.   1st th.   2nd th.   3rd th.   coda

16. Motivic aspects of large-scale chromaticism. One of the most fascinating aspects of great music is the way large-scale plan relates to detail—the way, for example, key areas project over a long span of time those pitch relationships that are most characteristic of the piece. Thus in Chopin's F♯ major Impromptu (Example 32-11), an expanded D major (♭VI) leads to V, the large-scale bass motion being D♮-C♯. Now, in the opening section of the piece, the motive D♯-C♯ occurs over and over, in all voices. Surely the inclusive bass progression D♮-C♯ and the repeated motivic detail, D♯-C♯, are not unrelated; Chopin probably chose D major as a key area partly because it made possible a huge enlargement of a basic motivic idea.

Motive and inclusive plan are even more closely correlated in the first movement of the "Appassionata." The movement is permeated to an almost unbelievable extent by the constantly recurring figure $\hat{5}$-$\hat{6}$-$\hat{5}$ (in F minor, C-D♭-C), sometimes shortened to D♭-C). The D♭ major goal in the development (Example 32-19) results from an enlargement of this figure. Furthermore, the unusual turn toward A♭ minor in the exposition permits a transposition of the basic motive to E♭-F♭-E♭*; the motion in major 3rds at the beginning of the development (Example 32-19) contains the transposed motive enharmonically reinterpreted (E♭-E♮-E♭).

In the first movement of the "Hammerklavier," the modulation to G major is connected with the recurrent chromatic progressions F♮-F♯ and B♭-B♮ (section 1 of this unit). And the strange modulation from A major to C minor in *The Creation* (Examples 32-16 and 32-17) has to do with the transformation of a motivic D♯-E ($\sharp\hat{4}$-$\hat{5}$) into a vastly enlarged E♭-D♯-E♮.

---

*See, for example, bars 41-50, bars 54 and 58, left-hand part, and so on.

For our final example we shall discuss a highly chromatic passage from the first movement of Mozart's Piano Trio in E, K. 542 (Example 32-21). The passage begins when a deceptive cadence on ♭VI (G major) prevents the expected resolution of the second theme to I of B major. The G major is not followed by a quick relaxation of tension; most surprisingly, it is inflected to become G minor (♭VI♭). A wonderful transitional passage, based in part on an enharmonically reinterpreted °7 (E♭ becomes D♯), leads to V and a strong authentic cadence.

32-21   Mozart, Piano Trio, K. 542, I

(accompanying parts omitted)

These events—and, in particular, the remarkable change to G minor—have their roots in a basic motivic element of the piece. The movement opens with a descending chromatic figure, B-A♯-A♮-G♯, which is quoted in the second (B major) section of the exposition. Example 32-22 shows two statements of this motive; compare bars 71 and 88, Example 32-21. If you now study the reduction of the chromatic passage presented in 32-22c, you will note the prominent chromatic line B♮-B♭-A-(G♮)-G♯. What is this but an expanded transformation of the motive, with the A♯ expressed as a B♭. Without the mixture of G major and minor, the melodic progression B♮-B♭ and the motivic reference could never have been achieved. But without the motivic implication, the G minor would make little sense, for it would lack any organic connection with the movement as a whole.

32-22

(a) Mozart, K. 542, I   **(b)**

(c) reduction of K. 542, I

It is interesting to compare this excerpt with the first example in Unit 1, also drawn from a work by Mozart—the C major Piano Sonata, K. 545. In their use of the tonal language, the two excerpts could hardly be more divergent, with the simplest diatonic relationships on the one hand and the most daring chromaticism on the other. Yet these passages are not only from works of the same composer, but from works completed within a few days of each other (on June 22nd and 26th, 1788). That Mozart could produce two such contrasting masterpieces at virtually the same time is testimony to the immense scope of his genius. It is equally a tribute to the tonal system that made possible the creation of so rich a repertory of masterworks. As for the system itself, it must rank among the great achievements of the human spirit.

POINTS FOR REVIEW

1. A type of modulation that sometimes accompanies the large-scale use of chromaticism is *modulation by chromatic inflection,* where the motion to the pivot chord involves a chromatic melodic progression such as F♮-F♯.

2. A *modulation by common tone* is one where there is no pivot chord and where a prominent common tone—usually in the soprano—forms the connecting link. Common-tone modulations sometimes also involve a chromatic inflection; frequently they occur in connection with a chord progression down a 3rd between two major triads (example: C major-A♭ major).

3. Two key areas can be connected by a *chromatic sequence.*

4. In an *enharmonic modulation,* the pivot chord is reinterpreted enharmonically. The two most important possibilities are those in which a diminished 7th chord is reinterpreted and those in which a V^7 becomes a German $^6_5$ or vice versa.

5. The expansion of chromatically altered chords forms an important possibility for large-scale chromaticism. Such expansions occur somewhat more frequently in major than in minor, expanded ♭VI being a particularly important possibility. Expanding the more remote alterations can enrich the possibilities for tonal variety; at the same time it can threaten the continuity and unity of a composition. The solution to this problem varies according to the individual character of a piece; one frequent solution is to relate the large-scale chromaticism to the motivic design.

EXERCISES

1. Preliminaries.

   a. Using a modulation by chromatic inflection, write a phrase or phrase group that modulates from G major to E major and back.

   b. Using a common-tone modulation, write a phrase or phrase group that moves from F♯ major to D major and that returns to the main tonic through an augmented 6th chord.

   c. Write a sequential progression that begins on a B♭ major triad and that briefly tonicizes every chromatic step from B♭ down to G major. Lead the G major chord to a cadence in B major; then think of the B major as ♭II of B♭ and return to the original tonic.

   d. Write at least six different modulations, each starting in A minor and employing the enharmonic reinterpretation of VII^{o7}. Remember that $^o7$ can move directly to a new tonic, that it can be an applied chord, that it can embellish a V^7, and that it can be a common-tone chord.

   e. Write a phrase that begins in C♯ minor and modulates to C minor using the enharmonic relationship between V^7 and the German $^6_5$.

2. Waltz. Set for keyboard, using typical waltz accompaniment. Don't forget the possibility of chromatically filled-in voice exchanges.

3. Figured bass. Set for keyboard, making use of the melodic ideas labeled (a) and (b). Depending on the setting of the soprano, you can interpret the given figures somewhat freely, especially with respect to the rhythmic placement of the notes.

4. Melody. Set for violin and piano. Common-tone chords are a feature of this exercise.

*parallel major here

APPENDIX:
KEYBOARD PROGRESSIONS

The following progressions illustrate the most important techniques covered in Units 6-32. They are designed to be played at the piano and are notated in C throughout for your convenience in transposition. Your goal should be to get them well enough into your head and fingers to be able to play them fluently through at least the first four sharp and flat keys, major and minor.

We have not attempted to include every possible soprano voice; finding other possibilities will be good practice for you. You can incorporate some of the shorter progressions into longer and more continuous ones, as we did in (d) of Unit 8, for example; in this way, you will gain experience in improvising phrases and phrase groups.

Unit 6: I, V, and V⁷

Don't forget to raise $\hat{7}$ in minor! In (e-h) pay particular attention to the resolution of the 7th.

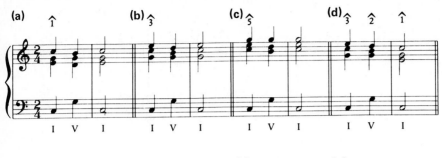

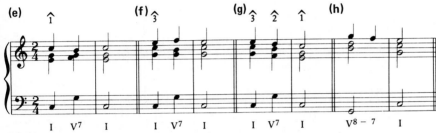

Unit 7: I⁶, V⁶, and VII⁶

Progressions (a) and (b) can function as expanded initial tonics and can lead to a V-I cadence; (c) can continue to a final I.

Unit 8: Inversions of V⁷

Many other sopranos are possible. Use these progressions to expand I, then lead
to either an authentic cadence or a semicadence.

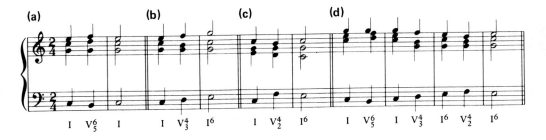

Unit 9: Leading to V: IV, II, and II⁶

The initial tonics of (a-d) can be expanded by the progressions of Units 7 and 8;
cadences using IV and II can follow.

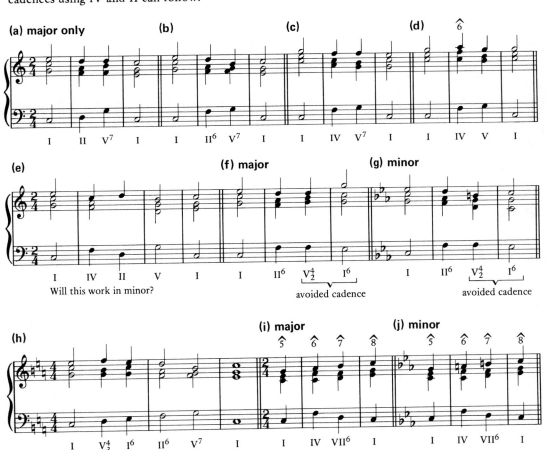

Unit 10: The Cadential $\frac{6}{4}$

Using progressions learned in Units 7, 8, and 9, play antecedent-consequent
phrase groups: both semi- and authentic cadences should feature 6 on V

Unit 14: V as a Key area

Many other possibilities exist for progressions that tonicize V and return to I. Invent progressions using other pivot chords than the ones used here.

major only

```
C:              V⁷  VI        V
       G: II      V      I
```

Unit 15: III and VII

The progression given here works only in minor. In addition, practice the scale
harmonization in Example 15-12.

```
I   VII   III   II⁶   V⁶₄ ‒ ⁷₄   I
```

Unit 16: $\frac{5}{3}$-Chord Techniques

Keyboard progressions using only $\frac{5}{3}$ chords are most common in sequences; they
will therefore be presented in the following group.

Unit 17: Diatonic Sequences

Other sopranos are possible for some of these progressions, especially (a), (c), (d), (e), and (g). In (d), the progression is easier in four voices if the left hand plays the tenor; alternatively, the tenor may be omitted.

(a) descending 5ths   **(b) $\frac{6}{3}$ variant of (a)**

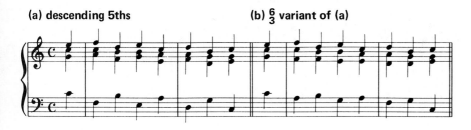

(c) ascending 5ths   **(d) ascending 5-6**

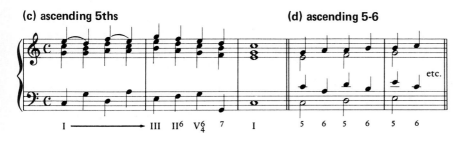

(e) $\frac{5}{3}$ variant of (d)   **(f) descending 3rds (g) descending 3rds (h) $\frac{5}{3}$ variant of (f)**

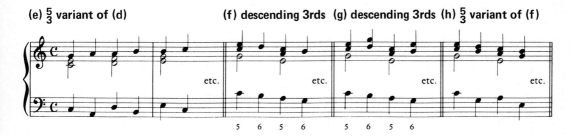

Unit 18: $\frac{6}{3}$-Chord Techniques

These progressions show the alternating doublings characteristic of parallel $\frac{6}{3}$ chords in four voices. Performance in three voices is also possible, omitting the tenor, but be sure to include the 3rd in $\frac{5}{3}$ chords.

(a)   **(b)**

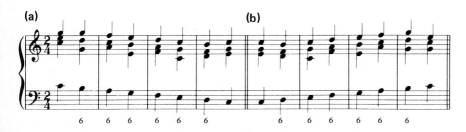

Unit 19: $\frac{6}{4}$-Chord Techniques

The most important $\frac{6}{4}$ usages are summarized in these progressions.

(a) accented $\frac{6}{4}$

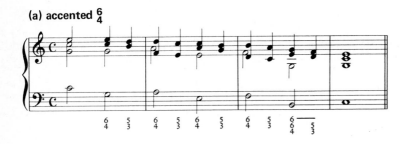

(b) neighboring $\frac{6}{4}$

(c) consonant and passing $\frac{6}{4}$ **(d) passing $\frac{6}{4}$**

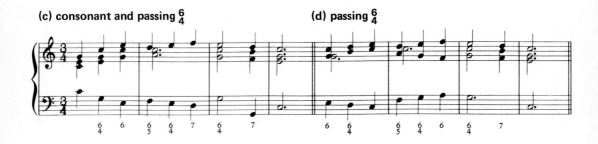

Unit 20: Melodic Figuration

These exercises are based on sequences already familiar to you. The first is a complete phrase; the others should be continued and led to a cadence.

Unit 21: Rhythmic Figuration

Lead these sequential progressions to cadences. At the cadences use anticipations
in the soprano where appropriate.

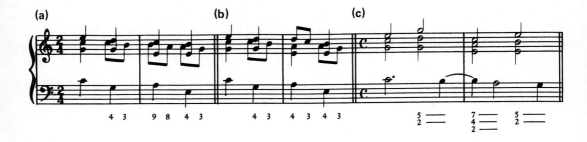

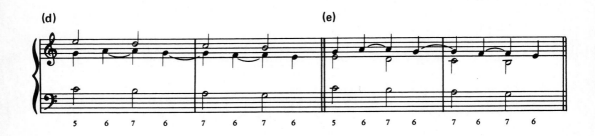

Unit 22: Mixture

Invent phrases in major followed by parallel phrases in minor.

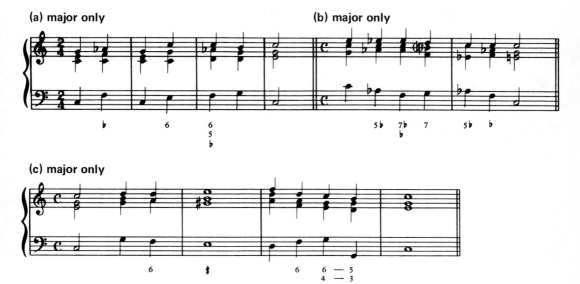

Unit 23: Leading-Tone Seventh Chords

In addition to playing (c) as written, alter the upper voices to produce °7 on the second and fourth chords.

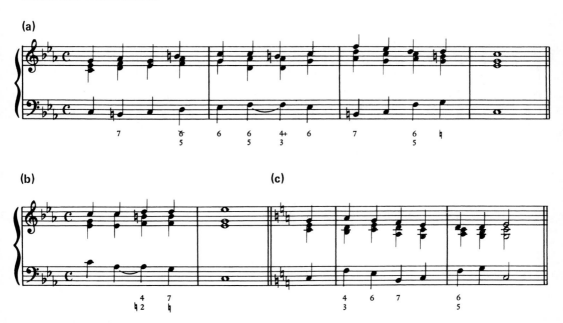

Unit 24: Remaining Uses of Seventh Chords

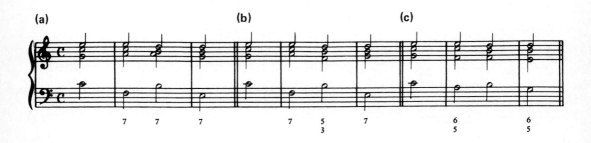

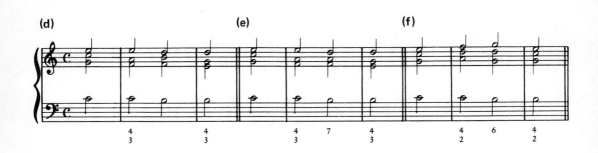

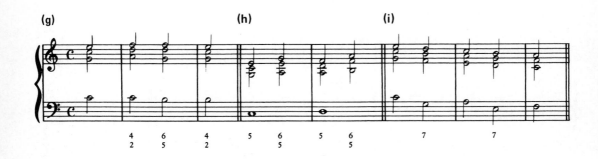

Unit 25: Applied V and VII

Play short progressions that begin as shown below. Lead each one to a cadence. Use different types of applied chords and sometimes lead the applied chords to triads in $\frac{6}{3}$ position.

I - applied chord - II (major only)
I - applied chord - III
I - applied chord - IV
I - applied chord - V
I - applied chord - VI
I - applied chord - VII (minor only)

(a) major only   **(b) major only**

(c) major only; °7 also possible   **(d) minor also possible**

(e) minor and °7 also possible   **(f)**

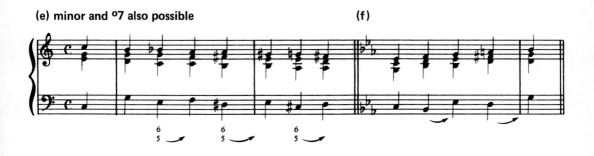

(g) major only

Unit 26: Diatonic Modulation

1. The following exercise in establishing keys can help you to acquire considerable fluency in modulation: Take a major or minor triad and lead it convincingly to an authentic cadence in every key to which it belongs. For example, besides being I in F major, an F major chord is:

> III in D minor
> IV in C major
> V in B♭ major (also minor)
> VI in A minor
> VII in G minor

And an F minor chord is:

> II in E♭ major
> III in D♭ major
> IV in C minor
> V in B♭ minor
> VI in A♭ major

Examples (a) through (k) illustrate progressions in all the keys listed above; the possibilities shown are by no means the only ones, but they are good ones. You should reproduce these, starting on other chords, before inventing other possibilities. Note that the progressions that begin on V do not move immediately to I—a procedure that would be most unconvincing. Instead they expand V and add a 7th to it in order to lead forcefully to I. If the V (in minor) is a *minor* triad, its 3rd must eventually be raised to form a leading tone. In most of the progressions, the V is intensified (and its dominant function made clear) by a form of II or IV immediately preceding it.

(a) **(b)**

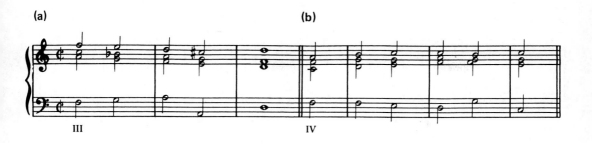

III   IV

(c) **(d)**

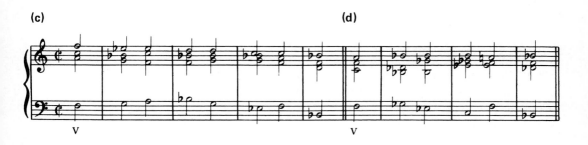

V   V

(e) **(f)**

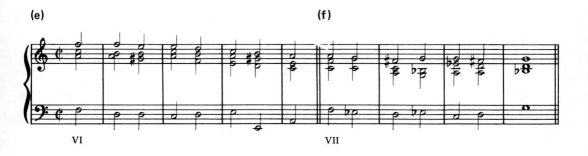

VI   VII

(g) **(h)**

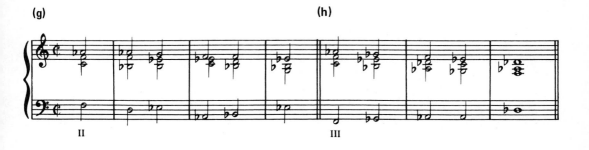

II   III

(i)   **(j)**

IV   V

(k)

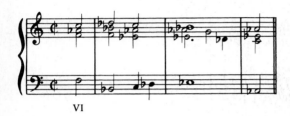

VI

2. Once you can play the above progressions easily and well, incorporate them into modulations. Establish the first key, move to the pivot, and lead to a cadence in the new key. Example (l) illustrates.

(l)

Ab: I ⟶ VI

Db: III II⁶   V⁶ $\begin{smallmatrix}8-7\\6-5\\4-3\end{smallmatrix}$ I

3. Invent more elaborate modulations, using sequences with applied chords to lead to the pivot chord.

4. Use "skeletal" progressions like the one shown in Example (l) as points of departure for improvising short phrase groups that include a modulation and a return to the home tonic. These phrase groups should follow the procedures outlined in Unit 14, section 13, except that they are no longer restricted to tonicizations of V in major. Example (m) illustrates such a phrase group.

(m)

G: I
b: VI

G: III⁶
b: I⁶

Unit 27: Seventh Chords with Added Dissonance

1. Prepare phrases, each in a different major or minor key, that incorporate the progressions of Example 27-4.

2. "Ninths"

(a)   **(b)**

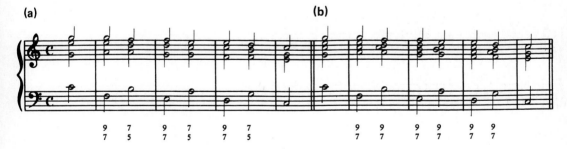

3. "Elevenths" and "thirteenths"

(c) major only   **(d)**

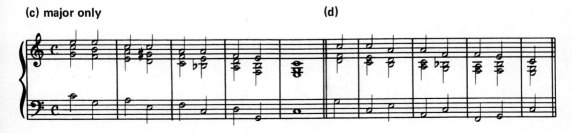

Unit 28: The Phrygian II (Neapolitan)

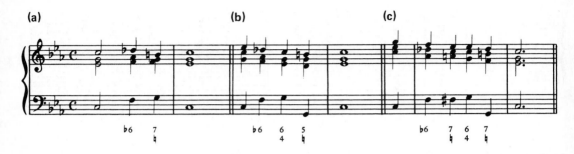

Unit 29: Augmented Sixth Chords

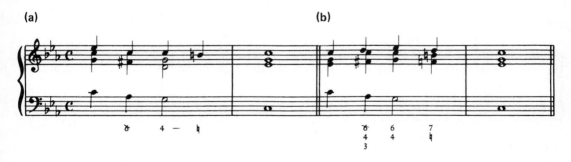

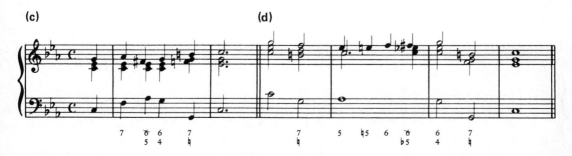

(e)   **(f)**

(g)   **(h)**

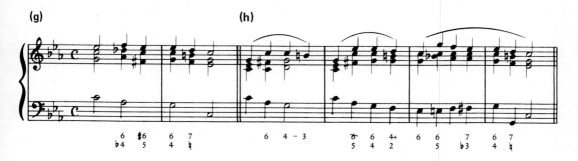

Unit 30: Other Chromatic Chords

(a)

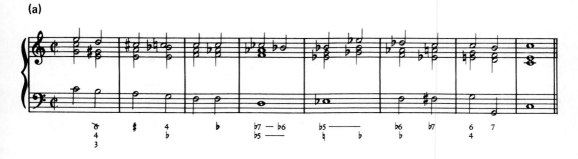

(b)   **(c)**

Unit 31: Chromatic Voice-Leading Techniques

In (a) and (b) the space between I and ♭II⁶ must be filled in by parallel chromatic chords. The sample for (a) shows ascending parallel $\frac{6}{3}$ chords; other possibilities are ascending chromatic 5-6 series and parallel augmented triads. Other possibilities for (b) include descending parallel $\frac{6}{3}$'s, chromatic 7-6 series, and consecutive °7 chords.

(d)

Unit 32: Chromaticism in Larger Contexts

The following progressions illustrate advanced modulatory techniques: modulation by chromatic inflection (a), by common tone (b), by chromatic sequence (c), and by the enharmonic reinterpretation of a diminished seventh chord (d). All of them are merely models, which you should vary and elaborate as well as, in (b) and (d), complete. In (a), the chromatic inflection transforms IV⁶ of C into II⁶ of E♭. Lead the F minor ⁶₃ to other keys; invent other progressions with chromatic inflection. The common-tone modulation (b) should continue sequentially until you arrive again at C major. The chromatic sequence (c) leads to an A major triad that functions as VI of c♯. Lead the A chord convincingly to four other keys. You should complete (d) in at least six different ways, each time to a different key and with attention to the many possible functions of °7. You should also use Example 32-10 as a model for enharmonic modulations based on the V⁷/German 6th relationship.

Index of Musical Examples

Italicized page numbers refer to examples that are mentioned but not notated.

Subject Index

ABA form, 207-8, 435
accent, 38-41, 43. *See also* meter;
    rhythm.
  and melodic figuration, 314-15,
    318-20
  and rhythmic figuration, 328-29,
    344
accidentals, 12. *See also* notation,
    chromatic.
  in figured bass, 52-53
active tones, 8-11, 29. *See also* scale
    degrees.
antecedent-consequent phrases, 147,
    187-88, 203-6, 212-13
anticipations, 44, 59, 345-48
apparent chords, 335, 343, 372-73,
    390-93, 409, 448-53, 461,
    469-70, 488-89, 513-14, 516,
    520, 533
apparent meter, 343
applied chords, 196-98, 214-15, 276-77
applied dominant (applied V and V^7),
    232-34, 255, 257, 276-77,
    396-417, 423, 426, 445-46,
    466, 468, 478, 509, 514-15,
    526, 528, 540-41, 543, 545-46,
    549-50. *See also* chords on
    individual scale degrees (tonic,
    supertonic, etc.).
  apparent, 409
  "back-relating," 417
  and cross relation, 398-400, 413
  doubling in, 397

in interlocking series, 410-11, 532
inversions of, 397-408, 410-17
and mixture, 509-10, 565-66
and parallel fifths/octaves, 412-13
in sequences, 410-17, 423, 446,
    468, 495, 526, 528, 559
and voice exchange, 399-400, 403-4,
    485, 540-41
applied leading-tone chord (applied VII
    and VII^7), 396-417, 423,
    457-58, 478, 509, 517, 550-51.
    See also chords on individual
    scale degrees (tonic, supertonic,
    etc.).
applied VII^6, 397, 401, 404, 406,
    415-16
  in sequences, 412-13, 415-17, 423
applied VII^{o7} (and inversions), 397-408,
    412-13, 417, 422-23, 457-58,
    490, 493, 510, 517, 533-34,
    540, 561
applied $VII^{\phi7}$ (and inversions), 397,
    402, 412
  and cross relation, 398-400
  irregular resolution of, 408-9
  labeling of, 400
appoggiatura, 43, 59, 320-21, 546-47
arabic numerals
  capped, for scale degrees, 6, 49
  for figured bass, 48, 52-53, 58-59
arpeggio, 8, 59, 71, 83, 310-13, 328,
    373, 486, 541. *See also* chordal
    skip; bass line.